Augmented Reality Law, Privacy, and Ethics

Law, Society, and Emerging AR Technologies

Augmented Reality Law, Privacy, and Ethics
Law, Society, and Emerging AR Technologies

Brian D. Wassom

Allison Bishop, Technical Editor

ELSEVIER

AMSTERDAM • BOSTON • HEIDELBERG
LONDON • NEW YORK • OXFORD
PARIS • SAN DIEGO • SAN FRANCISCO
SINGAPORE • SYDNEY • TOKYO
Syngress is an Imprint of Elsevier

SYNGRESS.

Acquiring Editor: Chris Katsaropoulos
Editorial Project Manager: Benjamin Rearick
Project Manager: Surya Narayanan Jayachandran
Designer: Matthew Limbert

Syngress is an imprint of Elsevier
225 Wyman Street, Waltham, MA 02451, USA

British Library Cataloguing-in-Publication Data
A catalogue record for this book is available from the British Library

Library of Congress Cataloging-in-Publication Data
A catalog record for this book is available from the Library of Congress

ISBN: 978-0-12-800208-7

For information on all Syngress publications
visit our website at http://store.elsevier.com/

Working together
to grow libraries in
developing countries

www.elsevier.com • www.bookaid.org

To the two mentors who had the most meaningful influence on the first 15 years of my professional career. The Honorable Alice M. Batchelder personifies integrity and excellence, and taught me to respect the legal system. Herschel P. Fink, Esq. taught me to love the law I practice, and to practice the law I love. Both gave me amazing opportunities to serve in ways that fundamentally shaped my career. I hope to pay forward to others all that I can never repay to them.

Contents

Endorsements xv

Author Biography xvii

Technical Editor Biography xix

Acknowledgments xxi

PART A UNDERSTANDING THE LANDSCAPE

**CHAPTER 1   What is "Augmented Reality Law,"
and Why Should I Care?** 3

What is "Augmented Reality Law"? 3

A Horizontal Study 3

The Law of the Horse 5

Why Study AR Law? 6

Inevitability 6

Follow the Money 13

Conclusion 15

CHAPTER 2   A Summary of AR Technology 17

Introduction 17

Defining our Terms 18

Augmented Reality 18

Synonyms 20

Variations on the Theme 20

Related Vocabulary 22

A Technology for All Senses 23

Vision 23

Touch 26

Hearing 27

Taste and Smell 28

Extra-sensory AR 29

Synthetic Synthesis 30

Supporting, or "Augmented World," Technologies 31

Mesh Networking and the Panternet 31

Mechanical Vision and Sensors 32

Taggants for Pinpoint-accurate Perception 32

Hand and Gesture Tracking 34

Facial Recognition 35

Levels of Adoption 36

Now: Emergence 36

The Near Future: Legitimacy 36

The Medium Term: Ubiquity 38

The Long Term: Maturity 39

PART B AR & THE LAW

CHAPTER 3   Privacy **43**
Introduction 43
Sources of Privacy Law 43
Backdrop: The First Amendment 43
The Common Law Right to be Left Alone 46
Eavesdropping and Wiretapping Statutes 48
Electronic Privacy Laws 48
Subject-specific Privacy Laws 49
Limitations on Government Intrusion into Privacy 49
Privacy Concerns Raised by AR 50
Facial Recognition and Other Biometric Data 50
Data Enhancement 55
Surveillance and Sousveillance 57
Passive Data Collection Through the Internet of Things 62
Using AR to Enhance Privacy 68

CHAPTER 4   Advertising, Marketing, and eCommerce **71**
Introduction 71
AR's use in Advertising and Marketing 71
How AR is Currently Used 71
How AR is Likely to be Used for Advertising in the Future 77
False Advertising and Unfair Competition 80
Sources of Law 80
False Advertising and Unfair Competition in AR 81
Business Defamation and Product Disparagement 89
Advertising Disclosures 90
Disclosures Required and Enforced by the Federal
Trade Commission 90
Making Appropriate Disclosures in the AR Space 92
Conducting Commerce 97
The Emerging Ability to Conduct Monetary
Transactions in the AR Medium 97
Consumer Protection and Contract Law 98
Conclusion 100

CHAPTER 5   Intellectual Property **101**
Introduction 101
Patents 101
The Nature of Patent Protection 101
Patent Protection in AR Inventions 102

The First AR Patent Infringement Case:
Tomita v. Nintendo..104
Patents as Weapons of Competition:
1-800-Contacts v. Ditto Technologies 106
The First AR Patent Troll: Lennon Image
Technologies 107
Trademarks 111
Trademark Basics...111
Expanding Trademark Law by Augmenting New Senses.....114
Keyword Advertising in the Augmented Medium 116
Fair Use and Free Speech...121
Copyright 125
Copyright Basics..125
Obtaining Copyrights..126
Reproduction and Derivative Works 131
Public Display and Performance..136
Moral Rights..136
Fair Use 137
Augmented Copyright Enforcement 138
Licensing 141
The Right of Publicity 143
The Basics of Publicity Rights...144
Facial Recognition as Infringing the Right of Publicity 145
Three-dimensional Capture of Entire Bodies:
Sex Appeal and the Right of Publicity 145
Virtual Assistants as Infringement 149

CHAPTER 6   Real Property Rights 153
Introduction...153
The Basic Rights at Issue..153
A Brief Overview of Real Property Rights 153
The Freedom of Speech 156
AR: Where Property Rights and Free Speech Collide..............157
Augmented Advertising – and More – Is Coming
to Real Estate Near You...157
Property-based Models of Controlling
Location-based Messages Break Down in AR......................158
In Many Cases, Free Speech Rights will Prevail 160
One Collateral Benefit for Land Owners: Digital Graffiti 163
Scarcity in Augmented Real Estate...165
When Everyone Wants to Use the Same Platform 165
Sacred Ground: When (Augmented) Worlds Collide............167

Other Intersections Between Property Rights and AR 169
    An Invitation to Trespass? 169
    Nuisance 171
    Physical and Virtual Easements 172
    Environmental Protection Laws 173

CHAPTER 7 Torts and Personal Injury **175**
Introduction 175
Intentional Torts 176
    Assault 176
    Intentional Infliction of Emotional Distress 179
Negligence 180
    The Elements of a Negligence Claim 181
    Augmented Reality Games and Physical Injury 182
    Augmented Distractions and Physical Injury 188
    Disrespecting the Physical 191
    Injury Due to Inaccuracy 192
Products Liability 193
    Eye Strain 194
    Blunt Trauma 195
    Motion Sickness 196
    Skin Irritation 198
    Cancer 198
    Retinal Projection 199
Automotive 200
    AR Mobile Phone Apps and Driving 201
    Driving with Digital Eyewear 202
    Achievements to Date with Augmented
    Windshields and Driver Aids 204
    Driving Amidst Ubiquitous Augmented Reality 207
Conclusion 208

CHAPTER 8 Criminal Law **209**
Introduction 209
Unintentional Run-Ins with the Law through AR 209
    Location-based Games 209
    Virtual Shooting Games 211
    Effect on Criminal Responsibility 212
Intentional Criminal Activity 213
    Augmented Weapons 213
    Surreptitious Data Collection and Hacking 215
    AR as a Disclosure of "Soft Targets" 217
    Repurposing the Infrastructure of an Augmented
    World for Criminal Purposes 220
    Criminal Collaborations Through AR Darknets 222

Law Enforcement Usage..226

Enhancing Situational Awareness 226

Harvesting Digital Information for Crime

Investigation and Prevention 230

Force Multiplication with Autonomous Drones....232

Turning the Cameras Backwards: Wearables

as a Means to Monitor Law Enforcement....................233

The Right to Hold Public Officials Accountable

is Enshrined in the First Amendment and Our System

of Ordered Liberty...234

The First Amendment Severely Limits Public

Officials' Ability to Assert Personal Privacy in their

Work-Related Speech...235

Police Officers are Particularly Subject

to Public Scrutiny..236

Massachusetts Shows What Happens if First

Amendment Rights are Not Protected...................238

Reprisals by Police Against the Citizens Who Record

Them are Inevitable without Clear Judicial Guidance..........239

Citizen Video Recordings are Effective in Curbing

Unlawful Conduct by Police.................................241

CHAPTER 9   Civil Rights... **243**

Introduction...243

The Current Requirements for Accommodating

the Disabled in Digital Media...................................244

The Governing Legal Framework 244

Digital Accommodation is Still in its Early Stages..............245

How AR can Meaningfully Improve the

Lives of Disabled Persons...249

The Deaf...249

The Blind..251

The Physically Handicapped.................................253

Those with Cognitive Impairments, Learning

Disabilities, and Emotional Trauma......................255

CHAPTER 10 Litigation Procedure **259**

Introduction...259

Gathering Evidence for Use in Legal Proceedings....................259

Mobile Video as an Intentional Means

of Gathering Evidence..260

Preserving Three-Dimensional Experiences in AR..............261

Gathering Evidence from Digital Remnants.................262

V-Discovery 264

    The Precedent of e-Discovery 264

    Orders of Magnitude More Data 265

    Tracking it all Down 265

    Making Sense of First-Person AR Data 266

    Preservation 266

Assisting Lawyers with Legal Research 267

Augmented Reality in the Courtroom 268

    Telepresence 268

    Immersing Judges and Jurors in the Evidence 269

Personal Jurisdiction 271

    Jurisdiction Requires a Meaningful Connection
Between the Defendant and the Forum State 272

    The Precedent of Today's Internet Law 273

    Exercising Jurisdiction Over Providers of Augmented
Reality Experiences 274

PART C AR & SOCIETY

CHAPTER 11 Politics and Civil Society 277

Introduction 277

AR as a Means of Mobilizing People for Social Good 277

    Rediscovering and Rebuilding Civic Identity 277

    Protests and Social Change 278

    Political Campaigns 279

    New Augmented Communities 279

AR and the Erosion of Civil Society 281

    The Devaluation of Physical Proximity
and Interpersonal Community 281

    Political Groupthink, or the "Echo Chamber" Effect 283

    Enforcement of Political Correctness 284

    Diminished Reality 287

    Labeling Others – Literally 288

Hope Remains 290

CHAPTER 12 Personal Ethics 293

Introduction 293

Will Augmented World Technologies Erode Our Ability
to Make Ethical Decisions? 293

    Self-monitoring Apps are Increasingly Giving
us Ethical Guidance 293

Will Augmented World Technologies Corrupt
our Ethical Decisions? 299

Sight...299

Infinity AR...300

Ex Post Facto..301

A Disturbing Unanimity...303

Will Augmented World Technologies

Lead us to Form Bad Habits? 304

The Inseparability of Fantasy and Reality 304

AR, Muscle Memory, and Desensitization 305

CHAPTER 13 Addiction and Pornography.............................**311**

Introduction..311

AR Addiction 311

Some People Will get Hooked on Augmented

World Technologies..311

What Can and Should be Done to Prevent Addiction? 314

Reasons for Optimism..315

Pornographic and Prurient Content 316

Pornography is Already Going Mainstream

through Today's Digital Media 316

Porn will be Plentiful in Augmented Media..........................317

Society will Suffer as a Result 322

Conclusion 330

Index 333

Endorsements

"Any techie that follows Augmented Reality knows that AR continues to surge under Moore's law. Brian Wassom is the indisputable, top legal expert in the realm of Augmented Reality. His perspective and legal lens continues to focus on AR and its journey to revolutionize technology. This book is a must read for any person looking to delve into the augmented world and absorb the rapidly changing legal and ethical landscape of cutting-edge high technology and its influence on society. This book is an unmatched AR resource that yields a powerful comprehension of an evolving mass medium."

–Joseph Rampolla – Cyber-crime expert/Augmented Reality Dirt Podcast creator/Co-author of Augmented Reality: An Emerging Technologies Guide to AR book

"Brian D. Wassom is my go-to resource on anything having to do with how Augmented Reality and emerging technology relates to legal issues. His writing is clear, impactful, and highly accessible regarding complex legal and technical issues. His book *Augmented Reality Law, Privacy, and Ethics* provides compelling evidence as to why Augmented Reality will drastically change culture over the next few years and how people need to prepare for what lies ahead. Brian's wisdom, humor, and insights make *Augmented Reality Law, Privacy, and Ethics* a pleasure to read, and a must-have resource for anyone wishing to understand how our vision of the future will be perceived through the lens of Augmented Reality."

–John C. Havens, Contributing writer for Mashable, Slate, and author of Hacking H(app)iness – Why Our Personal Data Counts and How Tracking it Can Change the World.

"We're at the precipice of the next, visual era, with smart glasses that will forever change how we look at the world. More than just a comprehensive look at the related legal, social, and ethical issues, this book will get you thinking about the full impact of what's to come."

–Dave Lorenzini, CEO of Arc

"As the mass-media industries adapt to the newest mass medium, Augmented Reality, the combined abilities of digital, mobile, social, and virtual, all produce a quagmire of challenges and threats – as well as opportunities. Brian's groundbreaking book is an invaluable guide to the treacherous ground that media owners, content creators, talent, news organizations, and others will face as they rush to stake their claims in the AR world. A must-read and invaluable resource for the next ten years."

–Tomi T. Ahonen, author of 12 books including "Mobile as 7th of the Mass Media."

"Brian Wassom is the world's leading expert on augmented reality (AR) law. Wassom's research pioneered the field of AR law and currently defines the way it is understood by developers. His writing points out the heart of the salient issues facing the rapidly growing field of AR. Wassom's texts are required reading for my Mobile AR graduate course at NYU."

– Mark Skwarek, a full-time faculty member at New York University (NYU) and the director of the Mobile AR Lab at NYU.

"Brian Wassom brilliantly illuminates some of the tricky issues of privacy, law, and ethics that will determine whether Augmented Reality results in an enhanced or degraded future for humanity."

–Tish Shute, Head of Product Experience at Syntertainment and cofounder and chief content officer of Augmented World Expo.

"Wassom thoroughly highlights most of the key issues facing AR today while establishing a clear path for analysis in the future. From advertising, to smart cars, to the augmented criminal organisations of the future, Augmented Reality Law, Privacy, and Ethics is must read for anyone looking to become deeply involved in AR over the next decade."

–Brendan Scully, Senior Business Development Manager, Metaio, Inc.

Author Biography

Brian D. Wassom litigates disputes and counsels clients from *Fortune 50* companies to startups concerning copyright, trademark, publicity rights, privacy, and related intellectual property and advertising issues. He is a partner in the law firm of Honigman Miller Schwartz and Cohn LLP, and chairs the firm's Social, Mobile and Emerging Media Practice Group. Brian authors a popular blog on emerging media at Wassom. com that features the section *Augmented Legality*®, the first regular publication devoted to the law governing augmented reality. Brian presents regularly to industry groups, legal education seminars, and conferences across the country on intellectual property, digital media, and related topics.

Technical Editor Biography

Allison Bishop is a highly experienced criminal reviewer with 10 years experience reviewing cases, criminal research, and criminal activity. Allison also works as a paralegal performing tasks such as briefing cases and reviewing case law and the working within the legal process. As an editor, Allison enjoys reviewing and editing works based on criminal justice, legal studies, security topics, and cybercrime. When Allison is not entrenched in studies, she loves to exercise, cook, and travel.

Acknowledgments

I am indebted to those who assisted in editing this manuscript, including Brian Coe and Karen Larson. My thanks as well to all those whose input shaped my outlook on, and understanding of, the augmented reality industry and all of the potential it holds, including Brian Mullins, Gaia Dempsey, Jay Wright, Joseph Rampolla, Ori Inbar, Tish Shute, Will Wright, Dave Lorenzini, John C. Havens, Trak Lord, Brendan Scully, Daniel Suarez, Dr. Mark Billinghurst, Dr. Steve Mann, Keiichi Matsuda, Mark Skwarek, Bruno Uzzan, Eric Mizufuka, Dima Kislovskiy, Cecilia Abadie, Brian Selzer, Robert Rice, Pete Wassell, Steven Petersen, Brad Waid, Drew Minock, the members of the AR Detroit Meetup Group, and so many more.

All thoughts, speculation, and analysis in this book – and especially any errors in fact or logic – are mine alone. This work is not intended as legal advice or a solicitation for legal representation, and does not reflect the views of my law firm or its clients. Moreover, although this book mentions several actual products and companies in the course of explaining augmented reality and related technologies, nothing herein is intended as a criticism of, or suggestion of wrongdoing involving, any mentioned product or company. To the contrary, this book is meant as a celebration of the technological advances that these pioneers represent, and to prepare society to better understand the world that such developments will usher in.

Understanding The Landscape

1 What is "Augmented Reality Law," and Why Should I Care? 3

2 A Summary of AR Technology. 17

What is "Augmented Reality Law," and Why Should I Care?

INFORMATION IN THIS CHAPTER:

- The "horizontal" nature of studying augmented reality law
- The inevitability of augmented reality technology
- The economic significance of augmented reality technology

WHAT IS "AUGMENTED REALITY LAW"?

One of the joys of writing the first book on a topic is having the freedom to frame the discussion however seems best to me. The topics of discussion in the following chapters are the ones that I find the most important to explore based on my own experience practicing law and spending time with members of the augmented reality (or "AR") industry.

But there are also downsides to a project like this. Among those is the need to justify the book's existence before convincing anyone to read it. In the case of AR law, I am often required to explain to listeners what "AR" even *is* before I can broach the subject of why the law governing it is distinct and significant enough to require its own book.

That is the function of this chapter and the next. Here, I will attempt to persuade you that the AR industry is one to take seriously, and that it will be important to understand (and to help shape) the law governing the use of AR technology. Assuming that you remain sufficiently open to these conclusions to follow me to Chapter 2, I will explain in greater detail the nature of AR and its related technologies. From that foundation, the rest of the book will survey a number of different legal and ethical topics that are likely to be, or are already being, implicated by AR.

I hope you will stick with me to the end, and agree that it was worth the ride.

A HORIZONTAL STUDY

If you are a student, then you are likely accustomed to studying one concept – such as contract law, chemistry, or grammar – at a time. Even in professional settings, individuals and entire companies often find themselves, consciously or unconsciously, thinking and operating within defined tasks, categories, or industrial segments, to the exclusion of all other subjects. We frequently refer to these areas of concentration as "silos" or "verticals," implying that the people inside them may build up quite a bit of knowledge of, or experience in, the given topic, but have relatively little idea how that topic relates to anything else. For example, an automotive engineer may spend years, even an entire career, immersed in the inner workings of a particular subsystem of a car, with no understanding or concern as to how that subsystem relates to or affects the rest of the vehicle. Similarly, many legal and medical professionals develop highly specialized (and expensive) skills in a niche practice area, but would not have the first clue how to help a random client who walks in off the street with a basic, everyday problem.

This is not such a study. "Instead of a deep 'vertical' look at one legal doctrine, this [book] will survey several disparate topics 'horizontally.'[1] In the current professional vernacular, it cuts across several verticals. Put another way, this book takes as its starting point one particular industry – the companies and innovators developing AR and related technologies – and surveys the various legal issues that members of that industry are likely to encounter. This approach has the advantage of being enormously more useful for the members of that industry and the professionals (like me) who would serve them, but it can be a bit disorienting (at least at first) for students accustomed to more abstract analysis.

That is not to say, by any means, that vertical studies of legal principles do not have their place in academia, or that students should avoid reading a book like this one. To the contrary, courses in basic legal doctrines provide the building blocks necessary for applying the law to complex problems. Horizontal exercises like this one can be ideal vehicles for transitioning from book learning to the ability to counsel clients in real-life situations. That is one reason why horizontal studies like this one are not uncommon during the third year of law school.

Perhaps the most direct audience for this book, however, is the growing ranks of those business people and technological dreamers who are out there, even now, literally building a new world around us all by means of what we currently call "AR" or "augmented world" technology. I have been privileged to meet and interact with scores of these innovators who are rapidly forming an industry out of concepts that were pure science fiction mere months earlier. They have the foresight to recognize just how much our world will change when we finally master the art of interweaving our digital and physical means of experiencing the world.

When I speak at AR conferences and events or counsel clients in this industry – usually after the audience has already heard from several entrepreneurs who cast grandiose visions of what can be done with the technology – I sometimes joke that it is my job as the lawyer in the group to crush their dreams and bring them back down to earth. Yet my actual intention (both there and here) is quite the opposite.

---

[1] I borrow this description from another exercise in horizontal legal analysis, the excellent e-casebook *Advertising & Marketing Law: Cases & Materials*, by Rebecca Tushnet and Eric Goldman. REBECCA TUSHNET & ERIC GOLDMAN, ADVERTISING & MARKETING LAW: CASES & MATERIALS, 1 (JULY 2012) (available at: http://blog.ericgoldman.org/archives/2012/07/announcing_a_ne.htm).

These innovators' dreams are so inspiring because they actually have a chance at being realized. But if AR entrepreneurs are going to successfully bring their visions to fruition, they need informed guidance from advisors who understand the realities and requirements of the legal and business worlds. These advisors must shepherd the innovators through the tricky landscapes and potential pitfalls of regulatory checklists, investment deals, IP protection, and all of the minutiae on which visionaries ought not spend too much of their time. I want more members of this industry to recognize their need for such guidance for the legal services industry to be better prepared to provide it.

This leads to two more currents that are important for me to mention at the outset. First, this book cannot, and does not attempt to, provide legal advice. Consult a lawyer directly before making business decisions. Second, the laws discussed herein are almost exclusively those of the United States. Although the AR community is truly worldwide and many legal and ethical principles cross national boundaries, it is the American legal system in which I practice and that forms the context for my analysis.

THE LAW OF THE HORSE

Today, there is almost no one who could honestly be called an "AR lawyer." This will remain true for some time, even as the industry begins to mature. One reason for this is that "AR law" is a concept much like a term I learned in my law school days: "the law of the horse." This phrase illustrates the difference between vertical and horizontal legal studies. The idea behind it is that there is no such thing as "horse law." Rather, if I own a horse and have a problem with the jockey, for example, I would seek counsel from an employment lawyer. If my shipment of hay doesn't arrive, I should consult a commercial transactions attorney. And if my neighbor complains about the smell of horse ranch, I might consult an attorney experienced in nuisance law.

Each of these lawyers would be practicing some aspect of "horse law," in some colloquial sense, but you would not call any of them a "horse lawyer," because lawyers do not usually hold themselves out in that manner. Lawyers typically market their services according to particular categories of legal doctrine or practice. Historically, relatively few lawyers have packaged their services according to the needs of a particular industry, even though it might be more efficient for our hypothetical horse owner to find a lawyer or law firm specializing in "horse law" than to seek counsel from different specialists on each issue.

I first heard this "law of the horse" analogy applied to "Internet law," to make the point that there was no such thing. Rather, the Internet and its use implicate virtually every legal vertical, depending on the context. "Internet law" is a horizontal subject (and thus not worthy of study in a law school, or so was the implication when I first heard the term used).

In the same way, "AR law" is also like the law of the horse. Defined literally, "AR law" encompasses all of those fields of legal practice that AR companies will encounter – including corporate, tax, intellectual property, real estate, litigation, and personal injury, among others. Indeed, if AR reaches even half of its potential, it is poised to revolutionize society at least as much as the Internet itself has done. It is inevitable, therefore, that such a sea change in how we conduct ourselves on a daily basis would also influence the laws governing that behavior and how they are applied. Yet, even today, we still see relatively few lawyers marketing their expertise in "Internet law," and virtually none have yet grasped the significance of AR as such.

Today, more lawyers and law firms recognize the value of organizing their services according to clients' needs rather than by traditional categories of practice. This, in part, is why many law firms have assembled "industry teams" focused on the needs of particular types of companies and comprising a number of specialists from relevant legal disciplines. Practice groups like these are one way in which legal professionals can more comprehensively and efficiently serve the needs of horse owners or any other given industry. Working within a general practice firm composed of lawyers working in dozens of different focus areas is another.

As only one such example, I help to lead my firm's "Social, Mobile and Emerging Media Practice Group," so named so as to encompass both the social media that presents today's most pressing digital media issues and tomorrow's emerging media such as AR. For several years now, I and other members of this team have gotten to know professionals within the AR industry and – together with other members of our general practice firm – helped them solve the issues they encounter across a broad spectrum of legal disciplines. It gratifies me to say that I am not personally aware of any other legal practice group as focused on the AR sector. As the inevitability of AR becomes more apparent, however, I expect that we'll see more such teams intended to serve this important industry.

WHY STUDY AR LAW?

If you are not already as enamored of the AR industry as I am, you may not yet be convinced that AR law is worth your time to study. In that case, allow me to recount some of the reasoning that led me to conclude that this field will be so important.

INEVITABILITY

In this chapter I have already used the word "inevitable" to describe the increasing prominence and impending ubiquity of AR. That is because I see AR not so much as a brand-new concept that will someday suddenly emerge onto the scene, but rather as a medium that has existed for decades and that is beginning to manifest itself with increasing speed as we finally see the development of the technology that can make it happen.

There are dozens of factors fueling the inevitability of widespread AR. Since consonance makes things more memorable, however, I will summarize them as the three C's of convenience, creativity, and capability.

Convenience

Not many years ago, humanity's best means of reading and recording data was on two-dimensional pieces of paper, which we stitched together and stored in books. When that data began to migrate onto computers, we displayed it on monitor screens, and books became files and folders. Over time, the screens became incrementally more aesthetically pleasing – flatter, higher-resolution, and more mobile – and even displayed some digital images that had the illusion of three-dimensionality. But the context in which these displays have appeared – the computer screen – has always been a two-dimensional rectangle.

AR is a unique step forward in the way we experience digital data, because it liberates that data from its two-dimensional box to make it truly appear (as far as human senses can perceive) to be three-dimensional. Granted, there will almost always be some medium (such as eyewear, a window, or a mobile device) through which we experience the display, and those media will remain two-dimensional for the foreseeable future. But AR creates the illusion that the display is present among, and even interacting with, our physical surroundings. Perception is reality, as the saying goes, and it is the perception of this illusion that we call "AR."

One fundamental reason that there will always be an impetus to experience data in this format is that physicality is intuitive to us. As children we have to learn to read and write, but playing with physical objects comes naturally. The less work our brains need to do in order to translate and process data, the more readily our minds will embrace it.

Take, for example, the yellow line of scrimmage and the blue first-down line that appear in most televised football broadcasts these days (Fig. 1.1). The technology to

FIGURE 1.1

NFL broadcasts contained some of the earliest examples of mass-market AR.

FIGURE 1.2

The Iron Man films are among the most popular depictions of AR.

create this illusion is actually one of the earliest forms of AR in mass media. Today it is even more sophisticated, with all manner of game statistics appearing as if they were on the football field itself. And the images themselves are so high-resolution and rendered so fluidly that the illusion of physicality is complete. The result has been to make it significantly easier for viewers not schooled in the rules of the game to comprehend the action. It's one thing to say "the offense needs to carry the ball 15 more yards to the 30-yard line"; it's another thing entirely to say "they need to reach that blue line." One statement takes significantly less mental processing to understand, which, for some viewers, is the difference between enjoying the broadcast and changing the channel. Indeed, I have heard from several people who attended their first live football game and were disappointed by the experience of trying to follow the game without the digital overlays on the field. For some children who have never watched a game on television without those overlays, the effect is jarring; they had never considered the fact that the lines weren't actually there!

For the same reasons, there is a certain level of understanding about a thing that we as humans cannot reach unless we experience the thing physically. In my line of work, when young litigation attorneys are arguing a case involving a specific place or product, they learn the value of actually visiting the place or holding the product in their hands. That experience does not always reveal more quantifiable data about the thing, but there is a qualitative level of understanding that the attorney gains. They feel as if they understand the thing better, and are therefore often better able to form and express arguments about it.

The *Iron Man* movies offer another example of the same truth. In each of the four films in which Robert Downey, Jr.'s version of the Tony Stark/Iron Man character has appeared to date, we see him use AR to design complex machinery, architecture, or landscapes (Fig. 1.2).[2] Whatever it is that he's studying, Stark views digital

---

[2]See, e.g., IRON MAN (Paramount Pictures, 2008).

FIGURE 1.3

Elon Musk acknowledged Iron Man as the inspiration for his own AR system.

renderings that are projected into the space in front of him. By means of poorly explained but fantastically acute holographic and motion-sensing equipment, he physically grasps, manipulates, and alters the data as easily as he would a physical object. (Actually, it's even easier, since a real physical object would offer resistance and could not hang motionless in empty space.) When Stark needs to study an object more closely, he sweeps his arms in broad gestures to expand the display to hundreds of times its original size. If Stark needs to walk among the digital objects as if they were surrounding him on all sides, he can do that.[3] Each such cinematic sequence comes at a point in the plot in which Stark needs to overcome a design problem or gain new insight that he could not grasp merely by reading lines of code or digital images on a computer screen. And each time, it works.

Despite all of the entertaining, fast-paced action and gee-whiz effects of the *Iron Man* movies, these AR design sequences have so stirred viewers' imaginations that they remain some of the most memorable scenes in the films. Perhaps that is because this way of interacting with data just feels so natural to so many people – and also so tantalizingly plausible that we wonder why we don't already have such devices in our own offices and living rooms.

No less than Elon Musk feels the same way. Musk is the billionaire entrepreneur behind Tesla Motors, SpaceX, and the proposed Hyperloop train that could carry passengers from Los Angeles to New York in half an hour. As such, he is already the closest thing that our actual reality has to Tony Stark. He cemented that parallel on August 23, 2013, when he tweeted: "Will post video next week of designing a rocket part with hand gestures & then immediately printing it in titanium." *Iron Man* director Jon Favreau responded, "Like in Iron Man?" Musk replied, "Yup. We saw it in the movie and made it real. Good job!" (See Fig. 1.3.)

---

[3]See, e.g., *Tony Stark Makes an Atom*, YouTube.com (July 22, 2010), available at: http://www.youtube.com/watch?v=6W8Q6wJ_TT8.

The next week Musk followed through, demonstrating on YouTube how SpaceX engineers were combing such devices as the Leap Motion gesture sensor, the Oculus Rift virtual reality headset, and a 3D projector to design rocket parts more or less exactly the way that Tony Stark would.

The point of this exercise was not merely to emulate *Iron Man* (or any of the other Hollywood films that depict AR being used in such a utilitarian manner, such as *Terminator, Serenity, Mission: Impossible – Ghost Protocol*, and *G.I. Joe: The Rise of Cobra*, just to name a few). Rather, Musk explained in his YouTube video that designing three-dimensional objects using "a variety of 2-D tools … doesn't feel natural. It doesn't feel normal, the way you should do things."[4] Interacting with digital objects that appear to be real, on the other hand, only requires a designer to "understand[] the fundamentals of how the thing should work, as opposed to figuring out how to make the computer make it work."[5] "Then," Musk said, "you can you can achieve a lot more in a lot shorter period of time."[6] In the terminology of this chapter, the AR experience becomes a more *convenient* way to interact with the data.

Notice the importance of *feelings* in Musk's explanation of the technology. His premise is that if an interaction *feels* normal and natural on an intuitive level, it will be a more efficient and effective interaction. And that is a difficult premise with which to argue. The fact that interacting with data in this manner just *feels* right is one reason that humanity will inevitably design its technology to function in precisely that manner.

Creativity

Another fundamental characteristic of human nature is the need to express ourselves as individuals. The unique potential of AR to fuel such creative expression also contributes to the technology's inevitability.

When a medium of expression is more convenient and intuitive to use – in other words, when we don't have to think about how to use it, but can focus more on what we want to do with it – the medium will be an effective means of expressing ourselves. At the same time, the depth of what we can express is also limited in many ways by our chosen medium. For example, coloring, pointing, screaming, and grunting all come to young children more naturally than actual words. But one reason kids soon turn to language is because they quickly reach the limits of how much they can express with these other forms of communication. On the other end of the spectrum, I have a good friend who is a master violinist. His instrument gives him a "voice" that can express emotion to a depth that mere words cannot reach. But only through years of rigorous training did that means of expression become natural enough for him that he could use the violin to express actual music, as opposed to the painful shrieks the instrument would emit if I tried to use it.

---

[4]*The Future of Design*, YOUTUBE.COM, available at: http://www.youtube.com/watch?v=xNqs_S-zEBY#t=18.
[5]*Id.*
[6]*Id.*

In a similar way, digital imagery has become a rich medium for creative expression. And although two-dimensional rendering still requires a significant amount of training and skill to do well, the means to create it is becoming cheaper and easier to use all the time. As we add more dimensions to those images, the potential for creative expression goes up, but so do the practical barriers to entry. High-quality three-dimensional imagery is still difficult to do well; just witness the difficulties that movie companies faced getting audiences to accept 3D movies, despite the constant pressure to make them commercially viable. Taking those three-dimensional images and making them appear to be physical objects that persist and adapt to human interaction over time – what some in the AR industry refer to as "4D" – remains an even tougher nut to crack.

The cornucopia of creative expression that awaits when the public at large is able to experience AR is a big part of what keeps innovators working on the technology. To illustrate the qualitative difference between creative expression in standard 2D versus 3D or 4D, picture (the original) General Zod and his Kryptonian cohorts taking bodily form again as they escaped their two-dimensional "Phantom Zone" prison in the 1980 movie *Superman II* (Fig. 1.4). Or, even more aptly, consider the "Space Liberation Manifesto" advocated by science fiction author and *Wired* columnist Bruce Sterling at the 2011 Augmented Reality Event in Santa Clara, California. There, as part of his keynote address, Sterling arranged for a group of "rebels" dressed in faux-futuristic jumpsuits to "hijack" the speech to spread flyers advocating a populist agenda for this new "blended reality." The manifesto – which Sterling promptly published in his *Wired* blog – read, in part:

> *The physical space we live in has been divided, partitioned and sold to the highest bidder, leaving precious little that is truly a public commons. The privatization of physical space brings with it deep social, cultural, legal and ethical implications. Private ownership of physical space creates zones of access and trespass,*

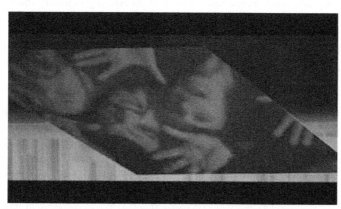

FIGURE 1.4

The two-dimensional Phantom Zone prison in *Superman II*.

participation and exclusion. Private use of physical space becomes an appropria-
tion of our visual space, through architecture, so-called landscape design, and
ubiquitous advertising whose goal is to be seen well beyond the boundaries of
privately owned property. Simultaneously, private space becomes the preferred
canvas for street artists, graffiti writers and other cultural insurgents whose works
seek the reclaimation [sic] of our visual space, the repurposing of private political
and commercial space for their alternative cultural messages.

The nature of SPACE is changing. In the past, space primarily meant physical
space – the three dimensional cartesian world of people and places and things.
Networked digital computing brought us the notion of cyberspace – an ephemeral
"consensual hallucination" that nonetheless appeared to have an almost physi-
cal sense of place, a separate and parallel universe alongside the physical world.
Today, as computing and connectivity become pervasive and embedded into the
world and digital information infuses nearly every aspect of the physical environ-
ment, space has become an enmeshed combination of physical and digital – a
'blended reality'. Cyberspace has everted; reality is enspirited.

This new physical+digital SPACE brings new characteristics, new affordances,
new implications for culture. Its physical dimensions are finite, measurable, sub-
ject to ownership and control, but its digital dimensions are essentially infinite,
subjective, and resistant to centralized control or governance. The new SPACE
opens tremendous opportunities for access, expression and participation, but also
for commercialism, propaganda, and crushing banality.[7]

Prolixity aside, this passage does a good job of foretelling the "tremendous opportunities" for creative expression in a world where the digital and physical can
be combined in a meaningful, perceptible way. The manifesto's example of graffiti illustrates the point well. When people are limited to physical means to express
themselves, one person's artistic appropriation of a given object (such as a brick
wall) necessarily conflicts with the interests of others who would use that object for
different purposes (such as the landowner). With AR, a potentially infinite number
of people could superimpose their own expression on the same physical wall without
changing anything about the wall in "real" space. As Sterling notes, this explosion of
creative democracy will, over time, have profound implications not only for our art
but for our culture as well.

Capability

Before society at large can experience the medium of AR, it first needs the technological capability to do so. The fact that we are now beginning to cross that practical threshold is what makes the future potential of AR an important consideration for the present.
Sterling's manifesto is right to note that "computing and connectivity [have] become
pervasive and embedded into the world,"[8] because it is that development that will lay

---

[7]Bruce Sterling, *Augmented Reality: Space Liberation Manifesto*, WIRED.COM (May 19, 2011), available
at: http://www.wired.com/beyond_the_beyond/2011/05/augmented-reality-space-liberation-manifesto/.
[8]*Id.*

the groundwork for ubiquitous AR. The sheer amount of computational ability that we all carry with us each day has reached a critical mass that enables some truly amazing experiences. And by application of Moore's law, which holds that processing power doubles roughly every 2 years, we can expect that potential to grow exponentially.

We are at the point where each step forward in computational ability promises an entire new layer of digital–physical interaction. Brian Mullins, president and co-founder of the industry-leading company Daqri, has often noted in his public presentations that it was the addition of a compass, accelerometer, and enhanced processing power to the iPhone 4 that allowed AR apps to make the jump from simply detecting QR codes and other 2D markers to recognizing three-dimensional objects and overlaying data onto them in four dimensions.

That device hit the market in June 2010 – 3 short years before this writing. Now Apple considers the iPhone 4 too antiquated to sell any longer. Virtually all of the devices the Elon Musk used in his *Iron Man*-esque YouTube video – e.g., the Leap Motion sensor and the Oculus Rift headset – have been introduced in the interim. If we have gone from relatively simple iPhone apps to gesture-controlled rocket design in 3 years, what will be possible in another year? In 3? Ten?

FOLLOW THE MONEY

The progression of digital technology to date and the multiple visions of our augmented future from people who understand the technology are persuasive evidence of AR's imminence. But these are not the only indicators. Investors and market watchers are also increasingly placing their bets on AR.

SmarTech Markets Publishing's revenue forecasts

In 2013, SmarTech Markets Publishing released a report called *Opportunities for Augmented Reality: 2013–2020*. Despite identifying a number of practical hurdles that must still be overcome, "SmarTech believes that there is enough in this analysis to suggest a strong and profitable future for AR."[9] Some of the reasons SmarTech offered for this conclusion include that:

- The "mobile industry" is already "huge" and "sophisticated."
- "AR is already out there as a deployed technology to some extent."
- "It also fits in well with other important trends such as the rise of tagging/RFID, NFC, location-based services, image recognition, and visual search."
- "Strong business cases can be made for AR using today's technology."
- "Many of today's backers are firms with deep pockets."[10]

The report lists several well-known companies in the AR industry that had already received recent venture capital investments of between $1 and 14 million, including Layar, Tonchidot, Total Immersion, Ogmento, Ditto, Wallit, Flutter, GoldRun,

---

[9]Smartech Markets Publishing, Opportunities for Augmented Reality: 2013–2022 [this should be a page number if you have access to the actual source] (2013).
[10]*Id.*

CrowdOptic, Blippar, and Wikitude.[11] In June 2013, shortly after the release of SmarTech's report, Daqri announced $15 million in private investment to support its own AR platform.[12]

These funds are called "investments" for a reason; the people making the investments expect a return on their money. The SmarTech report gives good reason to expect one. It forecasts revenue in the AR industry to exceed $2 billion by 2020, and to surpass $5 billion just 2 years later.[13]

Tomi Ahonen's predictions on AR usage

SmarTech is not the only prognosticator to talk in numbers of this magnitude. Tomi Ahonen is an oft-quoted consultant and author of 12 books on the mobile industry. He characterizes AR as the "Eighth Mass Medium" of human expression, following print, recordings, cinema, radio, television, Internet, and mobile.[14] He has followed the growth rates of these technologies, and come up with his own forecasts for the rate at which society will adopt AR. Ahonen predicts 1 billion users of AR across the globe by 2020, with that number climbing to 2.5 billion by 2023 (Fig. 1.5). Translated into revenue, these figures are more optimistic than SmarTech's prediction.

Even more notable, however, is the similar exponential growth curve in both charts. Whether expressed in terms of dollars or users, both forecasters see the technology catching on first with a core market, and then taking off like wildfire from there. The experience of the Internet and mobile industries over the last few decades lends credence to these predictions.

Gartner's estimations concerning workplace efficiency

In November 2013, the information technology research and advisory company Gartner estimated that digital eyewear had the potential to net field service companies $1 billion in savings by 2017.[15] "The greatest savings in [this field] will come from diagnosing and fixing problems more quickly and without needing to bring additional experts to remote sites,"[16] it said. But the report also saw "potential to improve worker efficiency in vertical markets such as manufacturing, field service, retail and healthcare."[17] Numbers like these are certain to catch the attention of professionals from several industries.

---

[11]*Id.* at [page number].

[12]Nick Summers, *DAQRI Raises $15M to Develop Its Augmented Reality Platform, Will Support Google Glass at Launch*, THENEXTWEB.COM (June 4, 2013), available at: http://thenextweb.com/insider/2013/06/04/daqri-raises-15m-to-develop-its-4d-augmented-reality-platform-will-support-google-glass-at-launch/.

[13]SMARTECH MARKETS PUBLISHING, supra, note 9, at [page number].

[14]Tomi Ahonen, *Augmented Reality—The 8th Mass Medium*, TED TALKS (June 12, 2012), available at: http://tedxtalks.ted.com/video/TEDxMongKok-Tomi-Ahonen-Augment;search%3Atag%3A%22 tedxmongkok%22.

[15]"Gartner Says Smartglasses Will Bring Innovation to Workplace Efficiency," Nov. 6, 2013, available at: http://www.gartner.com/newsroom/id/2618415.

[16]*Id.*

[17]*Id.*

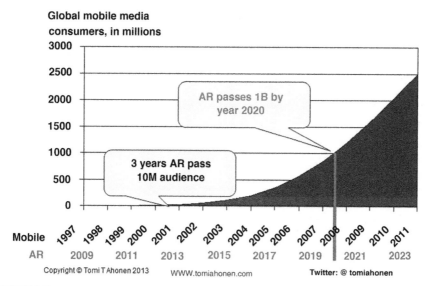

FIGURE 1.5

Tomi Ahonen's predictions on AR usage.

CONCLUSION

If you've read this entire chapter, the chances are good that you are becoming as convinced as I already am that the AR is poised to be a major force in American and global industry over the coming decade. If so, then follow me to Chapter 2 to learn in a little detail more about what the "AR" medium looks like.

A Summary of AR Technology

INFORMATION IN THIS CHAPTER:

- Defining terms
- Augmenting each of the senses
- Supporting technology
- Levels of adoption

INTRODUCTION

The goal of the previous chapter was to persuade you that augmented reality (AR), and the multiple ways in which it will intersect the law, are important. This chapter is meant to help you understand what AR actually is. After all, most good legal analyses begin by defining their terms.

More precisely, I want you to understand what I and the sources I will cite mean when we talk about AR, because the term means significantly different things to different people. Indeed, there are many within the AR community who do not care for the term "augmented reality" at all, believing that it sounds too stilted and artificial to ever be meaningful to the general public. Others have invented slightly different terms to refer to specific types of, or approach to, what could be considered AR.

Further, complicating this discussion is the fact that AR is not an island unto itself. If technologies that squarely fit within the definition of "augmented reality" are ever going to fully manifest themselves in society, they will require support from, and need to work in harmony with, panoply of related technologies that do not, in and of themselves, fit entirely within the "AR" box. A proper discussion of AR's role in society, therefore, must take these technologies into account as well.

Recognizing this fact, the industry's leading conference changed its name in 2013, from the "Augmented Reality Event" to the "Augmented World Expo." Following that lead, this book will likewise use the term "augmented world" to mean the full range of devices and technologies that work together to digitally enhance everyday life.

DEFINING OUR TERMS
AUGMENTED REALITY

Let's begin with the phrase "augmented reality". The subject of the phrase is "reality". That's the thing being "augmented" by AR technology. So, what do we mean by "reality" in this context? Obviously, we could answer that question in several ways. For example, when asked recently to give an example of "augmented reality" that the general public could easily understand, one commentator responded (perhaps jokingly): "drugs".

That's not what the emerging AR industry has in its mind. It doesn't encompass the dream worlds of such films as *Inception* or *Sucker Punch*, or a drug-enhanced vision quest. Poetic license aside, we're not talking about mental, emotional, spiritual, or metaphysical "reality" when we discuss the latest AR app. Instead, we mean the actual, physical world we all inhabit.

What, then, does it mean to "augment" that reality? Starting again with what it doesn't mean, it's important to note the distinction between AR and *virtual* reality, or VR. This, more familiar term describes a completely self-contained, artificial environment. Think *Tron* or *The Lawnmower Man*, or the web-based worlds of *Second Life* and *World of Warcraft*. The Oculus Rift headset that debuted in 2013 is another example of virtual reality because the display completely covers the user's eyes (Fig. 2.1).

FIGURE 2.1

Oculus Rift is a contemporary example of *virtual*, not *augmented*, reality.[1]

[1]© Flickr user Sergey Galyonkin, used under CC BY-SA 2.0 license. See https://creativecommons.org/licenses/by-sa/2.0/

ONLY FIVE SENSES?

Technically, biologists identify anywhere between nine and 21 separate physical "senses" in humans. Those outside the classical five sense understanding include pressure, itch, proprioception (body part location), nociception (pain), equilibrioception (balance), thirst, hunger, magnetoception, and time, among others.[59] An exploration of how these senses could also be digitally augmented would (and likely will) be fascinating, but is beyond the scope of this book.

[59] "How Many Human Senses are There?" wiseGEEK, available at http://www.wisegeek.org/how-many-human-senses-are-there.htm (last visited September 13, 2014).

The user's actual, physical surroundings don't enter into the experience. (That said, several developers have begun equipping the Oculus Rift with external, forward-facing sensors capable of incorporating the user's surroundings into their virtual environment, thereby enabling a true AR experience through the device.[2])

AR, then, is a blend of VR with plain old physical reality. The American Heritage Dictionary defines the verb "augment" as "to make (something already developed or well under way) greater, as in size, extent, or quantity."[3] That's what AR does. It uses digital information to make our experience of actual, physical reality "greater." It doesn't create a brand new, standalone plane of existence; it simply adds to the information we already process in the physical world. (This is an objective description, of course: whether AR makes our experience subjectively "greater" or promises to be a fascinating and very context-specific debate.) This book will frequently use the word "virtual" to describe the digital information displayed by AR devices. This is an accurate use of the word "virtual" – which means "existing or resulting in essence or effect, though, not in actual fact, form, or name"[4] – because AR often creates the illusion that digital information exists in, and interacts with, physical reality. But do not confuse the usage with "virtual reality."

Tying this understanding of "AR" with the word "reality" shows why it's important to define our terms. How does this technology increase the "size, extent, or quantity" of our physical reality? To answer that question, we need to recall how it is that we experience the physical world. And the answer, of course, is through our five senses: sight, smell, touch, taste, and hearing. "AR," therefore, is a technology that gives us more to see, smell, touch, taste, or hear in the physical world than we would otherwise get through our non-augmented faculties.

Again, it is important to recognize that even this definition of AR does not command universal consensus. When I first proposed the foregoing formulation in

---

[2] See, e.g., wizapply, "Augmented reality device for the Rift : Trial production," Oculus VR Developer Center, June 27, 2013, available at https://developer.oculusvr.com/forums/viewtopic.php?f=29&t=2042

[3] AMERICAN HERITAGE DICTIONARY (4th ed. 2000).

[4] Id.

March 2011, Bruce Sterling, the science fiction author and *Wired* columnist who has headlined several AR industry conferences and earned the nickname "The Prophet of AR," responded that he preferred a definition first articulated by Dr. Ronald Azuma, computer science professor at the University of North Carolina Chapel Hill. This definition "formally insists on some real-time interactivity with an augment in a registered 3D space." Otherwise, Sterling explained, "you get into trouble with adjunct technologies like 3D movies, digital billboards or projections. They have the AR wow factor, but, they're not using the core techniques of the field i.e. real-time processing of real 3D spaces."[5]

Sterling's point is a fair one. If we define our subject matter so broadly as to encompass too many commonplace technologies, then we dilute the significance of our conversation about AR, and we detract from the innovation currently underway in the AR field. At the same time, however, Sterling also admitted that, "in practice, these academic distinctions aren't gonna slow anybody down much."[6] We have laid out a sufficient understanding of what AR is to appreciate and what makes it special.

SYNONYMS

As I mentioned, some of the most prominent names in the AR industry do not care for the term "augmented reality" at all. For some, the concern is the one expressed above – that the phrase encompasses too many disparate technologies to be meaningful. To others, the term is such a mouthful that it shuts down conversation. Still others find "augmented reality" too reminiscent of "virtual reality," which they feel already lacks mainstream credibility, or else has too much of a science fiction ring to it. Underlying all of these views is the fear that, by using the wrong terminology, the AR industry will scare off too many potential consumers and unnecessarily stunt the technology's growth and its mainstream adoption.

For example, some commentators use such terms as "enhanced reality" or "reality with benefits."[7] As time goes by, assuming that AR experiences continue to become more prevalent, we may just call it another aspect of "reality," and leave it at that way. After all, twenty years ago, it was in vogue to refer to the internet as the "information superhighway," and the verbal imagery of on- and off-ramps was everywhere. No one speaks in such terms today.

VARIATIONS ON THE THEME

Some phrases that sound similar to "augmented reality" actually have a sufficiently different meaning to merit discussion. One such example is "augmediated" or simply "mediated" reality, terms preferred by University of Toronto professor and wearable

---

[5]Brian Wassom, *Defining Terms: What is Augmented Reality?*, WASSOM.COM (March 30, 2011) http://www.wassom.com/defining-terms-what-is-augmented-reality.html
[6]*Id.*
[7]See KTP Radhika, *Reality, With Benefits*, FINANCIALEXPRESS.COM (May 3, 2013) http://computer.financialexpress.com/features/1272-reality-with-benefits.

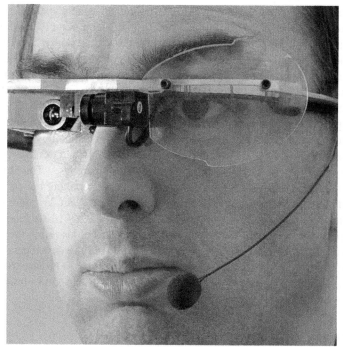

FIGURE 2.2

Steve Mann.[10]

computing pioneer Dr. Steve Mann. "[C]onsidered by many to be the world's first cyborg,"[8] Mann has worn one version or another of his EyeTap digital glasses for more than 20 years. In a 2012 interview, Mann said that "augmented reality doesn't make sense. Augmented reality just throws things on top, and you get a certain amount of information overloaded. We call it mediated reality." (See Fig. 2.2.)[9]

Mann expounded on the difference during his keynote address at the "2013 Augmented World Expo." As opposed to simply adding digital content, Mann's "augmediated reality" enhances things that are dark and filters out bright lights to allow the user to see the physical world more completely. For example, he used this technology to weld steel without wearing a conventional mask. He also gave the real-life example of standing in the headlight beams of an oncoming car and being able to see both the license plate and the driver's face. Of course, both examples fall neatly within

---

[8]Nick Bilton, *One on One: Steve Mann, Wearable Computing Pioneer*, THE NEW YORK TIMES, August 7, 2012, *available at* < http://bits.blogs.nytimes.com/2012/08/07/one-on-one-steve-mann-wearable-computing-pioneer/?smid=tw-share&_r=0 >.
[9]*Id.*
[10]© Steve Mann. Used under CC BY-SA 3.0 license. See http://commons.wikimedia.org/wiki/File:SteveMann_self_portrait_for_LinkedIN_profile_picture_from_dsc372b.jpg.

our definition of augmented reality as "making greater" one's visual perception of the world, even though the additional content that Mann perceived was physical rather than digital. His perception was nevertheless "augmented" and it was accomplished by digital means. Nevertheless, some people do use "AR" in the same narrow sense that Mann does, and it is valuable to understand the distinctions. If anyone has earned the right to be heard on the subject of how we speak about digital eyewear, it is Steve Mann.

Moving in the opposite direction, we encounter the phrase "diminished" or "decimated" reality. These terms refer to the use of AR technology to decrease the amount of content we perceive. Mann has used this term when describing a feature of his "EyeTap" device that filters out visual ads for cigarettes.[11] This, too, fits our working definition of "AR," if we think of such filters as making our perception of the world *qualitatively* greater. Will Wright, creator of the *SimCity*, *Sims*, and *Spore* video game franchises and another keynote speaker at the "2013 Augmented World Expo," spoke favorably of diminished reality as a means of lessening the amount of unwanted visual distractions in our lives. He encouraged the developers present to "add beauty to the world rather than using it as another way to browse the internet." Diminished reality will play a large role in this book's discussion of trademark law and civil society, among other things.

RELATED VOCABULARY

A few terms pop up often and uniquely enough in discussions of AR that are worthwhile to point out their meanings here. I'll introduce several during the course of the book, but a few are worth pointing out at the outset.

Chief among these is the concept of "immersion" or "immersiveness." This refers to the degree to which a user's mind subconsciously accepts a digital illusion as being physically real. Even when the user objectively understands that the digital representation is not tangible, their visceral experience of the content can still *feel* that way. The more immersive an "AR" experience is, the more effectively it has done its job. (Little wonder then, that one of the oldest companies in the AR field is named as "Total Immersion.")

"Geolocation" is a fairly self-explanatory term, but "geofencing" may not be. This refers to the establishment of invisible boundaries in real space, the crossing of which triggers a digital response. For example, the owners of a sports stadium may establish a "geofence" around the stadium's perimeter, allowing only those who cross inside to access exclusive content about the game. Advertisers establish "geofences" within a certain radius around a particular store to trigger advertisements to passersby.

"Digital eyewear" is a generic term I prefer, but that is not yet widely adopted in the mainstream press. "Smart glasses" have become a more popular synonym. Both

---

[11] *Id.*

terms are meant to include all forms of head-worn devices that directly intersect and digitally alter a user's field of view. Such generic language also sidesteps the debate about whether a particular device is truly "AR," and to avoid devoting a lopsided amount of attention to any one particular manufacturer or product. This is especially helpful now, when most mainstream press uses "Google Glass" as a stand-in for, or segue to, the entire AR field. "Google Glass" is ahead of the pack in terms of getting to market and in stirring conversation. But there is disagreement over whether it is truly "AR" (it isn't marketed as such), and it is only one limited expression of what digitally enhanced eyewear can achieve.

A TECHNOLOGY FOR ALL SENSES

Although we usually think of the visual sense when discussing and creating AR, our definition of the term encompasses digital enhancement of all five senses. Therefore, to round out our understanding of AR, let's survey some examples of how each sense could be, or is being, augmented.

VISION

A picture is worth a thousand words, and by some estimates, the brain processes visual imagery up to 60,000 times faster than text alone.[12] So, it is not surprising that most AR research has focused on how to augment the sense of sight. Yet this may also be the most difficult sense to augment well. Because our eyes perceive so acutely, it is difficult to trick them into accepting digital content as physically real. That is especially true because, with the exception of true holographic projections, digital displays must remain two-dimensional, and rely on some form of intermediary filter to create the illusion of three- (or four-, if you like) dimensionality.

AR developers are experimenting with several media to create this illusion. The earliest and simplest was the television screen. Leaving aside the academic debate of whether this truly fits the definition of AR, the digital scrimmage and first down lines that appear on the screen in every NFL broadcast are some of the earliest and most effective examples of digital content intermixed with physical reality in a way that our minds accept as real. As mentioned in Chapter 1, I personally know several people (most, but not all, of whom were children) who attended a professional football game in person, for the first time, only to feel cheated and disappointed that the lines were not actually there on the field. Their habit of reliance on this digital enhancement made it much harder to follow the action of the non-augmented game.

One of the earliest ways that actual AR was first distributed was through computer webcams. Programs running on desktops or laptops use the webcam to recognize a certain "target" – usually a printed code or special image, although it could also

---

[12]Media Education Center, Using Images Effectively in Media, available at < http://oit.williams.edu/files/2010/02/using-images-effectively.pdf > (citing research by 3M).

include particular body parts such as a hand or face – and then display digital content atop that target on the computer screen. Early examples included a promotion for the *Transformers* movies called *We Are Autobots,* which superimposed a robot's head over the user's, moving the image along with the user's in real-time video to create the illusion that he or she was really wearing the mask. (Fig. 2.3) Retailers have used a similar line of "virtual try-on" websites to allow users to see themselves on-screen wearing such products as rings, watches, eyeglasses, or clothes. In fact, as discussed in Chapter 5, these applications have been some of the first to spur patent infringement disputes related to AR.

The Lego company installed this same technology into in-store kiosks to promote its toys. A customer holding a Lego® box up to such a kiosk would see animated versions of the toys that could be constructed using the bricks in the box, moving around in three dimensions as if they were physically standing atop the actual box. Larger versions of the same concept have been installed on billboard-sized screens to promote various goods or causes.

Most AR available today exists in apps available for download and use on a mobile device. These perform a variety of functions, from displaying digital content on two-dimensional images, to augmenting physical objects recognized in the real world, to displaying walking directions directly atop the sidewalk a user sees through their device's video camera.

Navigation is also a prominent motivator for augmenting vehicle windshields, another potential medium for augmented displays. Pioneer has already launched its first version of an AR navigational aid, and more are sure to come. Several automotive companies have announced that they are developing technology for displaying driving directions over a driver's field of view, or for enhancing safety by highlighting roads in foggy weather or calling attention to road signs. A scene from *Mission Impossible: Ghost Protocol* even shows a car windshield with a proximity detector

FIGURE 2.3

The "We are autobots" promotion.

that displays the heat signatures of pedestrians in the vehicle's path. Toyota has also discussed the concept of augmenting the view for backseat passengers with all manner of entertainment content.[13] These applications are discussed more fully in Chapter 7.

The technology known as "projection mapping" also deserves mention here. This is the use of precisely positioned and timed digital projections to create the illusion of altering the illuminated object.[14] There are many who would not consider it AR, including Bruce Sterling in the above-mentioned quote. But, when done well (YouTube hosts a number of fine examples), projection mapping creates as complete an illusion of digital reality as any device I have seen. Adding to that, a projection mapping system currently under development at the University of Tokyo is capable of tracking fast-moving objects so precisely that it can project an advertisement on a bouncing tennis ball without missing a frame,[15] and I believe it accurate to describe the technology as "augmented reality."

Digital eyewear, however, is the real holy grail of visual AR. Users can only hold a mobile device out in front of themselves to see the augmented overlay in its video feed for so long before developing the feeling of exhaustion that AR developer Noah Zerkin aptly calls "gorilla arms."[16] Webcams and windshields are effective media, but not portable. Combining the best of both worlds requires a medium that is always in our field of vision, but that doesn't require any extra work or thought to stay there. Only digital eyewear fits that bill.

Unsurprisingly, developers have been working on such eyewear for at least three decades – as Steve Mann demonstrated in 2013 through his traveling exhibit of 30 years' worth of AR headwear. (Fig. 2.4) Now, several companies are poised to begin selling digital eyewear that is aesthetically acceptable and affordable enough to be enjoyed by the public at large – including Meta, a company Mann helps run. Most of the digital eyewear devices announced as of this writing are aimed at the consumer market. In September 2014, however, Daqri announced the "DAQRI Smart Helmet," a hardhat-like device designed to be used in industrial settings. "It has a transparent visor and special lenses that serve as a heads-up display, along with an array of cameras and sensors that help users navigate and gather information about their environment."[17] Once it hits the market, this device could help field service and similar

---

[13]See Dave Banks, *Toyota's "Window to the World" Offers Backseat Passengers Augmented Reality*, WIRED (July 29, 2011) *available at* http://www.wired.com/geekdad/2011/07/toyotas-window-to-the-world-offers-backseat-passengers-augmented-reality/

[14]See *Definition of Projection Mapping*, VJFORUMS (January 17, 2012) http://vjforums.info/threads/definition-of-projection-mapping.37607/ for a healthy debate on the meaning of this phrase and its relationship to AR.

[15]See < http://www.wimp.com/trackingcamera/>.

[16]Dan Farber, *The Next Big Thing in Tech: Augmented Reality*, C-NET (June 7, 2013) http://www.cnet.com/news/the-next-big-thing-in-tech-augmented-reality/

[17]Don Clark, "Augmented Reality Experts Unveil Hardhat 2.0," Wall Street Journal September 5, 2014, available at http://blogs.wsj.com/digits/2014/09/05/augmented-reality-experts-unveil-hardhat-2-0/.

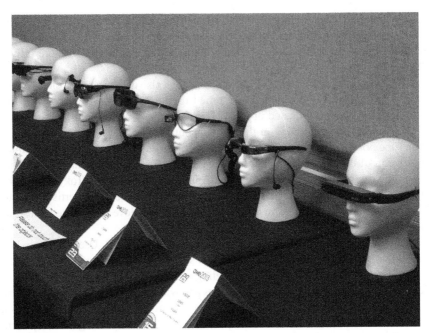

FIGURE 2.4

Steve Mann's traveling exhibit showcasing 30 years' worth of digital eyewear.

industries that would begin to realize the cost savings predicted by the Gartner report discussed at the end of Chapter 1 (Fig. 2.5).

TOUCH

Technology that enhances the sense of touch is better known as "haptic." After visual technology, this field has the most promise for delivering meaningful AR experiences. The Finnish company Senseg has been developing technology to turn touch screens into "feel" screens that generate any number of artificial textures, edges, or vibrations. It accomplishes this illusion through the use of touch pixels, or "Tixels™," that employ Coloumb's force, the principle of attraction between electrical charges. By passing an ultra-low electrical current into the insulated electrode, Senseg says that its "Tixels" create a small attractive force to finger skin. Modulating this attractive force generates artificial sensations.[18]

Scientists at the University of Tokyo have gone one step further and developed "a flexible sensor thinner than plastic wrap and lighter than a feather."[19] When overlaid

---

[18]See *A New Solution for Haptics*, Senseg.com, http://senseg.com/solution/senseg-solution (last visited May 27, 2014).

[19]John Pugh, *New E-Skin Brings Wearable Tech to the Next Level*, PSFK, (August, 14, 2013) *available at* http://www.psfk.com/2013/08/e-skin-university-of-tokyo.html

FIGURE 2.5

The DAQRI smart helmet.

on human skin, it creates an "e-skin" that is as persistent and imperceptible as modern AR eyewear is to the eye.

At 2013's ISMAR and Inside AR conferences, Disney introduced a different sort of haptic technology called "AIREAL." It uses precisely timed puffs of air to create physical sensations at defined points in open space.[20] And on September 9, 2014, Apple's announcement of the Apple Watch advanced the general public's understanding of what is possible with haptic feedback. "Right now, phones can provide physical feedback in one way: they buzz. But the Apple Watch can provide different kinds of haptic feedback and buzzing directionally to provide subtle directions or tapping lightly when a friend wants to say hello ...."[21] Apple also promised an eccentric feature that transmits the wearer's heartbeat to another person.

HEARING

Aural AR gets less attention, and would appear to hold less potential for innovation. Hearing aids, after all, have been digitally enhancing our aural sense for many years.

Yet there are those doing important work in this field. One of the most interesting-looking projects is run by Dr. Peter B.L. Meijer called "vOICe." This technology aims

---

[20]See Rajindwer Sodhi et al., AIREAL: Interactive Tactile Experiences in Free Air (2013) *available at* http://www.disneyresearch.com/project/aireal/

[21]Alexis Madrigal, "What Apple's New Products Say About the Future," The Atlantic, September 9, 2014, available at http://m.theatlantic.com/technology/archive/2014/09/what-apples-new-products-say-about-the-future/379907/.

to use and adapt sound waves into "synthetic vision through auditory video representations"[22] that allow totally blind individuals to effectively "see."

Others are working on next-generation hearing aids for use by people even with normal hearing. These would allow users to focus on a particular conversation in a crowded room, or automatically block sudden, unexpected loud noises. As of this writing, a start-up called Intelligent Headset is preparing to ship a pair of headphones by the same name with a type of aural AR it calls "3D sound," together with a variety of AR apps designed for gaming, education, and tourism.[23]

Meanwhile, some developers in the "quantified self" effort to collect even-more-detailed information about individuals' physical health have discovered that the ear is a much better location on the body for taking measurements than the wrist, where most present-day fitness devices are worn.[24] If this spurs manufacturers to sell, and users to wear, more ear-based devices, it is logical to expect that this will increase the demand to give these devices additional capabilities that actually effect, and augment, our hearing.

TASTE AND SMELL

Neither of these two related senses has ever offered much room for digital enhancement, but some work toward this end has been done. "The 'Tongueduino' is the brainchild of MIT Media Lab's Gershon Dublon. It's a three by three electrode pad that rests on your tongue … [and] connects to one of several environmental sensors. Each sensor might register electromagnetic fields, visual data, sound, ambient movement – anything that can be converted into an electronic signal. In principle, this could allow blind or deaf users to 'see' or 'hear' with their tongues, or augment the body with extra-human senses."[25]

The most prominent work in augmented taste is being done by Dr. Adrian Cheok and his students at the Mixed Reality Lab at Keio University. "Smell and taste are the least explored areas because they usually require chemicals,"[26] Dr. Cheok told an interviewer. But "we think they are important because they can directly affect emotion, mood, and memory, even in a subconscious way. But, currently its difficult because things are still analog. This is like it was for music before the CD came along."[27] Eventually, Dr. Cheok hopes to simulate smells in a digital manner, such as through magnetic stimulation of the olfactory bulb. The Mixed Reality Lab has even

---

[22]Peter B.L. Meyer, *Augmented Reality for the Totally Blind*, *available at* http://www.seeingwithsound.com/(last visited October 5, 2013).

[23]See https://intelligentheadset.com/.

[24]Rachel Metz, "Using Your Ear to Track Your Heart," MIT Technology Review, August 1, 2014, available at http://www.technologyreview.com/news/529571/using-your-ear-to-track-your-heart/

[25]Tim Carmody, *Trick out your tongue and taste the sensory-augmented world with Tongueduino*, THE VERGE) February 21, 2013) *available at* http://www.theverge.com/2013/2/21/4014472/trick-out-your-tongue-taste-the-world-with-tongueduino.

[26]Rick Martin, *The Next Step in Augmented Reality: Electrify Your Taste Buds*, SD JAPAN (June 21, 2013) *available at* http://www.startup-dating.com/2013/06/mixed-reality-lab-electric-taste

[27]*Id.*

FIGURE 2.6

Daqri's MindLight.

solicited papers for a workshop dedicated to augmenting the lesser-explored senses of touch, taste, and smell.[28]

Not far from this program, at the University of Singapore, another team of researchers is "trying to build a 'digital lollipop' that can simulate taste."[29] The group's leader, Dr. Nimesha Ranasinghe, says "a person's taste receptors are fooled by varying the alternating current from the lollipop and slight but rapid changes in temperature."[30] If the technology were perfected for commercial use, "[a]dvertisers might include the taste of a product in an add on your computer or television. Movies could become more interactive, allowing people to taste the food an actor is eating. [P]eople with diabetes [could] taste sugar without harming their actual blood sugar levels."[31] The team even hopes video game designers will offer players taste-based rewards and penalties in response to gamer's performance.[32]

EXTRA-SENSORY AR

Just when I thought I understood the boundaries of AR, I encountered the latest technology being developed by Daqri. The *New York Times* recently covered an application Daqri calls "MindLight," which detects a user's brainwaves using wireless EEG sensors connected to digital eyewear. [33] When the sensors detect that the user is concentrating on a light bulb, the bulb turns on or off. Think "The Clapper," but with brainwaves (Fig. 2.6).

[28]Bruce Sterling, *Augmented Reality: Touch, Tast, & Smell: Milti-Sensory Entertainment Workshop*, Wired, (August 17, 2013) *available at* http://www.wired.com/beyond_the_beyond/2013/08/augmented-reality-touch-taste-smell-multi-sensory-entertainment-workshop/

[29]Nick Bilton, "Getting to the Bottom of a Digital Lollipop,' *New York Times*, November 22, 2013, available at http://bits.blogs.nytimes.com/2013/11/22/getting-to-the-bottom-of-a-digital-lollipop/.

[30]*Id.*

[31]*Id.*

[32]*Id.*

[33]Quentin Hardy, *Thinking About the Next Revolution*, New York Times (September 4, 2013) *available at* http://bits.blogs.nytimes.com/2013/09/04/thinking-about-the-next-revolution/?_r=2.

FIGURE 2.7

Device interactivity through the Daqri Smart Helmet.

Flipping light switches, however, is the least impressive application of this revolutionary development. Daqri envisions "[t]his system increas[ing] the efficiency of industrial processes many fold by pointing workers toward targets for action in a specific sequence, measuring their concentration at critical junctures, and enabling pre-visualization of each action to reduce mistakes."[34] At the 2013 Augmented World Expo, CEO Brian Mullins demonstrated that the system could learn the brainwaves associated with many different images, allowing the images to be displayed as soon as the user thinks of them. The potential ramifications of this technology are simply astounding.

SYNTHETIC SYNTHESIS

Of course, the greatest potential in these separate means of augmentation lies in their combination. Just as we need all five senses working together with each other in order to fully appreciate our physical reality, so too will the effect and utility of AR be exponentially increased when multiple senses are augmented simultaneously. Such augmented experiences would be, in a word, far more *real*.

The initial teaser videos for the Daqri Smart Helmet provide a glimpse of one type of this interactivity between devices. The company intends that "users will have the ability to touch and control the interface through integration with new form factors, such as smart watches."[35] The video shows a worker viewing an augmented display hovering over his wrist, through which he can scroll by swiping his watch (Fig. 2.7).

---

[34]Gaia Dempsey, *Controlling Objects Through Thought: 4d And EEGs*, DAQRI BLOG http://daqri.com/2013/09/mindlight-controlling-objects-through-through-4d-and-eegs/#.UlG5LIash8E (last visited October 5, 2013).

[35]Daqri, *Smart Helmet Features*, available at http://hardware.daqri.com/smarthelmet/features.

SUPPORTING, OR "AUGMENTED WORLD," TECHNOLOGIES

Any discussion or implementation of AR also necessarily involves a variety of technologies that are not, in and of themselves, AR, but without which an augmented experience would not be possible. As explained above, I will refer to these as "augmented world" technologies.

MESH NETWORKING AND THE PANTERNET

I have come to believe that certain types of augmentation will not be practical on a mass scale until devices become much more autonomous, capable of sensing and interacting with each other, rather than relying on a single cloud server – or even a single internet – to provide all of the necessary data. This leads into a discussion of what is called the Internet of Things ("IOT"), an already emerging ecosystem in which digitally networked physical devices talk to each other and can register their geopositions in real time. At current rates, it will not be long before virtually every physical object we encounter on a daily basis will be hooked into the IOT.

But the concept I am aiming at here is also broader than the IOT. It also includes mesh networks – digital infrastructures "in which each node (called a mesh node) relays data for the network [and a]ll nodes cooperate in the distribution of data in the network."[36] Applied to AR, this means that an individual's wearable devices will be able to perceive and interact with networked devices the person encounters without having to rely on a connection to a central internet. This sort of infrastructure would greatly shorten the distance that data has to travel in order to become available to the user, and increase the number of pathways that data can take to get to the user, thus reducing potential lag time in transmission and eliminating devices' reliance on a steady Wi-Fi or LTE signal. In this environment, augmented user interfaces would be more reliable, and hence more likely to be adopted.

The slowly unfurling infrastructure to support networked automobiles is likely to spur development of this sort of technology. Networked vehicles will be expected to interact with fixed, roadside nodes in order to exchange data with a traffic control system. They will also be designed to communicate with other vehicles in order to reduce traffic accidents. Neither type of interaction can afford to be dependent on a strong Wi-Fi signal or a central cloud server.

Another step in this direction came in the form of the "goTenna," a phone-sized device that emits a wireless signal to create its own closed network, allowing participating devices to connect with each other. After another decade or so of miniaturization, one could imagine a similar capability being built into tiny, perhaps even microchip-sized devices and distributed broadly, allowing every business, family, or

---

[36]"Mesh networking," Wikipedia, available at http://en.wikipedia.org/wiki/Mesh_networking (last visited September 13, 2014).

social group to create its own ad hoc network independent of the internet.[37] Already, in September 2014, Sequans Communications and Universal Scientific Industrial announced their plans to release to market an all-in-one modem module capable of equipping IOT devices with the ability to transmit an LTE wireless signal.[38]

A related development is the steady progression toward universal, high-speed access to the internet at all points on Earth – what I will call the "Panternet." Both Facebook (through its Internet.Org project and a fleet of "drones, lasers and satellites") and Google (through "Project Loon, [an] effort [to] launch[] Internet-beaming antennas aloft on giant helium balloons"), among others, are working toward this goal.[39] That sort of infrastructure would also alleviate much of the connectivity issues that stand in the way of an always-on, instantly responsive infrastructure for the exchange of data in augmented form. It would still rely on a central network, and thus not be as robust and responsive as mesh networking, but it could support and be a backstop to such networks.

MECHANICAL VISION AND SENSORS

Mechanical vision is obviously important to the performance of AR eyewear because the devices must be able to detect that something is there before they can augment it. By the same token, the more advanced the eyewear becomes, the better it will need to be at tracking the movements of the user's eyes. Orienting displays so that they appear to overlap a particular physical object is notoriously difficult. To do it well, the device will need to know where the user is looking.

Location-sensing data will be important to the delivery of augmented content. Today's devices are mainly limited to using GPS signals, but those are only accurate to within a few feet and do not travel well through walls. Newer devices use near-field communication (NFC) or Bluetooth low-energy (BLE) sensors to detect location more precisely and indoors.

TAGGANTS FOR PINPOINT-ACCURATE PERCEPTION

My time involved with the AR industry has educated me on the enormous difficulty that computer vision applications have in precisely identifying the exact location, edges, depth, and identity of a three-dimensional object in uncontrolled environments, especially when the object (or sensor) is or is poorly lit. That is why even the most impressive vision-based AR devices rely on controlled environments, ample

[37]Jordan Crook, "The GoTenna Will Let You Communicate Without Any Connectivity," *Tech Crunch*, July 17, 2014, available at http://techcrunch.com/2014/07/17/the-gotenna-will-let-you-communicate-without-any-connectivity/.

[38]"New LTE Module for IoT," *Connected World*, September 11, 2014, available at http://connected-world.com/new-lte-module-for-iot/.

[39]"Facebook launches lab to bring Internet everywhere," Yahoo! News, March 27, 2014, available at http://news.yahoo.com/facebook-launches-lab-bring-internet-everywhere-221915445--finance.html.

lighting, and a high number of pre-programmed details about the image or object being recognized. These make for impressive displays under the right conditions, but not necessarily for robust AR applications suited for everyday use.

Nor is this a minor hurdle. Some of the best computer vision scientists in the world have been working on this problem for decades, and the technology still has an awfully long way to go in this respect.

This is why I have suggested that digital eyewear and other vision-based AR devices will soon rely on micro- or even nano-scale taggants to assist in locating physical objects.[40] As counter-intuitive as it may seem at first, it may actually turn out to be less practical to design computer vision sensors capable of perceiving the world as accurately as the human eye does than it would be to simply paint the entire world with location-aware dots that a machine could locate much more easily. "Taggants," according to one company that makes them, "are microscopic or nano materials that are uniquely encoded and virtually impossible to duplicate – like a fingerprint. They can be incorporated into or applied to a wide variety of materials, surfaces, products and solutions."[41] Some of the taggants available today can be detected from a distance; it is logical to expect that methods of remotely locating taggants will only continue to diversify and miniaturize.

Applied in a way designed to enhance visual AR, taggants might work in a way analogous to present-day radio frequency identification (RFID) tags, but a much smaller. RFID tags already "are tracking consumer products worldwide," reports the website *HowStuffWorks*.[42] "Many manufacturers use the tags to track the location of each product they make from the time it's made until it's pulled off the shelf and tossed in a shopping cart. Outside the realm of retail merchandise, RFID tags are tracking vehicles, airline passengers, Alzheimer's patients and pets. Soon, they may even track your preference for chunky or creamy peanut butter."[43] A British design student even called for "[i]ncorporating small, edible RFID tags embedded in your food."[44] Such a system would allow tracking food products along the entire food chain, from production to digestion, and even enable such devices as "smart plates" that scan your meal via Bluetooth and alert you to potential food allergens.

According to a 2011 *L.A. Times* article, "the Air Force asked for proposals on developing a way to 'tag' targets with 'clouds' of unseen materials sprayed from quiet, low-flying drones."[45] The paper quoted the president of one company that's

---

[40]"A Trillion Points of Light? Taggants as Ubiquitous AR Markers – Part 1," http://www.wassom.com/a-trillion-points-of-light-taggants-as-ubiquitous-ar-markers-part-1.html (June 2, 2011).

[41]Microtrace, *Taggant Technologies*, http://www.microtracesolutions.com/taggant-technologies/?gclid=CL7asN_Ok6kCFZQbKgod22OSdw (last visited November 29, 2013).

[42]Kevin Bonsor & Wesley Fenlon, *How RFIS Works*, http://electronics.howstuffworks.com/gadgets/high-tech-gadgets/rfid.htm (last visited June 8, 2014).

[43]*Id.*

[44]Kyana Gordon, Nutrismart: Edible Food Tags That Track Food Down the Supply Chain, (June 1, 2011) http://www.psfk.com/2011/06/nutrismart-edible-rfid-tags-that-track-food-down-the-supply-chain.html

[45]W.J. Hennigan Pentagon seeks mini-weapons for new age of warfare, Los Angeles Times (May 30, 2011) *available at* http://articles.latimes.com/2011/may/30/business/la-fi-mini-drones-20110531.

developing such nano taggants as saying that tagging, tracking and locating "is a hot topic in government work. It isn't easy tracking somebody in a crowded urban environment like what is seen in today's wars."[46]

According to that company's website, its "nano crystal taggants are deployable in solvents, inks/paints, and aerosols, allowing them to be easily integrated into various [military] applications. .. and customized for the unique needs of other operations [as well]."[47] It already makes "nano crystal security inks that can be incorporated directly into clear laminates, plastics, or appliqués[,] ... and dye- and pigment-based inks (including black inks) for use in banknotes, concert tickets, lottery tickets, or CDs – and even in varnishes and lacquer finishes." The transparent, "nanophotonic" taggants are optically clear, but can be designed to respond to a specific range of UV radiation.

Add these trends together, and what do you get? A technology capable of literally painting the world with AR markers. Micro- or nano taggants baked into paint, plastics, asphalt, ink, or even dust would be invisible to the naked eye, but capable of marking all manner of 3-D objects in a way that appropriately equipped AR optics could potentially be designed to recognize.

These technologies are especially exciting for those developing what AR enthusiasts call a "clickable world," in which a person can physically interact with a physical object and get a digital response. Just as a real estate developer needs an infrastructure of water pipes and power lines in order to build a subdivision of houses, so too will software developers need an infrastructure of geolocation-aware similar sensors in place before the augmented world truly takes shape.

HAND AND GESTURE TRACKING

One of the most important augmented world technologies is gesture tracking. Hand gestures and other physical movements are likely to become the most common way of interacting with digital objects that appear to be physical, if only because it is the most natural way to interact with physical things. As but one example, in 2012 Google obtained U.S. Patent No. 8179604 B1, titled "Wearable Marker for Passive Interaction." The patent describes "[a] wearable marker [in] the form of a ring, a bracelet, an artificial fingernail[, a fingernail decal,] or a glove, among other possible wearable items."[48] Sensors in a user's digital eyewear would "function together to track position and motion of the wearable marker via reflection, and by doing so can recognize known patterns of motion that correspond to known hand gestures."[49] For many, this means of interacting with digital data calls to mind scenes from *Minority Report* and similar sci-fi films (Fig. 2.8).

Closely related to tracking gestures is the ability of digital eyewear to register where the user's hand touches. In May 2014, German AR company Metaio, one

---

[46]*Id.*
[47]<http://voxtel-inc.com/> .
[48]U.S. Patent No. 8,179,604 B1 (filed May 15, 2012)
[49]*Id.*

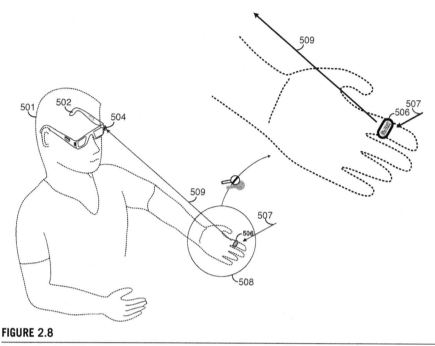

FIGURE 2.8

Illustration from Google's patent on a gestural interface device.

of the most prominent companies in the industry, demonstrated a prototype of the "Thermal Touch" technology it is developing.[50] "Consisting of an infrared and standard camera working in tandem and running on a tablet PC, the prototype registers the heat signature left by a person's finger when touching a surface."[51] Digital eyewear equipped with such technology "could turn any surface into a touch-screen."[52] Still very much in early stages of R&D, however, Metaio projects the technology to be ready for widespread use in 5–10 years.[53]

FACIAL RECOGNITION

Facial recognition technology will be another important augmented world technology. To date, industry-leading companies have shown remarkable restraint in implementing such features. Google has disallowed facial recognition apps on its Glass headset, and Facebook has refrained from rolling out the technology to the degree

[50]Metaio, "Press Release: Metaio unveils thermal imaging R&D for future use in wearable augmented reality headsets," May 22, 2014, available at http://www.metaio.com/press/press-release/2014/thermal-touch/

[51]*Id.*

[52]*Id.*

[53]*Id.*

that it could. But, as AR hardware proliferates, it will be impossible to keep this genie in the bottle. The potential commercial applications are just too numerous and profitable to expect such restraint from all service providers. AR concept videos are chock full of examples in which digital data – including links to their social media profiles, dating service information, even whether they're a registered sex offender – is seen hovering in the air over a person's head. As noted in Chapter 8, the law enforcement community is particularly eager to implement this technology. Facial recognition is by far the easiest and most direct means by which to associate such displays with a particular person.

LEVELS OF ADOPTION

The analysis in this book largely presumes a world that does not quite yet exist. Although the pieces for realizing a fully augmented world are either in place or about to be, there is still progress to be made before the technology penetrates all levels of society and reaches its full potential. I will occasionally contrast these various levels of adoption when discussing AR's legal ramifications, but it might be helpful to consider at the outset what these various stages might look like. These are only predictions, of course, and they get fuzzier the further out we go. But they are based on years of interaction with the people at the forefront of this industry.

NOW: EMERGENCE

The real world at the time of this writing is one in which AR is beyond its infancy, but not quite yet at its adolescence. There are hundreds of AR apps available for our mobile devices, and thousands of marketing campaigns have used the technology. Dozens of start-up companies are touting various AR innovations, and a few of those have received significant funding. Tech columnists write eager words about what's just around the corner in this field. Although AR concepts have shown up in mainstream entertainment for decades, the public is just starting to grasp the idea that this technology is real, thanks in large part to the buzz about Google Glass and a handful of other products.

THE NEAR FUTURE: LEGITIMACY

One of the primary themes at the 2014 Augmented World Expo was the industry's shift in emphasis from the consumer market to enterprise applications. Large companies like Daqri, Raytheon, and the Newport News Shipbuilding Company, among many others, have shown that AR can solve real problems and generate revenue. Investment from this sector will allow the technology to improve without being limited by the aesthetic whims and cost constraints of the consumer market. Within the next few years, AR technology should be able to cross the threshold from gimmicky marketing technique to an everyday method of consuming data used by a large segment of the general public.

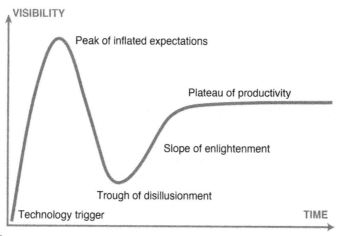

FIGURE 2.9

The Gartner Hype Cycle.[54]

At time of this writing, the most recent prediction of when we may see this transition is contained in the 2014 Gartner Hype Cycle. Gartner Hype Cycle provides a graphic representation of the maturity and adoption of technologies and applications.[55] The graph on emerging technologies charts the progression of various innovations through the phases of development that experience and collective wisdom have demonstrated virtually all technological developments to pass through. These have come to be known as "Innovation Trigger," "Peak of Inflated Expectations," the "Trough of Disillusionment," the "Slope of Enlightenment," and the "Plateau of Productivity." In the annual chart released in August 2014, augmented reality ranked within the middle phase, "the Trough of Disillusionment." In this phase, the buzz of expectation has begun to wear off as some promising early innovations failed to deliver, and unproductive start-ups begin to fold. "Investments continue only if the surviving providers improve their products to the satisfaction of early adopters."[56] (Fig. 2.9)

As the graph suggests, however, this is an inevitable, even healthy period for any new technology to pass through. Next comes the "Slope of Enlightenment," in which "more instances of how the technology can benefit the enterprise start to crystallize and become more widely understood. Second- and third-generation products appear from technology providers. More enterprises fund pilots; conservative companies remain cautious."[57] Finally, on the Plateau of Productivity, mainstream adoption starts to take off. Criteria for assessing provider viability are more clearly defined. The

---

[54]Used under CC BY-SA 3.0 license. See http://creativecommons.org/licenses/by-sa/3.0/.

[55]Gartner, "Hype Cycles," available at http://www.gartner.com/technology/research/methodologies/hype-cycles.jsp (last visited September 13, 2014).

[56]Wikipedia, "Hype Cycle," available at http://en.wikipedia.org/wiki/Hype_cycle (last visited September 13, 2014).

[57]Id.

technology's broad market applicability and relevance are clearly paying off."[58] Gartner's 2014 chart includes an additional notation that it will likely be 5 to 10 years before the technology reached the "Plateau of Productivity."

Once AR begins to approach the Plateau of Productivity, digital eyewear will have become a mainstream product category, available from half-dozen manufacturers or more. Indeed, these will be the centerpiece of the already emerging ecosystem of connected, wearable devices, including subtle gestural controls. Sales of mobile phones will begin to decrease as more consumers come to expect the data they consume to exist in midair rather than on a flat screen.

In this stage of AR's development, entertainment and advertising companies will have begun creating content intended to be consumed in augmented form. Consumers will expect to discover content this way, and the real world will begin to look like a vast, unused canvas ready to be digitally painted. That canvas will include people, as facial recognition and other biometric data become widespread means of identifying each other and associating people with digital content. There will be plenty of debate about when it is appropriate to augment certain people, places, and things, and who has the right to do so. Privacy, intellectual property and obscenity debates will be common (and are previewed in subsequent chapters of this book).

AR will also have become an indispensable tool in a variety of industrial settings, where AR can cut down on production and worker training costs. For the same reasons, augmented methods of teaching will be the hottest trend in educational circles as well. The word "augmented," though, will become less common, as people begin to think of AR as the natural way to consume digital data. But the technology will still have its kinks, in light of how difficult it is to precisely augment moving physical objects. People will complain of motion sickness, and visual augmentations will still rely on various forms of targets and assists to improve image quality, such as location sensors, tags, and projection mapping.

THE MEDIUM TERM: UBIQUITY

At this stage, no one uses "phones" anymore, and two-dimensional screens of any type are used only in rare, special-purpose applications. This will be celebrated as an aesthetic advancement, since physical signage is less necessary, but the virtually nil cost of digital advertising will mean that there is far more clutter in our field of view. AR starts to become reliable enough that, especially in combination with the now-commonplace self-driving cars, even traffic signs have started to become digital-only.

Most social interaction and consumer experiences will have an augmented digital component to them. Visual augmentation will finally have gotten to an acceptable level of acuity, and companies will be experimenting with prototypes of augmented contact lenses.

---

[58]*Id.*

There will also be a significant digital divide between those using the latest AR technology and those who cannot afford it or who are prevented from enjoying it by physical disabilities. We already hear talk of a "digital divide" today, but the implications of the inequality will grow into a full-fledged social justice issue as reliance on the augmented medium grows. Chapter 10 explores this issue from the perspectives of ethics and social science.

THE LONG TERM: MATURITY

At this stage – decades from now – AR is old hat. All digital data comes in augmented form, and we are so accustomed to receiving input by digital means through all five senses that to communicate by any other means will seem quaint. By then, society will be on to the next big thing, whatever that might be. Meanwhile, the ability to interact in this manner will have shaped our societal norms and ethics to a degree that is difficult to foresee. Our society may not be one that people living today would recognize or be comfortable in.

But enough about the far-flung future. Let us now begin to examine the legal principles that will govern the use of AR technology over the next few years.

AR & The Law

B

3 Privacy 43

4 Advertising, Marketing, and eCommerce 71

5 Intellectual Property 101

6 Real Property Rights 153

7 Torts and Personal Injury 175

8 Criminal Law 209

9 Civil Rights 243

10 Litigation Procedure 259

Privacy

INFORMATION IN THIS CHAPTER:

- Sources of privacy law
- Privacy concerns raised by AR
- How AR can enhance privacy

INTRODUCTION

Privacy is a hot topic these days, especially in connection with any sort of communications technology. In part, this is due to the lightning-fast pace at which information technology is developing. The less people understand how the technology works and how it can be used to gather information about them, the more apprehensive they are likely to feel about it. Privacy is as much about emotional reactions as it is about legal doctrine, and it is still a very amorphous concept from either perspective. There is much disagreement about just what the word means, what sort of rights it should include, and where those rights come from.

That said, however, there are various laws and court decisions that define and protect different types of privacy rights. Many of these are likely to be implicated by the development and implementation of augmented world technologies.

SOURCES OF PRIVACY LAW
BACKDROP: THE FIRST AMENDMENT

One basic reason that privacy is such a difficult concept to define and protect in the United States is that it runs counter to our fundamental commitment to free and open speech. Our country was founded on the expression of dissent, personal liberty, and the ability of each individual to participate in the political system. The American legal system still reflects those values in its hesitance to give government the power to prevent a citizen from saying whatever he or she chooses to say – or, putting it more precisely in light of modern communications technology, *conveying* whatever *information* he or she may choose to convey.

In the American legal system, virtually all laws concerning the conveyance of information are limited in their application, to some degree, by the First Amendment to the United States Constitution. This bedrock provision prohibits governments from "abridging the freedom of speech … or of the press."[1] After more than two centuries of interpretation by the courts, this simple statement has been fleshed out into a fundamental principle of free expression that undergirds our entire framework of participatory democracy. As long as the subject of one's speech has any arguable connection to issues that affect the well-being or interests of more than just those involved in the conversation – what the law calls "matters of public concern" – then the right to express that view will almost always be protected by the First Amendment. By contrast, "matters of *private* concern" are those that the law recognizes as not being the legitimate business of anyone other than those directly affected by them. These – and, for the most part, *only* these – issues the law will protect as "private."

The following excerpt from a 2011 Supreme Court opinion gives a concise summary this bedrock legal doctrine:

> *Speech on matters of public concern is at the heart of the First Amendment's protection. The First Amendment reflects a profound national commitment to the principle that debate on public issues should be uninhibited, robust, and wide-open. That is because speech concerning public affairs is more than self-expression; it is the essence of self-government. Accordingly, speech on public issues occupies the highest rung of the hierarchy of First Amendment values, and is entitled to special protection.*
>
> *Not all speech is of equal First Amendment importance, however, and where matters of purely private significance are at issue, First Amendment protections are often less rigorous. That is because restricting speech on purely private matters does not implicate the same constitutional concerns as limiting speech on matters of public interest. There is no threat to the free and robust debate of public issues; there is no potential interference with a meaningful dialogue of ideas; and the threat of liability does not pose the risk of a reaction of self-censorship on matters of public import.*[2]

The fact that this summary of the law preceded an opinion in which the Court ultimately upheld the right of radical protesters to display hateful messages at funerals illustrates the breadth of the phrase "matters of public concern." *Any* arguable connection to public affairs imbues speech with a nearly inviolable legal protection, no matter how controversial a particular speaker's point of view may be.

One corollary of this principle is that information in the public domain is free for all to use. In this context, data is more or less presumed to be public; it is a significant burden to prove that something should be free from public scrutiny. Even if information was once legally private, that privacy is gone for good after it is lost. For example, in the 2001 decision *Bartnicki v. Vopper*,[3] the United States Supreme Court

---

[1] U.S. Const. amend I. The actual text of the First Amendment applies only to Congress, but the courts have long ago established that the Fourteenth Amendment's guarantee of due process resulted in the same restrictions being applicable against state and local governments as well.

[2] *Snyder v. Phelps*, 131 S. Ct. 1207, 1215-16 (2011) (internal quotations, citations, and alterations omitted).

[3] *Bartnicki v. Vopper*, 532 U.S. 514 (2001).

refused to punish a newspaper for publishing video footage, even though a third party had obtained it in the first instance by illegal eavesdropping.[4] And in the famous *Pentagon Papers* cases of 1971,[5] the Supreme Court refused to prevent newspapers from publishing leaked classified military documents about the Vietnam War, even though the government warned that disclosure would lead to the death of Americans abroad. That is how sacrosanct the First Amendment principle against what the courts call "prior restraint" on publication has become.

This also explains why what some call the "right to be forgotten" is unlikely to ever take root in the United States as it is beginning to do in Europe. Various groups have advocated different types of legal proposals to give people a legal mechanism to have embarrassing information about them removed from the public record – particularly internet search engines – and to get others to stop repeating it, even if it was once newsworthy. Some American legal commentators have said that this "sweeping new privacy right ... represents the biggest threat to free speech on the Internet in the coming decade."[6] In 2013, California became the first American jurisdiction to grant a legal right to have personal information deleted from the internet, although the statute applies only to minors and is riddled with uncertainty as to how it will work.[7] But even if the statute survives legal challenge, First Amendment jurisprudence will not permit American regulators to run very far with this idea. The Supreme Court has struck down on free speech grounds more than one law intended to prevent child pornography, for example, and even refused to restrain newspapers from publishing the names of rape victims, so long as the information was legally acquired.[8]

That is why the First Amendment remains the elephant in the room during any discussion of American privacy law, even though the provision itself restricts only the government and not private citizens. It explains, for example, why privacy laws cannot prevent individuals from collecting and repeating information that is freely available in public places – such as overheard sights and sounds – including by recording them. The freedom of speech also explains why the penalties for even a *bona fide* invasion of privacy sometimes seem so anemic; the offender may be punished, but the ill-gotten information typically remains in the public sphere.

This is also why it has been so difficult to find a legal path toward a third category of information between "public" and "private." For example, philosophy professor Evan Selinger of the Rochester Institute of Technology in New York has proposed formalizing the idea of "obscurity" as a legal category for information that, while not

---

[4]*Id.* Similarly, on April 20, 2010, the Supreme Court held in *United States v. Stevens* that the government cannot hold criminally liable someone who distributes a tape of an illegal act (in this case, animal "snuff" films) that he/she was not complicit in committing. *United States v. Stevens*, 559 U.S. 460 (2010).
[5]*New York Times Co. v. United States*, 403 U.S. 713 (1971).
[6]Jeffrey Rosen, *The Right to Be Forgotten*, 64 STAN. L. REV. ONLINE 88 (February 13, 2012).
[7]See CAL. BUSINESS AND PROFESSIONS CODE § 22580–82 (West 2014).
[8]*Florida Star v. B.J.F.*, 491 U.S. 524 (1989).

entirely private, must still remain difficult to access.[9] Despite the attractiveness of this proposal, it is difficult to envision how obscurity could be lawfully enforced in a legal framework that forbids government restrictions on speech.

All of this said, however, the law will restrict *some* speech on *some* subjects under *some* circumstances. Exceptions to the freedom of speech are just as important to the healthy functioning of our democratic system as is the freedom itself. Certain types of information are so unrelated to the public concern, and some methods of expressing it are so disruptive to the public order, that some regulation by the courts is permitted. Moreover, we need spaces in our lives for private discourse, where we can actively explore our opinions with others without fear of public recrimination. Brazilian President Dilma Rousseff reminded the United States government of this point in the midst of news reports that the NSA had tapped her communications. "Without the right of privacy," she said, "there is no real freedom of speech or freedom of opinion, and so there is no actual democracy."[10]

Under most circumstances, however, government protection of individual privacy over free speech remains the exception rather than the rule. As a result, instead of having a single "right of privacy" in the United States, we have one central freedom of speech, together with a mismatched patchwork of state and federal laws occupying the spaces between and surrounding the boundaries of that freedom.

THE COMMON LAW RIGHT TO BE LEFT ALONE

Federalism is another reason for the lack of a uniform "law" of privacy in the United States. Our legal system is one historically based on limiting the powers of the national government, with all other powers of government being reserved for the states. The power to regulate and protect information about individual citizens was not one of the traditional powers of the Federal government, and (with narrow exceptions discussed below) the affirmative limitations on government power in the Bill of Rights do not have much to say on preventing encroachment on personal privacy. Traditionally, therefore, most of the laws protecting personal privacy have come from state legislatures – which retain the general power to pass virtually any law they choose within the very loose boundaries established by the Constitution – and from state courts, which have the inherent authority to go beyond the written statutes and declare principles of judge-made "common law."

The modern era of American privacy protection began in 1960 with the publication of a law review article by Dean William L. Prosser.[11] He summarized what

---

[9]Woodrow Hartzog and Evan Selinger, *Obscurity: A Better Way to Think About Your Data Than "Privacy"*, THE ATLANTIC (January 17, 2013) http://www.theatlantic.com/technology/archive/2013/01/obscurity-a-better-way-to-think-about-your-data-than-privacy/267283/.

[10]Colum Lynch, *Brazil's president condemns NSA spying*, Washington Post http://www.washingtonpost.com/world/national-security/brazils-president-condemns-nsa-spying/2013/09/24/fe1f78ee-2525-11e3-b75d-5b7f66349852_story.html (Sept. 24, 2013).

[11]William L. Prosser, Privacy, 48 CALIF. L. REV. 383 (1960).

by then was a burgeoning but chaotic body of common law decisions from courts across the country and distilled them into four distinct torts that have henceforth become the foundation of privacy law in virtually every state. Three of the four torts amount to variations on what is commonly called "the right to be left alone." They are as follows:

- Intrusion into Seclusion. This common law tort occurs when someone intentionally intrudes upon the private space, solitude, or seclusion of a person, or the private affairs or concerns of a person, if the intrusion would be highly offensive to a reasonable person. The classic example is a secret video camera installed in a changing room or bedroom. The tort occurs upon recording; no publication of the recorded footage is necessary.
- Publication of Private Facts. This separate cause of action arises when someone publicly disseminates little-known, private facts that are not newsworthy, not part of public records, public proceedings, not of public interest, and would be offensive to a reasonable person if made public. Typical examples here include private health matters and intimate sexual information.
- False Light. This cause of action is similar to the tort of defamation (also known as libel or slander), which punishes the unprivileged publication of demonstrably false assertions of fact that injure a person's reputation. The tort of false light is also designed to protect a person's reputation, but it deals with the publication of information that, while potentially true in some respects, is communicated in a manner that conveys something false. It requires a publication made with actual malice that places the plaintiff in a false light and would be highly offensive to a reasonable person.[12]

One common thread running through each of these causes of action is a prerequisite that the aggrieved party have a "reasonable expectation of privacy" under the circumstances alleged. The word *reasonable* is a legal term of art loaded with meaning. For one thing, it is an *objective* measurement. Although courts will often require a plaintiff to have subjectively expected privacy as well, the law does not deem something private just because someone wants it to be. A reasonable expectation of privacy is also one that is constrained by the boundaries of what other laws – such as the First Amendment – make public. A court will determine what the average, reasonable person would have expected under the circumstances, and judge the case according to that standard.

---

[12]Prosser also articulated a fourth means of invading someone's privacy—namely, by "misappropriation of [the person's] likeness" for commercial gain. Since then, however, the interest protected by this body of law has evolved to look much more like property that an individual can own, license and commercialize rather than simply a means to avoid unwanted attention. Today it is more commonly known as the "right of publicity," a phrase recognizing it as a power held by its owner, rather than by the phrase "misappropriation of likeness," which emphasizes the negative result of what the infringer takes away. For that reason, many treatises and courts treat the right of publicity as a matter of intellectual property rather than of privacy, and this book will do the same.

Although Prosser and others like him did much to bring order to the common law of privacy, it remains an inherently decentralized, flexible concept that evolves each time a court applies time-tested principles to the facts of a new case.

EAVESDROPPING AND WIRETAPPING STATUTES

Eavesdropping laws protect the right not to be surreptitiously recorded. More specifically, eavesdropping involves making an audio or video recording of other people under circumstances in which those persons had a reasonable expectation of privacy. Eavesdropping is prohibited by statute in virtually every state, and much of the same subject matter is covered by federal wiretapping statutes as well. It can be punished as a tort, a crime, or both, depending on the jurisdiction. The most recent and highly publicized example of eavesdropping through emerging digital media was the case of now-former Rutgers student Dharun Ravi, who was sentenced to 30 days in jail for using his webcam to secretly record and broadcast his roommate's intimate encounter – an invasion that ultimately led the roommate to take his own life.[13]

The boundaries of prohibited activity vary somewhat between states; for example, some punish only audio recording and not video. Some are "one party consent" jurisdictions, in which the recording is lawful as long as one participant in the conversation agreed to the recording. By contrast, "two party consent" states consider the recording to be eavesdropping unless *all* participants consent. And in both types of jurisdictions, defining "consent" is rarely a simple task.

ELECTRONIC PRIVACY LAWS

There is no one statute, court decision, or other authority that establishes the boundaries between public and private realms online. Instead, we have a patchwork quilt of various statutes intended to address distinct areas of concern. For example, the Electronic Communications Privacy Act[14] and the Stored Communications Act[15] created barriers to both the government and private citizens obtaining the emails of others. The latter statute has since been interpreted to apply to other types of electronic messages that were intended by their senders to be private, such as texts and Facebook direct messages.

Both federal and state authorities have also taken various actions to regulate the use of customers' personal information by the owners of commercial websites and mobile applications. Various federal agencies, including the Federal Trade Commission, Federal Communications Commission, and the National Telecommunications and Information Administration, have all issued their own set of "recommended" guidelines for protecting such interests. The FTC occasionally takes legal enforcement action against

---

[13]See *New Jersey v. Dharun Ravi*,Wikipedia (June 5, 2014)http://en.wikipedia.org/wiki/New_Jersey_v._Dharun_Ravi.

[14]18 U.S.C. §§ 2510–2522 (2012).

[15]18 U.S.C. §§ 2701–2712 (2012).

companies who violate these guidelines in a manner that it considers to be an "unfair" commercial practice.

Meanwhile, the absence of binding legislation from Congress on these issues has led numerous states to pass their own laws regulating other aspects of online privacy. By far, California leads the pack in this respect. In the last few years alone, it has adopted rules on mandatory disclosures of data breaches, requirements for mobile app privacy policies, the ability of minors to get their information taken down, and the responsibility to respect user requests not to have their web usage tracked.

SUBJECT-SPECIFIC PRIVACY LAWS

The foregoing laws protect privacy in broad strokes by establishing general boundaries for behavior or regulating who has access to particular communications media and under what circumstances. There are also laws aimed at safeguarding specific categories of information. For example, the Health Insurance Portability and Accountability Act of 1996 (HIPAA)[16] significantly increased protection for individuals' personal health information. The Children's Online Privacy Protection Act of 1998 (COPPA)[17] regulates the collection and use of information from children younger than 13. The Gramm–Leach–Bliley Act of 1999[18] governs the disclosure of financial data. Various other laws on the federal and state level govern the collection and use of social security numbers and other discrete types of information.

LIMITATIONS ON GOVERNMENT INTRUSION INTO PRIVACY

For the most part, the authorities described above limit how private individuals can collect and use information about other individuals. Our legal system also contains fundamental restrictions on the ability of governmental authorities to collect private information. The most basic of these is the Fourth Amendment to the United States Constitution, which restricts the government from invading "the right of the people to be secure in their persons, houses, papers, and effects, against unreasonable searches and seizures."[19] From this comes the prerequisite that law enforcement officials obtain a judicial warrant based "upon probable cause" before intruding into any place in which a person has a reasonable expectation of privacy. In June 2014, the Supreme Court re-affirmed the importance of this provision in the digital age by holding that the Fourth Amendment requires a warrant before police may examine data on a detained person's mobile device.[20]

---

[16]Pub.L. 104–191, 110 Stat. 1936 (1996)(codified as amended at 29 U.S.C. § 1181 et seq. and scattered sections of 42 U.S.C.).

[17]15 U.S.C. §§ 6501–6506 (2012) Pub.L. 105–277, 112 Stat. 2581-728(1998).

[18](Pub.L. 106–102, 113 Stat. 1338)(1999).

[19]U.S. CONST. amend. IV.

[20]*Riley v. California*, No. 13-132 (June 25, 2014), available at http://www.supremecourt.gov/opinions/13pdf/13-132_819c.pdf.

Of course, subsequent developments such as the USA Patriot Act[21] and NSA surveillance scandals of recent years may call into question the efficacy of these limitations on government power. And to be sure, the opportunities for data collection presented by augmented reality and its supporting technologies will sorely tempt law enforcement agencies to find new ways to monitor and collect individuals' electronic data.

With this legal framework in mind, then, let's consider how AR-related technologies are likely to test the boundaries of American privacy laws.

PRIVACY CONCERNS RAISED BY AR
FACIAL RECOGNITION AND OTHER BIOMETRIC DATA
The importance of facial recognition in an augmented world

There is nothing inherent to augmented reality that requires the collection of biometric data. It *is* ingrained in human nature, however, to seek interaction and companionship with other people, which explains how social media has so quickly become the single most popular function of the internet, and why we invent so many devices for calling, texting, tweeting, poking, tagging, friending, following, and liking each other. That is also why we have already seen several real and imagined apps that bring social networking into the augmented medium. It is safe to say, therefore, that we will use AR technologies for new forms of social media and interpersonal interaction.

In order for any AR device to interact directly with a person, the device first needs to recognize who and where the person is. At present, there is no realistic alternative for accomplishing that task in a social setting other than by facial recognition. Retina and fingerprint scans do and will most certainly have their place, but they require the subject to get a little too up close and personal with the scanner to be comfortable in most settings. By contrast, faces can be recognized passively and at a distance.

Even social technology that we use today demonstrates the inevitability of widespread facial recognition. The capability to implement facial recognition on a broad scale has existed for years, but has been held back. As of this writing, for example, Google still prohibits any app for its Glass eyewear that recognizes faces.[22] These companies are leery of sparking a privacy backlash – which is exactly what has happened each time Facebook has expanded its use of the technology. For example, in 2012 Congressional hearings, Sen. Al Franken grilled Facebook officials about their intentions for the use of these "faceprints."[23] In August 2013, Facebook changed its Statement of Rights and Responsibilities to give it the authority to add individuals'

---

[21]Pub. L. 107-56m 115 Stat. 272 (2001).

[22]Charles Arthur, *Google 'Bans' Facial Recognition on Google Glass - But Developers Persist*, THE GUARDIAN (June 3, 2013) http://www.theguardian.com/technology/2013/jun/03/google-glass-facial-recognition-ban.

[23]*Id.*

profile photos to its facial recognition database.[24] This move was met with probes from various European regulators and promises of additional scrutiny from Sen. Franken.

Yet Facebook continues to roll out facial recognition applications, bit by bit, and has refused Sen. Franken's invitation to promise that they won't use it even more widely in the future. It isn't alone. "Businesses foresee a day when signs and billboards with face-recognition technology can instantly scan your face and track what other ads you've seen recently, adjust their message to your tastes and buying history and even track your birthday or recent home purchase."[25] This prospect became eerily real for me aboard a cruise ship in the Fall of 2012. It used to be that ship photographers had to post their photos in a massive onboard gallery that patrons spent hours browsing through, trying to pick out the pictures in which they appeared. No more. This time, my digital folder was updated in near-real time with new photos every day, using software that had tagged my face or even the faces of others in my party. Chances are that I signed something at some point allowing the ship to do this, although I'm not sure US privacy laws would hold much sway in international waters anyway. But it brought the technology's power home in a visceral way.

It is more than commercial pressures driving the technology, however; criminal acts like the Boston Marathon bombing stoke the demand for law enforcement to have better facial recognition capability. "The FBI and other U.S. law enforcement agencies already are exploring facial-recognition tools to track suspects, quickly single out dangerous people in a crowd or match a grainy security-camera image against a vast database to look for matches."[26] Even more likely to gain public support are apps such as Baby Back Home, an AR app in China that uses facial recognition to allow average citizens to locate and identify missing and kidnapped children.[27]

Or it may be far more simple and personally gratifying applications that finally win the public over. Forbes contributor Tim Worstall recently echoed[28] an argument that I have made for years – that the real "killer app" for AR eyewear will be one that recognizes faces and calls to the user's field of view everything the user knows about that person – their name, the names of their spouse and children, and so on – all in order to avoid embarrassment at cocktail parties.

---

[24]Meghan Kelly, *Facebook May Use Your Profile Photo in its Facial Recognition Tech*," Venture Beat (August 29, 2013) http://venturebeat.com/2013/08/29/facebook-facial-recognition/.

[25]Sarah Freishtat, *Just a Face in a Crowd? Scans Pick Up ID, Personal Data*, The Washington Times (July 26, 2013) http://www.washingtontimes.com/news/2012/jul/26/just-a-face-in-a-crowd-scans-pick-up-id-personal-d/#ixzz2lR6KFeSs.

[26]*Id.*

[27]*Face-Recognition App Lets You Identify Kids That Might be Missing*, Advertising Age (May 31, 2013) http://adage.com/article/creativity-pick-of-the-day/face-recognition-app-lets-identify-kids-missing/241813/.

[28]Tim Worstal, *The Killer Google Glass App That Google Won't Let You Have*, Forbes (November 20, 2013) http://www.forbes.com/sites/timworstall/2013/11/20/the-killer-google-glass-app-that-google-wont-let-you-have/ .

Whatever vector the technology takes, the more such sympathetic and socially redeeming applications of facial recognition gain acceptance, the more inured and less apprehensive the public will be toward the technology. Businesses will then encounter less resistance to using it for more commercial purposes. At that point, society will grapple in earnest with the boundaries that privacy law can and should impose on facial recognition.

Regulating facial recognition

Of course, as mentioned above, regulatory agencies are not waiting until facial recognition becomes ubiquitous before they begin to regulate the technology. On October 22, 2012, the Federal Trade Commission released a report entitled "Facing Facts: Best Practices for Common Uses of Facial Recognition Technologies."[29] The FTC has had its eye on this technology for a long time–at least since the workshop it held on the subject in December 2011[30]–aware that it is being implemented by a wide variety of industries.

Among the privacy issues that concerns the FTC most is "the prospect of identifying anonymous individuals in public."[31] One fundamental consequence of First Amendment jurisprudence, however, is that there are no "anonymous individuals in public [places];" being publicly visible pretty well eliminates any expectation of legally protectable privacy one might hold. Indeed, even before facial recognition technology was dreamed up, the law never recognized a general right to remain an anonymous face in a crowd. This is an example of the proposed right to "obscurity" discussed above.

If anything, it has been the opposite; the law has recognized faces as an important means of identification. For decades, police have used line-ups to identify suspects' faces, and taken mug shots as a means of recording detainees' identities. Although the recent rise of websites that catalogue these mug shots for shaming and extortion purposes has caused some agencies to clamp down on their distribution, most courts still protect the public's right to access these files as public records. And in 2003, a Florida judge refused to allow a Muslim woman to obtain a driver's license unless she agreed to remove her veil and be photographed, ruling the state "has a compelling interest in protecting the public from criminal activities and security threats," and that photo identification "is essential to promote that interest."[32] Therefore, we are unlikely to see any significant regulation on the gathering and use of facial recognition information in public places, unless public outcry results in significant new privacy legislation.

---

[29]Federal Trade Commission, FACING FACTS: BEST PRACTICES FOR COMMON USES OF FACIAL RECOGNITION TECHNOLOGIES (2012).

[30]The Federal Trade Commission, *Face Facts: A Forum on Facial Recognition Technology* (December 8, 2011).

[31]Federal Trade Commission, *FTC Recommends Best Practice for Companies that Use Facial Recognition Technologies*, FTC.GOV (October 22, 2012) *available at* http://www.ftc.gov/news-events/press-releases/2012/10/ftc-recommends-best-practices-companies-use-facial-recognition.

[32]Peter Cosgrove, *Muslim Woman Cannot Wear Veil in Driver's License Photo*, USA Today (June 6, 2003) http://usatoday30.usatoday.com/news/nation/2003-06-06-license-veil_x.htm.

Such regulation may have a greater chance of surviving judicial scrutiny, however, to the extent that it targets purely commercial activity. As the Supreme Court has explained, commercial messages receive less vigorous protection than other speech, at least if they have the effect of misleading the public or fostering illegal activity:

> *The First Amendment's concern for commercial speech is based on the informational function of advertising. Consequently, there can be no constitutional objection to the suppression of commercial messages that do not accurately inform the public about lawful activity. The government may ban forms of communication more likely to deceive the public than to inform it or commercial speech related to illegal activity.*[33]

This is why courts are able to hear such causes of action as trademark infringement, unfair competition and false advertising – all of which involve activities that are, at their core, speech. Because unfair commercial activity is exactly the sort of activity that the FTC exists to regulate, it is a logical starting place for conversations about the use of facial recognition in commerce.

The FTC sees this as the perfect time to publish its expectations "to ensure that as this industry grows, it does so in a way that respects the privacy interests of consumers while preserving the beneficial uses the technology has to offer."[34] The FTC *Facing Facts* report does not have the force of law, but you can bet that it will influence the decision-making processes of FTC administrative law judges and others evaluating novel allegations of "deceptive advertising practices" involving facial recognition.

Although the report characterizes its recommendations as "best practices," it does not do much to actually reduce its discussion to practice. Rather, the report loosely follows the theme of the following three "principles":

1. Privacy by Design: Companies should build in privacy at every stage of product development.
2. Simplified Consumer Choice: For practices that are not consistent with the context of a transaction or a consumer's relationship with a business, companies should provide consumers with choices at a relevant time and context.
3. Transparency: Companies should make information collection and use practices transparent.

These "principles" strike me as so vague as to almost be counterproductive. They are intuitive to anyone making a modicum of effort to incorporate privacy concerns into a facial recognition application. As a result, this recitation is not likely to encourage anything more than a modicum of effort to protect privacy. The technology itself is so young that efforts to guide it remain purely speculative at this point.

---

[33]*Central Hudson Gas & Elec. Corp. v. Public Serv. Comm'n of NY*, 447 US 557, 563-64 (1980) (citations and quotations omitted).
[34]Federal Trade Commission, *supra* note 29, at 21.

I am not alone in being uncomfortable with this report. The FTC committee behind the report adopted it on a 4-1 vote. The dissenting commissioner, J. Thomas Rosch, wrote that "the Report goes too far, too soon." He made three points. First, he thinks that the report fails to identify any "substantial injury" threatened by facial recognition technology. Second, he finds it premature because there is no evidence that any abuses of the technology have yet occurred. Third, he believes the recommendation to provide consumers with "choices" anytime that the technology doesn't fit the "context" is impossible, given the difficulty in assessing consumer expectations. As a result, he says, this amounts to an overly broad "opt-in" requirement.

In the months since this report was released, politicians have not gotten any more specific as to how they would regulate facial recognition technology. Even Senator Franken's November 2013 pronouncement complaining about Facebook says only that he "will be exploring legislation to protect the privacy of biometric information, particularly facial recognition technology" and supports "conven[ing] industry stakeholders and privacy advocates to establish consensus-driven best practices for the use of this technology."[35] Likewise, in December 2013, President Obama announced that his administration would be "looking into" these concerns, but offered no more specifics than Sen. Franken did.

In January 2014, the National Information and Telecommunications Administration convened the industry stakeholder meetings called for by Sen. Franken. Its goal is to articulate consensus guidelines for the application of the President's Bill of Rights to facial recognition technology. I had the opportunity to personally participate in many of these sessions on behalf of the AR industry. As of this writing, those guidelines have not been finalized, and their ultimate utility remains unclear (Fig. 3.1).

The FTC report also expressed worry about facial recognition "data [being] collected [that] may be susceptible to security breaches and hacking."[36] These same concerns have already been expressed about electronic databases of all kinds, and we have seen the consequences of banks, credit card companies, and retailers having their information hacked. As a result, there are already several laws on the books (mostly at the state level) regulating the privacy of commercial databases and spelling out proper procedures to follow when that privacy has been compromised. The FTC also treats the failure of companies to adequately secure customers' personally identifying information as an unfair commercial practice, and occasionally brings related enforcement actions. For example, in May 2014, it settled charges it brought against Snapchat for failing to provide the advertised level of data security to users of its mobile video messaging app.[37]

---

[35]Letter from All Franken, Chairman of Subcom. on Privacy, Technology, and the Law, to Lawrence E. Strickling, Assistant Secretary for Communications and Information, U.S. Department of Commerce (November 21, 2013) *available at* www.franken.senate.gov/files/documents/131131NTIAFacebookLetter.pdf.
[36]FEDERAL TRADE COMMISSION, *supra* note 29, at 7.
[37]FTC, "Snapchat Settles FTC Charges That Promises of Disappearing Messages Were False," May 8, 2014, available at http://www.ftc.gov/news-events/press-releases/2014/05/snapchat-settles-ftc-charges-promises-disappearing-messages-were.

FIGURE 3.1

One of the NTIA's industry stakeholder meetings on the regulation of commercial facial recognition technology.

Indeed, one plausible scenario is that governmental agencies and courts will begin to treat the recognizable dimensions of one's face as another facet of the "personally identifiable information" that is already regulated by a variety of laws. Other examples of such sensitive data include Social Security numbers, mailing addresses, ZIP codes, phone numbers, and IP addresses. Under today's laws, businesses are not forbidden from asking for or collecting such information, but they must post privacy policies listing the information they collect and how it is used. They must also disclose when websites deposit "cookies" on users' computers that allow the user to be tracked by advertisers as he or she moves between various websites. Some effort is underway to legally regulate the use of cookies and enforce "do not track" protocols, but they have not been very successful to date.

DATA ENHANCEMENT

Mid-air augmented displays of virtual information also create new privacy concerns. Concept art of near-future AR applications is rife with examples of augmented data being displayed as hovering over or nearby individual people. In some cases this is social networking or other self-disclosed information about the person, or even digital advertising associated with the individual's apparel. In other cases, though, it is data about the person that is stored in a variety of disparate databases with varying degrees of public accessibility, and collected by the AR device into one unified display. These include credit scores, transactional information drawn from IOT-connected devices, political affiliations, and even whether the person appears on sexual offender registries. In these concepts, such displays are made possible by recognizing the person's facial features and using that identification to query other databases for information about the person.

The FTC has previously raised concerns about practices like these, which it calls "data enhancement."[38] It began by noting the vast amount of facial data already collected by social media companies, and that could easily be gathered by other commercial face recognition applications. The FTC then went on to cite a study by researchers at Carnegie Mellon University, which combined readily available facial recognition software with data mining algorithms and statistical identification techniques to determine an individual's name, location, interests, and even the first five digits of their Social Security number.[39] Powered by AR, this capability could ultimately make available to everyone virtually every fact known by anyone about someone, just by looking at that person. The ability to socially reinvent one's self at any point in life, already under threat by social media, would be essentially lost.

To address this concern, the FTC suggested such basic steps as reducing the amount of time that companies retain facial information and disclosing to the consumer how their data may be used. Aside from being difficult to enforce, however, these suggestions do very little to address the practice or policing of such data enhancement. If copious amounts of personal information ever become visible through the mere act of seeing someone's face, we can be certain that the resulting public outcry will lead to practical and legislative steps to curb abuses of this practice similar to the steps described elsewhere in this chapter to address similar concerns in analogous circumstances.

For the foreseeable future, then, the most productive avenue for protecting the privacy of one's face in public may be more practical than legal. There are already a variety of software products that purport to shield users from being tracked online. The free market will certainly meet the same demand with regard to facial recognition. Already, several innovators have proposed various types of camouflage and countermeasures to throw off facial recognition software. These include off-center masks, makeup, clothing covered in face-prints, and hats containing infrared lights that confound video cameras.

Software engineer Greg Vincent has even suggested the development of a wearable protocol similar to the robots.txt files that prevent certain websites from being indexed by search engines.[40] (Fig. 3.2) Using this protocol, says Vincent, "I can

---

[38]FEDERAL TRADE COMMISSION, PROTECTING CONSUMER PRIVACY IN AN ERA OF RAPID CHANGE, 45-46 (March 2012) *available at* http://ftc.gov/os/2012/03/120326privacyreport.pdf.

[39]The report was called "Faces of Facebook: Privacy in an Age of Augmented Reality" and authored by Alessandro Acquisti. It appears to no longer be available at the location to which the FTC's report cites, or on any other website that this author has located. But a lecture by Acquisti on a similar topic is available here: https://www.youtube.com/watch?v=Kcz0hUtYVXc.

[40]*Google Glass: What are Some Potential Solutions to Issues Regarding Google Glass and Privacy?* QUORA (June 6, 2014, 7:08 PM) <http://www.quora.com/Google-Glass-4/What-are-some-potential-solutions-to-issues-regarding-Google-Glass-and-privacy> (March 12, 2013); *see also Robots.txt for Your Face,* (March 23, 2013) http://stopthecyborgs.org/2013/03/23/robots-txt-for-your-face/>.

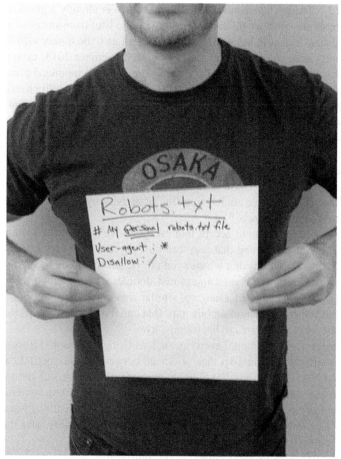

FIGURE 3.2

Greg Vincent's rough sketch of a robots.txt file for your face.

request that our conversation not be shared with anyone other than you and I ... [or] that I not be recorded for later use, that you not photograph me, that you not use facial recognition technology on me, or that you not record my voice."[41] As long as society retains its anxiety about facial recognition and the law remains unable to assuage that concern, we can expect the fashion and consumer electronics industries to fill the gap.

SURVEILLANCE AND SOUSVEILLANCE

All eyes on everything

Privacy advocates have long worried about "Big Brother" governmental agencies using advanced technology to spy on citizens. Such surveillance activity is inevitable,

---

[41]*Google Glass, supra* note 36.

as the 2013 NSA spying scandal has reminded us. It is already a given that surveillance cameras are everywhere in modern-day public life, from stores to gas stations to street corners to traffic lights. Those are so small as to be barely visible anymore, and we rarely even think about them. Indeed, in November 2013, even the City of Las Vegas – that self-proclaimed haven of anonymity – announced plans to install "Intellistreets" street lights that, among other things, have the ability to record sound and shoot video.[42] Knowledge is power, and it is the nature of governments to collect all the knowledge available to them.

But we are also entering an era where personal, wearable video recording devices are about to become ubiquitous. Wearable technology empowers individuals to record the words and deeds of themselves and others far more pervasively than any government could reach. Digital eyewear pioneer Steve Mann has coined the word "sousveillance" to describe such "recording of activity by a participant in the activity," or "inverse surveillance."[43]

We have already come to accept that everyone we meet is likely to be carrying a video-equipped cell phone that they can pull out at any moment. But the newest recording devices are ones that we wear on our persons. Among the earliest of these is the Looxcie, an over-the-ear camera that doubles as a Bluetooth headset. More recently, GoPro has launched a range of similar wearable cameras. Both companies' devices come with companion mobile apps that can transfer recordings to Facebook, or broadcast what a user sees to his friends, live.

The earliest forms of digital eyewear, such as Google Glass and Recon's ski goggles, represent a transitional species of device between simple digital cameras and true AR devices. They offer a heads-up display of information, but are not currently designed to truly augment our perception of the physical world by superimposing on our vision interactive digital images with the illusion of physicality. Photo and video capability are, however, an important part of their functionality, and they make it remarkably easy to record on the fly.

All wearable devices are designed to be comfortable, which can cause the wearer to forget they're there. California Lieutenant Governor Gavin Newsom wore the Glass prototype during a television interview. Newsom later told Wired, "You can easily forget you have them on, and sense the capacity of use in the future," adding the headset felt incredibly light, comfortable and inconspicuous on his head.[44]

Wearable devices are intended to let technology get out of your way so you can record life while still participating in it. This has fantastic upsides, and is something I have already enjoyed; I've made great, hands-free videos of my kids with my Looxcie and my Glass while continuing to play with them, rather than pull out my

---

[42]Chris Matyszczyk, *Street lights to spy on everything that happens in Vegas?* CNET (November 9, 2013) http://news.cnet.com/8301-17852_3-57611630-71/street-lights-to-spy-on-everything-that-happens-in-vegas/ .

[43]See Torin Monahan, Surveillance and Security: Technological Politics and Power in Everyday Lief 158 (2006)

[44]Roberto Baldwin, *Sergey Brin Finally Lets Someone Else Where Google Glass*, WIRED (May 29, 2012) http://www.wired.com/2012/05/sergey-brin-finally-lets-someone-else-wear--google-glass/.

camera and separate myself from the experience. But there are also easily foresee-able downsides to forgetting you're wearing a video camera on your head. I wore my Looxcie during a 2012 augmented reality conference, to underscore the talks I gave there about (among other things) this very subject. Even in that crowd–who are the movers and shakers in the industry that will produce these devices–I got a number of odd looks, turned heads, and derailed conversations.

And accidents do happen. While wearing my Looxcie, even I – someone who was keenly interested in the device's impact on privacy – forgot I was wearing it at times, and I ended up accidentally recording (and later deleting) at least one conversation that was supposed to be private, along with a couple inherently private situations. What if I had forgotten I was wearing the camera when I walked into a *public* bath-room, and recorded myself or someone else in a compromising position? Or worn it (accidentally or intentionally) into any other setting in which people expected pri-vacy, such as a family home, bedroom, or church confessional? Or read a confidential document or email? And worse, what if, instead of being set to merely record, my device was live-streaming to Facebook or some other audience?

At present, this is much more of a concern with a device like the Looxcie, which has a battery life of approximately five hours and is designed for continuous recording, than with the earliest digital eyewear. As of this writing, for example, Glass has a battery life of only 30 minutes when recording video,[45] and it lights up conspicuously when running – not to mention that activating the recorder requires a hand gesture or voice command. In other words, it is not at all a device designed for surreptitious recording.

But these are the types of concerns we will encounter in droves once true AR eyewear goes mainstream. Most of the buzz surrounding these devices centers on the digital images that they overlay onto the user's field of view. Less discussed so far, however, is the fact that, in order to truly augment the user's vision, the eyeglasses need to also see (and recognize) what the user sees. Thus, every prototype of AR eye-wear we have seen to date includes an integrated, forward-facing video camera. They have to. The earliest of these devices record only when necessary to run a particular app in order to conserve power. But as the augmented experience becomes more ro-bust, these cameras will need to remain on constantly in order to make the discovery of digital content more organic, spontaneous, and useful.

There are also audio-only devices that pose similar concerns. In October 2013, a wristband-like audio recording device call Kapture accomplished its fundraising goal on Kickstarter. Here's how the creators described its function:

> *Kapture functions as a 60-second buffered loop. The loop continuously overwrites itself until you tap the device to save a clip. The saved file is downloaded to your smartphone where the duration can be shortened and you can name, tag, filter, and even share it. Simple!*[46]

---

[45]Saul Berenbaum, *Google Glass Explorer Edition has a 30-minute battery life while shooting video*, DIGITAL TRENDS (April 25, 2013) http://www.digitaltrends.com/mobile/google-glass-30-minute-videobattery/#ixzz2lb9DqSYX.

[46]Kapture, *Kapture: The Audio-Recording Wristband*. KICKSTARTER (October 3, 2013) http://www.kickstarter.com/projects/1483824574/kapture-the-audio-recording-wristband.

Basically an audio-only version of Looxcie, Kapture's founders foresee it being used to preserve unrepeatable moments with kids or friends, or to record an epiphany while the user is driving.

But once the devices are in consumers' hands, there will be no way to limit the purposes for which they are used or the subject matter they are used to record. Even the users themselves are not likely to realize everything they're recording, even when they're subjectively aware that a recording is being made. The human ear has a marvelous ability to pick one voice out of a crowd and focus on it, ignoring all other conversations. Recording devices, on the other hand, pick up everything within earshot, even the confidential conversations that someone wearing the device may not even realize they're hearing.

Sousveillance and invasion of privacy

Wearable sousveillance technologies will prove enormously useful in many circumstances. Their use is not inherently incompatible with personal privacy. Nevertheless, they will make possible eavesdropping and common-law invasions of privacy on an unprecedented scale, to the point where these technologies will eventually force a redefinition of what the common law recognizes as private.

From a privacy standpoint, the biggest concern will be the devices that are always on and always recording, such as the Looxcie and the Kapture. Because these are designed to keep recording even without conscious intervention by the user, it becomes virtually inevitable that the user will wear them into situations where he or she would not otherwise think to pull out a recording device, and where he or she would not record if they had been thinking about it. Here I am referring to private conversations and intimate surroundings. The fact that these devices record over their buffers every so often is irrelevant from a liability perspective; it is the act of recording that constitutes eavesdropping and/or intrusion into seclusion. Taking the next step and broadcasting that recording to third parties – which, again, at least some of these devices can be set to do with or without conscious intervention – risks additional liability for causes of action such as publication of private facts or, depending on the context, false light.

Although other mobile AR devices *could* be used to make surreptitious recordings, the prospect does not seem materially greater than with the smartphones and other mobile recording devices already on the market. As long as the onus is on the user to manually activate the recording feature, they are functionally equivalent to any other form of recording device. Indeed, head-worn recording devices actually have less capacity for surreptitious recording, since they require the user to constantly look at the subject of the video recording and to be within earshot to hear the audio being recorded.

Privacy concerns can also be at least partially mitigated to the extent that the device in question makes it reasonably clear to third parties that it is recording. Eavesdropping and privacy rules generally cover *surreptitious* recordings, not those made with the knowledge of the person being recorded. The Looxcie, for example, turns on a small red light when it is recording. It is unclear as of this writing whether the

Kapture wristband or the various digital eyewear in production give any such warning. Of course, whether such warnings are sufficient to give fair warning of the recording, or whether users have made efforts to obscure them, will depend on the facts of each individual dispute, and may require litigation to sort out. The trouble is, going through all of the procedural steps necessary to sort out the facts of a case can be a long, complicated, and expensive process. I was once involved in an eavesdropping lawsuit that lasted for eight years, and one of the central questions throughout the case was whether the video cameras used to make the recording at issue, and the warning lights on them, were visible or not.

Over time, as wearable recording technology becomes more commonplace, the average person's expectations – and, therefore, the law's definition of a *reasonable* expectation – of privacy will change. Thirty years ago, shoppers in retail stores would not have expected to be filmed as they browsed the aisles. Now one cannot walk into the typical big-box store without being captured from every angle on hundreds of obscure security cameras. Twenty years ago, spies and oddballs were the only people we would expect to carry recording devices on their person, and to publish such footage in real time across the planet was unfathomable. Today, it's odd to meet someone who *doesn't* carry a device with all of those capabilities. We have accepted those developments, and our expectations of privacy have adjusted accordingly. Those expectations will continue to evolve along with our technology.

Surveilling the sousveillers

People in view of those wearing digital eyewear are not the only ones who can be recorded by the devices. Wearable devices are already being used to keep tabs on their users as well.

This potential will become especially apparent once eyewear becomes truly capable of augmenting our vision with data that overlays specific physical objects and places. To accomplish that feat, the devices will need to know not only where the object or place is, but also where the user's eyes are pointed, in order to maintain the illusion that the digital data is in a fixed physical location. Eye-tracking data is already of great interest to retailers and advertisers, who crave to know what draws customers' attention. If our digital devices can store and transmit that data, you can bet that advertisers will be clamoring to get their hands on it.

Similarly, employers will be keen to know how much attention their employees are paying to their assigned tasks at any given time. Being able to monitor employees' eye movements would offer a tempting means of measuring productivity and efficiency. Still other examples of potential uses for this data abound, as do other means of gathering it. As facial recognition technology improves, for example, retail displays will know not only who we are, but also what we're looking at. Thus will we fully enter into the commercial experience depicted by the groundbreaking futurist film *Minority Report*, in which augmented displays personalize shopping experiences based primarily on retinal data.

Following the movements of our eyes will not be the only way that a fully connected, internet of things economy will be able to track us, however.

PASSIVE DATA COLLECTION THROUGH THE INTERNET OF THINGS

The phrase "going off the grid" was coined to describe a lifestyle that intentionally avoids interacting with technology that leaves a trace of one's activities. As depicted by characters in popular fiction, this has heretofore been accomplished mainly by paying for things with cash instead of credit, using a false name, and talking on pay-as-you-go mobile phones. But how can one stay off the grid when every single physical device in existence has the capacity to gather and transmit digital data?

The IOT's sense of touch: beacons and taggants

As of this writing, Bluetooth Low Energy (BLE) technology is just starting to roll out to the public, most notably in the "iBeacon" feature of Apple's iOS7. It has been seen as a rival to Near Field Communication (NFC) technology (which iOS8 also embraces), or as a convenient way to pipe coupons into your phone. But history will look back at BLE as a major step forward in manifesting the Internet of Things (IOT), and in eroding any remaining illusions of privacy we have in our physical whereabouts.

BLE is a means of transferring data. "Beacons" – devices that use BLE – are tiny, wireless sensors that transmit data within a 10-meter range. At present, they support only low data rates and can only send (and not receive) small data packets, but these are perfect for interacting with iPhones and wearable computing devices such as smart watches and fitness trackers.[47] In light of the current proliferation in such devices, therefore, it's safe to say that in the near future we may carry a half-dozen devices or more that are equipped with BLE or similar technology.

One of the most obvious applications of BLE is micro-location geofencing. GPS technology is great for determining your approximate location to within a few feet, but it relies on satellites that can't see into buildings very well. A mobile device running BLE technology, however, can interact with nearby beacons to determine its precise location, even indoors.

Set up around a store, they can detect shoppers entering and exiting, and send them coupons (customized to your unique shopper profile) or even internal directions – *Minority Report* without the retinal scans. You will soon be able to even pay for goods without ever pulling out your phone, just like the newest vehicles will open their doors even when your key stays in your pocket. PayPal is already developing just such an app using BLE.

The real potential of BLE lies not in coupons, but in the IOT–the burgeoning trend towards making physical objects internet-connected and digitally interactive. Just like humans cannot meaningfully interact with the world around them without their five senses, so too will IOT-enabled objects lack interactivity without some means of sensing and communicating with their surroundings. BLE beacons are a major step toward providing that ability.

---

[47]Elyse Betters, "Apple's iBeacons explained: What it is and why it matters," *Pocket-Lint*, September 18, 2013, available at http://www.pocket-lint.com/news/123730-apple-s-ibeacons-explained-what-it-is-and-why-it-matters/

In all likelihood, some improved version of BLE technology, or its next-generation replacement with even broader capabilities, will be available either when this book is released, or shortly thereafter. Moreover, as discussed in Chapter 2, the need for digital sensors to precisely locate physical objects may lead to the deployment of beacons or taggants on the micro- or even nano-scale. Each of these devices – including present-day beacons and RFID tags as well as taggants and other future technologies – will be able, in theory, to have its own unique IP address on the internet. The migration begun in 2012 of the Internet Protocol address system from IPv4 to IPv6 increased the total number of IP addresses from a mere 4.3 billion – a number we've already reached – to 340 undecillion (i.e., 340 trillion trillion trillion). Now, literally every Barbie doll, toilet paper roll, and random chatski can have its own unique IP address on the internet. Each becomes a data point capable of reporting its exact physical location on a real-time, global map. Once more people are using this infrastructure, its consequences will become more apparent.

Aggregating our interactions with the IOT

Digitizing our physical interactions will create a digital record of our movements and whereabouts that had never previously existed. For advertisers and retailers, this will be a goldmine of information just like social media was before it–a brand-new trove of personal data that can be used to send out even more precisely targeted commercial solicitations. Without doubt, those providing IOT services will want not only to recognize who we are, but also to remember where we've been.

And just like we do online now, many users will consent to their information being collected in this manner. The convenience factor will be huge. Just as internet browsers use cookies and browsing histories to remember who I am without forcing me to re-type my password every time I re-visit a website, so too will I want my clothing store to remember my size, my restaurant to remember my favorite meals, my grocery store to remember the location of my favorite items, and the news feeds that I'll see projected everywhere to remember my favorite topics.

But others will be remembering that data as well. Thanks to Edward Snowden and others like him, the world is already aware of how much information private companies and the government collect about our emails and other online interactions. Law enforcement already does all it can to track a suspect's physical movements, whether through cellular towers, IP addresses, or GPS trackers. In the near future, the government will likely have access to high-resolution, constantly updated digital maps of the entire planet's surface; the Pentagon's National Geospatial-Intelligence Agency is already at work on an "orthorectified image skin" that would provide the base layer for a next-generation map.[48] Just like GPS and the internet itself, it will only be a matter of time before the private sector gets its hand on this geolocation data (Fig. 3.3).

---

[48]Ray Locker, *Pentagon Agency Creating Digital Map of the World*, USA Today (October 26, 2013) http://www.usatoday.com/story/nation/2013/10/25/nga-digital-map-world-updated/3189781/.

FIGURE 3.3

The defense agency working on next-generation digital maps.

When the government and the private sector have access to high-fidelity geolocation data and a geolocation-aware sensor infrastructure, merely walking down the street with one or more sensor-enabled devices on our persons will leave behind so much data about our physical location that it may well become possible to create precise maps of our every step going back hours, days, or even longer. Add to that the digital data we'll leave behind in each of the physical objects with which we interacted along the way. Everything we touch – the toothbrush we use in the morning, our clothing, doors through which we pass, the pavement we step on, even the plastic fork from the street-side falafel stand – could potentially be capable of not only recording their interactions with us, but also transmitting that data to one or more servers, which then collect, collate, and make the data available for reporting out.

Even this possibility could one day seem tame if a system of trackable nanotaggants ever truly becomes reality. With that technology, it could become possible for the first time to literally destroy the possibility of privacy altogether–at least when it comes to concealing your physical location. Consider: the nanotaggants that the military is reportedly developing are intended to be sprayed onto enemy combatants so they can be tracked in situations where direct surveillance is impossible, such as urban combat. Because these devices exist on a micro or nano scale, they're invisible to the human eye. Ideally, the soldier won't even know he's been tagged, let alone be able to find or remove all of the devices. The same technology could be used to track anyone. Even if you knew you were tagged, could you remove them all? A human skin pore is 200~250 nanometers wide, which easily allows nano-scale products to be absorbed into the skin. What if you inhaled or ingested them? Like Lady Macbeth, you'd wash and wash, but never get the damned nano-spot out.

Privacy regulations and IOT

Government regulators are only beginning to draw lines of privacy around data accumulated by the IOT. Certainly, where networked devices are used to surreptisously record the words and actions of third parties, existing causes of action for eavesdropping and common law invasion of privacy will be enforced, just as they are now with the "Peeping Tom" cameras that seem to regularly find their way into changing rooms, bedrooms, and other unambiguously private places.

In September 2013, the FTC took its first enforcement action related to IOT-collected information. TRENDnet, a company that markets video cameras designed to allow consumers to monitor their homes remotely, settled FTC charges that its lax security practices exposed the private lives of hundreds of consumers to public viewing online.[49] According to the FTC, TRENDnet marketed its numerous products as being "secure" when, in fact, the cameras had faulty software that left them open to online interception. The complaint further alleged that, in January 2012, a hacker exploited this flaw and made it public, and, eventually, hackers posted links to the live feeds of nearly 700 of the cameras. The feeds displayed babies asleep in their cribs, young children playing, and adults going about their daily lives. Once TRENDnet learned of this flaw, it uploaded a software patch to its website and sought to alert its customers of the need to visit the website to update their cameras.

"The Internet of Things holds great promise for innovative consumer products and services. But consumer privacy and security must remain a priority as companies develop more devices that connect to the Internet," said FTC Chairwoman Edith Ramirez.[50] Under the terms of its settlement with the Commission, TRENDnet was prohibited from misrepresenting the security of its devices or network, and was required to establish a comprehensive information security program designed to address security risks that could result in unauthorized access to or use of the company's devices. The company also was required to obtain third-party assessments of its security programs every two years for the next 20 years.

This first foray into protecting privacy in the IOT – which came only a month before the FTC hosted its first public seminar about the IOT – signaled that the FTC is likely to continue following its existing practices in this new technological field. That is, it will take a proactive role of facilitating public conversations on the topic, while at the same time reacting to the worst offenders in the field in order to set examples

---

[49]Edward Wyatt, *F.T.C. Says Webcam;s Flaw Put Users' Lives on Display*, THE NEW YORK TIMES (September 4, 2013) *available at* www.nytime.com/2013/09/05/technology/ftc-says-webcams-flat-put-users-lives-on-display.html?_r=0.
[50]*Id.*

for the rest of the industry. The FTC has done the same thing in recent years with social media endorsements and other fields that catch its interest.

There is every indication that regulators will continue to have plenty of opportunities to punish lax security practices in the IOT space. A 2014 study by researchers at Hewlett-Packard "identified an alarmingly high number of vulnerabilities" in the most popular IOT devices.[51] These insecurities ranged "from issues that could raise privacy concerns to serious problems like lack of transport encryption, vulnerabilities in the administration Web interface, insecure firmware update mechanisms and weak or poorly protected access credentials."[52] Sixty percent of the devices were vulnerable to common hacking attacks, while 70% used unencrypted networks and 80% used extremely weak passwords. [53] This reflects "the current nature of online services [to] provide[] few mechanisms for individuals to have oversight and control of their information, particularly across tech-vendors."[54] At some point, certain unfair practices may become so prevalent that Congress will feel the need to step in with new legislation.

The IOT will also implicate subject-specific privacy laws. Without question, IOT advancements will allow a greater range of devices to do such things as storing personal health information or sending messages that are intended to be private. When they do, new questions will arise about applying existing, subject-specific privacy laws like HIPAA and the Stored Communications Act. For example, the refrigerator is a device that many IOT enthusiasts talk about being networked. They often cite such advantages as the fridge being able to tell you when you're out of a particular item, or what other ingredient you might need for a recipe. But what if an insurance company sought access to our fridges' data logs to determine how healthy our diets are before determining what our health insurance premiums should be? The same could be asked of the panoply of health statistic-monitoring wearable devices that are now all the rage. In light of how strict many of the current regulations concerning health information already are, it would not be surprising to see the government severely limit who can access such information. The counter-argument will be made, however, that insurers should have access to this data in order to set rates that are fair to everyone.

Geolocation privacy

Geolocation data is something the courts have been trying to wrap their arms around for a few years now, with no clear boundary lines yet emerging. In January 2012, the United States Supreme Court decided *United States v. Jones*,[55] in which it unanimously ruled that the attachment of a GPS tracking device to an individual's vehicle

---

[51]Lucian Constantin, "Popular Internet-of-Things devices aren't secure," Computerworld, July 30, 2014, available at http://www.computerworld.com/article/2490587/networking/popular-internet-of-things-devices-aren-t-secure.html

[52]*Id.*

[53]*Id.*

[54]"The internet of things - the next big challenge to our privacy," *The Guardian*, July 28, 2014, available at http://www.theguardian.com/technology/2014/jul/28/internet-of-things-privacy.

[55]565 US ___, 132 S.Ct. 945 (2012),

by police, and subsequent use of that device to monitor the vehicle's movements on public streets, constituted a "search or seizure" within the meaning of the Fourth Amendment. Contrary to many news reports at the time of the decision, however, the *Jones* Court reached no conclusion on whether that search was unreasonable, or whether it required a warrant. The case produced three opinions from overlapping groups of Justices, some of whom found any degree of GPS tracking without a warrant legally dubious, while others would limit only long-term tracking, and still others so no problem with collecting such data as long as the police committed no physical "trespass" onto the person's property. This mish-mash of views illustrates the difficulty in applying eighteenth century legal principles to twenty-first century technology.

At least with regard to data collected by mobile phones, then, courts have generally concluded that "[u]nder existing law, … a user does not have a reasonable expectation of privacy as to geolocation data."[56] This is because, unlike the police-imposed "tracking devices" at issue in *Jones*, consumers carry mobile phones with themselves voluntarily, and are presumed to agree to their carriers' privacy policies that allow collection and sharing of this data. Presumably, mobile AR devices will come with the same broad policy provisions, and the same legal principles will apply to the data they collect.

Regulatory bodies are also paying attention to geolocation data privacy. On May 25, 2012, the Federal Communications Commission (FCC) released a report with the opaque title "Location-Based Services: An Overview of Opportunities and Other Considerations."[57] The report outlines the growing use of location-based services (LBS) in navigation, tracking, social networking, gaming, retail, real estate, advertising, news, weather, device management, and public safety applications, and government and industry efforts to address the privacy issues surrounding such services. It stemmed from a June 2011 workshop that the FCC hosted on the subject.

Like the FTC's efforts, this FCC report offered more general principles than concrete rules. In this case, the report highlighted "notice and transparency," "meaningful consumer choice," "third party access to personal information," and "data security and minimization" as its primary concerns. The FCC ended its report with a warning that it will "continue to monitor industry compliance with applicable statutory requirements and evolving industry best practices," and that "additional steps may be necessary if privacy issues are not met as effectively and comprehensively as possible or within reasonable time frames."[58]

What will be more interesting, though, is determining expectations of privacy in our digital interactions with IOT-connected physical devices. It is one thing to

---

[56]*In re Smartphone Geolocation Data Application*, 2013 U.S. Dist. LEXIS 62605, at *45 (E.D.N.Y. May 1, 2013); *see also United States v. Caraballo*, Case No. 5:12-cr-105 (D. Ver. August 7, 2013) (collecting cases).

[57]FEDERAL COMMUNICATIONS COMMISSION, LOCATION-BASED SERVICES: AN OVERVIEW OF OPPORTUNITIES AND OTHER CONSIDERATIONS (May 2012) *available at* http://apps.fcc.gov/edocs_public/attachmatch/DOC-314283A1.pdf.

[58]*Id.* at 2.

follow the legal fiction that everyone visiting a website or opening a particular software program reads and agrees to its terms of use, including the privacy policy that allows personal data to be collected. It will be another thing to apply that presumption to random devices we encounter in the physical world. Expecting every BLE-enabled beacon we will encounter on the sidewalk or within stores to carry a privacy policy that consumers can be expected to read and consent to seems impractical. The companies that provide service to our AR devices will likely seek to obtain from users a blanket consent to data collection on the front end, but even that consent cannot meaningfully apply to every party who will eventually have access to our interactions with the IOT.

USING AR TO ENHANCE PRIVACY

A new approach will need to be found. Here, in addition to new questions, AR also offers potential solutions.

Wearable technology in general has the potential to change individual users' attitudes toward data privacy. On today's internet, the providers of content and services do not go out of their way to offer individuals an opportunity to understand, much less control, how their data is collected or used. In most circumstances, any such effort is only the result of cajoling by regulators, and comes in the form of a dense privacy policy that offers little or no more information beyond what is legally required. After years of operating in this environment, users have become accustomed to the idea that controlling data privacy is beyond their reach.

With wearable and "pervasive computing, [however,] much of the technology becomes tangible and familiar. This makes issues of privacy more readily apparent to users. ... If you can physically witness aspects of data collection, it short-circuits what has traditionally been a long feedback loop between privacy risk and cumulative effect. The hope is that the increased awareness inspires action."[59] Moreover, as wearable devices make computing a more personalized experience, "it could also be used to provide individuals with the opportunity to take control of their personal data."[60]

By truly allowing users to *see* the data they exchanges, AR interfaces could go one step further than other wearable devices in bringing about this shift in users' mindset about their data. Because augmented display technologies will allow us to see large displays of virtual data floating in mid-air, rather than relying on size-constrained physical monitors, privacy warnings and dialogues can be made easier to notice. They will also be made easier to understand if they are displayed in physical proximity to the device being warned of, rather than on a remote, two-dimensional privacy document. So, for example, if the manufacturer of my refrigerator wishes to warn me that it will remember all of the food items I place inside the fridge, it can be programmed to display in my AR eyewear a large, red box containing this warning and floating in mid-air in front

---

[59]"The internet of things - the next big challenge to our privacy," *The Guardian,* July 28, 2014, available at http://www.theguardian.com/technology/2014/jul/28/internet-of-things-privacy.
[60]*Id.*

FIGURE 3.4

"Watch Your Privacy" by Sander Veenhoff.

of the refrigerator door. By gesturing a hand (which, at that point, will likely also be equipped with location-aware transmitters for just such a purpose as this) through the dialogue box, I can indicate my assent to this data collection and go about my business. Similarly, as I walk down the sidewalk, my AR eyewear could be programmed to display the geographic boundary lines around each store's BLE sensor network. These could be highlighted in predetermined colors, or annotated with the appropriate warning language, to indicate that by stepping over the line, the store's network will register my physical presence there and be permitted to digitally interact with me. In both examples, the consumer is able to make a decision that is orders of magnitude more informed than anything allowed by present-day digital privacy practice.

Software coder Sander Veenhof has actually already published the first attempt at a digital eyewear application that attempts to enhance an individual's privacy. Called "Watch Your Privacy,"[61] the app "visualises nearby privacy intrusions based on open data about surveillance cameras worldwide."[62] It also claims to map the real-time geo-location of other digital eyewear wearers who are using the app. In both cases, the goal is to inform the user as to the location of video cameras (both stationary and wearable) so that the user can make an informed choice as to whether or not they wish to be filmed. The screen capture included here as Fig. 3.4 demonstrates an augmentation showing red and yellow circles, indicating areas where a camera is or could be pointed, and green areas that are not being surveilled. Presumably, the same approach could be applied to beacons and other sensors capable of reading NFC, Bluetooth, Wi-fi, or other signals. Of course, this early implementation has a number of practical limitations; its database of camera locations will necessarily be incomplete, and the augmentations are likely only approximate. As a proof of concept, however, Veenhof's creation is a marvelous sneak peek at what AR could do to enhance personal privacy.

---

[61]"Watch Your Privacy," available at http://sndrv.com/watchyourprivacy/.
[62]*Id.*

Advertising, Marketing, and eCommerce

INFORMATION IN THIS CHAPTER:

- AR's use in advertising and marketing
- Unfair competition
- Disclaimers and disclosures
- Mobile commerce

INTRODUCTION

As augmented reality grows in importance as a medium, it will be used more heavily for advertising. That is an assertion so obvious as to hardly require support, but copious amounts of evidence can be found both in the prevalence of ad-supported content online and on the air, as well as the accelerating trend of AR ads already underway.

Less certain, however, is how the various laws and regulatory bodies governing commercial scruples will react to these innovations. Federal regulators have already been invited to limit the use of AR in advertising, but to date have refused to do so. As with web-based advertising before it, though, it can only be a matter of time until we see the development of new norms for fair advertising in the new medium of AR. Moreover, recent precedents in the regulation of internet marketing offer clues as to how AR is likely to be policed.

AR's USE IN ADVERTISING AND MARKETING
HOW AR IS CURRENTLY USED
Printed targets

For several years now, printed advertisements have contained "targets" that trigger augmented content on a computer screen when held up to a computer webcam or mobile device. The first of these usually took the form of Quick Response (QR) barcodes. The fact that these blocky boxes stood out from the surrounding text proved to be both an advantage and disadvantage; although they made it (relatively) clear to audiences that an interactive experience was available (once the public caught on to what QR codes were, that is), they were not the most aesthetically pleasing content to include in valuable print space.

Therefore, even though you will still find QR codes on printed advertisements today, it is much more common for augmented content to be triggered by images already present in the ads themselves. One early example of this technique was the newspaper ads that Universal ran in the January 28, 2010 issue of *USA Today* for its new "Wizarding World of Harry Potter" theme park.[1] The ad contained a two-dimensional sketch of the park. When held up to a webcam or mobile device, the park came alive, allowing readers to explore it in three dimensions.

Interactive print

This term describes an interactive, augmented experience with the pages of printed books, magazines, and promotional flyers. The concept is materially identical to the earliest print advertisements designed for webcams, except these are optimized for mobile devices and typically offer a wider range of real-time interaction and utility for the reader. Examples of this type of experience include:

- Science textbooks with molecules that appear to hover over the page, allowing the reader to physically interact with them;
- Products that hover in space above their print ads, allowing shoppers to inspect the device in three dimensions, make it move, and even hear audio of what the product sounds like when used;
- Two-dimensional floor plans that spring to life in three dimensions, allowing readers to look through virtual windows and to test how various light sources would illuminate a room;
- Instruction manuals that display assembly directions step by step, with three-dimensional animations;
- Handouts at automotive shows that show consumers three-dimensional models of cars that can be explored from every angle;
- Videos that appear to play on top of a printed page;
- Digital buttons that "pop out" from a physical page, allowing users to select new digital content by touching their finger to that portion of the page; and
- Pages that become the anchor for a broader digital display, such as by placing a page on a floor and stepping back for broader perspective, allowing the user's device to show what a life-sized piece of furniture, machinery, or floor tiling would look like in that space.

By taking advantage of the ever-increasing processing power of mobile devices and of the environment in which the typical user will encounter the printed material, interactive print represents a qualitative improvement in user experience over first-generation augmented advertisements.

---

[1] *Augmented reality map of Wizarding World of Harry Potter available in "USA Today"*, Orlando Attractions, (January 22, 2012), *available at* http://attractionsmagazine.com/augmented-reality-map-of-wizarding-world-of-harry-potter-available-in-usa-today/#sthash.AAqvMcLy.dpuf.

FIGURE 4.1

A child making and displaying augmented content with the "Disney Princess Ultimate Dream Castle."

Augmented products

The concept of interactive "print" can be, and has been, applied to three-dimensional objects as well as the printed page. Starbucks was one of the first retail brands to include augmented content on product packaging. During the holiday-themed promotions, customers using a branded app could view select coffee cups to see one of several different characters emerge and perform various actions.[2] Absolut did something similar with their "Absolut Truths" app, which encouraged consumers to locate targets on specially marked bottles to launch videos that "[e]xplore the unnecessary lengths we go to, to make our vodka good."[3] In 2014, McDonald's used Qualcomm's Vuforia AR software to augment its french fry containers. The associated app turned the containers into an interactive soccer game to promote the World Cup tournament.

Increasingly, AR apps are being launched in connection with toys. These differ from the aforementioned promotional campaigns in that the app is designed for repeated use by the consumer after purchase, rather than solely as an inducement to make the purchase. For example, Disney offers a "Magic Mirror" app that offers children the chance to discover a wide range of augmented experiences when used in connection with the "Disney Princess Ultimate Dream Castle."[4] (Fig. 4.1) Although

[2]Starbucks, *Starbucks Cup Magic*, YOUTUBE (November 8, 2011) http://www.youtube.com/watch?feature=player_embedded&v=RWwQXi9RG0w.

[3]Absolut Vodka, *Absolute Truths* (September 21, 2012) https://itunes.apple.com/us/app/absolut-truths/id492665840?mt=8.

[4]Disney, *Disney Magic Mirror* (September 23, 2013) https://itunes.apple.com/us/app/disney-magic-mirror/id591987216?mt=8.

nominally sold for $1.99, the castle toy comes with a code for a free download. At the 2014 Augmented World Expo, Qualcomm demonstrated a toy military vehicle that children could scan with a mobile device in order to "import" the toy into a digital universe. This is a variation on the *Skylanders* and *Disney Infinity* products that also feature physical toys that affect digital game play.

Offerings such as this turn AR into "added value" that makes the physical product more attractive to would-be purchasers – often at very little marginal cost to the manufacturer.

In-store kiosks

Lego pioneered the concept of importing the at-home webcam experience into retail stores (Fig. 4.2). Shoppers in select Lego Stores will find kiosks to which they can hold up certain boxes of Lego toys. When they do, the webcam displays a three-dimensional, animated depiction of the toy that the box of bricks is designed to create – and projects that depiction as if it is actually present on top of the box the customer is holding. Rotating the box allows customers to view the toy from multiple angles. In this case, the imagery already present on one entire face of the box serves as the target that triggers the augmented display. And although the application is limited to one, immobile device, it works instantly without the need for customers to pull out a mobile device or download a specific app. Therefore, although such kiosks perform only one function, they do it very well.

Public installations

Lego is not the only entity to make creative use of AR in a fixed physical space. Iowa's Simpson College drew attention by hanging a banner inside a local mall, then encouraging teens to view the banner through a custom app that augmented

FIGURE 4.2

The Lego store kiosk.

FIGURE 4.3

National Geographic AR installation in a shopping mall.

it with digital graphics, sound and video.[5] Several brands, including National Geographic[6] and the BBC[7], have set up billboard-sized video walls inside shopping malls that display the pedestrians in front of the wall, along with digital animals with which the shoppers can interact – not unlike a giant version of the *Kinectimals* game for the Microsoft Xbox Kinect[8] (which itself was an impressive step forward in mass-market AR). (Fig. 4.3) Victoria's Secret[9] and Disney[10] have done the same with augmented characters, while Nokia[11] and Ford Motor Company[12] have set up similar, somewhat smaller interactive mall displays.

Even non-commercial entities have taken advantage of AR's unique capacity for messaging. (Fig. 4.4) Apparently, public employees in the Netherlands frequently

[5]Karine Joly, *Beyond the boring #highered ad banner: Augmented reality done right by Simpson College*, College Web Editor (Mar. 25, 2013) http://collegewebeditor.com/blog/index.php/archives/2013/03/25/beyond-the-boring-highered-ad-banner-augmented-reality-done-right-by-simpson-college/

[6]David Kiefaber, *National Geographic Lets You Pet Dinosaurs at the Mall: Augmented Reality Goes Jurassic* (November 17, 2011) http://www.adweek.com/adfreak/national-geographic-lets-you-pet-dinosaurs-mall-136591.

[7]Yi Chen, *BBC Augmented Reality Brings Artic Animals to Life in Local Malls*, (June 1, 2012) http://www.psfk.com/2012/06/bbc-arctic-augmented-reality.html

[8]See Xbox Marketplace, *Kinnectimals Now With Bears!*, Xbox.com (October 1, 2011) http://marketplace.xbox.com/en-US/Product/Kinectimals/66acd000-77fe-1000-9115-d8024d5308b3#/Home.

[9]Malory Russell, *11 Amazing Augmented Reality Ads*, (January 28, 2012) available at http://www.businessinsider.com/11-amazing-augmented-reality-ads-2012-1?op=1.

[10]Disney Parks, *Disney Villans Take Over the Streeds of New York City*, YouTube (December 9, 2011) http://www.youtube.com/watch?feature=player_embedded&v=CGzkbx4EMR0.

[11]Xath Cruz, *Nokia's Augmented Reality Experience Hits Malls*, Creative Guerilla Marketing (November 29, 2012) http://www.creativeguerillamarketing.com/augmented-reality/nokias-augmented-reality-experience-hits-malls/.

[12]Aden Hepburn, *Ford C-Max Augmented Reality Billboards*, Digital Buzz Blog (February 28, 2011) http://www.digitalbuzzblog.com/ford-c-max-augmented-reality-digital-billboards/.

FIGURE 4.4

Dutch billboard using AR for public shaming.

encounter resistance – and sometimes even violence – while attempting to assist other citizens. Making matters worse, in several such incidents, passersby chose not to intervene on the public servants behalf. To combat this "bystander effect,"[13] the Dutch government took the creative approach of installing interactive video billboards over heavily trafficked public streets in Amsterdam and Rotterdam. The screens played pre-recorded scenes of public servants being attacked on the streets just below the signs, and overlaid onto these scenes real-time video from the same location, so that those watching the display could see themselves in the midst of the disturbing scene, yet doing nothing to stop the violence. The video was not inter-active, so there was nothing these passersby could actually do about the violence. Nevertheless, viewers gained a unique perspective on just how out of place a passive onlooker appears in that situation. "Whether or not it's achieving its higher pur-pose," wrote *Popular Science* magazine, "the technology is turning some heads on the street. It appears that being injected into an augmented reality without warning is just as jarring as it sounds."[14]

Projection mapping

As discussed in Chapter 2, projection mapping may not meet some people's defini-tion of "augmented reality." But when done well, its effect is every bit as immersive and impressive as any other form of digital augmentation.

---

[13]The "bystander effect," or "Genovese syndrome," is hardly unique to the Netherlands; it has been studied at least since the infamous 1964 murder of Kitty Genovese in New York, when thirty-eight neighbors heard the crime take place but took no action. *See Murder of Kitty Genovese*, WIKIPEDIA, http://en.wikipedia.org/wiki/Murder_of_Kitty_Genovese (last visited June 9, 2012)

[14]Clay Dillow, *Video: Augmented Reality Billboard Installed in Amsterdam, to Educate and Shame Passers-By*, POPULAR SCIENCE (April 29, 2010) *available at* http://www.popsci.com/technology/article/2010-04/dutch-psa-uses-augmented-reality-shame-citizens-not-helping-their-countrymen.

Advertisers have taken notice. Hyundai used projection mapping to spectacular effect to advertise their new Accent sedan. The company suspended an actual vehicle on the side of a building, then used projection mapping to make it appear as if the building itself moved and morphed into various roadways on which the car traveled.[15] Nike, BOX, the Tokyo City Symphony, Volkswagen, Nissan, Gillette, Samsung, Sony, Chevrolet, and Lamborghini, among others, have all employed similar technology for marketing spectacles.[16]

HOW AR IS LIKELY TO BE USED FOR ADVERTISING IN THE FUTURE

All of the foregoing technology will continue to have its place in marketing efforts, while at the same time continuing to evolve as advancing capabilities and new imaginations open the door to greater innovation. Each method currently shares the attribute of being new and unusual, which makes it easy for them to draw customer attention and increase engagement. That, in turn, translates into easily quantifiable results for advertising agencies that they can then use to convince more retailers to use the same concepts. As these methods become commonplace, however, something more than easy digital gimmicks will be necessary to capture consumers' attention.

The following seem like safe predictions to make regarding AR in near-future advertising.

More interactivity in more places

There are millions of static, flat surfaces waiting to be augmented, in the form of the exterior walls on buildings all around the world that generally do not change significantly over time. Billboards and other wall-sized advertisements are similarly durable flat surfaces that, although they change periodically, last long enough to structure a promotional campaign around them. The only thing keeping augmented advertisements from appearing (or, more precisely, being available to be made to appear by the viewer) on them is a lack of adoption by retailers and advertisers – which, in turn, is probably mostly attributable to inertia and the absence of a sufficiently attractive business model to overcome that inertia.

Insufficient adoption of wearable technology is another contributing factor. It is notable that many of the most impressive uses of AR in advertising discussed above employed large, static displays that allow viewers to interact with the digital content without needing to hold up a mobile device to view it, much less download a specific app for that device. Mobile AR will not create that same hands-free, immersive interaction until we no longer need to use our hands to operate the hardware.

Hardware capabilities also limit the range of immersive experiences a retailer can generate. Current digital AR technology looks for pre-determined "target" images on

---

[15]Discover Hyundai, *Hyundai Accent 3D Projection Mapping*, YOUTUBE (April 5, 2011) http://www.youtube.com/watch?feature=player_embedded&v=tu0TRA6a21Q.
[16]See DIGITAL BUZZ BLOG http://www.digitalbuzzblog.com/tag/3d-projection-mapping/ (last visited June 9, 2014).

which to display its content, and those images are often deliberately placed indoors, where lighting and position can be controlled. As sensors become better able to recognize a wider range of objects under less controlled conditions, advertisers will have a wider range of surfaces at their disposal to augment – including people walking down an outdoor sidewalk, moving vehicles, and the like.

Biometrics

Along with immersiveness, personalization is another characteristic that makes marketing more effective. The 2002 Steven Spielberg film *Minority Report* already showed us the path forward to hyper-personalized marketing: biometrics. Although we are not much closer to using retinal scans or fingerprints for mass-market commercial purposes, facial recognition technology is poised for widespread adoption. As discussed at length in Chapter 3, retailers are already implementing facial recognition technology in various settings and industries to remarkable effect, and this trend will only grow as the public becomes more inured to the attendant privacy implications. Accurate sensing and reproduction of other bodily features is similarly advancing. The combination of these technologies will not only allow for "magic mirror"-type augmented displays to sell apparel, but also make it easier for marketers to store and remember an individual's preferences and shopping history across multiple locations and platforms (again, as popularized by *Minority Report*).

Recent advancements have also suggested futures that even Spielberg did not foresee. For example, Google created a buzz in mid-2013 by receiving a patent[17] on "pay-per-gaze" advertising – a method that crosses the current "pay-per-click" model of online ads with the mobile AR enabled by Glass and other wearable devices. It would allow advertising service providers to charge an advertiser each time someone *looked at* their ad for a certain period of time through their wearable device.

But wait – there's more! The same patent described a similar payment model, except gauged on the viewer's *emotional reaction*, rather than on mere viewing. "Pupil dilation can be correlated with emotional states, (e.g., surprise, interest, etc.)," the patent notes, and a wearable device that tracks such reactions can also transmit them to the advertiser for analytic purposes.[18]

Other biometric data would likewise be available for tracking user reaction to advertisements. Chapter 2 explained recent developments in using head-mounted sensors to track a user's brain waves and correlate them with certain digital content. Similar sensors could correlate certain brain activity with particular advertising, creating a virtually foolproof record of the ad's true effectiveness. Researchers are already exploring the use of brain waves as a replacement for passwords;[19] commercial spin-offs of this technology would not be far behind.

---

[17]U.S. Patent No., 8,510,166, (filed May 11, 2011), *available at* <http://patft.uspto.gov/netacgi/nph-Parser?Sect1=PTO2&Sect2=HITOFF&u=%2Fnetahtml%2FPTO%2Fsearch-adv.htm&r=36&p=1&f=G&l=50&d=PTXT&S1=%2820130813.PD.+AND+Google.ASNM.%29&OS=ISD/20130813+AND+AN/Google&RS=%28ISD/20130813+AND+AN/Google%29> .

[18]*Id.*

[19]Kate Freeman, *Are Brain Waves and Heartbeats the Future of Passwords? [VIDEO]*, MASHABLE (April 24, 2012) *available at* http://mashable.com/2012/04/24/brain-waves-passwords/.

Location-based advertising

One attribute that, by definition, differentiates AR from other digital experiences is its interaction with the physical world. A necessary corollary of that feature is that virtually all devices providing AR experiences will constantly know their geolocation. The market research firm Forrester Research has already issued a report noting "that [such a] device's location-based technologies and services could be especially useful to advertisers that are attempting to develop more targeted campaigns".[20]

But ads are likely to target factors even more specific than mere coordinates. Google has even received a patent on a method for delivering "advertising based on environmental conditions."[21] Using this method, an advertiser "may obtain information on the environment (e.g., temperature, humidity, light, sound, air composition) from sensors [in the user's mobile device].) Advertisers may specify that the ads are shown to users whose environmental conditions meet certain criteria."[22] Those "environmental" conditions could even include the ambient noise at the user's location.

User-generated parody videos have already portrayed a world filled with a comically large degree of advertisements. (Fig. 4.5) Keiichi Matsuda's concept video

FIGURE 4.5

A parody depicting augmented sponsored advertising.

---

[20]Stephen Vagus, *Google Glass could serve as a new mobile commerce platform*, Mobile Commerce Press (July 1, 2013) http://www.mobilecommercepress.com/google-glass-could-serve-as-a-new-mobile-commerce-platform/857436/.

[21]U.S. Patent No. 8,138,930(filed January 22, 2008), available at http://patft.uspto.gov/netacgi/nph-Parser?Sect1=PTO1&Sect2=HITOFF&d=PALL&p=1&u=%2Fnetahtml%2FPTO%2Fsrchnum.htm&r=1&f=G&l=50&s1=8,138,930.PN.&OS=PN/8,138,930&RS=PN/8,138,930.

[22]*Id.*

FIGURE 4.6

Keiichi Matsuda's vision of a world saturated with augmented advertising.

Augmented (hyper)Reality: Domestic Robocop depicted a daily life literally saturated by augmented advertising (both visual and aural).[23] (Fig. 4.6) Real life may not end up looking like either of these depictions, but it seems certain that AR will cause the typical person's interaction with advertising to be fundamentally different than what we are used to.

With this understanding of how the advertising industry is likely to employ AR technology, we can explore some of the legal issues most likely to be raised.

FALSE ADVERTISING AND UNFAIR COMPETITION
SOURCES OF LAW

"Unfair competition" is a catch-all term for a wide variety of legal claims challenging deceptive or misleading commercial behavior. It encompasses such causes of action as false advertising, false designation of origin, false suggestion of sponsorship, and the like. The primary legal authority creating the right to sue for such actions is the Federal Lanham Act, 15 U.S.C. §§1101 *et seq.* – the same statute that regulates the use of trademarks. In particular, Section 43(a) of the Act (15 U.S.C. §1125) provides:

1. Any person who, on or in connection with any goods or services, or any
   container for goods, uses in commerce any word, term, name, symbol, or
   device, or any combination thereof, or any false designation of origin, false or
   misleading description of fact, or false or misleading representation of fact,
   which
   a. is likely to cause confusion, or to cause mistake, or to deceive as to the
      affiliation, connection, or association of such person with another person,

---

[23]See Keiichi Matsuda, *Augmented (hyper)Reality: Domestic Robocop* YouTube (January 6, 2010) www.youtube.com/watch?v=fSfKlCmYcLc.

or as to the origin, sponsorship, or approval of his or her goods, services, or commercial activities by another person, or

b. in commercial advertising or promotion, misrepresents the nature, characteristics, qualities, or geographic origin of his or her or another person's goods, services, or commercial activities, shall be liable in a civil action by any person who believes that he or she is or is likely to be damaged by such act.[24]

A cause of action for unfair competition may be brought by a regulatory agency or by a private party whose interests may be negatively affected by the challenged activity. The Federal Trade Commission, for example, has wide latitude to take action against marketing techniques that it deems misleading or deceptive, even if they are not explicitly prohibited by law. Although the immediate harm being alleged is *customer* confusion, the ultimate interest that the Lanham Act protects is the ability of businesses to compete with each other without undue advantage.

In addition to the Lanham Act, which can be asserted in either state or Federal courts, many states have consumer protection laws or common law that create similar or even greater protections. These include such causes of action as business defamation, which is a libel or slander claim as applied to a business or product rather than an individual.

FALSE ADVERTISING AND UNFAIR COMPETITION IN AR

With the various descriptions of AR technology given so far in this book, one can easily imagine a number of ways in which one could assert an unfair competition claim based on AR advertising.

False advertising

One likely candidate is a lawsuit alleging "false advertising" or some similar cause of action under Section 43(a)(1)(A) of the Lanham Act. As noted above, this includes "any false designation of origin, false or misleading description of fact, or false or misleading representation of fact, which … in commercial advertising or promotion, misrepresents the nature, characteristics, qualities, or geographic origin of his or her or another person's goods, services, or commercial activities."[25]

In order to prevail, a plaintiff must prove that the defendant made a false or misleading statement of fact about a product or service, and that this statement was likely to influence a customer's purchasing decisions. In reality, though, defendants responding to such complaints end up shouldering an expensive burden to show that their statements (or implications) were true and not misleading. Quite a few of these cases have been brought over the years. As of this writing, Prof. Rebecca Tushnet's *43(B)log*,[26] one

---

[24]15 U.S.C. §1125 (2012).

[25]*Id.*

[26]Rebecca Tushnet, Rebecca Tushnet's 43(B)log, http://tushnet.blogspot.com/ (last visited June 9, 2014).

of the leading resources on this area of law, is up to over 1360 entries under the "false advertising" category (and more in related categories).

How might AR be used to "misrepresent the nature, characteristics, [or] qualities" of goods or services? To answer that question, let's phrase it another way: how might representations made via AR get the facts wrong?

One obvious answer is "mistakenly." AR remains an emerging technology with a lot of developing yet to do. And there are currently a lot more ideas about how to apply the technology than there is hardware capable of implementing those ideas. It may seem to the general public that the camera capabilities of smartphones and tablets are maturing rapidly, but to AR developers waiting for markerless object recognition, millimeter-precise GPS, and stereoscopic machine vision capabilities, they're moving at a snail's pace.

Consequently, some over-ambitious AR apps may try to convey or recognize more data than they are able to – resulting in blocky, choppy, imprecise output. Under the wrong set of circumstances, that might end up conveying information that is false and has a material impact on a consumer (Fig. 4.7).

Another answer is "by cutting corners" or "over-polishing." Take, for example, the incident in the Summer of 2012 in which British regulators banned L'Oreal from running ads containing two photos of Julia Roberts and Christy Turlington. L'Oreal's marketers digitally enhanced both photos to the point that it could not prove to the regulators' satisfaction that the advertised makeup products were able to produce results like the ones shown. Fashion companies are also lambasted on a regular basis for altering photos of clothing models to give them physical features so extreme as to be anatomically impossible. The difficulty of precise 3D rendering – not to mention the same commercial and societal pressures that lend to the photo alterations – could likewise result in augmented ads that are similarly unrealistic.

By definition, digitally enhancing physical reality is a fundamental element of what AR does. This type of situation, therefore, is one that AR marketers could very

FIGURE 4.7

The L'Oreal ads banned by U.K. regulators.

easily get themselves into if they are not careful (and if they do not run their content by trained lawyers first.)

Ad replacement

Television broadcasts (especially of sporting events) are increasingly using "digital billboard replacement" technology to overlay advertisements in the physical world with digital ads from other companies. [27] Presumably, the companies that purchased the rights to depict the replaced physical banners bought only rights to the physical sign and not to broadcasts as well. And with the advent of such replacement technology, more stadia are likely to sell the two sets of display rights separately.

The ability to replace physical ads on a broad scale in other public venues, however, has not existed until now. And the first effort to implement it was driven not by commercial interests, but by *anti*-commercialism. The New York-based organization "Public Ad Campaign" believes "that public space and the public's interaction with that space is a vital component of our city's health, [and considers] outdoor advertising [to be] the primary obstacle to open public communications."[28] Its mission is to "air our grievances in the court of public opinion and witness our communities regain control of the spaces they occupy."[29]

One of Public Ad Campaign's several attempts to further this goal was a project called the "AR Ad Takeover." This smartphone/tablet app used feature tracking to recognize particular print advertisements that were then prominent across New York City. The app then superimposed original art on top of those ads, essentially replacing their commercial message with an expression of the Campaign's choosing. In April 2011, BC Biermann, founder of The Heavy Projects and one of the Public Ad Campaign's partners, launched a similar app that hijacked the movie poster for the film *Pirates of the Caribbean: On Stranger Tides.* The app morphed the face of "Captain Barbossa" (played by Geoffrey Rush) into that of Goldman Sachs CEO Lloyd Blankfein – who BC calls "the real pirate."

Each of these is a step in an "iterative process" toward an overall "philosophical" goal in mind with these efforts, said Biermann in an interview.[30] It is two-fold: first, to change the way people think about public space and second, to democratize the way public spaces are used for communication. Or, as BC Biermann says, "eradicating the last bastions of common space that you can't control." "AR can democratize messaging in public space," Biermann says. "I'm not against commercial messaging per se, but I'm opposed to commercial dominance."[31] Like most of us who write

---

[27]See *Miikka Kukkosuo, Supponor gets EUR 6M in Series A funding*, ARCTIC STARTUP (September 2, 2008) *a*vailable at http://www.arcticstartup.com/2008/09/02/supponor-gets-eur-6m-in-series-a-funding.
[28]Miss*ion,* PUBLIC AD CAMPAIGN, http://www.publicadcampaign.com/mission.html (last visited June 9, 2014).
[29]*Id.*
[30]Brian Wassom, *[Interview] BC "Heavy Biermann: Taking Back Public Spaces With AR*, WASSOM. COM (January 31, 2012) http://www.wassom.com/interview-bc-heavy-biermann-taking-back-public-spaces-with-ar.html.
[31]*Id.*

about the future of AR, Biermann envisions a world where people wear AR-powered eyewear that superimposes digital data atop our field of vision in a seamless, effortless manner. But for Biermann, the "killer app" for such hardware would be an "open environment platform that allows users to filter their environment according to their interests." Users of such a platform would not see the billboards and other commercial messaging that now occupy so much of our public space unless they chose to.

Just like the hundreds of stores selling "Occupy Wall Street" t-shirts, however, commercial interests will inevitably find ways to profit from this egalitarian ad replacement technology as well. Indeed, with digital eyewear now reaching the market, it is only a matter of time until ad replacement apps are available for these devices. Chapter 5 will explore the ramifications of these apps under the trademark-specific portions of the Lanham Act, but those inevitable trademark infringement claims will certainly be accompanied by allegations of unfair competition as well. Advertisers who thought they were getting a guaranteed degree of exposure by renting large, expensive billboards will receive a rude awakening when large numbers of digital eyewear users no longer see that content. This could occur in any number of ways. The users themselves could install apps that replace the physical advertising with other content, or that simply block them out. Or, the companies providing internet service to those devices could contract with other advertisers to overlay digital ads atop physical ones. Alternatively, owners of those physical spaces – the buildings and billboards housing the physical ads – could follow the example of sports stadia, and sell the rights to physical and digital advertising separately. (Such digital advertising would actually be subdivided even further, since users will have a theoretically limitless choice of channels through which to view the physical space, in the same way that there are a limitless number of websites on the internet.) The most realistic scenario is that some combination of all of these methods will occur.

Regardless, those with established business models do not appreciate having those models disrupted, and often resort to litigation in an attempt to preserve their interests. Expect to see disgruntled owners of physical advertisements sue to recover the value of their "lost" visibility, and to enjoin the further digitization of their signage.

False suggestions of endorsement or sponsorship

The ability to project meaningful, interactive digital content anywhere and everywhere will be both the biggest advantage and largest headache of AR. On occasion, the mere proximity of augmented content will itself be problematic. Allegations of false endorsement or sponsorship under the Lanham Act typically arise when two parties' trademarks or other distinctive content appears so near each other, or one party's content is used by a person not authorized to do so, that a question is raised in a viewer's mind as to whether the two parties have some sort of partnership, licensing agreement, or other formal relationship. Claims are brought by parties who do not wish to be associated with the other party, and who accuse the other party of free-riding on their goodwill.

Those sorts of boundaries are difficult enough to draw when dealing with physical materials or even websites. The democratic nature of AR content creation and projection, though, will allow anyone to locate their digital content literally anywhere in physical space that they choose, including directly on top of someone else's signage or commercial establishment. The fact that this content will be viewable only through certain devices will make it that much more difficult for the owner of the physical space to police the digital data associated with his property. These circumstances create a fertile breeding ground for claims of false suggestion of endorsement or sponsorship.

Allegedly deceptive advertising methods

The broad, flexible nature of unfair competition law was proven by the fact that the first actual legal complaint filed against an augmented reality advertising campaign was one that nobody saw coming.

On October 19, 2011, four consumer advocacy groups (The Center for Digital Democracy, Consumer Action, Consumer Watchdog, and The Praxis Project – to which I'll refer collectively as "CDD" – filed a complaint and Request for Investigation with the Federal Trade Commission against PepsiCo and its subsidiary, Frito-Lay. The complaint called on the FTC to investigate and bring action against these companies for allegedly "engaging in deceptive and unfair marketing practices in violation of Section 5 of the FTC Act." Together with their complaint, the CDD issued a press release and a detailed collection of case study videos – apparently from the advertisers themselves – explaining the challenged ad campaigns.

The CDD objected to several aspects of Frito-Lay's online ad campaign for its "Doritos Late Night" line of products. The ultimate point of the complaint was to argue that Frito-Lay's campaign deceives teens into eating too many unhealthy snacks, thereby contributing to the childhood obesity problem. For support, the complaint relied on a "scientific" report called "Digital Food Marketing to Children and Adolescents," conducted by National Policy & Legal Analysis Network to Prevent Childhood Obesity (NPLAN).[32] The report (non-coincidentally released on the same day as the complaint) began from the unstartling premise that "contemporary marketing practices are increasingly multidimensional" and rely on social and relational methods rather than hard-sell advertising.[33]

The report and the complaint went on to call out five specific forms of outreach to which teens are "uniquely susceptible." At the top of that list are "Augmented reality, online gaming, virtual environments, and other immersive techniques that can induce 'flow,' reduce conscious attention to marketing techniques, and foster impulsive behaviors."[34] The CDD's reasoning, therefore, was not limited to what Frito-Lay did. Rather, it indicted the very concept of using AR to market to teens.

---

[32]National Policy & Legal Analysis Network to Prevent Childhood Obesity, Digital Food Marketing to Children and Adolescents (October, 2011).
[33]*Id.* at 4.
[34]*Id.*

FIGURE 4.8

The Doritos Late Night AR ad campaign.

The complaint did, however, single out the Doritos campaign as "particularly problematic" (Fig. 4.8).

At least one, and arguably two, aspects of this campaign qualified as AR. Most notable is the "Late Night Concert" featuring the band Blink-182. Here's how the complaint describes it:

> *The Late Night music experience utilized "augmented reality," an immersive marketing technique featuring a vivid interactive experience that can be personalized for individual users. Bags of Doritos Late Night chips were printed with a special symbol to serve as a "ticket" for the concert. Flashing that symbol at their webcams would create the appearance of the stage popping out of the bag of chips.*[35]

The CDD also called out a related feature involving the music video for Rihanna's song, "Who's That Chick." The producers filmed two versions of the video with identical camera angles and choreography. The only difference is that the default video is shot with "daytime" lighting and costumes, while the "Late Night" version has a "darker" backdrop and wardrobe. Holding a Doritos Late Night bag up to a webcam while the video is playing will "unlock" the Late Night version and automatically switch between the two. By at least some definitions, this, too, is augmented reality.

The Doritos Late Night campaign appears to have been a success. According to the complaint and the video case studies, it cites, the website received almost 100,000 hits in its first week, with an average visit length of 4.5 minutes.

The CDD's complaint was not a lawsuit. Rather, what the CDD did was to gather all of the data it could find to support its argument, packaged the data in what it thinks is the most persuasive manner, and laid it all at the FTC's doorstep, asking the FTC

---

[35]Complaint and Request for Investigation at 26, Center for Digital Democracy, *et al.* before the Federal Trade Commission (October 19, 2011) *available at* http://digitalads.org/how-youre-targeted/case-studies/ftc-complaint

to do something about it. The FTC has no legal obligation to respond to such complaints. It can choose simply to do nothing. The FTC is "empowered and directed" by Section 5 of the FTC Act "to prevent persons, partnerships, or corporations ... from using unfair methods of competition in or affecting commerce and unfair or deceptive acts or practices in or affecting commerce."[36] In this context, "unfair practices" are defined as follows:

> *An act or practice is unfair where it:*
>
> - *causes or is likely to cause substantial injury to consumers;*
> - *cannot be reasonably avoided by consumers and;*
> - *is not outweighed by countervailing benefits to consumers or to competition.*
>
> *Public policy, as established by statute, regulation, or judicial decisions may be considered with all other evidence in determining whether an act or practice is unfair.*
>
> *An act or practice is deceptive where:*
>
> - *a representation, omission, or practice misleads or is likely to mislead the consumer;*
> - *a consumer's interpretation of the representation, omission, or practice is considered reasonable under the circumstances and;*
> - *the misleading representation, omission, or practice is material.*[37]

But it is up to the FTC itself to decide whether such methods are being used, and if they are, whether "a proceeding by it in respect thereof would be to the interest of the public."[38]

To reach that decision, the FTC usually conducts an investigation first. Even if the FTC does act, there is no deadline for action. It has been known in some cases to let investigations lie dormant for years, only to pick them up again and take action months or years later. After investigating, if the FTC decides to act, it has two options under Section 5. First, it can file a lawsuit in federal court against the allegedly deceptive marketers, seeking an injunction against the unlawful practices and penalties of up to $10,000 "for each violation." Second, it can hold an administrative hearing, in which the FTC files a complaint and the marketer may defend itself before the Commission itself. Any interested third party (e.g., the CDD) may petition to intervene and offer testimony. That process can also result in an order that the marketer cease the objectionable practice. In either scenario, the ruling may be appealed to a U.S. Court of Appeals.

Meanwhile, PepsiCo has little it can do but wait, and to parry the CDD's PR blitz. "We are aware of the filing to the FTC and believe it contains numerous inaccuracies and mischaracterizations," Frito-Lay spokesperson Aurora Gonzalez was quoted as

---

[36]12 U.S.C. § 45(a)(2) (2012).
[37]15 U.S.C. § 45
[38]12 U.S.C. § 45(b) (2012).

saying. "PepsiCo and its Frito-Lay division are committed to responsible and ethical marketing practices. Our marketing programs, which are often innovative, comply with applicable law and regulations."[39] As of this writing – nearly three years after the complaint was filed – there is no indication that the FTC has taken, or is inclined to take, any action concerning the Doritos Late Night campaign.

Those in the AR industry will recognize Doritos' webcam-based AR advertising model as entirely commonplace. Although the production values for the campaign appear quite high, the technique of holding a marker up to a webcam to activate content on a desktop monitor – even video content – is first-generation AR marketing. In other words, there is nothing about the technical aspects of this specific campaign that make it any more "problematic" than any other campaign of its genre. Rather, the CDD is on a mission to reduce the consumption of junk food by teens. This campaign used AR to sell teens such food, so the CDD attacked AR. Presumably, if the Ad Council were using AR to lower teens' inhibitions against quitting smoking, the CDD would not object.

But Doritos Late Night is far from the only campaign on the CDD's radar. At the same time the CDD filed this complaint, the CDD made it known that it was "likely to file other complaints in the next year or so."[40] The CDD's website about the complaint lists some specific examples of other campaigns it objects to. Some of the examples on that list were also successful AR campaigns. Although it has yet to file additional AR-related complaints, a CDD representative confirmed to me in February 2014 that the CDD still plans to file them.

The reasoning behind the CDD complaint doesn't stop at foods, either. Consider this passage from the complaint about the ills of "immersive" environments:

> *Frito-Lay's ability to disguise its marketing efforts is further enhanced by the use of "immersive" techniques. Immersive marketing is designed to foster subjective feelings of being inside the action, a mental state that is frequently accompanied by "intense focus, loss of self, distorted time sense, effortless action." Immersive environments can also induce a state of "flow," causing individuals to lose any sense of the passage of time. Immersive environments use augmented reality techniques to deliberately blur the lines between the real world and the virtual world, making the experience even more compelling, intense, and realistic. In such an emotional environment, a teen is even less likely to recognize that the game or concert event is marketing for the reasons discussed above.[41]*

The same reasoning could be applied to adults, and to the use of immersive AR to sell virtually anything. If the CDD or some other group makes any headway with this argument in fighting snack sales, who will use it next against some other use of

---

[39]Sheila Shayon, *PepsiCo Refutes Consumer Watchdog's Deceptive Marketing Complaint*, BRAND CHANNEL (October 20, 2011), http://www.brandchannel.com/home/post/2011/10/20/PepsiCo-Frito-Lay-Refutes-Complaint-102011.aspx.
[40]*Id.*
[41]Complaint and Request for Investigation, *supra* note 39, at 35-36

AR? "Immersion" is the *sine qua non* of AR. The CDD's line of attack, if successful, could pose a potentially existential threat to a large portion of the AR industry as we know it.

Even if this CDD complaint goes nowhere – which, by now, seems likely – it demonstrates that AR is on the radar of consumer watchdog groups. They see "immersive" as a code word for "deceptive." As a result, any AR advertising campaign targeting teens or other groups that are arguably more vulnerable to suggestion should be particularly wary of attacks by such groups. Future legal challenges, however, may not be limited to just this demographic.

This lesson also demonstrates that marketers should take care in how they describe their own campaigns. The CDD's complaint and website are chock full of quotes and excerpts from the Doritos advertisers' own case studies. Be aware that someone may try to use your own words against you. At the same time, starting AR marketers would do well to keep notes not only on how effective their methods are at influencing consumer decisions, but also about how the use of AR benefits consumers and the public. Above all, get legal advice about what constitutes "unfair and deceptive practices" while you are designing your campaign, not after it is over.

BUSINESS DEFAMATION AND PRODUCT DISPARAGEMENT

Advertisements sometimes depict more than the advertiser's own product, which can lead to more than just false advertising liability. The law of defamation (a.k.a. libel or slander) provides a cause of action against anyone who publishes a demonstrably false statement of fact that injures another's reputation. We usually think of this cause of action in terms of a slander against an individual's reputation. But businesses can also bring defamation claims against those whose false statements injure the reputation of their products or services. (Some courts recognize a distinction between "defamation" and "disparagement" of a business or its products,[42] but this book will use the terms interchangeably.) Therefore, inaccurate augmented representations of a product could potentially be alleged to defame that product's manufacturer, in addition to creating an unfair commercial advantage, if the augmented version is significantly less appealing than the real thing.

Imagine, for example, a scenario in which a business hopes to create a splash by being one of the first to use AR for comparative advertising – a type of ad in which the advertiser's product is compared side-by-side with a competitor's. In theory, this is a legitimate form of advertising, as several courts have decided over the years. But also suppose that the digital artists recreating the two products as three-dimensional digital objects did not replicate them precisely. Perhaps they cut corners, or the technology simply was not robust enough to render the exact dimensions of the products. The images are good enough to tell what the products are, but are not photo-realistic by any means. Moreover, let's assume that the artists creating the images are going

---

[42]See *U.S. Healthcare, Inc. v. Blue Cross of Greater Phila.*, 898 F.2d 914, 924 (3d Cir. 1990).

to pay more attention to detail on the product of the client paying them, as opposed to the competitor.[43]

This all-too-realistic scenario is a recipe for an allegation of business defamation (in addition to one of more Lanham Act theories). The aggrieved competitor would claim that the sloppy representation of its product created an unfairly negative impression of its product in the minds of consumers, especially as compared to the advertiser's product. Comparative ads are already an inherently confrontational method of advertising, and they have often provoked lawsuits from competitors chagrined by the ads' descriptions of their products.[44] The inevitable consumer buzz that will accompany the first uses of AR for this type of advertising will bring with it an equal degree of scrutiny by competitors targeted in such ads, making a lawsuit that much more likely. Regardless of who ultimately prevails, the answer will very likely not be obvious, and it will probably require quite a bit of expensive litigation to resolve.

ADVERTISING DISCLOSURES
DISCLOSURES REQUIRED AND ENFORCED BY THE FEDERAL TRADE COMMISSION

As mentioned above, the FTC is charged with policing the marketplace for advertising practices that deceive and potentially mislead consumers. In recent years, the FTC has given particular attention to digital marketing practices. In 2009, it created a stir across the blogosphere by announcing stricter rules requiring the disclosure of any "material connection" between a retailer and any online author – including average, everyday bloggers – who endorse the retailer's product, even as simple of a connection as receiving a free product to review. The idea was to make sure that the consuming public understood the potential for bias in an online review. In reality, the FTC's enforcement of this rule focused much less on individual bloggers than on the corporate interests that supplied them, but the announcement did much to educate online marketers and the blogging public about the importance of disclosing to online consumer all information that could be material to their purchasing decision.

In March 2013, the FTC released a new instructional guide called *.com Disclosures: How to Make Effective Disclosures in Digital Advertising.*[45] As explained

---

[43]I imagined a similar scenario in the first piece I published related to AR law—the short story "The More Things Change," published in 2007 by the State Bar of Michigan. See BRIAN WASSOM, THE MORE THINGS CHANGE (2007) *available at* http://www.honigman.com/media/site_files/1606_the%20 more%20things%20change.pdf.

[44]See, e.g., *Southland Sod Farms v. Stover Seed Co.*, 108 F. 3d 1134 (9th Cir. 1997) (litigating over ads comparing competing varieties of sod); *US Healthcare v. Blue Cross of Gr. Phila.*, 898 F. 2d 914 (3rd Cir. 1990) (litigating over claims about competing health plans); *Procter & Gamble Co. v. Chesebrough-Pond's Inc.*, 747 F.2d 114 (2d Cir. 1984) (litigating over comparative advertising of hand and body lotions); *American Home Products Corp. v. Johnson & Johnson*, 577 F. 2d 160 (2d Cir. 1978) (litigating over alleged differences in the performance of pain medication).

[45]FEDERAL TRADE COMMISISON, .COM DISCLOSURES:HOW TO MAKE EFFECTIVE DISCLOSURES IN DIGITAL ADVERTISING (March, 2013).

therein, "[t]his FTC staff guidance document describes the information businesses should consider as they develop ads for online media to ensure that they comply with the law."[46] Because the following summary succinctly captures the advice in the entire document, it is reprinted here with only minor editing:

1. The same consumer protection laws that apply to commercial activities in other media apply online, including activities in the mobile marketplace.
2. When practical, advertisers should incorporate relevant limitations and qualifying information into the underlying claim, rather than having a separate disclosure qualifying the claim.
3. Required disclosures must be clear and conspicuous. In evaluating this point, advertisers should consider the disclosure's proximity to the relevant claim; the prominence of the disclosure; whether it is unavoidable; whether other parts of the ad distract attention from the disclosure; whether the disclosure needs to be repeated at different places on a website; whether disclosures in audio messages are presented in an adequate volume and cadence; whether visual disclosures appear for a sufficient duration; and whether the language of the disclosure is understandable to the intended audience.
4. To make a disclosure clear and conspicuous, advertisers should:
   - place the disclosure as close as possible to the triggering claim; take account of the various devices and platforms consumers may use to view advertising and any corresponding disclosure; design the disclosure to prevent the ad from being misleading when viewed on any of the devices or platforms from which it may be viewed.
   - When a space-constrained ad requires a disclosure, incorporate the disclosure into the ad whenever possible. However, when it is not possible to make a disclosure in a space-constrained ad, it may, under some circumstances, be acceptable to make the disclosure clearly and conspicuously on the page to which the ad links.
   - When using a hyperlink to lead to a disclosure, make the link obvious; label it appropriately to convey the importance, nature, and relevance of the information it leads to; use hyperlink styles consistently, so consumers know when a link is available; place the hyperlink as close as possible to the relevant information it qualifies and make it noticeable; take consumers directly to the disclosure on the click-through page; assess the effectiveness of the hyperlink by monitoring click-through rates and other information about consumer use and make changes accordingly.
   - Preferably, design advertisements so that "scrolling" is not necessary in order to find a disclosure. When scrolling is necessary, use text or visual cues to encourage consumers to scroll to view the disclosure.
   - Keep abreast of empirical research about where consumers do and do not look on a screen.

---

[46]*Id.* at i.

- Recognize and respond to any technological limitations or unique characteristics of a communication method when making disclosures.
- Display disclosures before consumers make a decision to buy, e.g., before they "add to shopping cart." Also recognize that disclosures may have to be repeated before purchase to ensure that they are adequately presented to consumers.
- Repeat disclosures, as needed, on lengthy websites and in connection with repeated claims. Disclosures may also have to be repeated if consumers have multiple routes through a website.
- If a product or service promoted online is intended to be (or can be) purchased from "brick and mortar" stores or from online retailers other than the advertiser itself, then any disclosure necessary to prevent deception or unfair injury should be presented in the ad itself – that is, before consumers head to a store or some other online retailer.
- Necessary disclosures should not be relegated to "terms of use" and similar contractual agreements.
- Prominently display disclosures so they are noticeable to consumers, and evaluate the size, color, and graphic treatment of the disclosure in relation to other parts of the webpage.
- Review the entire ad to assess whether the disclosure is effective in light of other elements – text, graphics, hyperlinks, or sound – that might distract consumers' attention from the disclosure.
- Use audio disclosures when making audio claims, and present them in a volume and cadence so that consumers can hear and understand them.
- Display visual disclosures for a duration sufficient for consumers to notice, read, and understand them.
- Use plain language and syntax so that consumers understand the disclosures.

5. If a disclosure is necessary to prevent an advertisement from being deceptive, unfair, or otherwise violative of a Commission rule, and it is not possible to make the disclosure clearly and conspicuously, then that ad should not be disseminated. This means that if a particular platform does not provide an opportunity to make clear and conspicuous disclosures, then that platform should not be used to disseminate advertisements that require disclosures. Negative consumer experiences can result in lost consumer goodwill and erode consumer confidence. Clear, conspicuous, and meaningful disclosures benefit advertisers and consumers.[47]

AR marketers will be held to those same standards.

MAKING APPROPRIATE DISCLOSURES IN THE AR SPACE

As noted above, whenever digital content recreates or augments a physical object, there is an opportunity for inaccuracy or exaggeration in that depiction. This, in turn, can cause consumer confusion. To prevent these circumstances from being deemed

---

[47]See *id*, at i–iii.

unfair business practices and survive FTC scrutiny, advertisers will need to include certain disclaimers and disclosures in their augmented ads. But the medium will present unique challenges in this regard.

Including disclaimers in or with the claim

The FTC's *.com Disclosures* manual repeatedly emphasizes the importance of including required disclosures in the same context as the potentially misleading advertisement – to the point of suggesting that when Twitter posts require disclosures, some degree of disclosure must appear in the tweet itself, even though it is limited to 140 characters. Other authorities in this field have reached similar conclusions. In 2012, an arbitration panel of the Better Business Bureau's National Advertising Division took Nutrisystem to task for posting weight loss testimonials on Pinterest, but publishing the necessary "results are not typical"-type disclaimers on the page hyperlinked to the "pins," rather than in the pins themselves. Although *additional* information may be provided elsewhere, at least some degree of disclosure must generally be included directly adjacent to the potentially misleading content.

How this will work with augmented advertising remains to be seen. Consider ads that feature a digital object, such as a car or a washing machine that emerges from an interactive print publication. Regardless of how well-rendered these complex objects are, they are exceedingly unlikely to be photo-realistic using contemporary technology. If the discrepancies between the image and the real thing are material – that is, an attribute that would be important to a consumer's purchasing decision – then the potential for confusion should be remedied by an appropriate disclaimer. Which feature is material in any given circumstance will depend on the thing being depicted and why it matters to the consumer. If I'm using an interactive print object as an anchor to assess how a particular piece of furniture will fit in a room, for example, I will be primarily concerned with replicating the item's exact physical dimensions. On the other hand, if I'm shopping for a car, a three-dimensional image would be most helpful in judging its aesthetic appearance and interior layout.

The most liberal, straightforward interpretation of the FTC's guidelines would require annotations in the 3D image itself warning users about the potential material inaccuracies. But it is difficult enough to render a digital image in a way that creates some degree of illusion that it is a tangible, three-dimensional object. Inserting additional text boxes that explain each shortcoming in the image could disrupt the effect and mar the image so much as to make the ad worthless, or at the very least unappealing.

Of course, the same objections have probably been made by every advertiser in every media, yet the legal requirements remain the same. Necessity births innovative ways to incorporate disclosures without detracting from the message. It seems likely, for example, that disclaimers such as "objects may not be to scale," if necessary, will be displayed for only a finite period of time, probably while the image is loading. The messages could also be incorporated into an image's background; for example, if I see a virtual car driving on a moving road, the disclaimer text may appear as text painted on the "road" that disappears after the car drives "past" it. A persistent disclosure could also be printed on the physical target of an augmented display, even though that message would presumably be eclipsed once the augmented display begins. Or a dialog box could appear persistently in the user's field of view, and be designed to expand when selected to reveal more detailed disclosure information. This would be the closest AR analog to the current internet's use of hyperlinks to convey more disclosure data than can realistically fit within the advertisement itself.

Some limitations of the medium will be sufficiently obvious that no disclaimer is necessary. When I encounter 8-bit graphics of the kind employed in the *Minecraft* game, for example, I understand that any depiction of an actual object I see is going to be only the roughest imitation. Paradoxically, it is only as digital imaging technology improves enough that it can depict things accurately that the law will impose upon advertisers the responsibility to be more accurate.

It is also worth remembering that the assessment of when a disclosure is necessary, and how prominent it must be, is inherently subjective, and varies in importance depending on the nature of the transaction occurring. Many of the augmented marketing techniques employed to date are indirect, in that they generate consumer interest, build goodwill, and convey information rather than directly inducing a purchase. Even those that advertise a particular product rarely have the capability to make a direct sale; at best, they contain links to an ecommerce website. As augmented advertisements become more robust and directly commercial, the more important disclosures and disclaimers will become.

Moreover, just as was mentioned in Chapter 3's privacy discussion, AR may prove to be a boon, rather than hindrance, to accurate commercial disclosures. Color-coded objects or displays could communicate basic messages in immediate and non-jargonized ways, and customers could be required to indicate assent by physically interacting with the displays. Touching a virtual display could trigger an augmented call-out box that ties a particular warning or message to a specific portion of an image that has drawn the customer's attention. Unbounded by the size limitations of a particular device, advertisers could have more physical area in which to communicate messages so that consumers do not miss them in the fine print. Indeed, augmented displays could prove to be such an effective means of educating consumers that these methods could easily become the norm, and then become a legal requirement.

At the same time, advertisers should not get so carried away with the ability to display content beyond the physical page or object that the necessary disclaimer is placed so far away as to be unnoticed. The concept of "fine print" at the bottom of a 2D advertisement was born out of the advertisers' desire to meet the legal obligations while being as inconspicuous as possible. On websites, we see the same phenomenon when disclaimers appear in smaller print, different columns, in page footers, or on the other end of a hyperlink. The FTC's *.com Disclosures* called out a few of these examples, and warned that such placements are unlawful if they do not occur in the same cell or screen as the associated ad text. In AR, this could mean that ad copy visible through one's mobile device must make any disclaimers visible in the same field of view, instead of requiring the user to tilt their device in a different direction to see the disclaimer.

Distractions

Even if proper disclaimers of otherwise-sufficient prominence are included in an advertisement, they can fail to accomplish their purpose if the remainder of the display is so engaging that a user's attention is distracted (Fig. 4.9). On this point, the FTC's *.com Disclosures* gives the example of disclaimer text that appears in the correct place and size for a typical webpage, only to become obscured (and therefore ineffective) when the website owner employs a virtual shopping assistant who "walks" across the screen to interact with the user.

This example from the FTC was a bit novel as applied to the vast majority of websites, but is prescient in the context of AR. The very point of AR is to create the illusion of interacting with digital objects as if they were physical. This means that neither advertisers nor regulators can continue thinking about ad text as if it were merely words on a two-dimensional screen. Instead, ad composition will begin to look more like choreography than copy editing. To judge whether a particular element is sufficiently visible, one will need to consider the placement and movement of all elements of the three-dimensional, moving image, as well as the physical location and perspective of the viewer at any given time. If one digital image gets in the way of a user's view of required disclaimer text, that could render the entire ad unlawful.

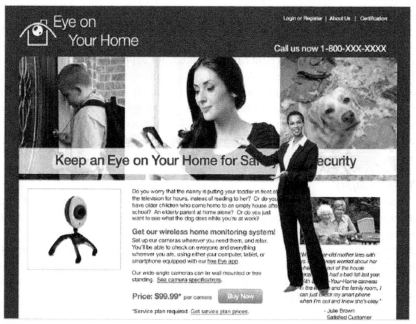

FIGURE 4.9

Distractions will be an inherent challenge with AR displays.

A scene from the epic sci-fi film *Star Trek II: The Wrath of Khan* illustrates the point. The movie's antagonist is a brilliant military tactician, but he is a transplant from the twentieth century and therefore accustomed to conflict on the flat surface of a planet, rather than the starship battle in which he finds himself. The twenty-third century heroes, who are used to space-based vehicles that travel in three dimensions, are therefore able to outwit their foe. Mastering the art of displaying ads and disclaimers in augmented reality will be a bit like that; those who learn to think in terms of all the medium has to offer will be more successful in using it to communicate effectively.

Empirical research and analytical data

One of the requirements listed in the FTC's *.com Disclosures* guide is that advertisers "[k]eep abreast of empirical research about where consumers do and do not look on a screen."[48] The results of such studies are often displayed as heat maps illustrating the parts of a screen to which users' eyes are drawn – such as the studies demonstrating that readers almost totally ignore banner ads on websites.[49] This FTC guidance does not directly require advertisers to conduct such research themselves.

Once again, however, the easier that certain steps become through advanced technology, the more likely they are to eventually become mandatory. One of the most attractive elements of augmented reality campaigns to retailers is not only the level of customer engagement they inspire, but also the richly detailed analytics they allow advertisers to gather. Many AR campaigns require precise geolocation, accelerometer information, and cloud-based content (among other data) to function properly, and all of that data can be tracked and aggregated to reveal quite a bit of insight into the consumer base viewing the promotion. At present, such data is competitive intelligence, and if regulators think about it at all, they do so in terms of user privacy, as discussed in Chapter 3. But it may become so commonplace that the FTC instead begins to require advertisers to collect it and study it in order to better understand how effectively certain disclosures are being communicated to users.

Physical injury

It seems doubtful that many, if any, digital advertisers have ever worried that a consumer might hurt themselves while viewing their ad. But what turns digital content into augmented content is its interactivity with physical places and things. So, as advertising moves into the augmented medium–especially if it includes "game" mechanics that require users to go looking for digital objects in physical space–marketers will need to pay close attention to the surroundings into which they ask consumers to go. Chapter 7 will explore this topic in greater detail.

---

[48]*Id.* at ii.
[49]Banner Blindness: Old and New Findings, Neilsen Norman Group, August 20, 2007, available at < http://www.nngroup.com/articles/banner-blindness-old-and-new-findings/>

CONDUCTING COMMERCE
THE EMERGING ABILITY TO CONDUCT MONETARY TRANSACTIONS IN THE AR MEDIUM

Point-of-sale payments in the United States are still carried out almost exclusively in cash or by credit or debit cards. As of this writing, mobile electronic payments via near-field communication (NFC) technology – although popular in many countries – had not yet caught on to any significant degree. That is likely to change very soon in light of Apple's September 2014 announcement that its next generation of devices would support NFC payments, and that a number of major retailers had already signed on to support such transactions. This is likely to jumpstart the development of an NFC payment infrastructure that other devices will be able to take advantage of as well.

Digital eyewear and other augmented world devices will benefit from such developments. Forrester Research has already suggested that AR technology "can be used … with Google Glass, allowing consumers to shop for products with Glass acting as a sort of virtual shopping assistant. Moreover, Google's strong interest in mobile commerce may herald the introduction of mobile payment services that are specifically designed for Glass."[50] Glass already allows users to take a photo simply by winking an eye. In the short film *Sight*,[51] a character wearing AR contact lenses pays for a meal at a restaurant by looking at the virtual representation of a bill and winking at it (Fig. 4.10).

FIGURE 4.10

Augmented commerce in *Sight*.

[50]Stephen Vagus, *Google Glass could serve as a new mobile commerce platform*, MOBILE COMMERCE PRESS (July 1, 2013) http://www.mobilecommercepress.com/google-glass-could-serve-as-a-new-mobile-commerce-platform/857436/.

[51]Patrick Bateman, *Sight*, YOUTUBE (July 23, 2012) https://www.youtube.com/watch?v=fSU0lTCMTZw.

FIGURE 4.11

Purchasing milk through the Tesco Google Glass app.

As mentioned above, in 2013, Google obtained a patent for "pay per gaze" and "pay per emotion" systems. Although these are described as methods for ISPs to charge advertisers based on a consumer's reaction to the ad, they could just as easily be adapted to take payments from consumers in order to access the advertising or other content. In February 2014, the company EAZE unveiled such a system. Dubbed "Nod to Pay," it enabled Google Glass wearers to pay merchants in Bitcoins by nodding their heads twice.[52] Similarly, in August 2014, British grocery chain Tesco released an app for Glass that allows individuals to scan the barcode of a product at home and use the app to purchase the product, which is then delivered straight to the user's home.[53] (Fig. 4.11)

CONSUMER PROTECTION AND CONTRACT LAW

The convenience of such payment methods and the fact that precursors already exist in today's technology make it highly likely that future devices will provide this payment option. Care will need to be taken, however, to avoid unintentional transactions. Experience has already demonstrated that unintentional winks can result in unintended photographs, so there will need to be some sort of additional safeguard where money is involved. This could be as simple as a virtual "Are you sure?" call-out box at which the user must wink for a second time. Even more ideally, it would involve a second source of input, such as making a hand gesture. Still – as in a public auction where bids can be placed by nodding, waving, or similar gestures – it seems inevitable that a certain percentage of individuals will end up challenging the legitimacy of a purchase registered by an augmented app, arguing that the app misinterpreted the user's gesture.

---

[52]See https://paywitheaze.com/.

[53]Jacob Kleinman, "New Google Glass App Lets You Order Groceries by Looking at Them," *Techno-Buffalo*, August 10, 2014, available at http://www.technobuffalo.com/2014/08/10/new-google-glass-app-lets-you-order-groceries-by-looking-at-them/?utm_content=buffer7857d&utm_medium=social&utm_source=twitter.

However these hurdles are overcome, it seems certain that payments through paper and plastic will wane. Augmented interfaces offer not only convenience, but also additional security, as they can easily be tied to the user's biometric data as well.

The issue of proper disclosures to customers is also pertinent to monetary transactions conducted in the AR space. Various consumer protection laws in various jurisdictions require all manner of information to be made conspicuously available to consumers, such as price, warranty information, return policies, dispute resolution procedures, shipping options, taxes, ingredients, and the like. On today's internet, many retailers accomplish these disclosures through lengthy, dense, written policies that the vast majority of customers never read. As discussed above, the augmented medium offers a much wider range of options for displaying such data, but the information itself is still likely to be lengthy and dense.

Some disgruntled purchasers challenge documents like these as "contracts of adhesion" that are "unconscionable" – legal terms of art for provisions that are so one-sided, unfair, and/or poorly disclosed that it would be fundamentally unfair to enforce them against a consumer with no bargaining power of their own. Occasionally, such arguments prevail, but not often. Instead, in the digital context, courts are likely to enforce even the most obscure contractual terms of purchase as long as the purchaser gave some indication of their assent to them. Typically this consent is conveyed by clicking a box that says "I agree." Hence, such provisions are called "click-wrap" contracts (a derivative of the "shrinkwrap" licenses that used to be printed on a sealed box, and that were deemed agreed to once a consumer opened the seal). Their antithesis is the "browsewrap" contract, which purports to be enforceable merely because a user visited a website, even if they never viewed the "contract" itself. Such terms are often not enforced unless it can be shown that the user assented to them.

What level of assent will be necessary to consummate a contract in the augmented medium? On the low end of the spectrum, the augmented equivalent of an unenforceable browsewrap agreement might be called a "glancewrap" – terms that purport to be enforced on an individual merely because they looked at a dialog box through their digital eyewear. A slightly more affirmative indication of assent would be the nodding, blinking, or waving used by the various apps mentioned above. Whether any or all of these gestures prove to be enforceable indications of assent will depend on the circumstances. Even more direct forms of agreement might include air-signing one's name, or speaking the words "I Agree" into one's wearable device.

In terms of the information available to consumers, however, at least one commentator has argued that AR[54] will substantially level the playing field between retailers

---

[54]Peppet uses the term "augmented reality" much more generically than this book does, to mean "the convergence of digital and physical space generally, not merely in the real-time augmentation of digital video." Scott Peppet, "Freedom of Contract in an Augmented Reality: The Case of Consumer Contracts," ___ UCLA L. REV. ____ (2012), Working Paper Number 11-14 at 2 n.9 (August 29, 2011), available at http://papers.ssrn.com/sol3/papers.cfm?abstract_id=1919013. Nevertheless, his insights are still relevant to the AR medium as it is more commonly understood.

and purchasers. Scott Peppet is a professor at the University of Colorado Law School. As a result of today's digital media, he argues, "[h]uge amounts of new information is now available to consumers, but it is not perfectly comprehensive. If information about a given product or contract is unavailable, consumers' ability to sort decreases and firms' temptations to include oppressive terms in their contracts increases."[55]

AR, however, makes it easier for businesses to convey more information to consumers. Peppet identifies at least four reasons why sellers will use AR to better explain their contractual terms. "First, firms can cheaply distribute text, audio, graphical, or video explanations to consumers at the point of sale.... Second, this distribution scale permits firms to centralize such legal explanation[,] ... [allowing] corporate counsel [to] control the message ... as it scales. [Third] ... in an augmented reality, firms can give consumers choice about whether to watch a given explanation of a product or contract term.... [Fourth], augmented reality gives sellers the ability to prove that consumers in fact watched their explanation."[56] Taking advantage of these opportunities would protect businesses from later assertions by a customer that they were deceived, by making it easier to prove that the customer got all of the information they needed to make an informed choice. The more effective such methods of disclosure prove to be, the more likely it is that courts and regulator will begin to require them, or at least apply extra scrutiny to retailers who do not use these methods.[57]

CONCLUSION

The augmented medium provides a broad range of options for communicating information. Commercial retailers will be among the first to use this medium as a new way to sell their goods and services. There will, however, be a transitional period in which retailer, regulators, and courts attempt to adapt existing standards of propriety to the new medium. In the end, the fundamental goal of commercial speech regulations and consumer protection laws will be the same as it is now – to protect individual consumers from being unfairly manipulated or deceived.

---

[55]*Id.* at 36.
[56]*Id.* at 38.
[57]See *id.* at 42.

Intellectual Property

5

INFORMATION IN THIS CHAPTER:

- Patents
- Trademark
- Copyright
- Publicity Rights

INTRODUCTION

Intellectual property laws protect ideas, creative expression, commercial good-will, and other intangible concepts. Although they cannot be seen or touched, these concepts have become some of the most valuable assets in our contemporary, knowledge-driven economy. They will remain just as important, if not more so, in a world with ubiquitous augmented reality.

PATENTS
THE NATURE OF PATENT PROTECTION

A patent conveys a property right to the inventor(s) of an invention. In the language of the statute and of the patent registration itself, the right granted by a U.S. patent is "the right to exclude others from making, using, offering for sale, or selling" the invention in the United States or "importing" the invention into the United States. To get a U.S. patent, an application must be filed in the U.S. Patent and Trademark Office (USPTO). Patent protection lasts for up to 20 years from the date of application, subject to the payment of appropriate maintenance fees for a utility patent.

Utility patents are the type of patents most relevant to AR. These may be granted to anyone who invents or discovers any new and useful process, machine, article of manufacture, or compositions of matters, or any new useful improvement thereof. In order to receive protection, the inventor must describe the method by which his or her invention would work. Until 1880, the USPTO required that inventors submit working models of their inventions.[1] Since that time, however, an applicant need only

---

[1]Teresa Riordan, *Patents; Models that were once required in the application process find a good home*, THE NEW YORK TIMES (February, 18, 2002) available at http://www.nytimes.com/2002/02/18/business/18PATE.html?pagewanted=all.

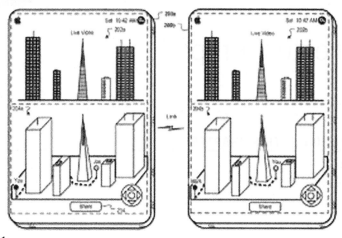

FIGURE 5.1

Apple's 2011 patent application showing AR on an iPad.

describe their concept in the patent application in order to receive protection; they need not actually create something in order to have invented it.

United States law also no longer entitles the one who first invents something to the patent protection on it. It used to be that even if someone else beat you to the punch in applying to register an invention, you could undo their patent by proving that you invented it first. No longer, thanks to the America Invents Act that President Obama signed into law on September 16, 2011. As of 2013, it is now the "first to file," not the "first to invent," who wins. That is the system that Europe and virtually the entire rest of the world already used.

PATENT PROTECTION IN AR INVENTIONS

Tangible, consumer-level AR applications have only recently begun to emerge because we have only recently devised the hardware and software required to make them commercially feasible. Many of these developments, however, have been anticipated for quite some time, which means that many creative minds have already had plenty of time in which to obtain patents on AR-related inventions.

On July 7, 2011, the USPTO published Apple's patent application US 2011/0164163 A1, for "Synchronized, Interactive Augmented Reality Displays for Multifunction Devices (Fig. 5.1)." [2] This news, and the accompanying drawings depicting AR at work on an iPad, caused quite a stir in the blogosphere and among AR enthusiasts, who took it as an indication that the era of mass-market AR was finally about to begin.

---

[2]U.S. Patent No. 8,400,548 (filed January 5, 2010) available at https://docs.google.com/viewer?url=patentimages.storage.googleapis.com/pdfs/US8400548.pdf.

a

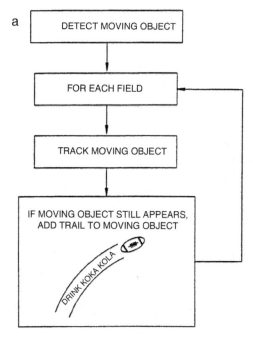

b

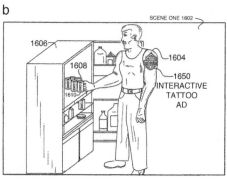

c

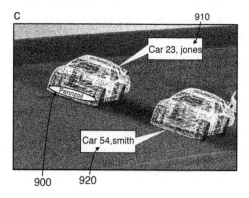

FIGURE 5.2

Additional excerpts from AR-related patents.

But AR has been in the process of "emerging" for years now – plenty long enough for all sorts of companies and inventors to get their ideas registered with the USPTO. These registered inventions include augmented tattoos, advertising on flying footballs, and adding virtual displays to live sporting events (Fig. 5.2).

There is, of course, still plenty of room for innovation in the augmented reality field – just not quite as much room as some might assume. As of Dec. 10, 2011, a search for "augmented reality" in the Google Patents search engine returned about 11,100 hits. In January 2014, that number was up to 160,000.

Moreover, as anyone reading the tech headlines in the past decade realizes, patent litigation is all the rage nowadays. Anyone and everyone with a patent, it seems, is suing or being sued by a competitor with a similar patent or product. In 2012, over 5,000 patent infringement lawsuits were reportedly filed – a spike of over 30% from the year before – and this trend "shows no signs of cooling off, either as a means of generating revenue or of protecting competitive advantage."[3]

This is especially true with respect to smartphones and tablets[4] – precisely the platforms on which consumer AR is just starting to take off. Therefore, we can expect patent litigation to be one of the first areas in which AR-related legal disputes arise in earnest.

THE FIRST AR PATENT INFRINGEMENT CASE: *TOMITA V. NINTENDO*[5]

As ominous as the trends of patent litigation can appear from a macro level, the facts of any particular case often seem entirely ordinary, even mundane. That was the case with the earliest recorded litigation activity related to AR.

On June 26, 2012, a judge of the U.S. District Court for the Southern District of New York issued what appears to be the first substantive decision in an AR-related patent infringement case. The device in question was one of the most popular AR-capable units then on the market: the Nintendo 3DS portable game console. Although the case had been first filed in June 2011, this was the first substantive decision from the court on the merits of the case, and the first to mention AR.

Plaintiffs ("Tomita") were the owners of U.S. Patent No. 7,417,664, issued in August 2008 and titled "Stereoscopic image picking up and display system based upon optical axes cross-point information." As described by the court, "the '664 patent attempts' to provide a stereoscopic video image pick-up and display system which is capable of providing the stereoscopic video image having natural stereopsis even if the video image producing and playback conditions are different."[6]

---

[3] CHRIS BARRY, ET AL., 2013 PATENT LITIGATION STUDY: BIG CASES MAKE HEADLINES, WHILE PATENT CASES PROLIFERATE, available at http://www.pwc.com/en_US/us/forensic-services/publications/assets/2013-patent-litigation-study.pdf.

[4] See *Topics, Patent Lawsuit*, MASHABLE, http://mashable.com/category/patent-lawsuit/ (last visited June 10, 2014) for articles discussing articles discussing patent disputes between major phone and tablet makers.

[5] *Tomita Techs. USA, LLC v. Nintendo Co., Ltd.*, No. 11-Civ-4256 (JSR), 2012 WL 2524770, (S.D.N.Y. 2012)

[6] *Id.* at *1.

Tomita alleged that the 3DS infringes this patent. The June 26, 2012 opinion rejected Nintendo's motion to dismiss the case. The court determined instead that there was enough evidence to allow the case to proceed to a jury.

Most of the discussion in the parties' arguments and the court's opinion focuses on how the 3DS's cameras work to capture 3D images. The patent describes a "means for measuring cross-point (CP) information on the CP of optical axes of [the] pickup means." The two cameras built into the 3DS are arranged in parallel, but the parties and their experts disagreed over whether the optical axes of these cameras would nevertheless intersect. The court agreed with Tomita that they would.

In addition, as described by the court and the parties, the system described by '664 patent includes a "manual entry unit" through which the viewer can change "the operation condition of the display control circuit." The 3DS has at least two modes: "Camera" mode and "AR games" mode. And it has two means of adjusting the three-dimensional image it displays: a circle pad and a "3D depth slider." In both the camera application and the AR games application, the 3DS's 3D depth slider only changes the display from a two-dimensional image (turning the three-dimensional display "off") to a three-dimensional one (turning the three-dimensional display "on"). The dispute over this feature was whether, by turning three-dimensional viewing on or off, the 3D depth slider operates as a "manual entry unit" within the offset presetting means' structure. To infringe the '664 patent, "the relevant structure" in the 3DS must "perform the identical function recited in the claim."[7]

The court found that "a reasonable jury could find that the 3DS's 3D depth slider constitutes a component of the offset presetting means' structure," performing one aspect of the identical function recited in the claim. "Specifically," it continued, the '664 patent notes that the "manual entry unit may be [a] switch... which is actuated by the viewer depending upon user's preferences for changing the operation conditions of the display control circuit." Both parties acknowledge that the 3D depth slider functions in the AR Games application as a "switch," allowing the user to exercise control over the display control circuit's operation conditions. Specifically, the 3D depth slider allows the viewer to determine whether the display circuit presents an offset at all. Thus, a reasonable jury could find that the manual entry unit, along with the circuits described in the '664 patent, performs the function of "offsetting and displaying" video images by allowing the user to determine whether the circuits will display an offset.[8]

On this basis, the court allowed Tomita to pursue its claim that, because the unit's 3D depth adjustment switch allows users to adjust the 3D image they see while in "AR Games" mode, the 3DS allegedly infringes the '664 patent.

On March 13, 2013, the jury returned a verdict in Tomita's favor, and awarded it $30.2 million in damages although the judge in the case had decided as a matter of law that Nintendo had not infringed the patent willfully. Both sides filed motions seeking to adjust these rulings. Nintendo prevailed on one important argument – the

---

[7]*Id.* at *3.
[8]*Id.* at *7.

amount of the damages award, which was based on the estimated value of a reasonable royalty payment by Nintendo to Tomita for use of the technology. The jury had apparently based its figures on the testimony of Tomita's expert, who used the "entire market value" of the 3DS as the royalty base for calculating the reasonable royalty rate. This led the jury to a rate of just under 3% of the 3DS's sale price.

In an August 14, 2013 opinion, the judge found this rate "intrinsically excessive," for a number of reasons. For one thing, the 3DS itself was not profitable. Nintendo makes its money on the sale of 3DS games, but the evidence showed that "the vast majority of games designed for the 3DS do not require or even utilize the technology covered by the '664 patent." It also struck the judge as unfair to consider the entire value of the 3DS game market when "the '664 patent's technology was used only in two features – the 3D camera and the AR games application – and thus was in some sense ancillary to the core functionality of the 3DS as a gaming system."[9] In other words, the court found as a matter of law that any AR functionality in the 3DS is an add-on, rather than a core feature, of the console.

As a result, the judge gave Tomita two choices – either accept a 50% cut in the jury's award, reducing it to $15.1 million, or else conduct a whole new trial on damages. The legal term of art for this ruling is "remittur."

I have reproduced the details of this litigation to demonstrate what patent infringement litigation looks like. Obviously, it hinges on the tiniest of details in the subject inventions and challenged products. Moreover, the ultimate decisions will be rendered by a judge or jury who is unlikely to be knowledgeable in the art, so much depends on how well the issues are explained to them. And in the end, the amount of money at stake in even the most inconsequential AR patents may be significant.

PATENTS AS WEAPONS OF COMPETITION: *1-800-CONTACTS V. DITTO TECHNOLOGIES*

Ditto Technologies launched in 2012 as an innovative leader in "virtual try-on" technology for eyewear. It employed webcam-based AR to show consumers what a particular pair of glasses would look like on them.

This apparently caught the attention of its more-established competitor, 1-800-Contacts. According to the Electronic Frontier Foundation, which came to Ditto's defense, "1-800-Contacts' CEO went onto Ditto's website the very day it launched, presumably to investigate the upstart competitor's new technology. Having seen Ditto's product, 1-800-Contacts then went out and purchased a patent from a defunct company that claims to cover selling eyeglasses over a network using a 3D model of a user's face." [10] At the time the lawsuit was filed, 1-800-Contacts still

[9]*Tomita Technologies USA, LLC v. Nintendo Co., Ltd.*, No. 11-cv-4256 (JSR), 2013 WL 4101251, at *10 (S.D.N.Y. August 14, 2013)

[10]Daniel Nazer & Julie Samuels, *UPDATED: Help Stop 1-800-Contacts from Abusing Patents to Squelch Competition*, ELECTRONIC FRONTIER FOUNDATION (April 17, 2013) https://www.eff.org/deeplinks/2013/04/1-800-contacts-buys-patent-squelch-competition.

did not offer a competing service, but said that it intended to launch one soon on its Glasses.com site. That app was eventually released for iOS and Android in January and February of 2014, respectively.

What angered the EFF even more was what it perceived to be the strategy behind the lawsuit. Rather than seeking a royalty from Ditto, said the EFF, 1-800-Contacts "seems determined to put Ditto out of business. Period."[11] 1-800-Contacts disputes EFF's characterizations, and claims it has tried to settle the case.[12] The parties actively litigated the case for several months, but in November 2013 it was stayed pending the result of Ditto's request that the U.S. Patent Office re-examine the patent's legitimacy – a long-shot procedural tactic available to defendants in these situations.

The attention given to this dispute contributed to the already active conversation about whether litigation like this and the patents underlying them threaten to squelch innovation in software development. No one entity has done more to raise alarm bells on that issue within the AR community, however, than Lennon Image Technologies, LLC.

THE FIRST AR PATENT TROLL: LENNON IMAGE TECHNOLOGIES

Lennon is what the patent world calls a "non-practicing entity," or NPE – more commonly referred to as a "patent troll." Such companies own patent rights, but do not use them to make or do anything; rather, their only business is to sue other companies for (allegedly) infringing the patents. The patent troll phenomenon is one of the primary drivers behind the explosion in patent infringement litigation; one report found NPEs responsible for more than half of the patent lawsuits file in 2012, compared to less than a quarter in 2007.[13] Yet only 16% of the cases actually decided by a court were filed by NPEs, "reveal[ing] a much higher tendency for NPE actions to be resolved without a formal court decision."[14] This corresponds to the anecdotal experience that most companies have with patent trolls; they leverage the threat of infringement liability and the steep expense of patent litigation to coerce an early, favorable settlement out of those they sue.

On July 16, 2012, Lennon filed six separate patent infringement lawsuits, all in the U.S. District Court for Delaware. Each is nearly identical to the other, and is based on the same patent: US 6,624,843 B2, issued Sep. 23, 2003.[15] The title of the patent is "Customer Image Capture and Use Thereof in a Retailing System." The abstract describes an AR "virtual try-on" experience very similar to what we see on websites from Ditto and several other retailers (Fig. 5.3):

[11]*Id.*

[12]Anthony Ho, "Ditto Defeats Patent Claim After Teaming Up With A 'Troll'," *TechCrunch*, October 12, 2013, available at http://techcrunch.com/2013/10/12/ditto-wins-defeats-patent-claim-after-teaming-up-with-a-troll/

[13]Chris Barry, et al., Patent Litigation Study, *supra* note 3, at 3.

[14]*Id.* at 3

[15]U.S. Patent No. 6,624,843 (filed December 8, 2000).

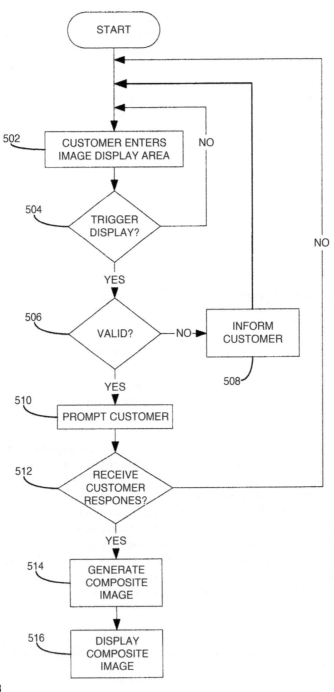

FIGURE 5.3

An image from Lennon's patent.

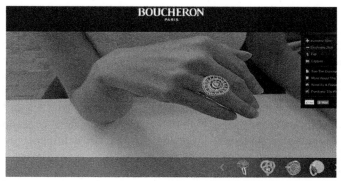

FIGURE 5.4

The Boucheron virtual try-on site shut down by Lennon Image Technologies' lawsuit.

> *In a retailing system, an image capture system is provided and used to capture refer-*
> *ence images of models wearing apparel items. At a retailer's place of business, an*
> *image capture system substantially identical to that used to capture the reference*
> *images is also provided. A customer has his or her image captured by the image*
> *capture system at the retailer's place of business. Subsequently, when the customer*
> *is in close proximity to an image display area within the retailer's place of busi-*
> *ness, a composite image comprising the customer's captured image and one of the*
> *reference images may be provided. The composite image may comprise full motion*
> *video or still images. In this manner, the customer is given the opportunity to virtu-*
> *ally assess the selected merchandise without actually having to try on the apparel.*[16]

Of course, one important difference between this abstract and what these defendants do is that current virtual fitting experiences happen online, rather than "within
the retailer's place of business." One wonders if that will make a difference in the
litigation.

Each of Lennon's complaints specifies a specific website using analogous virtual-
fitting technology. Among these is Mattel's BarbieDreamCloset.com, which an AR
company named Zugara designed and launched. This was the only complained-of
site that remained active in the days immediately following Lennon's suits, perhaps
because Zugara had recently obtained its own patent[17] for similar technology. Lennon's other lawsuits targeted jewellery-fitting sites run by Boucheron, Forevermark,
De Beers, and Tatler Magazine; a watch-fitting site run by Swatch's Tissot brand;
and Skullcandy's headphone-fitting site. On each of these sites, the "virtual try-on"
features were removed shortly after the companies behind them were sued (Fig. 5.4).

This illustrates another tactic commonly employed by patent trolls – suing
the end user of the technology, rather than the software company that designed

---

[16]*Id.* at 1.
[17]See U.S. Patent No. 8,711,175 (filed August 12, 2011) bool.html&r=1&f=G&l=50&co1=AND&d=P
TXT&s1=8,275,590&OS=8,275,590&RS=8,275,590

the website.[18] In each of these cases, the AR technology behind the virtual try-on component of the website was supplied by a relatively small software company, yet only the big-name brands publicly using the sites were named. The reason is simple: economics. Not only are these brands more likely to be able to afford to pay a monetary settlement, but they also have far less motivation to fight back against the lawsuit. To them, after all, these AR features were merely interesting but one-off promotional experiments. Losing them prematurely was inconvenient, but hardly significant to the retailers' overall bottom line. It made much more economic sense to pay an early settlement than to invest in defending costly litigation over another company's technology.

The AR companies, however, rely on the software they sell for their very existence, and are generally more likely to be start-ups without the liquid funding necessary to defend such litigation. Some of them may have settled, but if they could afford to fight, they would have been much more likely to resist the litigation to the bitter end and potentially defeat Lennon's asserted patent rights. None of that would have made economic sense for Lennon. So instead, Lennon delivered these companies a double whammy – not only did the lawsuits put an end to the AR companies' existing customer relationships, but they also likely scared away many potential clients who would not risk patent litigation.

And, of course, once the first round of defendants pay their settlement money, this gives the trolls cash on hand to fund another round of lawsuits. That is exactly what Lennon did in March 2013, filing six more identical lawsuits, this time in the U.S. District Court for the Eastern District of Texas. These lawsuits name Macys Inc., Bloomingdales, Fraimz LLC, Lumondi Inc., Luxottica Retail North America Inc., Safilo America Inc., and Tacori Enterprises. Again, the allegations revolve around "virtual try-on" and "magic dressing room" technology used by these retailers to give customers at home a chance to see on their computers in three dimensions what a product would look like on them. Just as happened after the prior round of lawsuits, the defendants appear to have deactivated the features on their websites as a precaution. Whether they launch again will likely depend on how the lawsuits resolve.

This sort of litigation activity is worrisome for the nascent augmented reality industry, which is still made almost exclusively of small, ambitious start-ups. "Magic mirror" and "virtual dressing room" technology has been a staple of early AR innovations, and (as these lawsuits demonstrate) has really begun to catch on with retailers and customers alike. On the other hand, developments like this were easy to anticipate. As AR starts to attract real money, we can expect it to give rise to at least as many patent fights as the mobile phone industry is currently dealing with.

Ditto became a poster child for this phenomenon. In a tragic twist of fate, in addition to its dispute with 1-800-Contacts, Ditto was also one of the companies sued by Lennon. This was one of the lawsuits studied in a subsequent study by Catherine Tucker, a professor of marketing at MIT's Sloan School of Business that attempted

---

[18]See Dennis Crouch, Patent Trolls by the Numbers, PatentlyO Patent Blog (March 14, 2013) http://patentlyo.com/patent/2013/03/chien-patent-trolls.html.

to quantify the economic impact of patent troll litigation on the economy. According to Tucker's study, even though Ditto eventually resolved Lennon's lawsuit, "the company was still being valued at $3 to $4 million less than it would be otherwise, and it was forced to lay off four of its 15 employees to pay legal expenses."[19] In total, Tucker estimated that lawsuits, the most active patent trolls, cost the U.S. economy more than $21 billion. Let us hope that litigation like this does not unnecessarily deter developers from pushing AR technology forward.[20]

TRADEMARKS

Although AR-related patent infringement has already begun, it is in the area of trademark law where I expect AR to begin breaking new ground in intellectual property law. Hundreds of innovators have already anticipated and sought patent protection for AR inventions, but the technology is only now entering into the consciousness of consumer-level retailers and marketing professionals.

TRADEMARK BASICS

A trademark is "a word, phrase, symbol, and/or design that identifies and distinguishes the source of the goods of one party from those of others."[21] Technically, a mark that distinguishes services rather than goods is called a "service mark," although the term "trademark" is often used to refer to both,[22] as it will be here. A mark need not explicitly identify the source of the goods or services – it may be suggestive, as many logos are – but the mark must be distinct enough to indicate one source and no other. In this way, trademarks perform an important role in our consumer-driven society, by providing consumers an efficient means to locate products from the providers they trust, and by allowing businesses to protect the integrity of, and goodwill in, their commercial identities.

A person or entity infringes upon the trademark rights of another by interfering with the trademark's ability to signify the goods or services of its owner. This can happen by adopting a mark that is so similar to a pre-existing mark that consumers are confused as to which mark signifies which source, or by using someone else's trademark in an unapproved manner. Courts assess whether trademark infringement has occurred by measuring the "likelihood of confusion" presented by the facts of a

---

[19]Joe Mullin, "New study suggests patent trolls really are killing startups," *Ars Technica*, June 11, 2014, available at http://arstechnica.com/tech-policy/2014/06/new-study-suggests-patent-trolls-really-are-killing-startups/.

[20]On September 15, 2012, a request was filed with the U.S Patent & Trademark office to re-examine Lennon's patent. As of this writing, that request had not yet been acted on. Meanwhile, several of the cases in Delaware and Texas remained ongoing.

[21]United State Patent and Trademark Office, *Trademark, Patent, or Copyright*, USPTO.GOV (January 18, 2013) http://www.uspto.gov/trademarks/basics/definitions.jsp.

[22]See *Id.*

particular case. The particulars of this test vary from court to court, but they always involve some variation of the following:

1. The similarity or dissimilarity of the marks in their entireties as to appearance, sound, connotation, and commercial impression.
2. The similarity or dissimilarity and nature of the goods. .. described in an application or registration or in connection with which a prior mark is in use.
3. The similarity or dissimilarity of established, likely-to-continue trade channels.
4. The conditions under which and buyers to whom sales are made, i.e. "impulse" vs. careful, sophisticated purchasing.
5. The fame of the prior mark.
6. The number and nature of similar marks in use on similar goods.
7. The nature and extent of any actual confusion.
8. The length of time during and the conditions under which there has been concurrent use without evidence of actual confusion.
9. The variety of goods on which a mark is or is not used.
10. The market interface between the applicant and the owner of a prior mark.
11. The extent to which applicant has a right to exclude others from use of its mark on its goods.
12. The extent of potential confusion.
13. Any other established fact probative of the effect of use.[23]

Not all of these factors may be relevant or of equal weight in a given case, and any one of the factors may control a particular case.

One obtains trademark rights by using the mark in commerce, but registering the mark with the U.S. Patent and Trademark Office gives the owner an even broader range of protection. Trademarks are governed on the Federal level by the Lanham Trademark Act of 1946, as amended,[24] as well as a variety of state laws. In a conflict between two trademarks, the one that began to be used (or was registered) first has priority over the other.

Not all trademarks receive the same degree of protection by the courts. In general, the more distinctive the mark is, the more protection it is afforded. In some cases, even a mark which is not by itself distinctive can still be protected because it has acquired "secondary meaning" in the market – in other words, a mark that is indistinct in the abstract can come to be generally understood as signifying a particular source. Courts place marks on a sliding scale of distinctiveness, generally dividing that spectrum into the following five categories:

- Fanciful: These receive the highest protection available under the Lanham Act. They have no logical meaning or alternative meaning and were invented solely to identify goods. Examples include KODAK and XEROX.

---

[23]See, e.g., *In re E.I. du Pont de Nemours & Co.*, 476 F.2d 1357 (C.C.P.A. 1973).
[24]15 U.S.C. §§ 1051–1141n.

FIGURE 5.5

The user-modulated AR ads in Keiichi Matsuda's video short, Domestic Robocop.

- Arbitrary: Slightly less protected than fanciful marks, but still considered a strong mark. These marks have no logical relation to the goods they are identifying. Examples include APPLE (as applied to computers), BLACKBERRY (for phones), and LOTUS (for software).
- Suggestive: Weaker than arbitrary marks, but still inherently distinctive. These marks evoke a characteristic of the good it identifies, but the viewer must make a mental inference to connect the mark to the product. Examples include CHICKEN OF THE SEA (for tuna), GREYHOUND (for buses), and COPPERTONE (for suntan lotion).
- Descriptive: Weaker than suggestive marks because they merely describe a characteristic of the product or service with no mental inference required. They are not protected as trademarks unless they have acquired a "secondary meaning" over time. Examples include SUDSY SOAP, ALL BRAN and VISION CENTER.
- Generic: These marks can never be protected as trademarks and are free to be used by anyone because they are basic, common descriptors for the category into which the product or service fits – such as "tape," "shirts," or "computers." Some marks that were once distinctive can become generic – and therefore unprotectable – by becoming publicly used as a generic term. Examples of words that were once trademarks but became generic include ASPIRIN and CELLOPHANE.

We can be certain that, as digital content gets published in augmented media, trademark-laden commercial content will follow. Perhaps the most extreme (and disturbingly plausible) depiction of "sponsored" augmented reality can be found in Keiichi Matsuda's short video *Augmented (hyper)Reality: Domestic Robocop.*[25] The

[25]Keiichi Matsuda, *Augmented (hyper) Reality: Domestic Robocop*, YOUTUBE (January 6, 2010) http://www.youtube.com/watch?v=fSfKlCmYcLc.

AR user in this video sees literally every flat surface in his modest kitchenette digitally plastered with branded advertisements. At one point he even manually raises the "advertising level" of his eyewear, suggesting that he's receiving micropayments or subsidized services for each ad he sees (Fig. 5.5).

With that consumer-facing communication come inevitable questions of how commercial goodwill is being used to attract consumer attention. That is the realm of trademark law. Because AR will enable various forms of communication that have not previously been seen, many of the related trademark questions will also be novel.

EXPANDING TRADEMARK LAW BY AUGMENTING NEW SENSES

Anything that distinguishes the source of a good or service can be a trademark. Although trademarks are often thought of as words or graphical designs, the term is also defined to include "symbols," which can encompass almost anything. Such exotic marks as such as scents, sounds, and colors have been registered in the past. Examples include the lion's roar at the beginning of MGM films, the sound a Harley Davidson motorcycle makes when it starts, and the tones at the end of an Intel commercial.

Emerging AR technologies have already inspired a wide variety of conventional trademarks, including words, logos, and phrases. Soon, though, technologies that augment our sense of touch may lead to a rush of trademark applications seeking to protect a wide variety of artificial textures. As discussed in Chapter 2, a number of companies from Senseg to Disney to Apple are experimenting with different means of tricking the mind into thinking one's skin is perceiving whatever haptic sensation a content provider wishes to convey. The potential of AR will never be fully realized until users can reach out and touch virtual objects through haptic interfaces. One way this technology seems likely to (literally) get into the hands of consumers is through retailers using haptic technology to further enhance the "feel" of their products. When that begins to happen, I believe we will witness a resurgence of interest in haptic trademarks. (Other trademark practitioners have called these "tactile," "texture," or even "touch" marks, but I prefer the more definitionally sound and technologically consistent term "haptic.")

Of the less-conventional trademarks, haptic marks are among the least common. Those commentators who have broached the subject in recent years[26] have only identified a handful of such federally registered marks. They include a registration by American Wholesale Wine & Spirits for "a velvet textured covering on the surface of a bottle of wine"[27]–specifically, its Khvanchkara brand of wine. In the course of

---

[26]See Steve Baird, *Touch Trademarks and Tactile Brands With Mojo: Feeling the Strength of a Velvet, Turgid, Touch Mark?*, Duets Blog (July 13, 2009) http://www.duetsblog.com/2009/07/articles/trademarks/touch-trademarks-and-tactile-brands-with-mojo-feeling-the-strength-of-a-velvet-turgid-touch-mark/.

[27]U.S. Trademark Application Serial No. 76,634,174 (Filed March 23, 2005) *available at* http://tsdr.uspto.gov/-caseNumber=76634174&caseType=SERIAL_NO&s.

convincing the U.S. Patent and Trademark Office to register this mark, American Wholesale distinguished its "velvety covering" from that of the more iconic Crown Royal bag by noting that Khvanchkara is "tightly encased within the fabric," and that the "FEEL of a LIMP bag is quite different from the FEEL of a TURGID velvety surface attached to a wine bottle."[28] Similarly, Touchdown Marketing has registered a trademark in the "pebble-grain texture" and "soft-touch feel" of its basketball-shaped cologne dispenser, and Fresh, Inc. has registered the "cotton-textured paper" that wraps its soap products.

Conceptually, a distinctive touch ought to be just as protectable by trademark law as any other unique indicator of source. Indeed, in 2006, the International Trademark Association (INTA) adopted "a resolution supporting the recognition and registration of 'touch' marks."[29] In practice, however, it is very difficult to separate the way something feels with the function that texture performs – and to come up with a texture that is truly "distinctive" of one product as opposed to other brands within the same category of products.

That is where haptic AR technologies like the ones proposed by Senseg and other companies come in. The ability to coat the surface of any product with a transparent layer of "tixels" capable of mimicking any arbitrary texture the manufacturer chooses would finally break the connection between a product's feel and the function it performs. Consider, for example, a book cover that feels wet, or a plastic squirt gun that feels metallic. There is no necessary correlation between what these products are or what they do, and the way they feel. There should, therefore, be no conceptual barrier to those manufacturers seeking trademark protection in those textures.

Of course, not every artificial texture will automatically be eligible for trademark protection. Many haptic enhancements may still be chosen for functional reasons. The maker of an automotive steering wheel or a baseball, for example, might choose to make their products artificially sticky to enhance performance. A cell phone might be designed to get warmer in one's pocket as it rings, in order to catch the user's attention.[30] And it could be that certain haptic enhancements still do not rise to the level of being sufficiently distinctive of a particular source to serve as a trademark. Still, by promising the ability to manipulate the sensation of touch independently from other aspects of a product, haptic AR technologies open up a new and exciting world of trademark possibilities. Consumers may soon reach out and touch … whatever retailers want them to.

---

[28]*Response to Office Action*, U.S. TRADEMARK APPLICATION SERIAL NO. 76,634,174 (April 17, 2006) available at http://tsdr.uspto.gov/documentviewer?caseId=sn76634174&docId=ROA2006041812151 4#docIndex=4&page=1

[29]Report of the World Intellectual Property Organization, Standing Committee On The Law Of Trademarks, Industrial Designs And Geographical Indications, Sixteenth Session, Geneva, November 13 to 17, 2006 at 10-11 (2006).

[30]Technically, as noted in Chapter 2, the ability to discern heat is distinct from the sense of touch. For simplicity's sake, however, this book will follow the popular approach of treating them as the same.

KEYWORD ADVERTISING IN THE AUGMENTED MEDIUM

The growth of the commercial internet over the past 20 years has been funded predominately by advertising revenue. We as consumers get to browse free content on millions of web pages and on various search engines in large part because advertisers have paid good money to insert their ad next to whatever we're reading. Odds are good that this funding model will continue well into the future.

The primary purpose of all commercial advertising is to draw potential customers to the advertised business or product, and away from its competitors. Moreover, as mentioned in Chapter 4, comparative advertisements – those that compare a product to its competition – have been around for decades. Courts have had opportunities to draw some basic lines between what is okay to say in such advertisements, and what is "deceptive" advertising. In a nutshell, it is permissible to describe your competitor's goods and compare one product to another, but you cannot say things that are likely to confuse customers into believing that you *are* your competitor. You cannot say something materially false or misleading about your competitor or your own product. And you cannot do anything to confuse reasonable consumers into mistakenly believing there's some sort of connection, sponsorship, affiliation, or endorsement between your companies or products.

These boundaries are not always easy to apply, however, and there are several contexts in which the courts have not been able to agree on how they apply. For example, the battle over "keyword advertising"–i.e., using an algorithm to display a "sponsored" ad whenever a user types a given term into a search engine–is still being fought, more than a decade after the practice began.

Google explained its own keyword advertising system, called "AdWords," this way:

> Google AdWords is Google's advertising program. AdWords lets you create simple, effective ads and display them to people already searching online for information related to your business. So how is it possible to show your ads only to the most relevant audiences? The answer is keyword-based advertising.
>
> When a searcher visits Google and enters a query – say, good beginner guitars – Google displays a variety of relevant search results, such as links to articles containing guitar purchasing advice, or websites dedicated to novice musicians. Google also displays AdWords ads that link to online businesses selling guitars, music lessons, or other products and services related to the query.
>
> For example, imagine that you own a music store carrying a large selection of guitars. You could sign up for an AdWords account and create ads for entry-level guitars in your inventory. For each of your ads, you might select keywords (single words or phrases related to your ad's message) such as beginner guitars or entry-level guitars.[31]

---

[31]See Google AdWords, http://www.google.com/adwords/learningcenter/text/18911.html (last visited March 23, 2009).

Company A potentially implicates trademark law when it purchases a search term that is also a trademark belonging to Company B. The fact that Company A's advertising appears when a user searches for Company B's trademark raises questions of whether Company A is "using" that trademark "in commerce" (most courts have said yes), and whether this use creates a likelihood that consumers will be confused regarding the potential association or sponsorship between the two companies or as to the source of Company B's goods or services.

Answers to this latter question have been mixed. Some courts over the past decade have found that ads triggered by a trademarked keyword search cause a likelihood of confusion – especially when the resulting ad also incorporates the trademarked term,[32] but even occasionally when it does not.[33] On the other hand, several recent cases have rejected the proposition that merely purchasing a competitor's trademark as a search term in and of itself creates confusion.[34]

This may suggest that the potential for confusion in many situations has decreased as online sponsored ads have become more commonplace.

Where the potential for confusion exists, though, the question of who is responsible for it also remains open. Rosetta Stone is one of several companies to sue a search engine for allowing competitors to use its marks in keyword ads. As most other courts had done in similar cases, the trial court dismissed the suit as a matter of law, finding that Rosetta Stone could not prove that the search engine was liable. But in April 2012, the U.S. Court of Appeals for the Fourth Circuit overturned that holding, finding it possible that the search engine's policy on the use of keywords in sponsored ads could amount to direct infringement, contributory infringement, or trademark dilution.[35] Other cases have likewise gone either way on liability depending on how the particular trademark at issue appeared in the header or text of a sponsored ad. But it is fascinating that, even as recently as 2013, one study found that more than 40% of search engine users were not able to distinguish sponsored ads from organic search results,[36] suggesting that the potential for confusion remains even more than a decade after this advertising model was adopted.

---

[32]See, e.g., *Storus Corp. v. Aroa Mktg.*, Civ. No. 06-2454-MMC; 2008 U.S. Dist. LEXIS 11698, at *12-13 (N.D. Cal. February 15, 2008) (finding infringement where defendant's sponsored ad was triggered by and incorporated plaintiff's trademarked "smart money clip").

[33]See, e.g., *Edina Realty, Inc. v. Themlsonline.com*, Civ. 04-4371JRTFLN; 2006 U.S. Dist. LEXIS 13775 (D. Minn. March 20, 2006) (finding liability where "Defendant purchases search terms that include the Edina Realty mark to generate its sponsored link advertisement"); *Fin. Express LLC v. Nowcom Corp.*, 564 F. Supp. 2d 1160, 1177 (C.D. Cal. 2008) (holding that defendant's purchase of keywords that "are identical or strikingly similar to the trademarks held by plaintiff" along with its offer of "services and products which are highly related to those offered by plaintiff" and "simultaneous use of the Web as a marketing channel" may result in consumer confusion).

[34]See, e.g., *1-800-Contacts, Inc. v. Lens.com, Inc.*, 722 F.3d 1229 (10th Cir. 2013).

[35]See *Rosetta Stone LTD. v. Google, Inc.*, 676 F.3d 144 (4th Cir. 2012)

[36]Graham Charlton, *40% of Consumers are Unaware that Google Adwords are Adverts*, Econsultancy Blog (February 28, 2013) http://econsultancy.com/blog/62249-40-of-consumers-are-unaware-that-google-adwords-are-adverts.

FIGURE 5.6

A campaign by the Public Ad Project and the Heavy Projects.

Augmented reality will take this jostling for position between advertisers to a new level. We already see this happening in TV broadcasts of certain sports games, in which "digital billboard replacement" technology is used to superimpose digital ads on top of the ones that are physically present in the stadium. The Public Ad Project and the Heavy Projects have demonstrated similar concepts on mobile devices by sponsoring campaigns that replace physical billboards with artistic images when viewed through a mobile device (Fig. 5.6).

But what happens when AR eyewear becomes ubiquitous, and digital ad replacement becomes commonplace? Will advertisers pay AR service providers for the ability to superimpose their ads on top of what consumers see? If the past 20 years of e-commerce is any indication, then the answer is "absolutely"–and in a number of creative ways. So, for example, a business may pay to superimpose its logo on top of signs advertising a competitor's products, completely blocking the physical ad from view. Or, the mere act of looking at Company A's ad through your AR eyewear may trigger a virtual ad for Company B to pop up somewhere else in your field of vision. The example of this that I typically give is of looking at a McDonald's sign through your digital device and instantly seeing a Burger King advertisement superimposed upon it.

Similarly, your decision to look at something may prompt suggestions for goods and services relating to the thing you're looking at. Self-described "pop culture hacker" Jonathan McIntosh captures all of these ideas in his parody video "ADmented Reality."[37] The video depicts a world in which every glance triggers another advertisement in one's digital eyewear, to the point where reality itself become obscured in a sea of sponsored content (Fig. 5.7).

---

[37]Jonathan McIntosh, *Admented Reality*, YOUTUBE (April 5, 2012) http://www.youtube.com/watch?v=_mRF0rBXIeg&feature=kp.

FIGURE 5.7

"ADmented Reality" Glass Parody.

Other commentators have also foreseen augmented advertising and the legal issues they will raise. John C. Havens discussed some of them his insightful piece for Mashable called *"Who Owns the Advertising Space in an Augmented Reality World?"*[38] Noting that Google had already applied for a patent for digitally replacing physical ads within the Street View feature of Google Maps, Havens wrote that "the importance of virtual real estate may quickly supplant actual signage for advertisers. This is especially true when virtual signage could be switched dynamically for individual eye traffic depending on a viewer's preferences."[39] He went on to quote Gabe Greenberg, director of social and emerging media at Microsoft, as saying that, "if the experience presents the ads in a way that makes sense for the augmented reality experience and the user's intention, this could be a powerful advertising tool for tomorrow's marketplace."[40]

These predictions are persuasive. As discussed in Chapter 6, I take issue with the idea of applying the law of real property to this scenario. That is not necessarily the end of the conversation, however, because the laws governing trademarks and unfair competition are not about property ownership. They are aimed at protecting commercial goodwill and avoiding confusion among consumers about the relationships between different products and businesses. Sponsored ads on search engines,

---

[38]John Havens, *Who Owns the Advertising Space in an Augmented Reality World?*, Mashable, (June 6, 2011) http://mashable.com/2011/06/06/virtual-air-rights-augmented-reality/

[39]*Id.*

[40]*Id.*

for example, do not do anything to obscure the results displayed on a search engine; they are merely displayed adjacent to that content. When Company A displays a sponsored ad next to Company B's trademark, it is not interfering with Company B's ownership of that mark. But – depending on the content of the ad, how it is displayed, and how it comes to appear on the page – Company A might be misleading consumers into believing there is some relationship between Company A and that trademark. This potential for confusion is what injures Company B and triggers the protections of trademark law.

The potential remains, therefore, that causing Company A's augmented ad to appear in a certain physical place – for example, on top of or next to Company B's physical billboard, place of business, or trademarked logo – may create a likelihood of confusion in the minds of consumers. It will be possible, therefore, for augmented advertising to infringe trademark rights.

At least in the short term, that result seems unlikely, if only because of the limited context in which AR experiences are currently available. Today, having an AR experience requires a user to download and open a particular, branded app on their device. These apps also usually offer only a very limited range of options in a predetermined number of situations. So, for example, as of this writing, the only way a user will see a Burger King ad atop the Golden Arches would be by using an app (or user-generated layer with an app like Junaio, Aurasma, or Layar) designed specifically for that purpose. In this situation, a trademark owner could object to the way that its trademark is being "used in commerce," and the way in which the app is portrayed could conceivably be confusing. Assuming that the user understands where the app is coming from, however, one can hardly expect the user to be surprised or confused by what they see through it.

The potential for confusion will come within digital services in which consumers expect to see advertising content from a variety of authentic sources within a viewpoint-neutral environment. One does not approach billboards, telephone directories, television commercial breaks, or internet banner ads *as such* with a predetermined expectation of the message those media will contain. Instead, one bases their determination about the source of a particular advertisement within those media based on the content and context of the ad itself.

For example, merely opening my internet browser tells me almost nothing about what sort of banner advertising I might encounter; I know by virtue of having surfed the internet that I will be served such ads by any random company that may have paid to place them there. But if I'm discerning, I will notice that certain types of websites are more likely to serve up advertisements from a particular point of view, and that the behavioral advertising cookies in my browser will sometimes deliver ads based on my prior online activity. Similarly, to the extent that anyone still reads telephone directories, they ought to expect to see advertisements for local businesses (especially personal injury lawyers) rather than for those located elsewhere.

When we have multi-user, viewpoint-neutral augmented reality browsers is when we should expect to see allegations of trademark infringement arise in earnest. The existing ability to digitally replace physical signs within mapping programs such as

Bing and Google Maps offers a glimpse of what such a world will be like. Ubiquitous, always-on AR will feel very much like moving around within a three-dimensional version of those contemporary mapping programs. Once we find ourselves there, what expectations will we have about the advertising we see? More than likely, we will realize that at least some of the augmented content we encounter is provided by the service provider itself (whichever company that turns out to be), while some is triggered by our personal activities and preferences. Just as with behavioral advertisements on the internet today, no two users of the service are likely to encounter all of the same ads.

Unlike the current web, however, augmented ads will necessarily correspond to physical places. It will be those relationships between digital and physical content that raise new and unique questions of when a likelihood of confusion may exist. Sticking with the fast food example, then, will it be permissible in *this* context for Burger King to deliver users an ad every time they look in the direction of a McDonald's restaurant or sign? If so, will the law of trademarks and unfair competition place limits on how obtrusive these ads can be? In other words, may they appear only in the periphery of a user's vision? May they hover in space next to the Golden Arches, or even be superimposed over them? Moreover, the degree to which a service provider makes these decisions – or allows users to adjust such settings – could well determine whether the service provider may be held jointly liable for any resulting infringement.

Courts deciding AR advertising cases in these contexts will apply the lessons learned in pre-existing media, including the reasoning of the search engine keyword cases with which today's courts are wrestling. Just as search engine algorithms use particular terms as keywords that prompt an ad to appear, so too can the physical objects that prompt similar virtual ads in AR devices be thought of as "keywords." Whether it's a billboard, logo, or some other trigger, any object that prompts an algorithm to display an ad is performing the same function that keywords do today.

A determination of whether that ad creates a likelihood of confusion will depend on how the likelihood of confusion factors apply to the particular case at hand. As with existing case law on sponsored advertising, moreover, courts are likely to be all over the map in how they decide such cases at first, until the model becomes more commonplace and a consensus forms about what boundaries it is fair to expect advertisers to observe in this space.

FAIR USE AND FREE SPEECH

Trademark ownership is not a complete monopoly on any and all uses of the word or symbol that forms the trademark. Although trademark rights are broad, they exist only to protect consumers from confusion and to safeguard business's goodwill. As restrictions on the rights of others' speech, moreover, trademark laws always exist in an uneasy tension with the First Amendment to the United States Constitution.

"Because overextension of Lanham Act restrictions in the area of [artistic expression] might intrude on First Amendment values," wrote the Second Circuit Court of Appeals in the frequently quoted opinion *Rogers v. Grimaldi*, "[courts] construe the Act narrowly to avoid such a conflict."[41] That case stands for the proposition that artists can freely refer to trademarked goods and services by name in the titles of their songs, films, and other creative expressions. Such issues will inevitably arise in the context of augmented works just as they do elsewhere. There are at least a couple situations, however, in which augmented content will stretch these legal principles in new ways.

Incorporating third-party trademarks into augmented content

Trademarks frequently show up inside of artistic works – especially in video games that attempt to create a realistic world in which players can immerse themselves. For the most part, courts uphold these uses as free speech, due in no small part to the United States Supreme Court's decision in 2011 that video games deserve First Amendment protection.[42]

Games and other immersive augmented reality environments will attempt to create similarly realistic digital worlds. In so doing, there will inevitably be some AR applications that recreate actual trademarks in the name of authenticity.

The one fundamental difference between the AR medium and traditional digital expression, however, is that AR content is inherently tied to real physical locations. This distinction adds a layer of risk to replicating someone else's trademark in AR because associating that trademark with a real place or object could, in many foreseeable circumstances, heighten the likelihood that someone will draw a connection between the trademark and the physical place or object with which it is digitally associated. For example, players may see the mark digitally displayed on the wall of a business not associated with the trademark owner, or the mark may appear (wither physically or digitally) on a real object designed to serve as a target within the AR app. In either circumstance, the mark is no longer confined within a virtual, fictional word created by the artist, but instead is being associated with real objects or places that may be businesses or products with which the trademark owner does not wish to be associated.

This could, in some cases, satisfy enough of the likelihood of confusion factors to add up to a real headache for both the trademark owner and the designer of the AR environment. Of course, it is equally possible – again, depending on the circumstances of the particular case – that the choice to make that particular association between trademark and physical place or thing could, in and of itself, be a creatively expressive decision that merits First Amendment protection. Regardless of result, however, use of trademarks within AR content will inherently raise an additional dimension of legal complexity beyond that found in other digital works.

---

[41]*Rogers v. Grimaldi*, 875 F. 2d 994, 998 (2d Cir. 1989).
[42]See *Brown v. Entertainment Merchants Ass'n*, 1313 S.Ct. 2729 (2011).

FIGURE 5.8

Mark Skwarek's "The Leak in Your Home Town" app.

Unauthorized augmentation of trademarks

For the first few years in which AR has been used in advertising, the technology required to create the experience has been more or less limited to corporations, agencies, and startups with substantial budgets, sophisticated software, and coding expertise. Even the first publicly accessible tools for creating user-generated AR contents have been slow to catch on, and required a significant learning curve. As this book nears completion during 2014, however, more user-friendly and robust creative tools are hitting the public market, democratizing AR even further. Before long, user-generated commentary is likely to be as ubiquitous in augmented form as video commentary currently is on YouTube.

When the subject matter of user-generated AR content relates to a particular brand, no object will be more tempting to serve as the trigger for that content than the very trademark that the brand owner uses to represent its goodwill to the public. Indeed, this has already happened least once. In 2010, Professor Mark Skwarek (of the NYU Polytechnic School of Engineering and, most recently, the creative lead behind the Kickstarter-funded app PlayAR) released the iPhone app "The Leak in Your Home Town" (Fig. 5.8). Through this app, one could view a physical sign bearing the BP logo at a local gas station, and see superimposed on that logo a digital broken pipe spewing oil, exactly like the one responsible for the then-current spill in the Gulf of Mexico.

These existing media also teach us that a sizeable portion of that commentary will be directed back toward the brands who advertise to us. For almost as long as companies have been setting up shop at <Company.com > , there have been detractors posting vitriol at <CompanySucks.com > . In today's social media, popular sites such as Ripoff Report and Pissed Consumer base their entire business models on naming and shaming commercial brands.

Although some early judicial decisions blocked these sites' ability to reproduce the trademarks of the companies they criticize, most courts and other trademark dispute resolution organizations recognize such content as fair commentary that trademark holders cannot prevent.[43] For example, in 2011, the United States District Court for the Eastern District of New York rejected a trademark infringement lawsuit that challenged the use of a reviewed company's trademarks in the sub-URLs, metadata, and text of PissedConsumer.com.[44] Despite copious use of the plaintiff's marks throughout the website, the court found it implausible that any reasonable person would believe the site's critical commentary to be sponsored by or associated with the trademark owner.

These are the types of precedents courts will look to when trademark owners begin to grapple with augmented repurposing of trademarks. They provide a strong basis for predicting that using corporate trademarks as triggers for AR content that criticizes the trademark owner will, in many cases, be permissible under U.S.

---

[43]See, e.g., *Taubman Co. v. Webfeats*, 319 F.3d 770, 777-78 (6th Cir. 2003) (no Lanham Act violation where gripe site with domain name taubmansucks.com that provided editorial on conflict between website creator and plaintiff corporation did not create any possibility of confusion); *Taylor Bldg. Corp. of Am. v. Benfield*, 507 F.Supp.2d 832, 847 (S.D.Ohio 2007) (gripe site with domain name taylorhomesripoff.com that served as forum for criticizing home builder did not create any likelihood of confusion "because [n]o one seeking Taylor's website would think — even momentarily — that Taylor in fact sponsored a website that included the word 'ripoff' in its website address"); *Bally Total Fitness Holding Corp. v. Faber*, 29 F.Supp.2d 1161, 1163-64 (C.D.Cal.1998) (gripe site with domain name www. compupix.com/ballysucks dedicated to complaints about Bally's health club did not create likelihood of confusion because no reasonable visitor to gripe site would assume it to come from same source or think it to be affiliated with, connected with, or sponsored by Bally's); *MCW, Inc. v. Badbusinessbureau.com, L.L.C.*, No. 02 Civ. 2727, 2004 WL 833595, at *16 (N.D.Tex. April 14, 2004) (Lanham Act unfair competition claims against consumer review websites called "ripoffreport.com" and "badbusinessbureau. com" that used plaintiff's trademarks in connection with allegedly defamatory posts dismissed because no visitor to websites would believe that plaintiff markholder endorsed the comments on sites); *Whitney Inf. Network, Inc. v. Xcentric Ventures*, No. 2:04-cv-47-FtM-34SPC, 2005 WL 1677256 (M.D.Fla. July 14, 2005) (unpublished memorandum and order) (dismissing trademark infringement and false designation of origin claims against "ripoffreport.com" because plaintiff mark holder, a seller of education courses, was involved in different field than defendant, who sold advertising space on site and helped aggrieved consumers reclaim lost money, and because no consumer would "be confused by a consumer watch-dog type website that is not selling any real estate investment course"); *Cintas Corp. v. Unite Here*, 601 F.Supp.2d 571 (S.D.N.Y. 2009), *aff'd* 355 Fed.Appx. 508 (2d Cir. 2009) (*per curiam*) (rejecting assertion by Cintas that the website < cintasexposed.com>, run by a labor union and dedicated to criticizing the company's labor practices, could cause customer confusion).

[44]*Ascentive, LLC v. Opinion Corp.*, 842 F. Supp. 2d 450 (E.D.N.Y. 2011).

trademark law. This conclusion is bolstered by considering the similarity between AR targets and hyperlinks, which will be considered in Chapter 6.

Of course, every rule has its exception. The circumstances of each situation will be different, and those differences will sometimes make a material impact on the outcome of a trademark infringement analysis. In cases where the augmented content that one associates with another's trademark is more akin to the competitive advertising discussed above than to critical consumer speech, the question of whether that content causes a likelihood of confusion will be much closer. Nor has this discussion taken into account the concept of trademark dilution, a cause of action that challenges the use of a famous mark in ways that diminish its distinctiveness or tarnish its goodwill, even in ways that do not cause a likelihood of confusion. The application of that doctrine to AR content will also vary widely depending on the circumstances.

What does seem clear, however, is that policing the use of trademarks in augmented reality will be significantly more complex than it first appears.

COPYRIGHT

AR-related copyright issues may not lead to litigation as quickly as patent and trademark disputes will. In the long run, however, I believe that AR is likely to raise a broader range of copyright matters than any other type of intellectual property issue. After all, the realm of copyright law is creative expression, an activity that (unlike innovation or the creation of commercial goodwill) is potentially available to all. AR is a medium in which all manner of creative ideas will be expressed.

COPYRIGHT BASICS

United States copyright law is a state-sanctioned, limited monopoly granted to the authors of creative expression. These authors receive the right to control some of the ways in which their works are used. In exchange, ownership of the work reverts to the public domain upon the expiration of the copyright term.

The U.S. Copyright Act specifies eight broad categories of creative "works" to which copyright protection applies:

1. Literary works;
2. Musical works, including any accompanying words;
3. Dramatic works, including any accompanying music;
4. Pantomimes and Choreographic works;
5. Pictorial, Graphic, and Sculptural works;
6. Motion pictures and other audiovisual works;
7. Sound recordings; and
8. Architectural works.[45]

---

[45]17 USC §102 (2012).

One could easily conceive of how each of these types of works could be expressed by augmented means.

United States copyright law affords to creators five basic rights with respect to their copyrighted work–the rights to control its reproduction, adaptation, distribution, public display, and public performance. These broad categories cover most, but not all of the uses one can make of copyrighted works. The copyright statute also carves out various categories of use over which the copyright owner should not have control. Chief among these is the doctrine of "fair use," which describes a range of activities that benefit society too much to allow copyright owners to squelch them.

OBTAINING COPYRIGHTS

Fixation in a tangible medium

Nothing inherent to the AR medium will prevent augmented content from receiving copyright protection. To qualify for copyright protection, the work must be "fixed in a tangible medium," meaning it must have some definite, perceptible form rather than just being evanescent sounds or an inchoate conception floating in someone's head. This requirement provides a measure of objectivity in the application of copyright law, without which society would not be getting anything in exchange for the legal monopoly it grants to a copyright owner. That said, this "fixation" requirement is a loose one. Storing an image in software form is enough; even projecting an image digitally onto a screen or loading software into temporary random-access memory is sufficient.[46] This is what allows digital representations to be copyright-protected in conventional two-dimensional media, and the same principle will apply when the same content is visualized by three-dimensional, augmented means. Even though augmented images are not actually in the physical environments in which they are made to appear, they nevertheless reside in a digital intermediary that is sufficiently "tangible" – such as on the lens of a head-mounted mobile device or in a cloud-based computer server. The "tangible fixation" element requires only that the works be stored in a media "from which they can be perceived, reproduced, or otherwise communicated, either directly or with the aid of a machine or device."[47] The specific type of device used to perceive the content is irrelevant.

A decision issued in September 2013 by the U.S. District Court for the Southern District of New York gives a preview of how AR copyright cases are likely to look. In *Firesabre Consulting LLC v. Sheehy*,[48] middle school technology teacher Cindy Sheehy purchased a set of islands within the virtual world *Second Life* for use in teaching students. Each island in the simulation starts off as a flat green rectangle, and the user can then change the topography and landscape of the island (known as

---

[46]For example, "all portions of [a video game] program, once stored in memory devices anywhere in the game, are fixed in a tangible medium." *Stern Elecs., Inc. v. Kaufman*, 669 F.2d 852, 855 n.4 (2d Cir. 1982).

[47]17 USC §102 (2012).

[48]*Firesabre Consulting LLC v. Sheehy*, No. 11-CV-4719 (CS), 2013 WL 4520977 (S.D.N.Y. September 26, 2013).

"terraforming") using a series of interactive tools provided by Linden. Firesabre – a consulting firm specializing in the educational use of virtual worlds – performed various terraforming services for Sheehy on those islands, including a train station, a café, music shops, and a volcano. When the relationship between the parties broke down, Firesabre claimed copyright ownership in all of the terraformed content. Allegedly, Sheehy continued to display the content within *Second Life* and copied some of it to another virtual world, all of which Firesabre asserted to be copyright infringement.

The court denied Sheehy's motion for judgment as a matter of law, holding instead that Firesabre had alleged plausible allegations of infringement. First, the court decided that the works had been "fixed in a tangible medium" because they existed on Linden's data servers and were visible within *Second Life* for a sufficient period of time to be perceived by the students who interacted with the islands.

Second, the court saw no reason to deny copyright protection to the terraformed works simply because others could come along later and modify them. "In this regard," the judge wrote, "I see no distinction between the terraforming designs and a drawing created on a chalkboard or a sculpture created out of moldable clay. That someone else could come along and, with or without permission, alter the original piece of art does not mean the art was too transitory to be copyrighted in the first place."[49] Therefore, even dynamic AR content will spark copyright law controversies.

Originality and the idea/expression dichotomy

Not every expressive work is automatically eligible for copyright protection. Both the U.S. Constitution and the Copyright Act require that the expression within the work be original to its author.[50] Originality is therefore said to be the "*sine qua non* of copyright.*" As explained by the U.S. Supreme Court, the word "original" in this context does not mean novelty (as is required by patent law), but rather that the work was independently created by the author as opposed to copied from other works, and that it possessed at least some minimal degree of creativity.[51] The author "must have made some contribution to the work which is irreducibly his own."[52]

A copyright is not a reward for mere effort or toil. A work that merely copies or compiles facts or the expression of others – no matter how much skill and effort that copying or compilation may require – cannot be copyrighted. This "idea/expression dichotomy" is the heart and soul of copyright law. That does not mean, however, that the expression must have any degree of artistic or aesthetic merit. As the U.S. Supreme Court held more than a hundred years ago, even "a very modest grade of art has in it something irreducible, which is one man's alone. That something he may copyright."[53] All that is needed is some creative spark, "no matter how crude, humble, or obvious."[54]

---

[49]*Id.*

[50]See *Feist Pub'lns, Inc. v. Rural Tel. Serv. Co.,* 499 U.S. 340, 346 (1991); 17 U.S.C. § 102 (2012).

[51]*Feist Pubs., Inc. v. Rural Tel. Serv. Co., Inc.,* 499 U.S. 340, 345-46 (1991)

[52]*Todd v. Montana Silversmiths, Inc.,* 379 F. Supp. 2d 1110, 1112 (D. Colo. 2005).

[53]*Bleistein v. Donaldson Lithographing Co.,* 188 U.S. 239, 250 (1903)

[54]*Feist,* 499 U.S. at 345.

FIGURE 5.9

The digital wireframes at issue in *Meshwerks v. Toyota Motors Sales USA, Inc.*

The application of these principles to augmented reality were foreshadowed in the 2008 case *Meshwerks v. Toyota Motors Sales USA, Inc.*,[55] which applied the age-old principle of originality to the relatively new technology: digital modeling (Fig. 5.9). In 2003, Toyota and its marketing partners decided to begin creating digital models of Toyota's vehicles for use on Toyota's website and in various other media. This approach offered significant cost savings over the prior method of obtaining vehicle images, which required a new photo shoot of entire fleets of vehicles each time even the smallest design element changed. Digital images, by contrast, can be edited with a few mouse clicks.

Toyota's marketing partners subcontracted with a company called Meshwerks to conduct the first two initial steps of the project – digitization and modeling. Meshwerks began this process by collecting hundreds of physical data points from the vehicles to be portrayed. Based on these measurements, modeling software (such as Maya) generated a digital "wire frame" image. Meshwerks personnel then fine-tuned the lines on screen to resemble each vehicle as closely as possible. According to Meshwerks, approximately 90 percent of the data points contained in each final model were adjusted by a person. Some areas of detail – including the wheels, head-lights, door handles, and Toyota emblem – could not be mechanically measured and instead were added by hand.

When Toyota and its partners later used these wire frame images in ways to which Meshwerks objected, Meshwerks sued, claiming that it owned a copyright in the images. Both the district court and the court of appeals, however, disagreed, holding that the wire frame models were merely copies of Toyota's products, and not sufficiently original to warrant copyright protection. The courts stressed that, despite the significant amount of effort Meshwerks invested in creating the images, it had never intended to create something original. To the contrary, its express intention was to replicate, as exactly as possible, the image of certain Toyota vehicles. That is the only way in which the images would have been useful to Toyota as substitutes for photographs of real vehicles.

Several other courts have likewise denied copyright protection in analogous cases, involving digital copies of physical facts and prior works of art. For example, in *Sparaco v. Lawler, Matusky, Skelly, Engineers LLP*,[56] the court denied copyright protection to the elements of an architectural drawing that conveyed "the existing physical characteristics of the site, including its shape and dimensions, the grade contours, and the location of existing elements, [because this portion] sets forth facts, [and] copyright does not bar the copying of such facts."[57] Other cases have denied copyright protection to catalog illustrations of transmission parts "copied from photographs cut out of competitors' catalogs,"[58] and to high-quality photocopies of

---

[55]*Meshwerks v. Toyota Motors Sales USA, Inc.* 528 F. 3d 1258 (10th Cir. 2008).

[56]*Sparaco v. Lawler, Matusky, Skelly, Engineers LLP*, 303 F.3d 460, 467 (2d Cir. 2002)

[57]*Id.* at 467

[58]*ATC Distr. Group, Inc. v. Whatever It Takes Transmissions & Parts, Inc.*, 402 F.3d 700, 712 (6th Cir. 2005).

paintings.[59] They have also denied protection to other examples of the "dimensional shifting" that Meshwerks did replicating a three-dimensional object in two dimensions. For example, courts have held that three-dimensional plastic toys[60] and costumes[61] based on pre-existing, two-dimensional cartoon characters were not original.

Anticipating the negative reaction to its decision that did, in fact, come from several sources, the *Meshwerks* court went out of its way to stress that "[d]igital modeling can be, surely is being, and no doubt increasingly will be used to create copyrightable expressions."[62] It even suggested "that digital models can be devised of Toyota cars with copyrightable features, whether by virtue of unique shading, lighting, angle, background scene, or other choices. The problem for Meshwerks in this particular case is simply that the uncontested facts reveal that it wasn't involved in any such process, and indeed contracted to provide completely unadorned digital replicas of Toyota vehicles in a two-dimensional space."[63]

Another example of the same issue is the recreation of real people. This is not hypothetical; there are already several companies publishing or working on augmented entertainment content that involves the replication of actual celebrities and historical figures. To the extent that these "characters" merely replicate the attributes of an actual person, they will not contain original, copyrightable content.

These cases illustrate the fine line between originality and reproduction for digital imitations of reality. Because AR content is meant to be perceived in conjunction with physical objects – often in a manner intended to create the illusion that the digital content is itself physical – we will be more likely to find digital content that straddles this line in AR than we are in other digital contexts. This will be increasingly true as the technology improves, creating higher-resolution images and more stable displays. (The fact that eligibility for copyright protection would decrease as the quality of the image increases understandably strikes some as a perverse result, but it is entirely consistent with the purposes of copyright law, as courts have repeatedly explained.) This could result in augmented environments that intentionally bear slight, digitized differences from their real-life inspirations – such as, for example, the flora and buildings in the Second Life islands in the *Firesabre* case – solely for the purpose of preserving original expression and therefore copyright protection. In other cases, though, it will simply mean that content creators will need to rely on other compensation models to reward them for their effort.

There may also come a day when augmented digital objects are so utilitarian that we come to think of them as functional tools rather than expressive works. Consider, for example, the menu layouts of most word processing programs, or the graphics used to symbolize such functions as "power on/off," "play," and "pause." If there were only one software program in existence that employed these arrangements and graphical works, they may well be considered copyrightable. In reality, however,

[59]*Bridgeman Art Library, Ltd. v. Corel Corp.*, 36 F.Supp.2d 191, 197 (S.D.N.Y. 1999)
[60]*Durham Indus., Inc. v. Tomy Corp.*, 630 F.2d 905, 910 (2d Cir. 1980).
[61]*Entm't Research Group, Inc. v. Genesis Creative Group, Inc.*, 122 F.3d 1211, 1221-24 (9th Cir. 1997).
[62]*Meshwerks v. Toyota Motors Sales USA, Inc.*, 528 F. 3d 1258, 1269 (10th Cir. 2008).
[63]*Id.* at 1269-70.

they merely represent methods of organization that are commonplace and critical to the function of thousands of programs. Although there is some room for minute variations in how these user interfaces are expressed, that room is so narrow that such variances will not be considered sufficiently original for copyright protection. (This is what copyright law calls the "merger doctrine." Both it and a related doctrine known as *scenes a faire,* or scenes that must be done, describes elements of an expression that are so common to its genre that they can no longer be considered original.) In an augmented world, we may come to rely on all sorts of augmented user interface designs that then become standardized *scenes a faire*, thereby depriving them of the ability to be protected by copyright.

REPRODUCTION AND DERIVATIVE WORKS

The foregoing section imagined augmented environments so similar to real-world objects that they cannot be protected by copyright. Much more frequently, however, augmented expression will reproduce other, pre-existing creative works – and therefore infringe their copyrights.

Duplicating copyrighted works

In order to prove infringement, a copyright owner must show a "substantial similarity" between the copyrightable expression in the two works. When one work entirely copies another that is an easy showing to make. Because so many AR applications will rely on video technology – particularly wearable devices with video recording capability – replicating copyrighted expression will always be a concern. After all, before digital eyewear is able to add digital content to our view of the world, the devices must first be able to know what we're looking at.

One of the earliest examples of this concern occurred on January 18, 2014 in Columbus, Ohio. That's when Federal agents from the Department of Homeland Security and local law enforcement officials allegedly yanked a customer out of a movie at AMC Theaters and interrogated him for several hours. His crime? Wearing Google Glass in a movie theater. The moviegoer was released only after demonstrating that he had not activated the recording function of the device during the film.[64]

Of course, this concern is by no means unique to wearable technology. In all likelihood, more than 90% of the other patrons in the theater were carrying smartphones, any one of which had both video recording capability *and* enough battery power to last throughout the film – something Glass definitely does *not* have. There was no word on how many of them were interrogated. Nevertheless, the emerging revolution in wearable and Internet of Things technologies will certainly multiply the number of recording devices in the wild, and with that will come concerns that copyrighted works are being reproduced.

---

[64]Julie Streitelmeier, *AMC movie theater calls 'federal agents' to arrest a Google Glass user,* THE GADGETEER (January 20, 2014) http://the-gadgeteer.com/2014/01/20/amc-movie-theater-calls-fbi-to-arrest-a-google-glass-user/.

Other exact replicas of copyrighted works may be deliberate. In order to create an immersive augmented experience of a far-away place, for example – as some companies are already contemplating – the location will need to be exactly duplicated. That would likely include any copyrighted artwork that may be visible in the scene.

Even transferring a work from one medium to another, without more, is a mere reproduction (and hence infringement) of the copyrighted expression in the original. In *Meshwerks*, the thing being copied was not a copyrighted work, so the only consequence of this copying was that the new work lacked originality. Where the thing being copied is copyrighted, however, the reproduction is an infringement of that copyright. A U.S. Court of Appeals reached a very similar conclusion in *Gaylord v. United States*.[65] There, the U.S. Postal Service issued a (two-dimensional) stamp depicting the (three-dimensional) Korean War Veterans Memorial in D.C. The creator of that sculpture successfully argued that the stamp merely copied his expression and reproduced it in a different medium.

Many artists will see AR as a medium in which they can "bring to life" existing works, especially those that currently only exist in two dimensions. If they are not careful to add their own expression to those recreations, however, a court may find them to be mere reproductions – infringements – of the copyright in the existing work.

Adding to existing works

Substantial similarity becomes more challenging to demonstrate when the copies are not exact. "[T]he copying [must be] quantitatively and qualitatively sufficient to support the legal conclusion that infringement (actionable copying) has occurred. The qualitative component concerns the copying of expression, rather than [non-protectable elements].... The quantitative component ... must be more than '*de minimis*.'[66] Neither threshold is particularly high, but it is ultimately a subjective determination by the court.

The exclusive right to make "derivative works" is closely related to the idea of making an inexact, but substantially similar, reproduction. A derivative work is simply the addition of new expression to an existing work. In either case, a substantial portion of the original work exists in the new one, and the copyright owner's rights have been infringed.

Since the very definition of "augment" is "to make greater," augmented reality tools carry with them an inherent risk of creating derivative works. In its most straightforward form, visual AR involves overlaying digital data on top of physical things in order to add content to it or change its appearance.

A few examples capture the point:

- In the books *Daemon* and *Freedom*™ by Daniel Suarez, a character nicknamed "The Burning Man" is memorialized by a statue. To the naked eye, it appears to be a conventional sculpture. Viewed through AR glasses, however, it become wreathed in three-dimensional flames, and studded with links to videos and tributes.

---

[65]*Gaylord v. United States*, 595 F. 3d 1364 (Fed. Cir. 2010).
[66]*Castle Rock Entm't v. Carol Publ'g Grp.*, 150 F. 3d 132, 138 (2d Cir. 1998).

- As part of their 2011 Re + Public collaboration, the Heavy Projects and the Public Ad Campaign used AR to "filter" outdoor advertising and replace it with original street art. Looking through an AR app, outdoor commercial advertisements were overlaid with political or artistic messages. One such pointed message caused the image of "Captain Barbossa" in the poster for *Pirates of the Caribbean 4* to morph before a user's eyes into the face of Goldman Sachs CEO Lloyd Blankfein conveying the artist's message that he is the "real pirate" (Fig. 5.10). Similar projects have superimposed digital content onto public murals in a form of augmented graffiti.
- Artist Amir Baradaran published a mobile app called "Italicizing Mona Lisa." It is designed to display on your phone as you hold it up to a physical version of the iconic painting, creating the video illusion that the woman depicted there wraps herself in the Italian flag.
- "Projection mapping" uses three-dimensional video to animate stationary objects, usually the sides of buildings. When done well, projection mapping creates the powerful illusion of a building actually coming to life and moving in three dimensions.

Do these digital animations infringe the copyright of the physical art they augment?

In the typical "augmented substitution" scenario, in which content on a mobile screen simply overlays or complements the existing work, no infringement is likely. That is because the digital content is not actually doing anything to the original work. It is not making a copy of or altering the original. Even though the physical display acts as a trigger for the digital content, and even though the user's mobile device causes the digital content to appear as if it exists in the real world in place of the

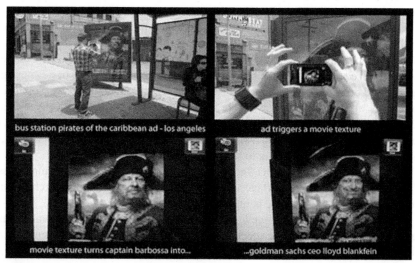

bus station pirates of the caribbean ad - los angeles

ad triggers a movie texture

movie texture turns captain barbossa into...

...goldman sachs ceo lloyd blankfein

FIGURE 5.10

From *Pirates of the Caribbean* to "the Real Pirate."

original, it doesn't actually exist there. It's an effective illusion for creating an immersive experience, but it's an illusion nonetheless. The content stays on the mobile screen, where it is a separate digital work that exists apart from the physical display.

But the question gets more complicated when the digital content actually makes the physical display appear to morph, as in the *Pirates of the Caribbean* and *Mona Lisa* examples. That is because, more likely than not, the AR software has already stored a reference copy of the original and altered versions of the physical work. In other words, the programmer may have created a reproduction and a derivative of the physical work long before anyone uses the program to interact with the physical artwork. In order to create the illusion of movement in the physical painting, the AR programmer first reproduced the artwork, then created a digital alteration of it. That doesn't raise any copyright concerns with public domain works like the Mona Lisa, but artists who digitally copy and morph copyrighted works are taking a risk.

Augmented architecture

Projection mapping and other means of augmenting architectural works add another layer of nuance. Today, this technology is confined to elaborate, after-dark advertisements on the sides of buildings. After AR becomes ubiquitous, however, I doubt that there will be many buildings that are not animated in one way or another. Unlike contemporary projection mapping, the effect will be superimposed by the user's AR viewer, instead of light being physically projected onto the surface of the building. Those who design these experiences will no longer be limited to the actual physical dimensions of the brick-and-mortar edifice. Instead, you could find a building actually wrapping its (simulated) arms around you, or see (virtual) flames spewing from its windows, or any other effect one can imagine. All of which leads a curious IP attorney to wonder: could any of this activity infringe the architectural copyrights of the person who designed the building?

One type of creative expression in which copyright may inhere is an "architectural work"–i.e., "the design of a building as embodied in any tangible medium of expression, including a building, architectural plans, or drawings."[67] But Congress also recognized that allowing architects to fully enforce all five of the basic copyright rights could cause all manner of logistical nightmares throughout society. So it pared back some of the protections available in architectural works. Specifically, Section 120 of the Copyright Act[68] allows people to make, distribute, and display pictures of public buildings. It also lets the owners of a building alter or destroy the building, if they so choose, without needing to first get the architect's permission.

With these things in mind, let's consider whether projection mapping impermissibly adapts (or, in copyright parlance, "creates a derivative work of") the architectural work embodied in the building being projected upon.

The short answer, in my view, is "no." With the caveat, the outcome of any particular case depends on the specific facts at issue. It is difficult to imagine a realistic scenario in which projection mapping (as it's currently done) would create an

---

[67]17 USC §101 (2012).
[68]17 U.S.C. § 120 (2012).

infringing derivative work. At least two reasons come to mind. First, nothing is actually being done to the architectural work (i.e., the building design) itself. Instead, the presentation involves two separate "works"–the building, and the video. Yes, the video is designed to take advantage of the unique design of the specific building that it's being projected upon. Its effect would be far less impressive if it were projected onto any other surface. And that effect is meant to create the illusion that the building design is changing. But it's only an illusion. No actual alteration to the architectural work ever occurs.

Second, even if a creative litigation attorney argued that simply creating the perception of a morphing building was enough to create a derivative of the building design, such an "alteration" should fall within Section 120's exception. Although there is very little case law interpreting Section 120, one court accurately observed that "Section 120(b) does not expressly contain any limitation upon the manner or means by which a [building owner] may exercise his right to alter the structure. Presumably, no such limitations were intended by Congress, else they would be expressed in [that section]."[69] The one catch here is that, as written, this statutory exception allows only the "owner" of a building, not anyone else, to authorize an alteration to the building. So the projection mappers would need to have the owner's permission; guerilla marketers would not have this statutory defense. Again, though, there would not appear to be any actual alteration made in the first place.

But would the result be the same if the illusion of an animated building were accomplished through AR smartphone/eyewear instead of an actual video presentation? Yes–for the most part. Whether the video image is actually projected on a building or only overlaid over the viewer's perception via AR, there is still no alteration of the actual building occurring.

There is a potential catch, however, depending on how the AR effect is accomplished. If the data superimposed on the building consists solely of original imagery designed to overlay the building, that's conceptually equivalent to existing projection mapping. But what if the AR designer copies the actual building design into virtual space, then alters that design, in order to create the end result? That would complicate things from a copyright perspective. An architectural work can be embodied either in 2-D written drawings or in a 3-D manifestation. Making a copy of the design is infringement, unless an exception applies. Section 120 allows people to make "pictures, paintings, photographs, or other pictorial representations of the work." A virtual recreation may very well fit that description. But the statute does not expressly allow the person who makes that pictorial representation to then alter the picture. Arguably, that could be creating a derivative work.

Even under those circumstances, potential defenses are available. For example, at least one court[70] has found within Section 120 an implied right to copy and alter a building's plans for the purpose of creating an owner-approved alteration to the

---

[69]*Javelin Investments, LLC v McGinnis*, CA H-05-3379, 2007 US Dist Lexis 21472 (S.D. Tex. January 23, 2007).

[70]*Id.*

building. Otherwise, the court reasoned, an architect hired by a homeowner to renovate a home would be forced to do so without the benefit of written plans–a dangerous prospect. A similar argument could be made in the AR space, depending on the purpose of the alteration. A different court,[71] however, has disagreed that any such implied right to copy plans for the purpose of altering a building exists.

PUBLIC DISPLAY AND PERFORMANCE

Public display and performance rights will also be at issue, in sometimes novel ways. Because most AR content will be experienced through individual mobile devices, one might presume those experiences to be private, rather than public, displays and performances. But AR programs that are aware of a user's geolocation and that are designed to portray content as being physically manifest at that location challenge that presumption. For example, the British Museum released a mobile app designed to show users historical London photos in the actual, public location where they were taken. The photo itself never leaves the confines of the mobile device, but its display is triggered by the user's physical location.

The same issue is presented by performances of location-aware video content. In 2011, tech news outlets reported on a man who had tattooed on his arm a target marker image used by a Nintendo 3DS game to represent an animated dragon. To the outside world, the tattoo was simply an uninteresting, approximately square-shaped symbol. When viewed through the 3DS device, however, it came to life as a three-dimensional, moving dragon.

Is that a "public" display and performance? And if so, has the app developer or end user acquired from the copyright owner the appropriate license rights for that public display? The case of the dragon tattoo seems likely to have exceeded whatever license may have come with the 3DS device for displaying the content. Entire industries were forced to confront the limitations of their licenses when the internet became a new medium for republishing old content; AR will present similar challenges. User-generated content and social media will guarantee that works get publicly displayed in all sorts of unanticipated ways. Such questions will grow in importance as our surroundings become populated with triggers for all sorts of digital data.

MORAL RIGHTS

The collection of rights known as "moral rights" are quasi-copyright protections entitling the creator of an artistic work to protect the integrity of their creation, regardless of who may come to own the work. This is primarily a European concept not recognized in U.S. law, and therefore is beyond the scope of this book. A form of moral rights, however, can be found in the Visual Artists Rights Act, which, among other things, gives artists a limited right "to prevent any intentional distortion, mutilation, or other modification of that work which would be prejudicial to his or her honor or reputation."[72]

---

[71]*Guillot-Vogt Associates, Inc. v. Holly & Smith*, 848 F.Supp. 682 (E.D. La. 1994)
[72]17 USC 106A (2012).

Whether the VARA or similar rights will ever apply to AR content remains to be seen. Case law interpreting this right is scarce, and by its very nature it cuts against the grain of the Copyright Act's design. United States copyright law places the power to control a work in the hands of whomever owns its copyright, as opposed to the original artist who created the work and then only within the five exclusive rights of a copyright holder. Moreover, digital augmentations of a physical work typically will not alter the actual physical work. Nevertheless, the foregoing *Mona Lisa* example illustrates how convincingly a physical work of art can digitally be made to appear as if it is being distorted. It is easy to foresee a visual artist taking umbrage to such augmentation, and resorting to every creative legal means available to enjoin it.

FAIR USE

Each of the foregoing examples of scenarios that may be considered copyright infringement are subject to affirmative defenses that may defeat the claim under particular circumstances. Among those is the defense of fair use. The Copyright Act identifies certain activities that are presumptively permissible under this doctrine – including "criticism, comment, news reporting, teaching (including multiple copies for classroom use), scholarship, or research."[73] This list of preferred activities derives directly from First Amendment case law, as each of these is an example of speech that contributes in one way or another to conversation about issues of public importance. It is a recognition that free speech rights ought to trump intellectual property protections in some circumstances.

Unlike most statutory exceptions to copyright infringement liability, however, whether any particular use is "fair" under any given set of circumstances can only be determined on a case-by-case basis by applying four subjective principles:

1. The purpose and character of the use, including whether such use is of a commercial nature or is for non-profit educational purposes;
2. The nature of the copyrighted work;
3. The amount and substantiality of the portion used in relation to the copyrighted work as a whole; and
4. The effect of the use upon the potential market for or value of the copyrighted work.[74]

In practice, most fair use cases center on the first and fourth factors. Many courts tend to cast the first factor in terms of whether or not the challenged use somehow "transforms" the purpose or character of the original work. Some of the foregoing examples, such as the augmentation of the *Pirates of the Caribbean* poster, have an obvious political message, which is a presumptively preferred "purpose and character" of use. Another popular (although not always successful) line of argument is that a use "transforms" the original by "mashing" it up in a display with multiple other works. For example, *Cariou v. Prince*[75] involved relatively crude and

---

[73]17 USC 107 (2012).
[74]17 USC 107 (2012).
[75]*Cariou v. Prince*, 714 F.3d 694 (2d Cir. April 25, 2013).

simplistic physical augmentations made to photographs. The iconic example from that case involved a guitar and psychedelic face mask that the defendant slapped on top of the photo of a Jamaican man. The Second Circuit held that even these simple additions were sufficient to fairly transform the original. Similarly, in June 2014, the Second Circuit held that Google's massive project to scan books into an enormous, searchable database was a fair, "transformative" use of the books because the originals were not capable of being searched. If these decisions hold as precedent for future cases, they could open the door to all manner of digital augmentations to other works.

The fourth factor – which assesses the impact of the defendant's work on the original's commercial value – will be difficult to ascertain, especially in early cases. The medium of AR is so nascent, and there are so few business models based on it, that there will be very few reliable facts from which a court can draw a conclusion. This uncertainty will cut both ways. In some cases, the lack of evidence will lead a court to conclude that there is no market for the original in the AR medium. Other courts, however, will reach the opposite conclusion, afraid that the defendant's use will have foreclosed the plaintiff's ability to exploit the limitless possibilities available for creating value in this yet-to-be-defined market.

The most significant drawback of the fair use defense is always its uncertainty. Someone proposing to use another's copyright work without permission cannot reliably determine ahead of time whether the use is fair; instead, the decision may only be made by a judge or jury in response to a copyright infringement lawsuit. Therefore, although fair use is commonly invoked to justify all manner of uses, it is never a reliable safeguard.

AUGMENTED COPYRIGHT ENFORCEMENT

Copyright enforcement will also be a major challenge in the AR medium. The mass lawsuits of the past two decades against file-sharers and signal pirates have required a significant amount of detective work and discovery to connect individual users to allegedly infringing downloads. Pursuing legal action against those who share infringing content in the augmented medium will not differ categorically from these efforts. After all, augmented content only *appears* to exist in three dimensions; in reality, it will still reside in a hard drive, device, or server somewhere that can be located and tracked. Indeed, the earliest versions of digital eyewear available now have relatively little on-board memory or processing power, and only connect to the internet by means of a connection (some hard-wired, some wireless) to a mobile phone, and many of their apps reside in the cloud.

As augmented content proliferates across the Internet of Things – and especially the types of distributed, *ad hoc* mesh networks described in Chapter 2 – the substance and sources of data will become that much harder to track. The entire world will eventually

FIGURE 5.11

Excerpts from *A Read-Only Future.*

become a giant peer-to-peer sharing network; think of AR channels as bit torrent sites that users can walk through, see, and touch. So-called "darknets" – sealed digital communities with no visible connection to the internet – will become much more common.

One can imagine that it will become even more difficult to prove that a particular user viewed a particular work when the "display" occurred entirely within a mobile headset. As discussed in Chapter 10, I expect that many litigators will soon be conducting "v-discovery," in which they must determine not only the device to which virtual data was routed, but also where individual users were located, and in what direction they were looking, when the data was displayed.

On the other hand, AR eyewear could also be used as a copyright *enforcement* mechanism. The YouTube video *A Read-Only Future*[76] depicts life through the eyes of someone wearing digital eyewear that is regulated by the entertainment industry (Fig. 5.11). His glasses recognize copyrighted content in the user's field of view or range of hearing – such as a photo hanging on the wall or a song being played on the sidewalk – and obscures it unless he agrees to a micro-license payment. Just as in concept videos for actual digital headsets, the eyewear in this video is able to share content directly to Facebook, but these will refuse to do so if they detect unlicensed content. They even alert the authorities if the user stumbles across an unauthorized reproduction published by someone else. Excerpts from copyright skeptic Larry Lessig feature prominently in *A Read-Only Future*, which plays out as if it was Lessig's nightmare.

This scenario is entirely plausible in light of how most AR apps function today. A mobile device scans the ambient world looking for one of the targets it is preprogrammed to recognize. Each time it captures a view, the device sends that image to the cloud to check against the portfolio of targets. If a match is found, the cloud server sends back the digital content associated with that target. Several non-AR apps operate in a similar way; for example, the popular mobile app Shazam listens to ambient music and identifies it in real time, allowing users to purchase a copy of the song or follow along to the lyrics. A few months before this book went to print, Shazam became available on Glass.

It would be child's play to simply add a roster of copyrighted works to a cloud-based catalog of targets. Every time the cloud server recognizes one of the protected files in its database, it could be set to trigger a request for micropayment, or obscure the work, or even issue a warning to law enforcement or the copyright owner itself. The fine print in our mobile app stores already prohibits us from using the apps to commit copyright infringement; this would be going one step further to turn mobile devices into the eyes and ears of the copyright police.

Such an enforcement mechanism could potentially be so effective, and offer such a unique functionality not available by any other means, that the company able to provide it would be foolish not to monetize it. Today, mobile devices (including digital eyewear) receive their internet connections through such providers as AT&T, Verizon, Sprint, and the like. In the near future, we may instead get online directly through the "panternet" mass wireless signals emitted by Google or

---

[76]*A Read-Only Future*, YOUTUBE (March 16, 2013) https://www.youtube.com/watch?v=f8bDg2qewFA.

Facebook and discussed in Chapter 2. Whichever company provides that service could easily sell to copyright owners the ability to police copyright compliance through the network of AR-capable devices they serve. Internet service providers (ISPs) would then become analogous to the performance rights organizations (PROs) of today – ASCAP, BMI, and SESAC – which rely on human investigators to overhear unlicensed public performances of copyrighted music. Indeed, these PROs could contract directly with ISPs to enforce their entire catalogs – deputizing every AR app user as investigators.

With such an arrangement in place, ISPs might even share the wealth in order to incentivize users to cooperate. Imagine if AR users received a micropayment each time they used their device to report an observed copyright infringement. Knowing that anyone you meet is a potential copyright cop would certainly be a powerful disincentive to would-be casual infringers. Five years from now, instead of movie theaters detaining and interrogating digital eyewear users, they may be rewarding them.

LICENSING

As with anything else, copyrights can be enforced through either carrots or sticks (or a combination of the two). If the aggressive enforcement action described above is the stick, then the carrot would be offering licensed content. In the early 2000s, digital music piracy was rampant, and CD sales were in free-fall. Not because the internet and digital music were inherently unlawful, but because the traditional publishers of copyrighted music offered no satisfactory alternative to meet the demand for digital music. Not until Apple introduced iTunes in 2003 did consumers finally have a digital marketplace robust enough to meet their needs. Since then, digital distribution (through iTunes, more often than not) has become the default means of obtaining new music.

It remains to be seen how much of a problem copyright piracy will be in the AR medium. Establishing an infrastructure for lawfully obtaining a wide variety of desirable content, however, will still be the means by which content creators will be able to make money from AR. In October 2013, NYU Polytechnic professor Mark Skwarek (who also created the "Leak in Your Home Town" app described in the foregoing trademark discussion) introduced the first augmented Halloween masks (Fig. 5.12).[77] Trick-or-treaters wearing a four-inch target in their hat or hair would be seen by users of Skwarek's AR app as if they were wearing giant, virtual masks. Once enough devices are in place to make the ability to perceive such content sufficiently ubiquitous, companies could easily begin selling entire lines of virtual Halloween costumes. The same infrastructure would allow sales of augmented clothing year-round, along with augmented ornaments, décor, signage, toys, games indeed, a digital analog of almost anything that exists physically.

---

[77]Mark Skwarek, *Still Wearing a Real Mask this Halloween?*, POLYTECHNIC SCHOOL OF ENGINEERING (October 28, 2013) https://engineering.nyu.edu/press-release/2013/10/28/still-wearing-real-mask-halloween.

FIGURE 5.12

Prof. Mark Skwarek's Augmented Halloween Mask.

Copyright owners could also license the right to make particular uses of augmented content. Today, for example, owners of musical works sell "sync" or "soundtrack" licenses to filmmakers, which convey the right to "sync" a particular song with video content into an audio-visual film. There is no logical reason why copyright owners could not likewise license the ability to sync their works with any physical object via the augmented medium. Want passersby to see a copyrighted dragon image on your arm (as in the foregoing example of the man with the tattoo of a Nintendo 3DS marker)? Pay the license fee. Are you a University of Michigan fan and you want other drivers (using augmented windshields) to see your car as if it were a giant, blue-and-maize-wearing wolverine? Pay the license fee. Want to see Mickey Mouse ears on the moon each time it rises? The list of examples is limited only by one's imagination.

On today's internet, copyright enforcement blends with licensing in the form of paywalls – websites that cannot be accessed without making a micropayment or purchasing a subscription. When it comes to augmented content, we could easily encounter similar paywalls – including some that we perceive as actual, physical walls – literally everywhere we go. Digital entertainment and other content could be made available floating in mid-air, on the side of a building, or anywhere else – but only accessible for a micropayment. As discussed earlier, the infrastructure for such payments is already being constructed. In 2013, Google obtained a patent for "pay per gaze" and "pay per emotion" systems. Although these are described as methods for ISPs to charge advertisers based on a consumer's reaction to the ad, the concept could just as easily be adapted to take payments from consumers in order to access the advertising or other content. Chapter 4 described multiple ways in which companies are already beginning to explore such "commARce" solutions.

Of course, too much reliance on such business models could have adverse social consequences. Retailers have always known the power of "impulse purchases," as well as how to position and price their content attractively enough to entice users to buy. It is a profitable model for retailers, but not exactly conducive to consumers maintaining a disciplined budget. If large quantities of copyrighted content – news reports, public art, television shows, and the like – became available only behind AR paywalls, it could deprive society as a whole of valuable experiences and encourage excessive spending. At this point, however, these remain only long-term, hypothetical concerns. How the new economic models shake out remains to be seen.

THE RIGHT OF PUBLICITY

Just as trademarked objects can easily serve as triggers for digital content, so too can the physical characteristics of individual people. The simmering debate over facial recognition technology and privacy summarized in Chapter 3 is a preview of the concerns we are likely to face when a large segment of the population is wearing eyewear capable of recognizing the faces of others.

The main concern voiced about this technology to date has been "privacy," although society in general seems to have no consensus about what that word actually means. But I also expect that the right of publicity – that weird, state-law transitional species between the common law of privacy and intellectual property – will play an increasingly prominent role in this debate going forward.

THE BASICS OF PUBLICITY RIGHTS

The right of publicity is a state-law right that emerged from the common law of privacy to become more or less recognized as a form of intellectual property. It is the fourth of Dean Prosser's four causes of action for invasion of privacy discussed in Chapter 3. Although the particulars vary slightly from state to state, it is essentially the right of an individual to control the commercial exploitation of his or her likeness. The best summary of the right of publicity as generally understood across the United States comes from the *Restatement (Third) of Unfair Competition* section 46: "[o]ne who appropriates the commercial value of a person's identity by using without consent the person's name, likeness, or other indicia of identity for purposes of trade is subject to liability." Each clause of this definition holds legal significance.

Commercial value

The "commercial" aspect of this right is intentional. It is what distinguishes the use of someone's likeness in creative expression like a movie or song – which is generally free speech privileged by the First Amendment – from commercial speech designed to advertise and sell goods or services, which is more akin to a trademark, and hence within the realm of governmental regulation and property rights. In order to prevail on a publicity rights claim, therefore, a plaintiff must generally prove that her identity has "commercial value" – i.e., that there is reason to believe that her identity would be worth something to an advertiser, or that a customer might be more likely to pay attention to a product because the plaintiff's identity was associated with it.

For that reason, courts had long ruled that the right of publicity was only available to "celebrities," and not the rest of us. Today, the rise of digital (and especially social) media makes it entirely realistic to argue that we can all attain commercial value in some context. One argument for establishing "commercial value" in social media is the value of personal relationships. On many social media sites, the identity of the person with whom one interacts in social media both incentivizes people to participate in the site and adds qualitatively significant value to the experience. And the more such interactions that occur on a particular social media site, the more benefit the owner of that site derives (in terms of advertising revenue, search engine tie-ins, or whatever the site's business model may be).

Therefore, in a very direct and measurable way, some would argue, digital (and especially social) media is a context in which literally every user's identity has potential commercial value. Two judicial decisions stemming from lawsuits filed against Facebook in recent years have given some credence to this view,[78] as did a lawsuit over a banking executive's LinkedIn profile.[79]

---

[78]*Cohen v. Facebook, Inc.*, 798 F. Supp. 2d 1090 (ND Cal. 2011) and Fraley v. Facebook, Inc., 830 F. Supp. 2d 785 (ND Cal. 2011).
[79]*Eagle v. Morgan*, No. 11-4303. (E.D. Penn. 2013)

Likeness

In this context, one's "likeness" typically takes the form of one's physical appearance, name, signature, or voice. The restatement expressly lists two examples of ways in which a person's identity can be "indicated": their "name" (which typically includes both the name itself and the person's signature) and their "likeness," or personal appearance. But the common law includes in that term any other "indicia of identity." So a famous race car driver's likeness was infringed by using a picture of his distinctive car, and Johnny Carson's right of publicity was infringed by the product name "Here's Johnny Portable Toilets" because the phrase "Here's Johnny" had come to be associated with Carson.

FACIAL RECOGNITION AS INFRINGING THE RIGHT OF PUBLICITY

Before long, someone is going to file a lawsuit arguing that facial recognition technology infringes the publicity rights of the person being scanned. I am actually surprised that, as of this writing, no one seems to have yet made this argument in court. Right of publicity law regulates the commercial exploitation of a person's identity, which is generally thought to include at least their physical appearance. The same commercial forces that guarantee the expansion of facial recognition will also provide plenty of evidence demonstrating the commercial value of the data. It will not take a scholar to connect the dots and argue that the people scanned should recoup a portion of any money made from their biometric data.

Whether this argument gains any traction is another matter. Biometric data is already widely used for entirely utilitarian (and especially security) purposes – witness, for example, the fingerprint scanner introduced in the iPhone 5S. Entire social networks and other user-generated content may come to rely on the ability to use facial recognition to identify specific individuals. As facial recognition capability becomes more democratized, allowing not only corporations to scan and store such data, the First Amendment may come to protect an individual's right to identify and annotate their knowledge of others in this manner. Allowing people to own intellectual property rights in that data might complicate matters too much for that technology to remain useful, to the detriment of society as a whole.

THREE-DIMENSIONAL CAPTURE OF ENTIRE BODIES: SEX APPEAL AND THE RIGHT OF PUBLICITY

Traditional biometric indicators may not be the only way in which augmented technologies catalog and exploit individuals' physical attributes. Mass-market devices like Microsoft's Kinect are already designed to recognize entire bodies. A few years ago, artists in Spain set up a booth that used three Kinect cameras to scan individuals from head to toe. That data was relayed to a 3D printer in order to make a personalized figurine of the person right there on the street. Today, there are companies simultaneously using more than 60 sensors more precise than the Kinect to digitally render individuals in real time with amazing accuracy. Moreover, the year

2014 saw the introduction of the Kickstarter-funded Structure Sensor – an iPad accessory that allows the device's camera to capture three-dimensional imagery from its surroundings in real time – and Google's Project Tango, an experimental depth sensor that also renders ambient surroundings in 3D.

AR applications will take advantage of such capabilities in order to superimpose digital data on a person's entire body. Many of these will be benign; entire markets will develop for virtual clothing and accessories, for instance. Security professionals already scan entire bodies for contraband, and have made progress in identifying individuals based on their gait as well.[80]

Other applications, however, will go beyond merely analyzing images of bodies to storing and repurposing those images. In an age where sexting is an epidemic among teens and states like California are forced to outlaw the salacious repurposing of such content (i.e., "revenge porn"), it does not require much imagination to conceive of the unsavory uses to which 3D personal imaging technologies could be put. (I would be surprised if, by the time this book sees print, there have not already been instances of three-dimensional sexting.) To date, in courts across the country, one of the most frequent reasons for invoking the right of publicity has been to enjoin the prurient use of girls' and women's images, which are often recorded unwittingly. It is logical to expect the same laws to be applied when those images are collected and manipulated by new digital media.

How effective this right will be in these new augmented realms remains to be seen. The right of publicity has always existed in tension with the First Amendment's protection of free speech, and often finds itself pre-empted by the Copyright Act as well. Both of these more-established bodies of law are likely to keep publicity rights from expanding too broadly. But there is still quite a bit of conduct that falls within the gray area between these areas of law, where the boundaries have yet to be definitively drawn.

"Profiting directly from their sex appeal"

In 2009, a 22-year-old college student calling herself Natalie Dylan sold her virginity to raise money for grad school. The bidding, conducted online for services to be rendered in Nevada, where prostitution is legal, went as high as $3.8 million. While her decision received a fair amount of criticism and moral approbation, she was also congratulated by the CEO of a Fortune 500 company for her "entrepreneurial gumption."

Explaining her decision, Dylan wrote: "it became apparent to me that idealized virginity is just a tool to keep women in their place. But then I realized something else: if virginity is considered that valuable, what's to stop me from benefiting from that?... I took the ancient notion that a woman's virginity is priceless and used it as a vehicle for capitalism."[81]

---

[80]"Gait biometrics shows promise," *Homeland Security News Wire*, September 8, 2011, available at http://www.homelandsecuritynewswire.com/gait-biometrics-shows-promise

[81]Natalie Dylan, *Why I'm Selling My Virginity*, THE DAILY BEAST (January 23, 2009) http://www.thedailybeast.com/articles/2009/01/23/why-im-selling-my-virginity.html.

"I might even be an early adopter of a future trend," Dylan predicted. "These days, more and more women my age are profiting directly from their sex appeal."[82] She was right. The following year, the UK press profiled an 18-year-old Romanian girl who sold herself in exactly the same manner (but for far less money), citing Dylan as inspiration. Search engines reveal hordes of similar copycats. Still, Dylan concluded that "society isn't ready for public auctions like mine – yet."[83]

She's right about that, too. But are we moving in the direction of women commodifying themselves in order to "profit directly from their sex appeal," as Dylan suggests? There are reasons to believe we are – and that the right of publicity is providing the legal framework in which it can happen.

Publicity rights as shields against prurient publications

Several courts have used the right of publicity to stop others from using plaintiff's image in a sexually suggestive manner. For example, Bret Michaels and Pamela Anderson won a lawsuit to block publication of their sex tape on this and other grounds.[84] More recently, Kim Kardashian argued that a sex doll bearing a striking resemblance to her violated her right of publicity.[85]

In 2004, Catherine Bosley, a local newscaster in Ohio, sued when a video of her participating in a wet t-shirt contest found its way online and went viral.[86] She won, but the reasoning the court used to reach that result raises some questions. For reasons I've discussed elsewhere in more depth, the logical implication of the court's holding is that, despite her pre-existing status as a "regional celebrity," Bosley's commercial value had nothing to do with her unique, personal "identity," as right of publicity case law has traditionally required. Rather, it came solely from the prurient value associated with her taking her top off. Several cases involving "Girls Gone Wild"-type situations have reached similar results. The implication of each ruling is that commercial value came from the plaintiff's body, not her identity.

In my home jurisdiction of Michigan, these questions were raised in the case of *Arnold v. Treadwell*.[87] There, a young aspiring model in Detroit posed for a photo shoot with local photographers, then sued them after some of those pictures (several of which were racy to begin with) ended up in a racy magazine, allegedly without her permission. She lost in the state trial court. But the Michigan Court of Appeals reversed, reasoning that the evidence could show "that there is value in associating an item of commerce with plaintiff's identity." The evidence supporting that finding? That "plaintiff has contracted to model clothing in a fashion show, to play an extra in

---

[82]*Id.*

[83]*Id.*

[84]*Michaels v. Internet Entm't Grp., Inc.*, 5 F. Supp. 2d 823 (C.D. Cal. 1998)

[85]Lisa Prince, *Keeping Up With The Kardashians: Kim Kardashian Reacts To Sex Toy Doll*, REALITY TV MAGAZINE (September 22, 2010)http://realitytvmagazine.sheknows.com/2010/09/22/keeping-up-with-the-kardashians-kim-kardashian-reacts-to-sex-toy-doll/.

[86]*Bosley v. WildWett. Com*, 310 F. Supp. 2d 914 (N.D. Ohio 2004).

[87]*Arnold v. Treadwell*, No.2007-080617-CZ, 2009 WL 2136909 (Mich Ct. App. July 16, 2009) (unpublished opinion)

a music video, and to work as an exotic dancer"[88]–all activities that involve exploiting her body, not her identity.

Only days after this ruling, a local Federal judge likewise refused to dismiss Arnold's parallel "false endorsement" claims under the Lanham Act.[89] The court's reasoning was slightly different than the state court's. The court only went so far as to note that Arnold had "a present intent to commercialize her identity." In other words, as long as Arnold had opened the door to commercially exploiting her own appearance, she would be allowed to make her case that her identity did, in fact, have commercial value. Nevertheless, there was still no discussion of the distinction between "likeness" and "identity."

Taken together, therefore, these cases demonstrate that the right of publicity (and related claims) can be an effective basis for attractive people to prevent others from publishing prurient images of them without permission. The means of achieving that result, however, is to think of those plaintiffs' bodies in purely commercial terms, and to legally equate their physical appearance with their identity as people.

My body, my intellectual property

I am not necessarily suggesting that these cases were wrongly decided based on legal precedent, or even that their results are inevitably bad for society. To the contrary, judges have understandably latched onto publicity rights as one of the few effective mechanisms for putting an end to revenge porn and other exploitative content. It is an easier solution than copyright law, since copyrights vest by default in the person taking the picture, rather than the person depicted in the picture. Until we have better laws, or better judicial precedents, to rely on, the right of publicity may remain the best tool courts have for combatting revenge porn and other unquestionably destructive behavior.

But I do want to raise the question of whether, in the long run, using this doctrine in this way creates precedents that will ultimately make it easier for individuals – primarily young women – to exploit themselves in ways they will later come to regret. Admittedly, this is not an entirely new concept. Sex sells. That's a basic fact of human nature. Advertising a product by associating it with an attractive model is Marketing 101. Thousands of people have pursued modeling as a career, and there is nothing inherently questionable about that.

What rights should modeling get someone? Arnold was no supermodel – people who, in today's culture, are "celebrities" in every sense of the word. Rather, she had appeared in one, very local modeling show, as an extra in a music video, and as an exotic dancer. No one reading the magazine she sued over had any idea who she was; they only saw what she looked like. But the mere fact that she (and the plaintiffs in each of the other cases discussed above) was attractive enough to appear in a magazine (or video) gave her legally enforceable rights to profit from the publication of her image.

---

[88]*Id.*

[89]*Arnold v. Treadwell*, 642 F. Supp. 2d 723 (E.D. Mich. 2009).

With that principle established, the right of publicity increasingly forms the basis of a reliable business model for any reasonably attractive person looking to "profit directly from their sex appeal." And they don't even have to go as far as Natalie Dylan did in selling her actual body; images will do just fine. The right of publicity has been in the news a lot lately, thanks to pop stars like Kim Kardashian and Lindsey Lohan, actors like Sandra Bullock, Julia Roberts, and George Clooney, and the estates of Tupac Shakur, Elvis, and Marilyn Monroe. Especially in the face of high youth unemployment and a sagging economy, how long until more young people start putting two and two together, like Natalie Dylan or the protagonists of *The Full Monty* did?

Of course, whether and how much this happens depends on a lot more than intellectual property laws. It's a product of moral and ethical norms, societal attitudes, and much more. But having the legal mechanism in place to guarantee a profit may make it easier.

VIRTUAL ASSISTANTS AS INFRINGEMENT

Apple has Siri. Microsoft has Cortana. Google has the yet-to-be-anthropomorphized Voice Search. The Oscar-nominated film *Her* featured Samantha, while Ender Wiggins (in the sequels to *Ender's Game*) had Jane. Vital to each iteration of the starship *Enterprise* was the Computer.

Futurists have long anticipated the day when humans could interact with computers using the same conversational speech we normally reserve for other people. In order to offer truly two-way interaction his type, however, the programs need to be able to respond in kind. In other words, they need to seem more human. The virtual assistants available as of this writing are beginning to approximate that experience. Siri has already reached its second generation, and some of its original creators are already at work on a next-generation competitor named "Viv" that is intended to be "blindingly smart," "infinitely flexible," "omnipresent," and "embedded in a plethora of Internet-connected everyday objects."[90]

But users and UX designers alike crave a more human-like interaction. AR will offer a unique avenue for achieving this goal by adding visual (and perhaps other sensory) elements to our digital companions. In the very near future, we will have available Siri-like assistants that we can actually see and communicate with face-to-face, via our digital eyewear. This sort of synthetic companion raises a variety of issues, some of which we will revisit in Chapters 7 (re personal safety) and 13 (re pornography). Here, however, I want to suggest that those designing virtual people will inevitably mimic real people, and that this will potentially infringe the publicity rights of their muses.

The simple case in this hypothetical is the company that offers the likenesses of recognizable celebrities as "skins" for a virtual assistant. (This is already beginning to happen; in November 2013, the company behind the crowdsourced navigation app

---

[90]Steven Levy, "Siri's Inventors Are Building a Radical New AI That Does Anything You Ask," *Wired*, August 12, 2014, available at http://www.wired.com/2014/08/viv/.

FIGURE 5.13

Olivia holding "Eve."

Waze announced a deal with Universal Pictures to allow the app to give directions in a celebrity's voice. The first such voice made available was that of comedian and actor Kevin Hart.[91]) That would amount to a commercial exploitation of an identity with defined monetary value, a straightforward infringement. But what if the real-life inspiration behind the program is less recognizable, the similarity is less than exact, or the imitation is unauthorized?

These questions were explored in (of all places) *Drop Dead Diva*, a legal dramedy on the Lifetime Network. The June 2012 episode "Freak Show" begins with the premise of a woman named Olivia, who is bitter over the fact that her husband has been preoccupied with "Eve," the virtual assistant program that he created and is about to bring to market (Fig. 5.13). Eve runs on a tablet computer and is clearly inspired by Apple's Siri. When Olivia fails to convince a judge that this amounts to infidelity, her lawyers then realize that Eve is programmed with a variety of biographical details–including her birth date, her hometown, her highest level of schooling – that all correspond to the Olivia's.

Olivia then uses these details to allege that Eve infringes her right of publicity. She cites the actual 1992 decision in *White v. Samsung Electronics America, Inc.,*[92] in which a Samsung commercial depicted a future *Wheel of Fortune* game show involving a faceless robot wearing a blond wig turned the letters. Vanna White prevailed on a claim that the robot misappropriated her likeness, even though the robot was an allusion to Vanna's occupation rather than her personal identity (Fig. 5.14).

---

[91]"Waze debuts new feature where celebrities give you driving directions," VentureBeat, November 23, 2013, available at http://venturebeat.com/2013/11/23/waze-debuts-celebrity-voice-navigation-feature/.
[92]*White v. Samsung Elec. Am., Inc.* 971 F. 2d 1395 (9th Cir. 1992).

FIGURE 5.14

Vanna White and her alleged doppleganger.

As it happens, *White v. Samsung* represents the outer boundaries of publicity rights law. In a vocal and well-reasoned dissent, Judge Kozinski lamented that "every famous person now has an exclusive right to anything that reminds the viewer of her." Both the Sixth and Tenth Circuits have explicitly rejected, and refused to follow, *White*'s logic. So its value as a basis for evaluating new technologies is questionable at best. Moreover, the facts of "Olivia v. Eve" would almost certainly fail to pass muster even under *White*'s version of the right. Even conceding that Eve could capture Olivia's "essence" even without mimicking her physical appearance, the overlap would have to be enough to at least suggest Olivia's identity to a rational consumer. Yet the only "data points" we're told of that match up are what even Olivia's intrepid lawyers describes as "totally random stats." No one other than Olivia and her lawyers are likely to ever make the connection between Eve and Olivia. Nor does the episode give any reason to believe that Olivia's identity has any commercial value to speak of.

Nevertheless, digital avatars will be fertile grounds for right of publicity claims. These theories are likely to have greater resonance with respect to virtual assistants because of the commercial, utilitarian nature of the function that they perform. To be sure, similar issues will arise in more artistic contexts as well. In fact, we've already seen several analogous claims in recent years, involving "holograms" of such deceased celebrities as Tupac Shakur, Marilyn Monroe, Amy Winehouse, Freddie Mercury, and Michael Jackson. Publicity rights objections by Winehouse's heirs in 2014 put a stop to her hologram before it began. College athletes in both New Jersey and California won publicity rights lawsuits against video game manufacturers that incorporated the players' likenesses into football games. And several celebrities, including Bette Midler, Tom Waits, the Romantics, and Arnold Schwarzenegger, have asserted publicity rights claims against those with sound-alike voices. Nevertheless, these artistic expressions raise much more convincing First Amendment defenses than non-expressive uses of celebrity identities.

Real Property Rights

6

INFORMATION IN THIS CHAPTER:

- Whether owners of real property can, or should be able to, control the augmented content associated with their property
- The intersection of free speech and property rights in AR
- AR's effect on trespass, nuisance, easement, and environmental protection principles

INTRODUCTION

The primary question considered in this chapter is this: can an owner of real property stop someone else from creating an augmented layer associating digital content with that property? At first blush, this question seems to present issues of property law. Because the content being overlain upon this property is both expressive and intangible, however, we cannot answer the question without also considering the law of free speech.

We will also briefly consider additional ways in which augmented world technologies may impact other real property rights, including in the areas of trespass, nuisance, easements, and environmental protection.

THE BASIC RIGHTS AT ISSUE
A BRIEF OVERVIEW OF REAL PROPERTY RIGHTS

In light of the various ways in which this book uses the word "real," it may be helpful to note that "real property" is the term of art that distinguishes a physical parcel of land from other sorts of property, such as portable objects (personal property) or abstract, intangible expression (intellectual property). From a legal perspective, ownership of real property is the right to possess and exclude others from a parcel of land. Such rights may be complete or limited in some respect.

In modern society, ownership rights in most parcels of land are limited by a variety of "nonpossessory interests," which are rights to make certain uses of the land (or to limit use by others) without actually physically occupying it. Centuries ago, for example, property rights were understood to extend from the land upwards all the way into space and down to the center of the earth. This legal concept is captured in the Latin maxim *Cuius est solum, eius est usque ad caelum et ad inferos* ("For whoever owns the soil, it is theirs up to Heaven and down to Hell"), which dates back to medieval Roman law and continued to be followed by English courts well into modern times. The latter half of this principle is what allows land owners to sell mining rights to the earth underneath their property.

The first half of that maxim – what can generally be called "air rights" – became a source of conflict soon after the development of aviation technology; land-owners began demanding the right to exclude aircraft from flying over their property, or to at least charge them for doing so. Faced with a balkanization of airspace that would have made development of an aviation industry impossible, Congress passed the Air Commerce Act of 1926, later replaced by the Federal Aviation Act of 1958. The latter Act provides that "[t]he United States Government has exclusive sovereignty of airspace of the United States,"[1] and that "[a] citizen of the United States has a public right of transit through the navigable airspace."[2] Currently, the general rule is that aircraft must fly high enough so that, in the event of an engine failure, the pilot can land the plane without undue hazards to persons or property on the ground. Specifically, in congested areas, aircraft must remain 1,000 feet higher than any obstacle within a 2,000 feet radius of the aircraft. In non-congested areas, or over bodies of water, the pilot must remain at least 500 feet from any person, vehicle, vessel, or structure. These requirements are reduced during take-off and landing. Thus, the demands of modern society have reduced the individual's historical sovereignty over their property. ("Some nations still assert a similar principle when objecting to satellites entering the orbital space above them."[3])

Air rights became a source of profit in urban centers when those who owned relatively short or underground structures realized they could sell to others the rights to construct buildings on top of theirs. Railroad companies in particular have made significant amounts of money selling the rights to build on top of railroad stations. The Madison Square Gardens arena, for example, is built above New York City's Pennsylvania Station (Fig. 6.1).

---

[1] 49 U.S.C. § 40103(a)(1).

[2] 49 U.S.C. § 40103(a)(2).

[3] Moreover, the tragic downing of a Malaysian Airlines jet over Donetsk, Ukraine – which occurred as this chapter was being finalized – is a stark reminder that not all groups share the same respect for common access to the skies.

FIGURE 6.1

Madison Square Gardens.[4]

This idea of alienating one's air rights has also contributed to the idea of the "Transfer of Development Rights" ("TDR"),[5] a concept within zoning law. There are several forms of TDR, but as applied to air rights, it describes a system in which a municipality sets an arbitrary cap on how high structures can be. A developer may exceed that cap, however, by purchasing from other landowners the right to develop the space between their existing buildings and the cap. The purchaser may then exceed the cap by the amount of purchased space. Therefore, although the height of individual buildings will vary, the average height of all structures remains below the cap. In contemporary urban life, people are often referring to TDR when they use the phrase "air rights."

The law provides various remedies for violations of a landowner's rights. If a person enters onto someone else's land without permission or privilege to do so, for example, they have committed trespass, and the owner could bring a cause of action to eject the trespasser and recover any damage that may have been caused. On the other hand, a landowner owes certain duties to protect the well-being of those who enter his property. Those duties vary based on how much of a right the person has to be there. Logically, trespassers are the group least entitled to the owner's protection. Nevertheless, under some circumstances, even someone who is injured while trespassing may still sue the owner for negligence (a concept discussed in more detail in Chapter 7).

Property rights may also be infringed without ever stepping foot on the land. That is because property ownership is also understood to include the right of "quiet and peaceful

---

[4]© flickr user russavia, used under CC license.

[5]Rutgers University – New Jersey Agricultural Experiment Station, *What Is a Transfer of Development Rights (TDR) Program?* Available at http://njaes.rutgers.edu/highlands/tdr.asp (last visited August 29, 2014).

enjoyment" of the land. A substantial and unreasonable interference with this right is called a "nuisance," and landowners may bring a cause of action in court to remedy it.

THE FREEDOM OF SPEECH

As touched upon in Chapter 5, the First Amendment to the U.S. Constitution forbids Federal, state, and local governments[6] from "abridging the freedom of speech, or of the press." There has never been consensus, however, on the precise meaning of these words.

Over the more than 200 years in which courts have been interpreting these phrases, they have relied on various rationales to explain the First Amendment's role in American society. Some argue that speech must not be restrained because "the best test of truth is the power of the thought to get itself accepted in the competition of the market"[7] – what's called the "marketplace of ideas" theory. Other rationales focus on the vital role that the free flow of ideas plays in a democratic society: "[T]o decide matters of public policy … voters … must be made as wise as possible. [And] this, in turn, requires that so far as time allows, all facts and interests relevant to the problem shall be fully and fairly presented to the meeting [so] that all the alternative lines of action can be wisely measured in relation to one another."[8] Still others argue instead that "[the] value of free expression … rests on its deep relation to self-respect arising from autonomous self-determination without which the life of the spirit is meager and slavish."[9] Regardless of its exact purpose, however, modern courts have agreed on one thing: the freedom of speech is one of the most cherished, fundamental principles in our legal system.

That is why, even though some limits on expression will be "permitted for appropriate reasons,"[10] those limits will be defined narrowly, and justifying a limitation on speech requires meeting a high burden of proof. Some established exceptions include content-neutral rules that curb the "time, place, and manner" in which expression may occur, and words that pose a clear and present danger of "inciting or producing imminent lawless action."[11] Some classes of expression have been deemed to have no First Amendment value at all, such as disclosures of purely private facts and obscenity. Similarly, commercial speech – i.e., advertising that proposes a commercial transaction – has been held to have less societal importance than most other speech. Therefore, courts are more willing to allow governments to regulate advertising than speech on political or personal ideas. This explains why trademark, false advertising, and similar laws are constitutional, and will also impact the regulation of commercial speech in the augmented medium.

---

[6]The text of the amendment, as written in the eighteenth century, applies only to "Congress." Subsequent interpretation by the courts and expansion of the right to due process of law by the Fourteenth Amendment, however, have made clear that this principle applies equally to state and local authorities as well.

[7]*Abrams v. United States,* 250 U.S. 616, 630 (1919) (Holmes, J.).

[8]A. Meiklejohn, FREE SPEECH AND ITS RELATION TO SELF-GOVERNMENT 15-16 (1948).

[9]Richards, *Free Speech and Obscenity Law: Toward a Moral Theory of the First Amendment,* 123 U. Pa. L. Rev. 45, 62 (1974).

[10]*Elrod v. Burns,* 427 U.S. 347, 360 (1976).

[11]*Brandenburg v. Ohio,* 395 U.S. 444 (1969).

AR: WHERE PROPERTY RIGHTS AND FREE SPEECH COLLIDE
AUGMENTED ADVERTISING – AND MORE – IS COMING TO REAL ESTATE NEAR YOU

As mentioned in Chapter 5, the augmented medium will allow advertisers to post commercial messages literally anywhere the eye can see. The past generation has already seen commercial sponsorship creep into such unlikely venues as grocery store floors and car wraps. Advertising dollars have largely underwritten much of the public internet's growth, including the rise of Google, the internet's most prominent titan. Google itself has told the government that the industry will soon be displaying ads in such novel places as refrigerators, automotive dashboards, and thermostats,[12] which represents a quantum leap in the pervasiveness of commercial messaging beyond what we experience today.

But that discussion is still about advertising that is physically transmitted by digital pixels and screens. Augmented advertising will enable commercial messages to appear as if they are physically present on top of almost any surface, without anything physical needing to change about that surface. Recall Keiichi Matsuda's "Domestic Robocop" visualization, discussed in the prior chapters, in which an individual wearing AR eyewear sees advertising plastered on nearly every flat surface within his apartment kitchen – and is even able to manually adjust the density of the messages to make the physical objects on those surfaces more or less visible amidst the digital clutter.

Now apply that same mechanism to the world outside that kitchen, and you have a sense of what augmented advertising could become. A person walking down a city sidewalk wearing AR eyewear could be shown advertising digitally plastered over every surface within view – sidewalks, buildings, park benches, passing cars, lamp posts, the clothing of passersby. City life is already thought of as dominated by commercial advertising because of the number of ads on billboards and building faces, yet such a physical infrastructure for commercial advertising will seem painfully quaint and outdated – not to mention expensive to maintain – in an augmented world.

This sort of urban experience will take time to manifest, and there will be stepping stones along the way. Current models of digital eyewear, for example, do a poor job (compared to the human eye, anyway) of recognizing the physical world around them, so visual messages are more like heads-up displays at optical infinity rather than "augmentations" that appear as if they are overlain on the plane of actual physical surfaces. Over time, the devices will catch up to where other mobile AR apps are now, able to recognize more pre-programmed surfaces in the physical world so long as those objects appear in just the right lighting and orientation. Those targets are likely to be mostly commercial symbols because the technology will need funding in order to expand. (And, as discussed in Chapter 5, these interactions will lead

---

[12]Rolfe Winkler, *Google Predicts Ads in Odd Spots Like Thermostats,* Wall Street Journal (May 21, 2014), available at http://blogs.wsj.com/digits/2014/05/21/google-predicts-ads-in-odd-spots-like-thermostats/ (last visited August 29, 2014).

to squabbles between brands, such as when the coupon triggered by one company's logo is for a competitor's product.) Ubiquitous, on-the-fly augmentations of anything and everything are still several years away. But it is coming because it is the logical conclusion of all of the various trends we see today in digital technology and advertising models.

PROPERTY-BASED MODELS OF CONTROLLING LOCATION-BASED MESSAGES BREAK DOWN IN AR

Before the advent of AR, if I wanted an advertisement to appear above a certain piece of land or the side of a particular building, I had only one option: to erect a physical sign there. That sign could take the form of a poster, a billboard, or a digital screen, but it would need to be a physical object located on the parcel of land. For that, I would need the landowner's permission. (For night-time-only ads, I could also project them against a physical surface on the parcel from afar, but that is only a temporary solution and may also infringe the landowner's rights in some cases.)

In the augmented medium, however, all I need to cause a digital message to appear as if it is plastered on a particular building or place is the right software and mobile hardware. No intrusion onto the physical space itself ever occurs, so the landowner's right to exclude me from his property is never triggered. Nor am I entering the airspace above the building, even if the digital message appears to be there, so air rights are not being violated. Nevertheless, AR is designed to create the illusion of physical presence, and ads virtually plastered onto physical places may *feel* like an intrusion, so resort to the law of property to regulate them is an understandable impulse.

Other commentators have also foreseen augmented advertising and the legal issues they will raise. John C. Havens, for example, discussed them and some of the legal issues they raise in his insightful piece for *Mashable* called "Who Owns the Advertising Space in an Augmented Reality World?"[13] Noting that Google had already applied for a patent for digitally replacing physical ads within the Street View feature of Google Maps, Havens wrote that "the importance of virtual real estate may quickly supplant actual signage for advertisers. This is especially true when virtual signage could be switched dynamically for individual eye traffic depending on a viewer's preferences." He went on to quote Gabe Greenberg, director of social and emerging media at Microsoft, as saying that, "if the experience presents the ads in a way that makes sense for the augmented reality experience and the user's intention, this could be a powerful advertising tool for tomorrow's marketplace."

These predictions are persuasive. As discussed in Chapter 4, advertisers will absolutely make use of the augmented space to customize and expand upon their messaging. This medium will offer so much more functionality than physical signage that it is likely to quickly become the dominant means of advertising, even

---

[13]John C. Havens, "Who Owns the Advertising Space in an Augmented Reality World?", *Mashable*, June 6, 2011, available at http://mashable.com/2011/06/06/virtual-air-rights-augmented-reality/.

more quickly than digital billboards have begun to overtake the printed variety. Where my view diverges from this article's (or headline's, anyway) approach, however, is in tying this means of augmented advertising to air rights. As discussed above, air rights are a subset of real property rights used to determine who may occupy the airspace immediately above a particular parcel of land. When (as in the scenario painted by the *Mashable* article) the land owner permits the advertising, air rights are not implicated. They only come into play when a third party seeks to impose its content on someone else's airspace. May the property owner control *that* type of advertising?

In my view, such questions will not typically be determined according to who owns the air rights. Applying air rights to control third-party augmented content would reflect a particular assumption – specifically, that the physical location in which the augmented ad appears to the consumer should determine who gets to control the content of that ad. In other words, an owner of real property should get to determine which, if any, digital advertisements that users can see projected upon their property. An advertiser could not build a physical billboard on a plot of land without the landowner's permission, after all; this viewpoint applies the same thinking to augmented ads.

This means of conceptualizing augmented advertising has been common in my experience because it parallels the laws that apply to the current media with which we are familiar. As the market for augmented advertising develops, however, I think it will become clear that an approach based on the law of real property does not work in this context. Property ownership is the right to exclude people and things from occupying a particular space. This model is logical – even necessary – when applied to physical objects because only one object can occupy a given physical space at any particular time.

But that model breaks down when applied to augmented content. Unlike a physical billboard, augmented content does not actually occupy the physical space in which it appears. AR is, in this respect, a mere illusion. Regardless of how convincingly the user's mobile device conveys the impression that a tangible, three-dimensional object exists in a particular physical place, it is *not actually there*. A limitless number of mobile apps can be programmed to display an infinitely diverse range of content on top of the same physical space. The digital content does nothing to interfere with the property owner's use or enjoyment of the physical property in which it appears to exist.

Therefore, property law does not help us think accurately about the AR experience. Rather, when my digital device recognizes a person, place, or thing and is triggered to augment my view of it with digital information, the experience is much more like clicking a hyperlink on a web page – except that the "web page" is the physical world around me, and the hyperlinked "text" is the person, place, or thing that triggered the display. And just as with a web page, there is someone responsible for writing the short piece of link code, for choosing to associate it with that person, place, or thing in the program being run by the digital eyewear, and for determining what information the link code will deliver to me.

IN MANY CASES, FREE SPEECH RIGHTS WILL PREVAIL

Consider the possibility, then, that the choices a coder makes in associating digital content with a tangible object is itself speech protected by the First Amendment's prohibition of laws that "abridg[e] … the freedom of speech, or of the press." We can get a sense of how courts will answer this question by thinking like judges do – in analogies. When courts encounter unique factual circumstances (what they call "cases of first impression"), they draw from cases dealing with the most analogous facts they can find, and from there new case law emerges.

A good way to understand the three-dimensional "clickable world" is by analogy to the two-dimensional World Wide Web with which we interact every day. The United States Supreme Court has long recognized the internet as a "dynamic, multifaceted [medium] of communication." Its 1997 decision *Reno v. ACLU*[14] struck down part of the Communications Decency Act of 1996 for infringing online free speech rights. In that case, the Court drew its own analogy to underscore the importance of online speech when it observed that, online, "any person … can become a town crier with a voice that resonates farther than it could from any soapbox. Through the use of Web pages, mail exploders, and newsgroups, the same individual can become a pamphleteer." Soapboxes and pamphlets are historic forms of political expression that were sacrosanct to those who wrote the First Amendment.

The Court's use of these analogies conveyed its conviction that digital speech should receive just as much protection as any form of communication. Hyperlinks are a key mechanism by which internet users convey information. Whereas an activist 250 years ago would have stood at the street corner handing out written pamphlets, today's activist conveys his message by posting a tweet containing a hyperlink to a page with more information. By pointing internet users to another publication, a hyperlink says, "look here for evidence that supports what I'm saying." It is little wonder, then, that people have long viewed hyperlinks as key tools for expression. Tim Berners-Lee, the father of the Internet, said it best in 1997: "[t]he ability to refer to a document (or a person or anything else) is in general a fundamental right of free speech to the same extent that speech is free. Making the reference with a hypertext link is more efficient but changes nothing else."[15]

Although courts have not addressed the First Amendment's application to hyperlinks as often as one might expect (perhaps because the conclusion is obvious), there is judicial support for the proposition.[16] The form of augmented reality I am considering in this chapter (in which viewing certain physical places triggers the display

---

[14]521 U.S. 844 (1997).

[15]Tim Berners-Lee, *Links and Law: Myths,* W3C (April 1997), available at http://www.w3.org/DesignIssues/LinkMyths.html (last visited August 29, 2014)

[16]For example, a federal court in Washington affirmed a student's right under the First Amendment to criticize a teacher by posting a link to a YouTube video about the teacher. *Requa v. Kent Sch. Dist. No. 415,* 492 F. Supp. 2d 1272, 1283 (W.D. Wash. 2007); see also *Universal City Studios, Inc. v. Corley,* 273 F. 3d 429, 449-50 (2d Cir. 2001) (holding that "computer code conveying information is 'speech' within the meaning of the First Amendment," but also that such speech may be regulated in a content-neutral manner by intellectual property laws, just like any other form of speech).

of pre-determined digital content) is little more than a system of three-dimensional hyperlinks – the World Wide Web stretched into a genuine webbing over the world. How users "click" on these links will vary. The first smartphone-based AR apps used QR codes as the physical "markers" that trigger the automatic display of digital content. Today's AR technology no longer relies solely on QR codes; "markerless AR" looks for any pre-programmed shape or pattern and displays the appropriate digital content when it recognizes the object. Visions of an AR-infused world have long included scenes in which one can walk down the street wearing AR eyewear and seeing digital objects blended into the real world just by looking around. Exactly as with two-dimensional hyperlinks, however, what a user sees through her AR eyewear when looking at a physical "trigger" depends entirely on the coder's choice of digital information with which to "link" it.

In most conceivable circumstances, that choice will involve some level of expressive "speech" – especially because the person writing the code can choose from literally any content in the world when making that connection. More often than not, the coder will intend to communicate some sort of message through his choice of digital content and in his choice of who or what to associate that content with. For example, as part of their 2011 Re + Public collaboration, the Heavy Projects and the Public Ad Campaign used AR to "filter" outdoor advertising and replace it with original street art. Looking through an AR app, outdoor commercial advertisements were overlaid with political or artistic messages. One such pointed message, as discussed in Chapter 5, caused the image of "Captain Barbossa" in the poster for a *Pirates of the Caribbean* movie to morph before a user's eyes into the face of Goldman Sachs CEO Lloyd Blankfein – conveying the artist's message that he is the "real pirate".

We will see plenty of user-generated content associated with, and displayed on top of, physical places as well. Much of this will be a mere extension of today's social media. For example, the current Foursquare app keeps track of my location via GPS and pushes me user reviews of establishments when I arrive at them. (Fig. 6.2) Adding AR to that app would simply provide another way to display the data (and perhaps use the geofencing infrastructure of an AR network to trigger the alerts more accurately.)

Of course, this technology could (and will) be implemented in creepy, offensive and invasive ways, as well. For example, popular illustrations of our augmented future have shown facial recognition technology and AR being used to convey messages about people such as "Don't trust this guy!" or "Slutty Ex-Girlfriend." (Fig. 6.3) A scene from Daniel Suarez's novel *Freedom*™ has characters using AR glasses to see credit scores and banking information floating over the heads of everyone around them. Others have depicted geotags used by thieves to indicate when residents are away from home or have just purchased something worth stealing.

But the possibility that speech rights can be abused is why the courts have never applied the First Amendment's command that there be "no law" abridging the freedom of speech in an absolutely literal way. The law has continued to regulate expressive activity that goes beyond the bounds of what we recognize as "free speech," including defamation, false advertising, criminal conspiracy, and infringement of

FIGURE 6.2

Foursquare already provides location-based user-generated content.[17]

intellectual property rights. The same legal boundaries that have governed speech in pamphlets and Twitter feeds will continue to apply in the augmented space. So to answer the question of whether the First Amendment will protect the right to augment reality, the answer must be "yes – to the same extent that it protects speech in any other format." In order to make sure we use the right legal principles and afford the

FIGURE 6.3

An illustration of potential ways in which real-time augmented data will be associated with places and people.

proper level of protection to augmented content, it will be important to think clearly about that content and recognize it for what it is: speech.

ONE COLLATERAL BENEFIT FOR LAND OWNERS: DIGITAL GRAFFITI

Another Re + Public campaign highlights a potential upside to AR for land owners and the public alike: digital graffiti.

There is a wall at Houston & Bowery Street in New York City that has been the site of street art for decades. The first mural was painted there in 1982, but soon afterwards it was overrun with advertisements and graffiti. In 2008, however, the owner collaborated with a number of artists to create a new series of murals. In June 2012, as part of the Re + Public collaboration, the Heavy Projects used augmented reality to create a virtual history of the famous mural site, allowing users to view each piece as it originally appeared.[18]

The Bowery Wall project highlights several aspects of augmented public art that could be beneficial for all involved. First, it demonstrates a way to add value to a

---

[18]The Heavy Projects, *heavy project,* available at http://theheavyprojects.com/projects (last visited August 29, 2014).

FIGURE 6.4

A screenshot from the Heavy Projects' Driskill Hotel Takeover.

building at relatively low expense – even (and perhaps especially) those that are otherwise nondescript and out of the way. The promise of "hidden" art could draw foot traffic to a location that translates into additional revenue for the business within.

Second, an artist working in AR has options that were never before available. He doesn't need to worry that his work will be lost the next time someone else comes and paints over the wall. If the work is created and preserved digitally, it will remain available, as long as it is associated with the appropriate physical cues necessary to trigger the experience. What's more, he has three-dimensional and perpetually moving elements at his disposal that cannot be achieved with mere paint. Several of the Heavy Project's murals, for example, depict imagery floating in the air and pouring out of the augmented wall (Fig. 6.4).

Third, AR allows graffiti artists to mark up a wall to their hearts' content without ever changing its physical appearance. Those who don't wish to experience the imagery won't ever need to see it. Those who do, however, may enter into one of several available digital experiences in the same location. In either event, unlike traditional graffiti, the art does nothing to impinge upon the property rights of those who own the physical surfaces.

Indeed, augmented graffiti could conceivably contribute to better preservation of physical walls because more people will have a stake in preserving them. Consider: as long as AR apps require a visually recognizable surface to trigger an augmented display (and that will be true for some time), then none of the AR artists whose content is visible on a particular wall will have their art seen if the wall becomes so altered that the AR app being used can no longer recognize it. In other words, one vandal can ruin the expectations of a limitless number of other street artists, not to mention the landowner. Therefore, each one of those stakeholders will have an interest in preventing undesirable physical graffiti on that wall. The more people who have that motivation, the less likely it will be that the wall gets physically "tagged."

SCARCITY IN AUGMENTED REAL ESTATE

Property values are driven by scarcity. As the old maxim goes, land is one thing "they ain't making any more of." Although the following observations do not deal with real property rights *per se*, they illustrate how the same principle will work in AR.

WHEN EVERYONE WANTS TO USE THE SAME PLATFORM

So far, this discussion has assumed that anyone who wants to will be able to create their own digital experience on the same physical surface or geolocation. Technically, that will always be true because someone can always create a new app (or a new "channel" within an app such as Layar, junaio, or Aurasma) in which to deliver their content. That is the predominate model for today's nascent AR market.

As more people begin to consume AR content, there will inevitably be consolidation around a finite number of more popular apps. That is human nature. For example, according to Nielsen, the average U.S. home now receives 189 television channels, a record-high number that has jumped up from 129 in 2008. But the average number of TV channels watched is 17.[19] Humans simply cannot handle choosing between too many options.

We see a similar phenomenon online. No matter how many generic top-level domains are added to the Web, companies still fight for access to the ".com" associated with their name – because that is still where customers instinctively look first. And despite the fact that almost every commercial website seems to have some social functionality to it nowadays, people still conduct the vast majority of their online interactions through a select few social media sites. (As of this writing, those are primarily Facebook, Twitter, LinkedIn, and Pinterest). Which of those are the most popular at any given time may change rapidly in a short amount of time, but again, people can only handle so many options to choose from. Moreover, most of these sites need a sufficiently large user base before any one user can truly get the most out of the experience. By necessity, only a select number of sites will attract that many users.

The same will be true in AR. Although the same piece of property could be augmented by thousands of bespoke apps and channels, that will almost never happen – because no one will use the vast majority of them.

Current AR apps vary in how they manage overlapping content. In some, targets are available for augmentation on a first-come, first-served basis. All users (or, at least, all those who don't pay for more options) see their content through the same app. If one person associates digital content with a particular physical place or thing first, that target is no longer available to other users through that app. Other apps offer a visual discovery function that will display each of the available options for

---

[19]Andrew Burger, *Nielsen: Despite Hundreds of Choices, Average Number of TV Channels Watched is 17,* telecompetitor (May 9, 2014), available at http://www.telecompetitor.com/nielsen-average-number-of-tv-channels-watched-is-17/ (last visited August 29, 2014).

objects that have been augmented more than once. In the current version of Layar, for example, a list of layers and campaigns that have augments on top of the same target will be shown first after the visual search. Users can choose which layer or campaign they would like to see from the results and launch it separately.[20]

Either way, viewing options within individual apps will be limited. And with limitations come conflict. How will we decide who has the right to augment a particular place or thing through a particular app? And how will we regulate the digital "land rush" within those platforms, particularly if any of those platforms are publicly owned?

The analogy to domain names suggests potential solutions. When domain names became available to the general public, the Internet Corporation for Assigned Names and Numbers (ICANN) created the Uniform Dispute Resolution Policy (UDRP). This procedure, which most domain name registrants agree to as part of the terms and conditions of their registration, offers a relatively inexpensive means of combatting cybersquatters – those who rush to buy the ".com" or ".net" version of a name in order to sell it to the person to whom it rightfully belongs. Congress also passed the Anti-cybersquatting Consumer Protection Act in 1999,[21] designed to give rights holder clearer protection online. Of course, these mechanisms are designed to protect intellectual property (primarily trademark rights), rather than real property interests. But the analogy to "squatting" on "land" has always been apt.

Whether similar protections will be needed or useful in virtual space depends on how the market for such content, and the means of distributing it, unfolds. If AR continues to be just one of many forms of digital content delivered via the internet, then it will continue to be governed by the same rules that apply to any online content. As long as AR stays within the walled gardens of private apps, the policies for determining who gets to augment what and how will remain up to the app's owner – at least until the point where a particular augmentation infringes on someone else's intellectual property or other rights. For example, as of this writing, virtually every business in the developed world wants to have its own Facebook page. Facebook is free to adopt its own means of policing (or not policing) how its Page names are allotted, and it has experimented with allowing trademark owners to reserve Pages under their respective names. Ultimately, though, in order to stop someone from using a name, it is up to a trademark owner to prove that their mark is being infringed, whether that occurs on Facebook or anywhere else.

The rules will get more complicated when (as I think is inevitable) AR becomes a "mesh" experience, combining content from the internet along with signals generated by wearable devices and the Internet of Things infrastructure. In that scenario, those who own the land or equipment from which the signals are generated may retain some ability to control how those signals are used. Even at that point, however,

---

[20]Layar, *Layar Vision FAQs,* available at https://www.layar.com/documentation/browser/howtos/layar-vision-doc/layar-vision-faqs/#can-i-augment-several-parts-of-the-same-reference-image (last visited August 29, 2014)

[21]15 U.S.C. §1125.

legal limitations on the content will depend on what basis others have to claim rights in what someone else is doing. How that applies to such a hypothetical mesh network remains to be seen.

Only to the extent that the public comes to depend on a common network for delivering AR content will the rules governing the triggering of that content come to resemble today's governance of internet domain names. And such a system may very well become tied to real property rights in interesting ways. For example, imagine all governmental AR information being distributed on a network called ".gov.ar," except that what comes before the ".gov" portion is not a trademark or other name, but rather a physical address. So, for example, residents jogging through New York City's Central Park might use the "centralpark.nyc.gov.ar" channel to visualize directions to all available pedestrian paths, while the same ".gov.ar" channel might display property tax information over your home or the details of local ordinances whenever you cross municipal boundaries. Switch to ".social.ar" in any of those venues, however, and you might see the past and present locations of your friends, along with the virtual tags they've left for each other. "PublicSafety.ar," on the other hand, might visualize crime statistics for any given address.

The actual content and number of channels would be limited only by bandwidth, funding, and imagination. Within each channel, it would then be necessary to adopt a means of arbitrating who has the rights to associate virtual content with a particular physical location.

SACRED GROUND: WHEN (AUGMENTED) WORLDS COLLIDE

For a brief time several years ago, I got to be part of a legal team helping a Native American tribe attempt to protect a particular piece of land. This land was the site of an impressive rock formation (Fig. 6.5). To the company who owned the mineral rights to that land, that rock was the most convenient place to drill an access tunnel to the mine underneath. But to the tribe, it was sacred. Their ancestors had performed religious ceremonies on that particular rock formation for centuries. The culture and beliefs that the tribe held dear required that the ceremonies continue to be held there. To them, this location was irreplaceable, and neither side saw room for compromise.

Although augmented uses of physical places are not likely to have the same depth of religious or cultural significance anytime soon, I do expect many analogous disputes to arise as a result of AR, and that some of them will be contested with similar intensity. One of the defining characteristics of AR is its interconnectedness with physical places and things. In addition, AR's early adopters still constitute a subculture defined by their shared passion for the medium, which reinforces their collective sense of identity. These factors can combine to create intense loyalties to a shared AR experience.

The best example of this phenomenon that I've seen to date in the augmented space is the passionate community that has built up around the sci-fi themed AR game *Ingress*. Players' social media posts are constantly updated with comments and

FIGURE 6.5

Sacred ground.[22]

developments within the game. "Factions" of players exist all over the world, crossing generational, gender, and ethnic boundaries. I've heard first-hand tales of how the game's requirement to get out and physically interact with virtual "objects" has contributed to in-person meet-ups and genuinely enriched human relationships. It is, by all accounts, a vibrant community.

Imagine, then, what would happen if another AR game with a completely different vibe and culture were to superimpose itself over the same physical locations used by *Ingress* players. (This is actually a realistic possibility, as "the developers of Niantic Labs intend to implement a whole platform for Ingress augmented reality games. Their plan is to use a variety of operating time and the elements to create a series of Ingress API, through which third-party developers can create their own game projects."[23]) If two overlapping games – say, a techno-thriller mystery and a *Dance Dance Revolution*-esque flash mob – require players to show up at the same times and places, clashes of personality are bound to ensue.

---

[22]© flickr user thecombjelly; used under CC BY-SA 2.0 license. See https://creativecommons.org/licenses/by/2.0/

[23]Saroi Kar, *Google's Ingress Platform Paves the Way for Other AR Games,* Silicon Angle (December 20), available at http://siliconangle.com/blog/2013/12/30/googles-ingress-platform-paves-the-way-for-other-ar-games/ (last visited August 29, 2014)

Now multiply that scenario by a dozen, a hundred, or even a thousand. The beauty of AR is that an infinite series of digital experiences can be overlain atop the same physical place, but that will sometimes prove to be its bane as well. Like loquacious moviegoers, the way in which some people enjoy one augmented experience in a place may be inherently disruptive to someone else's ability to appreciate a different digital experience in the same place.

One solution to this problem will be in the hands of those who own the physical property on which the experience takes place. To varying degrees, they will have the power to prescribe rules of conduct, and to eject those who refuse to follow those rules. If a particular location proves to be a popular locale for augmentation, owners may require all comers to quietly respect all others, or else make it easier for members of a particular group to enjoy their own augmented experiences over others. Of course, unless the owner is also the experience provider, they will expect compensation for their efforts, and will likely coordinate them so as to maximize foot traffic to any businesses located on the property. Before long it may become customary for a parcel of commercial real estate to have both physical *and* digital developers, and those may not be the same people.

Ingress and other games tend to locate their digital objects in public places. This brings its own limitations on personal conduct, as well as on the government's ability to prohibit expression based on its content. Could we soon see a First Amendment lawsuit challenging censorship of augmented activity on public land?

Ultimately, the most effective solution in cases of conflict between different augmented uses of a place will come down to common courtesy. As we'll explore further in Chapter 11, though, the basis for such norms will lose some of their "commonality" the more our experiences of the physical world become digitized. At least when two people are together in the same physical place – without digital distractions – they innately recognize on some level the concept of shared experience and, hopefully, responsibility. They recognize that both will suffer if one person does something destructive to the shared space, and, conversely, that respecting the other person's interests will likely lead them to reciprocate.

We lose some of that sense when our attention is given over to a digital world that is ours alone to control and experience. This phenomenon is already evident with mobile phones and game consoles, so we can expect it to multiply when groups of people are competing to digitize the same space. This does not mean that civility is impossible, but it does mean that acting civilly will become more of a conscious choice and less of an instinct.

OTHER INTERSECTIONS BETWEEN PROPERTY RIGHTS AND AR
AN INVITATION TO TRESPASS?

The flip side of "digital developers" and planned AR gaming activities is when people congregate on someone's property for the same activities uninvited. Physically entering land that someone else has the right to possess is called trespass. Once a trespasser is on someone else's land, they are liable for any damage resulting from their presence. Avoiding those circumstances is very likely one of the major reasons why *Ingress* and other AR experiences drive their users to publicly owned lands. Although the person trespassing would be the one most directly responsible for trespassing onto private property, it is not difficult to imagine circumstances in which an AR experience designer is held jointly liable for the trespass (and any resulting damage) because the AR experience led users to onto the private property.

Designers should also keep in mind how users are likely to access an intended destination, even if it is located in a public or otherwise permissible location. If the only, or the best, way to access the destination is by crossing private property, or if it's reasonable to expect that more people will arrive than the destination can accommodate, then trespasses are bound to occur.

Trespasses can pose legal risks for land owners too, in narrow circumstances. For example, a landowner may be held liable when he knows people are trespassing on his property and that there are hidden dangers they might encounter, but does nothing about it. This may be a particular concern if, instead of chasing AR-using kids off his lawn, a property owner instead provides digital content from his own location. If the augmentation is inviting enough, yet masks hidden dangers or otherwise poses risks that minors may not recognize, then it could pose what's called an "attractive nuisance."

The prevailing view of the attractive nuisance doctrine is set out in Section 339 of the Restatement (Second) of Torts. Under that standard, a possessor of land is liable for physical harm to trespassing children where the injury is caused by an artificial condition on the land if:

a. The place where the condition exists is one on which the possessor knows or has reason to know that children are likely to trespass;
b. The condition is one of which the possessor knows or has reason to know and which he realizes or should realize will involve an unreasonable risk of death or serious bodily harm to such children;
c. The children, because of their youth, do not discover the condition or realize the risk involved in intermeddling with it or in coming within the area made dangerous by it;
d. The utility to the possessor of maintaining the condition and the burden of eliminating the danger are slight as compared with the risk to children involved; and
e. The possessor fails to exercise reasonable care to eliminate the danger or otherwise to protect the children.

To put this in context: I recently experienced "artificial conditions" that had "attractive nuisance" (figuratively) written all over them. Walking through a public garden area in a major American downtown, I saw steep cement walls with narrow steps just begging to be climbed (Fig. 6.6). There were small, obligatory signs warning people not to do so, of course, but nothing that a minor would recognize. Likewise, the same park featured expansive retaining pools that certainly looked like swim-

FIGURE 6.6

A public water garden.[24]

ming pools, although the water was little better than sewer runoff. Again, the tiny signs nearby did nothing to stop hordes of young people from wading right in.

How might this doctrine apply in an augmented world? That depends entirely on how its digital infrastructure develops. I've included this discussion, however, because it's easy to picture circumstances in which large visualizations of digital signage, game elements, characters and other displays are made to appear over land that isn't meant to be physically entered – the middle of a road or a construction site, for example – but that nevertheless pique the curiosity of children beyond the point of resistance. In those circumstances, land owners would be well-advised to take stock of potential dangers and use reasonable care in preventing injury.

NUISANCE

Nuisance is an intentional or wrongful act that substantially and unreasonably interferes with a land owner's use and enjoyment of a property. Typically, this takes the forms of sound, light, vibrations, or even smells that disturb people on a particular parcel, even though nothing tangible invades the property in a way that would constitute a trespass. Substantial interference is easy to find when it can be shown to diminish the market value of the land, but it can also occur when residents persuade a judge that it prevents them from conducting regular activities on their property (like sleeping and socializing) as they used to do.

Where I live, it's often difficult to get to sleep at night during the summer because people are always setting off large fireworks – the classic definition of a nuisance. It's easy to picture digital content also causing disturbances on adjacent properties, especially if there is an audio component to the augmentation that can be overheard, or if it draws large groups of people nearby or at odd hours. Even if the augmented

---

[24]© Andreas Praefcke / GNU License.

experience itself is personal and evanescent, the hardware that creates it may not be. The infrastructure of an augmented world could conceivably create hums, eyesores, vibrations, and other nuisances to neighbors.

Light may also constitute a nuisance, especially at night. If the augmentation consists of projection mapping or other plainly visible displays, that light could easily spill into unwanted places. In the still-distant future, when AR technology matures and becomes an integral part of everyday life, we could even see things become nuisances because they diminish or interfere with digital, rather than physical, enjoyment of a property – such as by causing signal interference that impairs a home's virtual assistant, or by overtaxing the local digital infrastructure so that property owners can't get the content they need.

Whether any interference with the enjoyment of land is sufficiently "substantial" and "unreasonable" to constitute actionable nuisance is a case-by-case determination. Interference with an owner's interest is unreasonable if the seriousness of the harm outweighs the utility of the defendant's actions.

PHYSICAL AND VIRTUAL EASEMENTS

Although the concept of a landowner having complete dominion over their property is simple in theory, in practice people often need to make certain uses of land belonging to others. That's where easements come in. An easement is a limited right to make use of someone else's land. Typically, these arise by private agreements, but they can also be implied by circumstances in situations of strict necessity. Once granted, easements typically become part of the rights that "run with the land," meaning that subsequent owners will be bound by them.

In contemporary American life, by far the most prevalent examples of easements are those granted to cable companies and utilities to run wires, pipelines, and similar infrastructure through, over, or under a property. Those "affirmative" easement rights may also impose "negative" easement restrictions on the landowner, such as not being able to plant trees near an underground pipeline.

The augmented world will see its share of these sorts of easements. Work is already underway in places like Oakland County, Michigan to construct the infrastructure necessary for connected vehicles to communicate with each other and with a central, public network. That infrastructure will likely consist of digital devices placed at regular intervals along county roads, not unlike the road signs and traffic lights already present. As the applications for augmented municipal and commercial services grow, these networks will need to be expanded. To the extent such infrastructure needs to be installed on, through, or under private property, easements will need to be obtained (or, in the case of public projects, imposed through condemnation).

Similarly, to the extent that the industry adopts the micro and nanotaggant devices I have predicted (in which tiny machines that serve as signal routers and pinpoint accurate location beacons become implanted in virtually everything), the property law implications will get especially interesting. More than likely, permission will be needed from every landowner in the entire area where such devices are installed. Depending on how easy it is to detect and control such devices, however, it may be very difficult to control their distribution. And if the digital communications networks of tomorrow become as dependent on such microscopic devices as today's systems are dependent on the internet's backbone of transoceanic cables and server farms, then property law may lose its ability to regulate such devices, just like it lost its control over airplanes plying overhead.

It will also be interesting to see if property law will ever allow or require virtual easements for the display of digital information over a particular piece of land. Much of this chapter has already been dedicated to establishing the proposition that augmented digital information does not occupy the physical space in which it is depicted, and thus is outside the bounds of real property law. If (and only if) specific augmented information became so important and universally relied upon – the equivalent of today's traffic control system for automobiles, for example – could the prospect of applying real property law to digital information ever make sense. Only in that case would one particular display of digital information in a certain physical location displace, and be mutually exclusive with, the display of any other digital content in the location. In effect, the law may actually treat such digital content as if it were just as physical as it pretended to be. Even in that case, however, our legal system would need to moderate its perspective of digital content as expressive speech rather than as a utilitarian object. That would be a doctrinal sea change, and thus is unlikely anytime soon.

ENVIRONMENTAL PROTECTION LAWS

The foregoing discussion mentioned the property law implications of ubiquitous mechanical taggants of microscopic or even nano-scale size, distributed throughout the physical environment. Such a system would implicate more than just property law, however. It is also far too easy to imagine the potential effects that such devices would have on human health and the natural environment.

Indeed, even though AR-capable nanotaggants may accelerate the problem, there are already enough nanodevices in use for people to be talking about these issues. This is actually an area where, for once, the government is ahead of the game. In 2000, it created the National Nanotechnology Initiative,[25] which "serves as the central point of communication, cooperation, and collaboration for all Federal agencies engaged in nanotechnology research." In 2008 and 2011, the NNI published a *Nanotechnology Environmental, Health, and Safety Research Strategy*,[26] which is intended to provide a research framework in the core areas of human exposure, the

---

[25]See National Nanotechnology Institute website, available at http://nano.gov (last visited August 29, 2014).

[26]National Nanotechnology Institute, *Environmental, Health, and Safety Issues,* available at http://www.nano.gov/you/environmental-health-safety (last visited August 29, 2014).

environment, human health, and measurement tools, and risk assessment and risk management, along with research needs in predictive modeling.

Nevertheless, experts already see a lot of nanotech litigation coming.[27] "Product liability and toxic exposure attorneys," says Ronald Wernette, author of the Nanotort Law Blog, "suggest that the first civil tort suits will be filed within the next five years. They anticipate a variety of claims, including consumer claims based on the fear of future physical harm. At issue could be whether manufacturers of consumer products appropriately tested nanomaterials, whether the government approved the product, and whether the potential harms were adequately disclosed. ... Employees of nano-material manufacturers are likely to bring exposure claims, and ... theories applied to nanotechnology claims will include defective design, defective manufacturing, and failure to warn claims."[28]

This could all actually be positive news for companies thinking about constructing a nanotaggant network; maybe by the time the taggants are ready for prime time, either the NNI or the courts will have established some helpful guidelines for avoiding liability.

Even when digital information masquerades as physical, it is important to remind ourselves of the important differences between the two. This chapter has explored one of those reasons – namely, that certain legal principles apply only to real property. The next chapter discusses another difference – namely, the fact that only physical objects can hurt you.

---

[27]Peter E. Masaitis, *Not Such a Small Thing: The Litigation Risks of Nanothechnology,* Industry Week (September 18, 2009), available at http://www.industryweek.com/companies-amp-executives/not-such-small-thing-litigation-risks-nanotechnology (last visited August 29, 2014).

[28]Ron Wernette, *The Rise of Nanotech Litigation* from the Winter 2010 Issue of the ABA Section of Litigation magazine, Litigation News – "The Rise of Nanotech Litigation," Nanotort Law Blog (February 3, 2010), available at http://www.nanotortlaw.com/2010/02/03/the-rise-of-nanotech-litigation/ (last visited August 29, 2014).

Torts and Personal Injury

7

INFORMATION IN THIS CHAPTER:

- Intentional torts
- Negligence
- Products liability
- Automotive safety

INTRODUCTION

This chapter addresses the different ways in which augmented reality experiences could contribute to, or help avoid, individuals becoming physically injured. When injuries happen, civil lawsuits, known as "torts," often follow. Although "some torts are also crimes punishable with imprisonment, the primary aim of tort law is to provide relief for the damages incurred and deter others from committing the same harms."[1]

Torts are generally subdivided into three general categories, according to the mental state of the person committing them. "Intentional" torts are exactly what they sound like: unlawful acts done on purpose and designed to injure another person. There are also "strict liability" torts, which are imposed upon those who commit them regardless of the defendant's mental state or even awareness that they were doing something unlawful. Copyright infringement, for example, is a strict liability tort; it isn't necessary to prove that the infringer intended to copy the copyrighted work.

The most common, however, are torts of negligence – in which a defendant is held liable for an injury even though they did not intend to cause it. This type of liability is imposed when, in the eyes of the law, the defendant should have both foreseen the risk of injury and done something to prevent it. These sorts of torts take various forms, including slip-and-fall incidents, automobile crashes, and product liability. This chapter will primarily focus on these types of claims. The unique manner in which the medium of augmented reality blends digital and physical data together is likely to lead to all manner of unintended – yet logically foreseeable – accidental injuries of each variety.

---

[1]Cornell University Law School, Legal Information Institute, *Tort,* available at http://www.law.cornell.edu/wex/tort (last visited August 29, 2014).

INTENTIONAL TORTS

Before diving in to the many ways in which AR might accidentally lead to injury, it is worth considering whether it could be done on purpose.

ASSAULT

In common speech, the word "assault" is almost never heard apart from the term "battery." We use them together in a phrase to describe a physical attack on a person. Because AR deals with the non-corporeal, it may seem strange to suggest that one could use digital imagery to commit an assault.

Between the two terms, however, only "battery" actually describes a physical touching. "Assault" is an act intended to, and which directly or indirectly does, cause a person to reasonably *apprehend* an imminent harmful or offensive contact. In other words, it is the act of causing someone to fear they are about to be hurt. Raising my fist at someone is an assault; actually punching them is a battery.

Understood in this way, we can begin to see how an illusion projected in AR could startle someone into believing they are about to be harmed. For this theory to work, however, the context would have to be just right. That is because the victim's fear of imminent contact must be a "reasonable" one. "Reasonable" is a legal term of art indicating an objective, not simply subjective, standard. A silly, impaired, or inattentive person might fear an 8-bit *Minecraft* character that appears to be jumping out of a screen, but a reasonable person would not.

In order to create a reasonable fear of contact, then, the illusion would have to be both *believable* and *unexpected*. The graphical resolution must be sufficiently high that the image could pass, at least for a moment, as for being physically tangible. That is exactly the degree of realism that most creators of AR content strive for, so it is reasonable to expect a fair amount of such content to be available, hardware allowing. It must also be unexpected because it would not be reasonable to be startled by something you already know is coming.

Both of these requirements could be met by an experience that is sufficiently immersive. And unlike other forms of digital imagery, immersion is exactly the type of experience that AR is intended to create. By definition, a user immersed in an augmented experience subjectively loses touch with the distinction between the digital and physical aspects of his experience. It is in that state when the user could be expected to mistake a digital object coming at him as something capable of inflicting physical harm. But the immersion would need to be complete for a tort claim to have any credibility. It is difficult to foresee a circumstance in which a digital object seen only through a mobile phone or tablet could reasonably be mistaken for something real; more than likely, digital eyewear or a physical installation would be required.

"Intent" is another important element of this claim. Creators of augmented experiences should not take undue comfort in their lack of subjective intent to assault anyone. Tort law distinguishes between the intent to do an act from the intent to cause the resulting harm. Here is where foreseeability comes into play. If someone does something on purpose, and should have known that it would cause a harmful

FIGURE 7.1

Screenshot from a Ghost-in-the-Ad video.[3]

consequence, that person can be held liable for an intentional tort. In this context, therefore, if an experience designer programs a digital creature to jump out in front of a user, and should have known that this would cause a reasonable user to believe, even if just for a moment, that they were in danger of physical harm, the creator could be exposed to liability for the intentional tort of assault.

The types of applications most likely to include such content – for example, Halloween-themed haunted house augmentations or a ghost storybook[2] – are also those in which the user is most likely to see it coming, or at least to have taken upon themselves the risk of being frightened. But humor being what it is, spooks and scares often crop up in the most unlikely places. Take, for example, the viral "fake ad" videos easily found on YouTube. These follow the common theme of peaceful music playing over a bucolic scene – often a car driving through rolling plains – for several seconds, which is suddenly and jarringly interrupted by a ghost or other scary figure jumping up in the foreground and shrieking. Many of these are so well-designed that it's difficult not to at least jump, even when you know what's coming (Fig. 7.1).

Similar humor has already emerged in the augmented medium. For example, in March 2014, one major retail brand secretly installed video augmentation in the transparent glass sidewall of a London bus stop. A popular online video shows fallen meteorites, alien attacks, sea monsters rising out of the sewers, and pouncing Bengal tigers – along with the predictably startled pedestrians waiting inside. Some of the scenes, like the laser-blasting robot walking down the street, are obviously

---

[2]See, e.g., "Scary Ghosts Come To Life In New Augmented Reality App From Goosebottom Books," Social Times, September 4, 2012 http://socialtimes.com/scary-ghosts-come-to-life-in-new-augmented-reality-app-from-goosebottom-books_b177104

FIGURE 7.2

Screenshot from the augmented bus shelter.

fantastical,[3] but others are not so easy to discern. According to a report in the London Mirror, "With the regular street appearing 'as normal' through the glass passersby have no reason to suspect a Kraken emerging from the sewers isn't real. The brilliant stunt seemed to fool some, with many of the reactions downright hilarious."[4] Indeed, some pedestrians are shown literally jumping out of their seats and running from the apparent danger (Fig. 7.2).

Moreover, ads designed to surprise pedestrians have already led to physical injury and legal claims. In 2013, a woman using a staircase in New York City's Grand Central Station fell and broke her ankle, allegedly because a spooky advertisement on the front-facing portions of the steps startled her. The poster was a close-up of "Dexter" star Michael C. Hall with cellophane covering his face. According to her lawsuit, Ajanaffy Njewadda was distraught as she descended the staircase looking for her husband, from whom she had gotten separated. When she turned around to go back up the stairs, the advertisement frightened her. She lost her balance and fell, resulting in a broken ankle and a concussion.[5]

With augmentation of physical installations becoming more common, similarly shocking AR ads are bound to start popping up. Whether any of them are so immersive

---

[3]Then again, Orson Welles probably thought the same thing in 1938 when he performed his original War of the Worlds radio broadcast, but that didn't prevent large numbers of people from panicking. Stejan Lovgen, *"War of the Worlds": Behind the 1938 Radio Show Panic,* National Geographic News, (June 17, 2005), available at http://news.nationalgeographic.com/news/2005/06/0617_050617_warworlds.html (last visited August 29, 2014).

[4]Ben Burrows, *Video: Watch incredible augmented reality bus stop that scares Oxford Street commuters stiff,* Mirror, (March 21, 2014), available at http://www.mirror.co.uk/news/weird-news/video-watch-incredible-augmented-reality-3268061 (last visited August 29, 2014).

[5]James Fanelli, *Woman Scared by 'Dexter' Ad Sues MTA for Subway Fall,* DNAinfo New York, (June 25, 2014), available at http://www.dnainfo.com/new-york/20140625/midtown/woman-scared-by-dexter-ad-sues-mta-for-subway-fall (last visited August 29, 2014).

or frightening as to cause a reasonable apprehension of immediate and unwanted physical contact remains to be seen. But it seems likely that the providers of at least some displays may need to defend themselves against such claims before long.

INTENTIONAL INFLICTION OF EMOTIONAL DISTRESS

This tort, known as "IIED" for short, is a relatively new development in tort law. Courts have historically been hesitant to recognize and compensate injuries that are purely emotional, rather than physical, in nature. Such harm is difficult to verify and quantify. Perhaps as a result, the standard one must meet to prevail on an IIED claim is intentionally demanding. A plaintiff must prove extreme and outrageous conduct that intentionally or recklessly causes severe emotional distress. Hurt feelings or rudeness is not enough. A classic way that courts have traditionally explained the standard of proof is that the conduct must be such that it would cause a reasonable person to exclaim "Outrageous!" in response.

Despite the demanding level of proof required, it is actually easier to imagine scenarios in which creators of augmented experiences could be held liable for this tort than for the tort of assault. That is because society is already rife with individuals who intentionally bully, stalk, harass, abuse, and intimidate others in outrageous ways. AR would simply be another medium into which such people could extend their activity.

Take, for example, the phenomenon of student bullying. Whether or not one agrees with the prevailing wisdom that this activity is pandemic in contemporary society, it cannot be denied that many teens already use technology to harass and pick on others. There have been several high-profile examples in recent years of young people committing suicide after being targeted for ridicule through digital media. In 2010, a Rutgers University freshman jumped to his death after his roommate, Dharun Ravi, used Twitter and iChat to publish live video of the freshman kissing another man.[6] In 2013, a 12-year-old Florida girl killed herself after being relentlessly harassed through online message boards and texts by as many as 15 girls.[7]

Such poor judgment is not limited to teens. In 2010, Michigan couple Scott and Jennifer Petkov reportedly used Facebook (among other means, such as driving in front of the girl's house with a truck adorned in hateful messages) to taunt and harass a terminally ill child – even going so far as to post photoshopped pictures of the young girl's face above crossbones, and of her late mother in the embrace of the Grim Reaper (Fig. 7.3). Certainly, if any conduct could provoke an involuntary outcry of "outrageous," it would be that. Yet it is also uncomfortably reminiscent of other hate-motivated crimes that many individuals have historically inflicted on entire groups of people on account of their race, ethnicity, sexuality, and other attributes.

---

[6]Wikipedia, *Suicide of Tyler Clementi,* available at http://en.wikipedia.org/wiki/Suicide_of_Tyler_Clementi (last visited August 29, 2014).

[7]Fox News, *Girls, 12 and 14, arrested in death of bullied Florida girl who killed herself,* (October 15, 2013), available at http://www.foxnews.com/us/2013/10/15/girls-12-and-14-arrested-in-death-bullied-florida-girl-police-say/ (last visited August 29, 2014).

FIGURE 7.3

One of Jennifer Petkov's hateful Facebook images.

Anyone with a motivation to intimidate and easy access to AR-creation tools is likely to be tempted to use the medium for hateful purposes. The same aspects of augmented expression that make it so attractive to artists, industrialists, and advertisers will also offer new opportunities for harassment. Today, for example, students often create fake social media profiles for people they wish to target. Tomorrow, they may create augmented content visible on the targeted person themselves – the digital equivalent of a "Kick Me" sign on their back. Tomorrow's Jennifer Petkov might litter her neighbor's lawn with augmented taunts, while a racist down the street may target an ethnic minority's home with digital burning crosses. Augmented reality is simply a medium; what a society chooses to publish in that medium will be a reflection of the messages that society wishes to convey – just as we see in social media today.

One issue that today's digital media providers largely do not need to concern themselves with is the risk of accidental injury due to the use of their publications. The unique blend of digital and physical that defines AR, however, brings such concerns to the forefront.

NEGLIGENCE

"Negligence is one of the greatest sources of litigation (along with contract and business disputes) in the United States."[8] Anyone who has picked up a telephone directory, driven past a bus stop, or watched daytime television understands this intuitively

---

[8]Law.com, *Negligence,* available at http://dictionary.law.com/default.aspx?selected=1314 (last visted August 29, 2014).

because there is never a shortage of personal injury attorneys soliciting new clients. But what exactly *is* negligence?

THE ELEMENTS OF A NEGLIGENCE CLAIM

Although each state has its own body of law on the subject, negligence is generally defined as "failure to exercise the care toward others which a reasonable or prudent person would do in the circumstances, or taking action which such a reasonable person would not."[9] In order to recover on a claim alleging injury caused by a defendant's negligence, a plaintiff must typically prove:

1. The defendant owed plaintiff a duty of care, which usually means that the risk to plaintiff was reasonably foreseeable, and that defendant should have taken precautions to prevent the injury. There are also situations in which defendant owe a special duty to the plaintiff, whether by agreement or by operation of law under the circumstances.

2. The standard of care that the defendant owed. Generally, this will be the duty of acting as a reasonable person would act under the circumstances. This is an objective standard, but can sometimes be influenced by the circumstances of the case.

3. The defendant breached the standard of care. This requires proof of what the defendant did and why those actions failed to live up to the duty required of them. Under limited circumstances, circumstantial evidence can be used to prove what the defendant must have done, even though no direct evidence exists. This is known as the doctrine of *res ipsa loquitur*, which is Latin for "the thing speaks for itself."

4. The defendant's breach of their duty caused plaintiff's injury. This is often one of the more difficult factors to prove, especially when plaintiff's injuries were only an indirect result of defendant's actions. The plaintiff must prove not only that defendant was the factual cause of the injury – in other words, that the injury would not have happened but for defendant's actions – but also that defendant was the "proximate cause." This is basically a legal policy judgment of whether there was a sufficient link between a "cause" and its indirect "effect" that it is fair to hold the defendant liable. Issues of proximate cause come into play when there are multiple steps that occur between what the defendant did and what happened to the plaintiff. At some point, the indirect consequences of a defendant's actions become so remote and unforeseeable that it would no longer be just to hold defendant accountable for the result.

5. The plaintiff suffered damages as a result of the negligence. Damages are not presumed, as they are by some other legal theories. Typical types of damages in negligence cases include pain and suffering, medical expenses, and lost income. The court will also consider what the plaintiff should have done to mitigate their own injuries.

---

[9] *Id.*

With this understanding of what it takes to prove a negligence claim, how might augmented reality lead to negligence liability?

AUGMENTED REALITY GAMES AND PHYSICAL INJURY

I love games, especially the type that really engage your mind and force you to solve problems creatively. By all indications, I'm not alone. In 2013, the video game industry reportedly made $21 billion in the United States alone.[10] In March 2014, as online game company King Digital Entertainment prepared to go public, its runaway hit *Candy Crush* claimed 408 million active monthly users.[11] When *Grand Theft Auto V* – a game that cost $265 million to make – hit the market in September 2013, it reached $1 billion in sales in only *three days*.[12]

So you can bet that games will be among the first commercially successful augmented reality applications. Indeed, it has been persuasively argued[13] that it will be games that take AR into the mainstream. In 2010, Australian media professional Gary Hayes wrote: "Expect lots and lots of horror, crime and murder mystery ... locative AR games popping up in the next few years and months given the ease in which those genre can be adapted to 'location' points around any urban area and hunt for clue or task based play."[14] As one example, he pointed to "Operation SC Revelation," a transmedia campaign supporting the launch of Ubsoft's *Splinter Cell* video game. The promoters "set up an extra level in augmented reality ... a real-life fox-hunt played by walking through Amsterdam whilst looking through a smartphone that used the Layar-AR-browser. Layar showed what was around the players by displaying augmented reality seen through the camera of their smartphone."[15] A more recent example is the massively multiplayer game *Ingress* from Niantic Labs, which is easily the most popular entry in the genre to date. Thousands of players across the world, divided into two factions, compete to either protect or destroy virtual "portals" whose locations are tied to an actual, physical landmark. In order to manipulate a virtual object, a player must be in close physical proximity to its assigned location.

---

[10]Kate Cox, *It's Time to Start Treating Video Game Industry Like the $21 Billion Business It Is,* Consumerist, (June 9, 2014), available at http://consumerist.com/2014/06/09/its-time-to-start-treating-video-game-industry-like-the-21-billion-business-it-is/ (last visited August 29, 2014).

[11]Matt Krantz, *Candy Crush King IPO: $22.50, Trades Wednesday,* USA Today, (March 25, 2014), available at http://www.usatoday.com/story/money/markets/2014/03/25/candy-crush-king-ipo-price/6879681/ (last viewed August 29, 2014).

[12]Kate Cox, *It's Time to Start Treating Video Game Industry Like the $21 Billion Business It Is,* Consumerist, (June 9, 2014), available at http://consumerist.com/2014/06/09/its-time-to-start-treating-video-game-industry-like-the-21-billion-business-it-is/ (last visited August 29, 2014).

[13]Ori Inbar, *3 Reasons Why Games Are the Killer App for Augmented Reality,* Games Alfresco, (August 30, 2010), available at http://gamesalfresco.com/2010/08/30/3-reasons-why-games-are-the-killer-app-for-augmented-reality/ (last visited August 29, 2014).

[14]Gary Hayes, *Future of Location Based Augmented Reality Story Games,* Personalizemedia, (October 25, 2010), available at http://www.personalizemedia.com/future-of-location-based-augmented-reality-story-games/ (last visited August 29, 2014).

[15]*Id.*

But AR games carry at least one risk that the console-based games never did: physical injury.

The risks inherent in location-based AR games

Many digital games that incorporate some degree of AR pose no discernible risk of physical injury, because they do not require anything more from players than any other mobile game does. These include the dozens of "AR" games that are little more than a regular game superimposed on a live video feed. It also includes games that require the player to remain stationary, such as Total Immersion's 2011 release "SkinVaders," which used magic mirror-type technology to superimpose invading aliens onto the user's face.

Rather, the risk of injury comes with games that involve movement and genuine interaction with the player's physical environment. In these cases, injured players of AR games will argue that, by directing players to travel to various locations and perform certain tasks, the game designers undertook a duty to ensure that those activities would not place the players at undue risk of injury. These lawsuits will involve ascertaining just what duty the game designers owed to their players, whether they breached that duty, and whether the breach was the proximate cause of the player's injuries.

To date, one of the most vivid illustrations of the risks inherent in this type of game is the 2011 trailer published online for *The Witness*, an AR game that billed itself as "The First Movie in the Outernet" (Fig. 7.4). As described by the trailer, *The Witness* is much more like a mobile version of an online role-playing / mystery game than like anything one would currently think of as a "movie." Using AR-equipped video phones, players roam the physical world "collecting data" and "communicating with other players." Like a walking, talking version of a *Choose Your Own Adventure* book, the game directs players to different locations based on the choices

FIGURE 7.4

Scene from the trailer for *The Witness*.

they make – eventually solving the mystery, or else meeting one of a variety of alternate endings to the story.

But unlike someone playing a similar detective game on a board, console, or (non-location-based) mobile device, a player of *The Witness* faces potential dangers in the real world as well. The trailer shows players in seedy hotels and bars, a disheveled office, climbing stairs in a parking garage during winter, and scurrying through an abandoned warehouse – complete with barking guard dogs – in order to collect the clues necessary to "stay in the game."

In all likelihood, these scenes were probably amped up for dramatic effect. And there may have been safety measures in place that the trailer doesn't mention. As depicted, however, they just scream with the potential for personal injury. One scene shows a player scanning a room with his phone, looking for clues. What if he gets distracted and trips over something, or something falls on him while he's rooting around under a desk? Will the guard dogs always be there, and if so, will there be a staff member there 24/7 to make sure they don't bite anyone? Suppose a player gets mugged in one of these abandoned buildings, or falls on poorly-maintained stairs? The possible scenarios for injury multiply with every new setting.

On September 13, 2012, Dreamworks' Director of Global Interactive Chris Hewish gave a wide-ranging keynote address on Hollywood's use of augmented reality at *Vox: the 4D Summit*, an event for creatives that Daqri hosted in Long Beach, California. One of the examples he cited was *The Witness*, and he played the trailer for the audience.

During the talk, Chris shared these thoughts on whether games like *The Witness* posed a risk of injury, and whether anyone in Hollywood was yet thinking about these issues:

> *I think we're still really early on, and what you're seeing here are great examples of pioneers, who tend to be outside of the normal boundaries, willing to take risks and not as worried about the consequences. Which is great, and that's how you push the medium.*
>
> *I think in order for big Hollywood companies to get onboard, they're going to want to do something that has zero liability potential. And that's where I think you'll see these sorts of things become prevalent in established location-based entertainment. So, if you're able to go to Disneyland and participate in the equivalent of* The Witness *in a safe, controlled environment, now you're talking. Now you've avoided a lot of those risks.*
>
> *There's also the fact of a low barrier to entry. People are already used to going to Disneyland, so you don't have to convince them to go somewhere that's strange or new. You're just bringing them to somewhere they're familiar with and building on that experience.*

In other words, even if they've never had to worry about their viewers hurting themselves before, major content producers creating their own, self-administered immersive experiences are both smart and risk-averse. They are not likely to send users off to remote locations outside the company's control, for a host of safety- and business-related reasons. On the other end of the spectrum, start-up entertainment companies with shoe-string budgets may not ever worry about (or even consider) the risk of getting sued if players looking for digital data physically hurt themselves in the process.

But as Chris suggested, there will still be plenty of creators who take risks in order to push the medium forward. Those who do so and who have enough assets to create a very attractive location-based AR experience will create a tempting litigation target for would-be plaintiffs. Those entrepreneurs should not be afraid to continue innovating, but should get informed legal advice before encouraging their users to take any sort of risks in the real world.

Other games already in existence demonstrate the inevitable physical risks that come from requiring players to move from place to place. I have interviewed the players of some of these games. One admitted to slipping on ice and twisting their ankle; the other got themselves a bit scuffed up while searching through bushes for the exact coordinates of a virtual object. Additional potential avenues for mishaps were spotted and avoided. For example, they told me about one digital object that was originally located in the driveway for a hospital emergency room. This was reported to the game's designers, who moved it out of the way. Lessons like these should help future game designers avoid similar issues.

I have also wondered whether AR games will put players in dangerous situations that make them more vulnerable to criminal activity. It turns out that there is already a healthy debate on this very point among my new friends' community of players. Some say yes, and are wary of going certain places at certain times. Others argue that encouraging presumably law-abiding gamers to visit areas they don't normally frequent will have a "neighborhood watch" effect, essentially deterring crime in those areas. Time will tell on that point, and both arguments are likely to find supporting examples as time goes on.

On the plus side, though; AR games are already liberating players from their couches and getting them into the real world. My new friends report that they already get more exercise and have visited more local landmarks than they otherwise would have.

When might game designers be liable for physical injury?

AR game designers should consider the foreseeable ways in which players could injure themselves while playing the game, and take reasonable steps to minimize that risk. The most obvious way of satisfying this duty is to convey appropriate disclosures and warnings to users before they play. As of this writing, for example, the guidelines for *Ingress* players warn against trespassing onto private property, unwanted physical contact with others, unwanted recording of others, and insulting other players. They also include such blanket statements as "you are responsible for your own conduct and content while using the Products, and for any consequences thereof. You agree to use the Products only for purposes that are lawful, proper and in accordance with the Terms."[16]

---

[16]Ingress, *Ingress Terms of Service: Last Modified November 14, 2013*, available at https://www.ingress.com/terms (last visited on September 4, 2014).

In the absence of such precautions and warnings, however, an AR company may bear some measure of risk whenever it directs users to travel to a new location. The nature of the gaming experience can amplify that risk. *The Witness*, for example, says that players will need to "overcome their fear," as "the borders between reality and fiction dissolve completely." All of which makes the game that much more engaging and enjoyable; suspension of disbelief and an immersive experience are what every good storyteller aims for. But when you're walking around in the real world, you rely on those "borders between reality and fiction" to avoid hurting yourself.

We don't need to wait for mainstream AR gaming to see how courts might apportion liability for game-related injuries. Consider the 2000 decision of the Washington Court of Appeals in *Anderson v. American Restaurant Group*.[17] Plaintiff Anderson "suffered injuries when she slipped and fell while running across the bathroom floor at the Black Angus restaurant in Bellevue to retrieve a piece of toilet paper for a restaurant-sponsored scavenger hunt." Even though a wet bathroom floor is the type of dangerous condition that one might expect to be obvious, the appeals court reversed the trial court's judgment in favor of the restaurant. "[A] jury could conclude," the court explained, "that Black Angus should have expected that patrons darting into the bathroom would not discover or realize the danger of a wet floor because they would be focused elsewhere and in a hurry."

In a similar vein – but with much more severe consequences – is the case of Bob Lord. He was an internet entrepreneur and first-time player of "The Game," a private, invitation-only, immersive role-playing game remarkably similar to the Michael Douglas movie of the same name. As summarized in a September 14, 2008 *Seattle Times* article, "The Game" was an annual "adventure scavenger hunt" in which adult players "would scuba dive, rock climb, sing karaoke with a drag queen and fire automatic weapons … decode the Declaration of Independence inside a prison and befriend a white rat named Templeton, whose shivering little body carried a message."[18]

The 2002 version of The Game also involved searching for particular GPS coordinates inside "the Argentena Mine complex, a warren of abandoned openings left over from a 1927 silver-mining operation." Lord had gotten little sleep over the 28 hours before the time he entered the mines. Confused by the Game's ambiguous directions, he entered the wrong shaft, and fell 30 feet head-first, crushing his vertebrae and becoming a C3 quadriplegic for the rest of his life. When Lord's family discovered that the Game planners had been warned about mine's dangers beforehand, Lord sued them, and eventually settled for $10.6 million.

More recent are the examples of Kim Flint and Chris Bucchere, two California bicyclists who were involved in fatal accidents in 2010 and 2012, respectively.[19] Flint lost control while descending down a steep road and suffered fatal injuries. Bucchere struck Sutchi Hui, a 71-year-old pedestrian, killing him. Both riders were also active

---

[17]No. 44488-3-I (Wash. Ct. App. November 6, 2000).

[18]Jonathan Martin, *The Game,* The Seattle Times, (September 14, 2008), available at http://seattletimes.com/html/pacificnw/2008177548_pacificpendgame14.html (last visited on September 4, 2014).

[19]David Darlington, *The Strava Files,* Bicycling, available at http://www.bicycling.com/news/featured-stories/strava-files (last visited on September 4, 2014).

users of Strava, the mobile app that tracks riders' speeds and elevations and allows them to share results with each other through social networks. Riders who achieve the top speed on any given segment re awarded the title of KOM or QOM (King, or Queen, of the Mountain). Flint's family sued Strava for negligence, arguing that the company "breached their duty of care by: (1) failing to warn cyclists competing in KOM challenge that the road conditions were not suited for racing and that it was unreasonably dangerous given those conditions; (2) failing to take adequate measures to ensure the KOM challenges took place on safe courses; and (3) encouraging dangerous behavior." A judge ultimately dismissed the lawsuit in 2013, finding that responsibility for safety lay with the riders themselves.[20] Many of those following the case were not so convinced, however. The Flint family's attorney explained the theory of their case this way:

> *"The social network is a secondary function of their true business, which is profiting on what they call segments. The goal of these segments is to obtain the fastest pace. If you want to not call it a cycling race and call it a segment, that's fine,"* she told VeloNews. *"Our main point was that, look, Strava is behaving a lot like a race course organizer, bringing people together in some capacity. ... Why should Strava not be held to the same standards of any race organizer? They're making money based on faster and faster times. Sounds like a race organizer, right? It's a difficult case to make, but my overall sense of it is that something doesn't smell right."*[21]

One has to wonder how different the facts would have had to be before the case came out differently.

The typical AR game of the near future will almost certainly not involve circumstances as dangerous as those in The Game or injuries as severe as Flint's. But as the *Anderson* case demonstrates, even a condition as mundane and obvious as a wet bathroom floor can become a source of potential liability when game players are sent out into the physical world hunting for clues and competing against other players under short deadlines. AR game designers – including marketing stunts that require individuals to search for clues within a physical environment – must take these risks into account when creating their fictional experiences. Although it may present frustrations on a creative level, designers must take all due care not to sacrifice gamers' physical safety for the sake of an immersive gaming experience.

The special case of underage users

Location-based augmented reality games are growing in popularity. This mainstream appeal has led to some chance encounters that have some players wondering whether they could get in hot water for making the wrong sort of teammates.

---

[20]Brian Holcomb, *Strava wins dismissal of civil suit over Berkeley death,* VeloNews, (June 4, 2013), available at http://velonews.competitor.com/2013/06/news/strava-wins-dismissal-of-civil-suit-over-berkeley-death_289714 (last visited on September 4, 2014).
[21]*Id.*

For example, when one of these games recently graduated from beta testing, droves of curious players flocked to try it out. But this led an anonymous local player to recently share with me the following thoughts:

> One of the old timers ... was talking to a new player in the in-game team chat system ..., doing what we all often do for new players... offering to drop them gear to help them level up, and even going on an "AP run" which is the ... equivalent of a lioness chewing up a wildebeest a little so her cubs can learn to catch it.
> Other players were trying to get his attention because they knew the new player in question was a 12 year old girl.
> So yeah, some 30-something guy was unknowingly soliciting a rendezvous with a young minor. Honest mistake, but it opens up a number of questions.
> You probably know better than me that I think all player interactive games have an EULA requiring them to be at least 13 years old. So while 13 year olds game against 30 year olds every day, forming clans, chatting on audio services like TeamSpeak, that has come to be accepted as okay as long as someone isn't trying to do something illegal.
> But now you have a game in physical places you must physically be at. On one hand it seems stupid and silly for it to be taboo for say a 16 year old with a couple twenty-somethings to walk around and hit some public portals. But people are really touchy, so... dammit I don't know.

So, could adult players end up in trouble for using AR games to schedule a rendezvous with a minor? Should teens be wary of playing the games (to the extent that teens are wary about anything)?

The best answer to both questions is probably "only to the same extent they would in other, non-game circumstances." But players of all ages should remain aware about these and other issues. Just because it's a game doesn't necessarily make it a good idea to meet up with strangers at night, for example. And if you're an adult who happens to connect with a younger person, it's probably smart to remain in public view at all times.

Designers of AR games should likewise take into account the anticipated age range of their users when establishing game protocols. In many cases, it may well be that no further action is necessary on the game company's part other than to rely on the terms of use in the app stores that provide the game, or to include language in the game's terms of use that forbid underage users (much like Facebook and other social media platforms currently do.) Depending on the circumstances of a particular game, however – especially if it is intentionally marketed to a younger audience – greater care may be required to avoid putting minors in harm's way.

AUGMENTED DISTRACTIONS AND PHYSICAL INJURY

Just like the challenges of walking and chewing gum that came before it, today's generation has encountered its share of incidents associated with walking and texting on a mobile device. Some of those have been spectacularly "epic fails," to use the vernacular. In March 2012, for example, Michigan resident Bonnie Miller became an international poster child for the dangers of walking and texting when she walked straight off the end of a pier while checking her phone.[22] In 2009, Alexa Longueira, a teenager from Staten Island, New York, fell into an open manhole while reading a text on her friend's cellphone. According to a local news report, she fell 6 feet into four inches of raw sewage.[23] YouTube also has its share of local news broadcasts containing footage of falling pedestrians.[24]

With this in mind, how will a new class of augmented wearable devices affect pedestrian safety? On one hand, transparent digital eyewear may actually be safer than today's mobile devices, which require users to look down at them. Writing in the *MIT Technology Review*, cognitive science professor and designed Don Norman notes, "[u]nlike 'immersive' displays that capture your full attention, [Google] Glass is deliberately designed to be inconspicuous and non-distracting. The display is only in the upper right of the visual field, the goal being to avoid diverting the user's attention and to provide relevant supplementary information only when needed."[25] Among the current crop of digital eyewear either on the market or promised soon, Glass is the least "immersive" of the group in this way, and partially for this reason.

"Even so," Norman argues, "the risk of [any digital eyewear] distracting the user is significant." [26] That is because the modern virtue of "multitasking" is a myth. "Numerous psychology experiments show that when two relatively complex tasks are done at the same time, performance deteriorates measurably."[27] A 2013 study from Carnegie Mellon, for example, noted that juggling email, texts, and social media while in the office notably decreased the efficiency of employees, even when they knew ahead of time that they would be interrupted.[28] Moreover, the device manufacturer has only limited control over the user experience. Once third parties start providing software applications for the device, users will be able to customize their experience.

Used intentionally and effectively, however, wearable technology can actually enhance concentration and retention. Thad Starner is a founder and director of the Contextual Computing Group at Georgia Tech's College of Computing, where he is a professor. He has been a wearable computing advocate for almost 25 years, and has given examples of how the devices improve his ability to remember details, even

---

[22]Deborah Netburn, *For some, texting and walking don't mix,* Los Angeles Times, (March 26, 2012), available at http://articles.latimes.com/2012/mar/26/business/la-fi-tn-warning-texting-while-walking-20120326 (last visited on September 4, 2014).

[23]*Id.*

[24]See, e.g., theChomchom10, *Girl falls texting on live news,* YouTube, (uploaded on February 15, 2012), available at https://www.youtube.com/watch?v=g3jOlQqDPzQ (last visited on September 4, 2014).

[25]Don Norman, *The Paradox of Wearable Technologies,* MIT Technology Review, (July 24, 2013), available at http://www.technologyreview.com/news/517346/the-paradox-of-wearable-technologies/?goback=%2Egde_4437607_member_260638211#%21 (last visited on September 4, 2014).

[26]*Id.*

[27]*Id.*

[28]Dan Bowens, *Study: Downside of Digital Multitasking,* my foxny.com, (Posted: May 15, 2013), available at http://www.myfoxny.com/story/22265626/study-downside-of-digital-multitasking (last visited on September 4, 2014).

years later, by allowing him to take detailed notes in real time.[29] Maintaining Starner's level of focus, however, may be more difficult for the average user. "Without the right approach, the continual distraction of multiple tasks exerts a toll. It takes time to switch tasks, to get back what attention theorists call 'situation awareness.'[30] It will also "be difficult to resist the temptation of using powerful technology that guides us with useful side information, suggestions, and even commands,"[31] with the result that it will become clear to those around us that our attention is divided.

These opposing factors create a paradox in which, according to Don Norman, "we will tread uneasily as we risk continual distraction, continual diversion of attention, and continual blank stares in hopes of achieving focused attention, continual enhancement, and better interaction, understanding, and retention."[32] As with anything else, how an individual uses wearable technology ultimately depends on that person. Norman, however, is not entirely persuaded even by that conclusion. Noting the power that even today's instant-access, internet-enabled devices already have, he asserts that "[t]he providers of these technologies must share the burden of responsible design."[33]

Plaintiffs' attorneys representing those injured by distracted users will certainly agree. In an interview I conducted with a successful personal injury attorney, he admitted that he and others in his practice would look for any chance they could find to name the product manufacturer as a defendant in such a case. Their argument would be that the product itself was unreasonably designed, so as to cause an unacceptable risk of distraction and injury. In the terminology of negligence law, the argument would be that the manufacturers owed a duty to those affected by the wearers of the product to design the experience in a way that maximally reduced the likelihood of injury.

A simple online search confirms that personal injury lawyers across the country are virtually frothing at the mouth to be the first to sue someone over their use of digital eyewear. New York personal injury lawyer Eric Turkewitz declared in his well-read blog that:

> "The chances of [digital eyewear] being a factor in people being maimed and killed is approximately 100%. .. Cocky [eyewear] users will walk into intersections and be hit by cars because they are getting a Facebook update on the latest cat video, or tweeting about the latest basketball buzzer beater. There won't be sympathy for them, of course, as people chalk this up to the culling of the masses with Darwinian behavior."[34]

---

[29]Don Norman, *The Paradox of Wearable Technologies,* MIT Technology Review, (July 24, 2013), available at http://www.technologyreview.com/news/517346/the-paradox-of-wearable-technologies/?goback=%2Egde_4437607_member_260638211#%21 (last visited on September 4, 2014).

[30]*Id.*

[31]*Id.*

[32]*Id.*

[33]*Id.*

[34]Eric Turkewitz, *Will Google Glass Kill?* New York Personal Injury Law Blog, (Posted March 13, 2013), available at http://www.newyorkpersonalinjuryattorneyblog.com/2013/03/will-google-glass-kill.html (last visited on September 4, 2014).

Similarly, a California law firm includes the article "[Digital] Glasses Could Cause Car Accidents" on its website.[35] This advertising smacks of opportunism and is noticeably devoid of direct factual support for the claim made in its headline. These ads demonstrate the mindset of eager lawyers looking for the next big revenue stream, and not necessarily the extent of any actual liability that digital eyewear manufacturers will face. Whether lawsuits over such basic digital eyewear use – especially over the more obvious risks that are inherent to all digital devices – could ever succeed remains to be seen.

The potential for such assertions of liability, however, is exactly why many of today's providers of augmented experiences include safety warnings with their products. For example, Qualcomm's Vuforia software is one of the most popular visual recognition tools in the AR industry. As of May 2014, over 100,000 developers of augmented reality experiences were using Vuforia code.[36] The terms of use governing Vuforia software instruct those developers to advise end users "of the hazards of using a camera based application while driving, walking, or otherwise by being distracted or disoriented from real world situations."[37] Similarly, when Google introduced Glass to its first sets of Glass Explorers, it warned them "not to use Glass while driving, biking, using sharp objects, or playing sports, and to use caution while walking and crossing streets. If they have any concern about the safety of using Glass, Google asks participants to stop using them and return them immediately."[38] These companies are forward-thinking enough to anticipate the risks discussed in this chapter and to take steps to avoid them. Other companies may not be as proactive.

DISRESPECTING THE PHYSICAL

Within the AR community, reference is sometimes made to Plato's theory of forms, also known as Platonic Realism. This view postulates that all material objects are merely copies or imitations of the abstract concept, or form, of the shape, and that it is the forms that are ultimately "real." AR's ability to depict seemingly physical objects in evanescent digital space has resurrected and given a new immediacy to the debate over the relative significance of the physical or digital versions of an object, or whether perhaps they are equally important.

There is one sense, however, in which the physical will always be more significant. Physical forms are able to injure a person if they collide hard enough, and

---

[35]Thomas G. Appel, *Google Glasses Could Cause Car Accidents,* Appel Law Firm LLP, (November 14, 2013), available at http://www.appellawyer.com/blog/google-glasses-cause-car-accidents/ (last visited on September 4, 2014).

[36]David Beard, *Vuforia Ecosystem Reaches 100K Registered Developers,* Qualcomm developer Network, (May 27, 2014), available at https://developer.qualcomm.com/blog/vuforia-ecosystem-reaches-100k-registered-developers (last visited on September 4, 2014).

[37]*Vuforia 2.8 License Agreement,* Qualcomm Vutoria Developer Portal (Rev. December 10, 2013, available at https://developer.vuforia.com/legal/license/2-8 (last visited September 4, 2014).

[38]Pete Pachall, *Google Glass Developer Conference Has Ultra-Strict Rules,* Mashable, (January 25, 2013), available at http://mashable.com/2013/01/25/google-glass-nda/ (last visited on September 4, 2014).

may be capable of supporting a person's weight if stepped on. Neither of these things is true of digital images or of abstract concepts. That fact is elementary, but it is worth remembering as we proceed toward more widespread adoption of AR throughout society.

Some AR environments may be so well-rendered that it becomes difficult for users to distinguish physical from digital. Making the wrong guess about whether an object is one or the other may lead to injury. Moreover, the very fact of being repeatedly presented with that ambiguity may eventually prove to have significant psychological consequences for many.

Some AR professionals have raised concern about what effect widespread adoption of AR may eventually have on peoples' subconscious appreciation of this very important distinction. Marianne Lindsell, an AR professional in the United Kingdom, raised this concern in an online conversation about a blog post of mine. She wrote: "This may have the potential to make users subconsciously learn to treat solid objects with less respect, with dangerous results." If, psychologically, individuals train themselves to recognize and manipulate 3D digital imagery as if it were part of their physical environment, will they occasionally forget that the digital images aren't actually there, or start treating physical objects (through inattention or misapprehension) as if they were insubstantial? Will they step on (and fall through) a digital floor panel, not realizing it's only digital? Or run into a very physical wall, having grown accustomed to being surrounded by digital representations of walls?

This is a subject worthy of additional study. The results may inform what legal duty the creators of AR environments have to remind users of what is real and digital.

INJURY DUE TO INACCURACY

Anyone who has used an AR app on a mobile device has likely had their enthusiasm for the medium tempered a bit by the unsteadiness of the digital image. An article in an Australian publication captured that feeling in the following quote from architect Rana Abboud, who has studied the technology's potential for the construction trades: "In some of the places I went to, the marketing around it was really glossy and amazing," Abboud said. "But you actually tried the application and things didn't quite work as planned. For instance, the Museum of Vancouver put out an app that we trialed and the tracking was not quite there, and things would disappear on you and then re-appear. It wasn't stable enough."[39]

Today's technology still predominately relies on visual recognition of either a 2D marker or other distinct physical object to act as the image's anchor in the real world. If the device's camera loses sight of that target for even a split second, the image may disappear or lose its physical orientation, requiring the user to start over. Similarly, images that rely on GPS or other location awareness technology are often unsteady

---

[39]Andrew Heaton, *Major Obstacles for AR on Construction Sites,* Sourceable, (April 8, 2014), available at http://sourceable.net/major-obstacles-for-ar-on-construction-sites/ (last visited on September 4, 2014).

or jerky, jumping around in different directions as the device struggles to maintain pinpoint accuracy.

Both types of errors create a risk of injury for anyone who relies on the accuracy of the image's location. If a court later determines that it was objectively reasonable for the injured party to have relied on the location data, the creator of the AR experience may be found liable for the injury. So, for example, if (as in the foregoing example from The Game) a user is following augmented walking directions that are marketed as being accurate, and those directions lead the user to fall in a hole, the provider of those directions may be held liable.

The injury resulting from locational inaccuracy might be economic as well. Abboud's study highlighted a number of potential uses for AR in construction, such as visualizing future additions, discovering the position of hidden or obscured elements within a structure, and increasing worker efficiency by using mobile devices to overlay modeling information over their field of view onsite.[40] "Incorrect, incomplete or out-of-date data, [however], could have serious consequences if it showed the wrong location for a hidden pipe, wall stud or cable."[41] Expenses from such construction errors as a result of sensor or GPS inaccuracy could potentially rival the savings from using the technology in the first place. For that reason, although Abboud sees the technology's use in construction as inevitable, it will not likely take hold for another 5-10 years.[42]

PRODUCTS LIABILITY

Another facet of tort law imposes liability on the manufacturers and distributors of commercial products that cause injury to users. These claims are typically grounded in the principles of negligence law, although the laws of various jurisdictions also create statutory and breach of warranty causes of action.

In order for liability to be imposed, the product must first be defective. Broadly speaking, there are three different types of defects: manufacturing, design, and marketing.[43] Manufacturing defects result from errors in the creation of a particular unit of a product that cause it to not meet the quality standards the product is designed to meet. By contrast, a defectively *designed* product behaves as it is intended to, but that intended function is one that causes an unacceptable risk of harm.

Marketing defects generally refer to a manufacturer's failure to warn users against hidden dangers. Unless the injury is one for which the law imposes strict liability, manufacturers can often avoid liability for many "defects" in design by clearly communicating the risk to the users.

What sort of arguments might be made by future plaintiffs alleging that an AR device or similar wearable technology caused them injury? The following discussion collects some of the more likely theories. Here again, it is worth repeating the

---

[40]*Id.*
[41]*Id.*
[42]*Id.*
[43]James Henderson, et al, The Torts Process 561 (Little, Brown & Co., 1994).

disclaimer that none of this discussion should be read to suggest that any one particular product is defective at all. The fact that some products have reached market before others means that critics and the press have tended to focus most of their speculation on those early entrants. As with each chapter in this book, however, this is speculative discussion of the augmented reality industry as a whole.

EYE STRAIN

As of this writing, Google Glass has been available for more than a year. Thousands of users, myself included, use them on a regular basis without ill effects. Some users, however, have complained about eye strain.

Dr. Eli Peli, M.Sc., O.D. is the Moakley Scholar in Aging Eye Research at Schepens Eye Research Institute, Massachusetts Eye and Ear, and Professor of Ophthalmology at Harvard Medical School.[44] He also consulted Google about the potential side-effects of using Glass. In May 2014, Dr. Peli started quite a buzz when he was quoted by *BetaBeat* as saying that prolonged use of the device would cause "a discomfort in the eye muscles,"[45] because the act of looking up – where the Glass display sits – is the least-comfortable eye movement. "If you're looking at the Glass for a minute," said Dr. Peli, "you're holding it there for sixty times longer than normal."[46]

Not long after the *BetaBeat* article was published, Dr. Peli took to his Google+ account to clarify his position:

- First and foremost, I have researched both HMDs and Glass for years and have found no evidence of any health risks.
- Relative to the thousands of people using Glass, very few have reported that they've had an issue with eye discomfort or headaches.
- For most, the discomfort usually goes away after a day or two as they get used to the device.
- This adaptation phenomenon is similar to the initial discomfort some people have when wearing a new pair of prescription glasses, which eventually goes away.
- Like any piece of technology, from TVs to smart phones, it's important that people find what's comfortable for them. That's why Explorers are encouraged to ease into Glass.
- Glass is designed for micro-interactions rather than long interactions like reading a book or watching a movie. The Glass team makes this clear in their Help Center.[47]

---

[44]*Eli Peli, M. Sc., O.D.,* Vision Rehabilitation Library, available at http://serinet.meei.harvard.edu/faculty/peli/ (last visited on September 4, 2014).

[45]Jack Smith IV, *Google's Eye Doctor Admits Class Can Cause Pain,* BetaBeat, (May 19, 2014), available at http://betabeat.com/2014/05/googles-eye-doctor-admits-glass-can-cause-pain/ (last visited on September 4, 2014).

[46]*Id.*

[47]Eli Peli, post on #Glasses, Google +, (May 21, 2014), available at https://plus.google.com/u/0/109037277404485472366/posts/WbJDtZ7CYVY (last visited on September 4, 2014).

Google itself likewise responded to the *BetaBeat* article by noting:

"When anyone gets a new pair of glasses or starts wearing them for the first time there is always an adjustment period until people get used to them. For some it's the same with Glass. We encourage Explorers to ease into Glass, just as they would a new pair of glasses. As we note in our Help Center, Glass is designed for micro-interactions, not for staring into the screen, watching Friday night movie marathons or reading 'War and Peace.'"[48]

That isn't to say that others haven't raised similar concerns. "Sina Fateh, an ophthalmologist who has filed at least 30 patents related to wearable displays, told Forbes that these types of devices can put unnecessary stress on the eyes."[49] Read together, however, these competing viewpoints establish an uncontroversial proposition: using digital eyewear more heavily than intended, especially if the user isn't accustomed to it, could cause discomfort. This is true of existing eyewear, and will be true of the digital variety. To simply identify a means by which users may possibly misuse a product, however, falls far short of suggesting any defect in its design.

It also remains to be seen how the design of future devices compares to those available now. Telepathy, a Japanese company, worked for years on a device that sits above the eye like Glass does. Vuzix, on the other hand, sells similarly monocular eyewear that sits below, rather than above, the eye. Other manufacturers have touted stereoscopic eyewear in varying shapes, sizes, and fits. The industry standard is certainly far from being set.

BLUNT TRAUMA

Anytime a device sits close to one's eye, the potential exists that it could impact the eye, causing injury. Of course, this is true of any eyewear, digital or otherwise. "Penetrating injuries are [already] widely reported with spectacle related eye trauma," reported the *British Journal of Opthalmology*, and "the trend for small frames and frameless spectacles and may place patients at [increased] risk of serious ocular injury."[50]

Therefore, merely making eyewear digital should not necessarily increase that risk. Dr. Farooq Ashraf, MD, FACS, medical director at Atlanta Vision Institute, has been quoted as saying "the risk of eye damage [from Glass] is minimal, especially when the wearer uses common sense and avoids situations where his or her eye could

---

[48]Jack Smith IV, *Google's Eye Doctor Admits Class Can Cause Pain*, BetaBeat, (May 19, 2014), available at http://betabeat.com/2014/05/googles-eye-doctor-admits-glass-can-cause-pain/ (last visited on September 4, 2014

[49]Lisa Eadicicco, *The Doctor Who Said Google Glass Causes Eye Pain Now Says There's NO Evidence of Health Risks,* Business Insider, (May 29, 2014), available at http://www.businessinsider.com/google-glass-complaints-2014-5 (last visited on September 9, 2014).

[50]J Clarke, R Newsom, and C Canning, *Ocular trauma with small framed spectacles,* Br J Ophthalmolv.86(4);(April 2002), PMC1771106, available at http://www.ncbi.nlm.nih.gov/pmc/articles/PMC1771106/ (last visited on September 4, 2014).

be impacted."[51] Here again, whether future devices accentuate this risk at all remains to be seen.

MOTION SICKNESS

As the capabilities of digital eyewear expand, they will offer users an increasing amount of visual information that they were not previously accustomed to receiving. What's more, different devices will vary in how acutely they deliver this information. These variances could make a significant difference in how users react physically to what they see.

A 2011 article in the *MIT Technology Review* called "Could Augmented Reality Be Hazardous to Your Health?"[52] focused on the research of Eric Sabelman, a functional neurosurgery bioengineer at Kaiser Permanente. According to Sabelman, ubiquitous digital information floating around our field of view is bound to have a range of physiological effects on AR users. For some, it may be no more than a minor contributor to ADD; for others, it may contribute to "simulator sickness" – like watching *The Blair Witch Project* on a queasy stomach. "Mixing fixed elements into a dynamic real environment could ... lead to 'simulator sickness' in some users," the MIT article reports. This "extra load to our visual processing" could simply be too much for some users to handle – especially if we're moving. "[There is] no problem with a static image in the corner of your eye if you are at a desktop, but it will present conflicting information if you are walking or driving," Sabelman said.

According to Sabelman's research, the fact that digital data in our peripheral vision remains stationary while the world in front of us moves – kind of like the opposite of reading in the car – could be one factor causing these physical reactions. On the other hand, "the eye rapidly 'accommodates' to an image at a fixed location on the retina, rendering it invisible. Keeping interface elements visible could require jiggling them subtly, which might lead to further visual confusion as the user's brain interprets such movement as movement of their real-world surroundings."

We've already seen versions of this same effect in several other digital devices. For example, Apple's iOS 7 operating system introduced parallax backgrounds and zoom animations throughout the user interface. Several users immediately reported that the devices gave them "motion sickness." Dr. George Kikano, division chief of family medicine at UH Case Medical Center in Ohio, was quoted as saying "there's some validity to this, for people who are susceptible. But it's not the zoom animations that are responsible. It's a new 'parallax' function that causes the background

---

[51]*LASIK Surgery Enhances Latest Tech Craze: Google Glass,* The Atlanta Vision Institute, available at http://www.atlanta2020.com/blog2/lasik-surgery-enhances-latest-tech-craze-google-glass/ (last visited on September 4, 2014).

[52]Christopher Mims, *Could Augmented Reality be Hazardous to Your Health?,* MIT Technology Review, (April 22, 2011), available at http://www.technologyreview.com/view/423811/could-augmented-reality-be-hazardous-to-your-health/ (last visited on September 4, 2014).

of the phone to subtly move back and forth, a feature that leads to an effect not unlike car sickness."[53]

"It's no different than being in an IMAX theater," Kikano said. "The inner ear is responsible for balance, the eyes for vision. When things are out of sync you feel dizzy, nauseous. Some people get it, some people don't, and some people get used to it."[54]

Indeed, as more digital devices increasingly seek to mimic and overlay the real world, the effect is only likely to become more common. Some news outlets have gone so far as to proclaim that "[d]igitally induced motion sickness caused by iPhones, 3D films and computer games will become the biggest occupational illness of the 21st century."[55] Even those experts who have been skeptical of the physiological impact from small screen devices concede that more advanced displays will pose a risk of causing motion sickness. For example, Charles Oman, a former director at NASA who has studied motion sickness for over 15 years, was quoted as saying that, "if it were an immersive environment, like a headset or an IMAX screen, then I can believe it, but it's a little harder to believe on the small screens."[56] The more recent introduction of the Oculus Rift virtual reality headset proves Oman's point. Many of its users have reported that the slight lag between head movement and corresponding movement of the display has caused the motion sickness, and the device's creators have conceded "that the problem is one which may never go away."[57]

Of course, more complete immersion is the holy grail of augmented reality, so this concern will continue to loom on the horizon for the foreseeable future. Moreover, veterans of the industry know that precisely overlaying digital information onto physical objects – especially if those objects are moving or poorly lit – is exceptionally difficult to do at all, let alone to do perfectly. And it is the slight imperfections in almost-accurate renderings that cause so many to feel ill. Managing that side effect and making sure that users are properly forewarned, therefore, will remain a challenge for the industry.

---

[53]Jeremy A. Kaplan, *Apple iOS 7 is sickening users, doctor confirms,* Fox News, (September 27, 2013), available at http://www.foxnews.com/tech/2013/09/27/is-apple-ios-7-actually-sickening-users/ (last visited on September 4, 2014).

[54]*Id.*

[55]Aaron Sharp, *The rise of digital motion sickness: Video games, 3D film and iOS 7 set to make condition the 21st century's biggest occupational disease,* Mail Online, (September 28, 2013), available at http://www.dailymail.co.uk/sciencetech/article-2436638/Video-games-3D-films-iOS7-Why-digital-motion-sickness-tipped-21st-centurys-biggest-occupational-disease.html (last visited on September 4, 2014).

[56]Jon M. Chang, *Apple iOS 7 Literally Making Some Users Sick,* abc News, (September 26, 2013), available at http://abcnews.go.com/Technology/apple-ios-literally-making-users-sick/story?id=20385379 (last visited on September 4, 2014).

[57]Aaron Sharp, *The rise of digital motion sickness: Video games, 3D film and iOS 7 set to make condition the 21st century's biggest occupational disease,* Mail Online, (September 28, 2013), available at http://www.dailymail.co.uk/sciencetech/article-2436638/Video-games-3D-films-iOS7-Why-digital-motion-sickness-tipped-21st-centurys-biggest-occupational-disease.html (last visited on September 4, 2014).

SKIN IRRITATION

Many, if not most, wearable digital devices will come in contact with users' skin. This necessarily introduces the potential of skin irritation. For example, in April 2014, news outlets reported that "thousands" of people had complained that the Fitbit Force digital bracelet had given them "a bad rash."[58] By March 2014, "the Consumer Product Safety Commission issued a recall and Fitbit stopped [selling] the Force altogether."[59] Ultimately, the company determined that 1.7% of its users experienced the reaction because of an allergic contact dermatitis, which the company initially blamed on an allergic reaction to nickel, but later said "could stem from the stainless steel, materials in the strap, or adhesives used in its assembly."[60] A class action lawsuit against the company was filed shortly thereafter.

Similarly, in July 2014, the medical journal *Pediatrics* released a study suggesting that one 11-year-old boy's persistent rash turned out to be due to the frequent use of an iPad.[61] The author concluded that the child was allergic to the nickel in the device's exterior casing. The report prompted news coverage across the country and the world, which also suggested that such allergies are on the rise.[62]

While this is a very small sample set, these incidents are a sobering reminder of how little we truly understand about the consequences of prolonged contact between skin and hardware. It seems unlikely that the materials in the Fitbit Force were dramatically different than many other digital devices on the market. Other wearable technology manufacturers should learn a lesson from Fitbit's cautionary example and invest in enough physiological research before marketing a product to ensure that the risk of similar incidents is acceptably low.

CANCER

To date, none of the digital eyewear devices on the market or announced as in production contain a cellular radio. Without this capability, the devices cannot make phone calls or connect to LTE networks on their own. Instead, every device launched so far connects to a mobile phone or tablet, either by wireless Bluetooth connection or by a physical cord, or to Wi-Fi. Certainly, a do-it-all device would be more efficient, so why the two-step process?

---

[58]Liz Collin, *Digital Bracelet Company May End Up In Court After Rash Reports,* CBS Minnesota, (April 8, 2014), available at http://minnesota.cbslocal.com/2014/04/08/digital-bracelet-company-may-end-up-in-court-after-rash-reports/ (last visited on September 4, 2014).
[59]*Id.*
[60]*Id.*
[61]*Medical Journal: Electronic Devices Can Cause Nickel Allergies to Flare Up,* CBS New York, (July 14, 2014), available at http://newyork.cbslocal.com/2014/07/14/medical-journal-electronic-devices-can-cause-nickel-allergies-to-flare-up/ (last viewed on September 4, 2014).
[62]AP, *Is your iPad giving you a rash? Nickel in tablet case linked to uncomfortable skin inflammations,* Mail Online, (July 14, 2014), available at http://www.dailymail.co.uk/news/article-2691169/Itchy-rash-Could-iPad-Nickel-tablet-case-linked-scaly-eruptions-patients-body.html (last viewed on September 4, 2014).

One reason that multiple commentators have pointed out is the ever-controversial potential link between radio frequency (RF) fields and brain cancer. To date, government regulators and scientific studies have generated mixed information over whether phone signals contribute to this disease. Officially, the World Health Organization classifies RF fields as "possibly carcinogenic to humans."[63] But another reason the data remains inconclusive is that regulators (especially the US Federal Communications Commission, or FCC) have already acted to reduce potential exposure.

Therefore, introducing a line of RF-capable devices designed to be worn on one's head all day long could, as one article put it, "become the definitive test of whether or not cell phones cause cancer, and not in a good way."[64] It seems unlikely, however, that any device manufacturer will be eager to become the guinea pig whose device tests the theory. Such devices may also violate the regulations already issued by the FCC.

RETINAL PROJECTION

"The unprotected human eye is extremely sensitive to laser radiation and can be permanently damaged from direct or reflected beams."[65] Nevertheless, various proposed AR-related devices rely on laser projection to either recognize physical objects (which could potentially jeopardize others) or to relay digital information to the eye, which could injure the user. A 2012 post on *Hack a Day*, a do-it-yourself resource, reported on "a DIY retina projector,"[66] which is a device that "focuses laser light though beam splitters and concave mirrors to create a raster display on the back of your eye." What's troubling about the project is that it emits a 200 milliwatt beam, which the site reports to be 100 times the intensity of commercial retina projectors and "more than enough to permanently damage your eye."[67]

Of course, in one way or another, all digital displays must transmit light into the user's eye, whether in the form or laser light or more conventional screens. Some designs even go so far as to "modify the eyeballs"[68] themselves, such as Innovega's iOptik system. This device relies on projectors inside eyeglass frames as well as specially designed contact lenses that focus the display. As of this writing, the last

---

[63]Christopher Mims, *Cancer fears could prevent Google Glass from ever becoming a phone,* Quartz, (February 27, 2013), available at http://qz.com/57312/cancer-fears-could-prevent-google-glass-from-ever-becoming-a-phone/ (last visited on September 4, 2014).

[64]*Id.*

[65]Osama Bader, M.D. and Harvey Lui, MD, FRCPC, *Laser Safety and the Eye and Practical Pearls,* Lions Laser Skin Centre Division of Dermatology, Vancouver Hospital and Health Sciences Centre, and University of British Columbia, Vancouver, B.C., (February 1996), available at http://www.dermatology.org/laser/eyesafety.html (last visited on September 4, 2014).

[66]Brian Benchoff, *Projecting video directly on the retina,* Hack A Day, (April 9, 2012), available at http://hackaday.com/2012/04/09/projecting-video-directly-onto-the-retina/ (last visited on September 4, 2014).

[67]*Id.*

[68]Evan Ackerman, *Innovega Delivers the Wearable Displays that Science Fiction Promised,* IEEE Spectrum, (January 9, 2014), available at http://spectrum.ieee.org/tech-talk/consumer-electronics/audiovideo/innovega-delivers-the-wearable-displays-that-science-fiction-promised (last visited September 4, 2014).

hurdle to broad commercial introduction of this system is approval of the contacts by the Food and Drug Administration.

Presumably, the FDA's seal of approval should go a long way toward insulating Innovega from most hypothetical future claims of injury by iOptik users. Most other devices, however, are unlikely to receive that level of regulatory scrutiny before being introduced to the public. It would be wise, therefore, for manufacturers of digital eyewear devices to think carefully about all foreseeable risks associated with their devices, and to mitigate them through re-design or warnings, as appropriate.

AUTOMOTIVE

The line of propriety between wearing digital eyewear and driving a car has been debated for several years already, including on my blog since 2011. The mainstream public conversation on the issue, however, has been sparked by two more recent developments. The first was the introduction of Google Glass, including the media hype surrounding its Explorer program. Eager to ride this wave of public fascination, legislators in multiple jurisdictions proposed or introduced legislation to ban use of digital eyewear while driving.

The second event occurred on October 29, 2013, when San Diego, California-based Explorer and Glassware developer Cecilia Abadie received a traffic ticket for wearing her Glass while driving. The incident galvanized an amazing amount of media coverage, and strong opinions on both sides. On January 17, 2014, Abadie's ticket was dismissed for lack of evidence that the display had actually been turned on while she was driving. By default, Glass remains off unless the user activates it with a tap or by tilting the head upwards. Abadie maintained that the device "was not on when she was driving, but was activated when she looked up at the officer during the stop."[69] Nevertheless, Abadie has also argued that wearing Glass was far less of a distraction than using a mobile phone while driving, and others have argued that digital eyewear and other AR devices can actually enhance driver safety. For its part, Google simply warns users to follow local laws and to use common sense:

> "As you probably know, most states have passed laws limiting the use of mobile devices while driving any motor vehicle, and most states post those rules on their department of motor vehicles websites. Read up and follow the law! Above all, even when you're following the law, don't hurt yourself or others by failing to pay attention to the road. The same goes for bicycling: whether or not any laws limit your use of Glass, always be careful."[70]

The following section will discuss the role of wearables and AR in driving.

---

[69]Jennifer Jensen, *Google Glass user Cecilia Abadie acquitted in ticket case: Ticket is dismissed*, abc10 News, (Posted January 16, 2014), available at http://www.10news.com/news/trial-begins-in-google-glass-ticket-case-011614 (last visited on September 4, 2014).

[70]*FAQ*, Google Glass, available at https://support.google.com/glass/answer/3064131?hl=en (last visited on September 4, 2014).

AR MOBILE PHONE APPS AND DRIVING

The discussion earlier in this chapter about the potential for AR to distract from safe walking and other tasks applies equally to (and sometimes referenced) driving – particularly the Sabelman study cited in the 2011 *MIT Technology Review* article cited above. According to Sabelman, there is "no problem with a static image in the corner of your eye if you are at a desktop, but it will present conflicting information if you are walking or driving."[71] "I suppose we could learn to [walk or drive and use an AR system at the same time]," he said, but the author of the article concluded that "we might have to someday expand on those no texting while driving laws."[72]

Those commonplace laws already recognize driver distraction as an epidemic. Simply talking on your cell phone while driving used to get people up in arms, and it is still restricted in some areas. But now those who text while driving are the new pariahs – and not without reason. Multiple mass transit disasters and notable deaths have been blamed on texting. Some studies show that texting while driving is more dangerous than driving drunk. Yet large percentages of drivers can't help but continue to do it.

My home state of Michigan is one of several jurisdictions to ban the practice as a primary offense. The Detroit suburb of Troy went one step further to prohibit not only texting and calling, but also "any other activity that can distract a driver and affect their ability to safely operate the vehicle. Activities under this classification include, but are not limited to, eating, grooming, reading, writing, or any other activity that prevents someone from having control of the vehicle with at least one hand on the wheel."[73]

How would AR devices measure up by these standards? For starters, it seems clear that using an AR app (or any other app, for that matter) on your smartphone while driving is the functional equivalent of texting. You may not be inputting information into the phone, but you've still got your eyes on it rather than the road. This is only slightly less true if you're a driver peering through your smartphone to augment the view directly ahead of you. It may be the digital equivalent of looking at signs, a map, or a billboard while you drive, which can be distracting but not illegal (except maybe in Troy). But the app doesn't know you're driving, and can put an awful lot of information between you and what's in front of you.

What about smartphone apps that are *designed* to be used while driving? Just because someone wants you to use it behind the wheel doesn't make it a good idea. Take the "Augmented Driving" iPhone app,[74] for example, which was first released in

---

[71]Christopher Mims, *Could Augmented Reality be Hazardous to Your Health,* MIT Technology Review, (April 22, 2011), available http://www.technologyreview.com/view/423811/could-augmented-reality-be-hazardous-to-your-health/ (last visited on September 4, 2014).
[72]*Id.*
[73]"New distracted driving law is now in effect in Troy," WXYZ, July 29, 2010, available at http://www.wxyz.com/news/region/oakland-county/new-distracted-driving-law-is-now-in-effect-in-troy
[74]imaGinyze, *Augmented Driving,* iTunes Preview, (Updated October 28, 2013), available at https://itunes.apple.com/us/app/augmented-driving/id366841514?mt=8 (last visited on September 4, 2014).

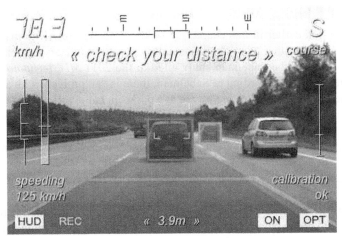

FIGURE 7.5

The "Augmented Driving" app.

2010 (Fig. 7.5). It "detects your lane and other vehicles in front of you and provides useful information for your driving situation," but only "in good lighting conditions during daytime for visible lane markings on highways and country roads and for detection of regular cars. For operation, a fix mount is required." (A similar app called iOnRoad, introduced in 2013, makes similar claims.[75]) But suppose I encounter an "irregular" car on a partly cloudy day? Or I want to see a wider view than what's visible through my front-mounted, 3.5″ screen?

Maybe there's more to this app than initially meets the eye. But relying on, and looking through, a mobile phone to detect other vehicles while driving seems like a dubious proposition.

DRIVING WITH DIGITAL EYEWEAR

There seems to be a growing interest in digital eyewear as a boon for driver safety. That certainly seems to be the prevailing conclusion among Glass Explorers, at least based on my own unscientific sampling of the Explorer Community message boards. In contrast to Cecelia Abadie's experience, at least two other Explorers have reported that the police officers who pulled them over saw and disregarded their Glass devices.[76] "I ... said I thought it was okay to drive with Glass because they were hands-free," wrote one. "That seemed to fly with him so after he ran my ID he let me go without a ticket!" Of course, such results may be influenced by the fact that (as discussed in Chapter 8) many law enforcement departments have themselves begun to wear Glass in the field.

[75]ionRoad, *Augmented Driving Lite,* Google Play, (October 29, 2013), available at https://play.google.com/store/apps/details?id=com.picitup.iOnRoad&hl=en (last visited on September 4, 2014).

[76][need Google account] https://www.glass-community.com/t5/Discussions/Driving-with-Glass-Hello-Johnny-Law/m-p/122602/highlight/true#M33803

FIGURE 7.6

Glass makes directions available to the driver without looking away from the road.

Automakers themselves are getting in on the game. Tim Mahoney, global CMO for General Motors' Chevrolet brand, confirmed that Google held a demonstration for the automaker.[77] "I think it's pretty cool," Mahoney was quoted as saying. "The demo that I saw was pretty fascinating.... It's going to come at some point."[78] Similarly, Mercedes-Benz is reportedly working to integrate both Glass and Siri, the voice-activated interface from Apple's mobile devices, into the same system with its in-car infotainment systems.[79] The idea would be to allow travel destinations stored in the user's mobile or wearable device to automatically transfer to the in-car navigation systems when the driver enters the vehicle.

The same arguments raised in opposition to Cecilia Abadie's example have been marshaled in response to these plans as well. Jurisdictions from the United Kingdom to West Virginia have moved to ban the use of digital eyewear while driving, concerned that they may be distracting, particularly for young drivers.

For its part, however, Google has expressed its intention to design Glass for safety. "It's early days and we are thinking very carefully about how we design Glass because new technology always raises new issues," Google has said. "Our Glass Explorer program, which reaches people from all walks of life, will ensure that our users become active participants in shaping the future of this technology."[80] And again, my own first-hand experience using Glass in the car shapes my perspective (Fig. 7.6).

[77]Michael McCarthy, *Do Chevy Execs See a Future With Google Glass?* Advertising Age, (October 4, 2013), available at http://adage.com/article/news/chevy-execs-a-future-google-glass/244555/ (last visited on September 4, 2014).

[78]*Id.*

[79]*Mercedes Benz integrating Google Glass into its cars,* Fox News, (July 30, 2013), available at http://www.foxnews.com/leisure/2013/07/30/mercedes-benz-intergrating-google-glass-into-its-cars/ (last visited on September 4, 2014).

[80]Michael McCarthy, *Do Chevy Execs See a Future With Google Glass?* Advertising Age, (October 4, 2013), available at http://adage.com/article/news/chevy-execs-a-future-google-glass/244555/ (last visited on September 4, 2014).

In Glass' favor is the fact that the device displays navigation information where the driver need only glance up to see it, rather than down to a mobile device, in-dash display, or physical map. The device does not remain on or impede the user's direct line of sight; instead, it chimes on when a turn is approaching, but otherwise remains off. Moreover, the interface is voice-driven. Directions are retrieved (and recited) by voice, rather than requiring the driver to type them into a keyboard. This too is a factor making the device less distracting than the alternatives.

It may be that regulators someday ban all digital interactions by a driver inside a car, including hands-free calling, map programs, and wearable technology. As long as navigational aids are allowed, however, it is difficult to see how digital eyewear is any more distracting than other, currently acceptable alternatives.

ACHIEVEMENTS TO DATE WITH AUGMENTED WINDSHIELDS AND DRIVER AIDS

One product has consistently been inserted between the driver and the road for the past century: the windshield. Automakers have experimented with projecting speedometer data and other information in heads-up displays on windshields for decades. And for at least the past several years, these same companies have been experimenting with truly interactive, augmented displays in this medium as well. A 2010 news report, for example, described a project by General Motors "to develop a working next-generation heads-up display that turns an ordinary windshield into an augmented reality information dashboard."[81] This approach used night vision, navigation sensors and cameras to gather data about the driver's surroundings – such as the location of road boundaries and speed limit signs – and ultraviolet lasers to project corresponding images onto the windshield surface.

In 2011, a company called Autoglass published a concept video for a similar windshield display system it suggested could be ready by 2020. It is unclear, however, how much actual progress the company has actually made in the interim toward achieving this goal.

Hollywood has foreseen the usefulness of displaying truly interactive, augmented data in this medium. In the 2011 film *Mission Impossible: Ghost Protocol*, for example, Tom Cruise's character drives a luxury sedan through a crowded intersection (Fig. 7.7). When pedestrians pass in front of the vehicle, heat signatures in the shape and location of their bodies flash onto the windshield.

Pioneer has actually demonstrated working prototypes of similar technology. In 2011, its Japanese arm announced the AVIC-VH09CS, ostensibly the world's first in-car, AR navigation system,[82] complete with "targeting" icons that encircle and

---

[81]Barb Dybwad, *Awesome Augmented Reality Windshield [video]*, Mashable, (March 18, 2010), available at http://mashable.com/2010/03/18/gm-ar-windshield/ (last visited on September 4, 2014).

[82]Serkan Toto, *Pioneer Shows Augmented Reality-Powered Car Navigation System*, TechCrunch, (Posted May 9, 2011), available at http://techcrunch.com/2011/05/09/pioneer-shows-aumented-reality-powered-car-navigation-system/ (last visited on September 4, 2014).

FIGURE 7.7

A scene from *Mission Impossible: Ghost Protocol.*

FIGURE 7.8

Pioneer's augmented navigation display.

identify other vehicles without obstructing them, and direction arrows that appear to hover over the intersection in real time and in three dimensions (Fig. 7.8). The images are displayed in a dash-mounted video display, however, rather than over the driver's actual point of view. In 2013, the company introduced Cyber Navi, an updated version of the same system.[83] This iteration includes the same in-dash AR system, as well as a heads-up display that replaces the driver's sunshade. Lasers project real-time navigational information onto the display so that they appear to the driver to be a few feet in the air in front of the vehicle.

A company named MVS-California, LLC has demonstrated a different, more minimalist approach to the augmented windshield. Called the Virtual Cable™, the device "presents a wayfinding line visible right through the windshield; presenting the information as a natural part of the landscape. [T]he line appears to be stretched over the road for several hundred yards in front of the car, above the street-level

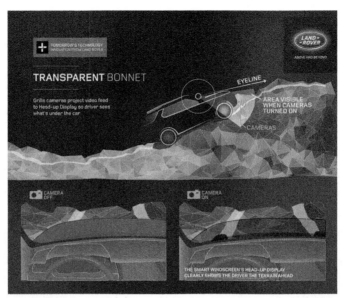

FIGURE 7.9

Land Rover's transparent bonnet system.[85]

activity of traffic."[84] Very similar to the red line followed by Daniel Suarez's protagonist in *Daemon* and *Freedom*™, the system is also capable of displaying logos of businesses along the route and other trip-related information.

In 2014, Land Rover took augmented windshields in a unique direction. Rather than adding augmented digital information to the driver's view of the road, its "Vision" concept employed a diminished reality technique to partially remove the vehicle's front end, or "bonnet." The result was to allow the driver to "see" the front wheels and the road underneath them, thus enhancing the driver's knowledge of driving conditions – especially on steep or uneven terrain (Fig. 7.9).[86]

The same technology would also be capable of augmenting the driver's situational awareness in all directions, as well as the car's ambiance. "The clear glass roof of the [Land Rover] Concept has 'mood screens' that behave like the screensaver on a computer. It's possible to change the roof from displaying a starry night to a sunny day…. The wing mirrors [also] have cameras that can project parts of the ground difficult to see onto the glass when parking."[87]

---

[84]*Follow the Virtual Cable,* MVS-California, LLC, available at http://mvs.net/ (last visited on September 4, 2014).

[85]Image © Jaguar Land Rover Ltd. Used with permission.

[86]Hunter Skipworth, *Land Rover Discovery Vision Concept: Hands-on, augmented reality in car,* Digital Spy, (May 21, 2014), available at http://www.digitalspy.co.uk/tech/feature/a572533/land-rover-discovery-vision-concept-hands-on-augmented-reality-in-a-car.html#~oEXyIcuPQVUVS3 (last visited on September 4, 2014).

[87]*Id.*

Such news is enough to give hope that AR could soon improve our driving experience in a meaningful way soon. In the not-too-distant future, AR windshield systems like this might be sufficiently effective that they become required by law, just like seat belts and scores of other safety features are today, and as car-to-car wireless communication will be within the next few years.

DRIVING AMIDST UBIQUITOUS AUGMENTED REALITY

Assuming that autonomous vehicles have not fully displaced human-driven cars by the time AR technology is ubiquitous throughout society, there are a number of ways in which a mature digital infrastructure could enhance the driving experience.

Transparent buildings

A January 2010 concept video from *New Scientist* magazine[88] demonstrates how a network of cameras synced with an AR windshield could allow drivers to literally see through walls, and thus spots potential dangers lurking around corners:

A system that works as smoothly as the one depicted in the video would certainly be a boon to driver safety, especially in urban settings with lots of blind corners. But it may be some time before the technology is that seamless. Latency and off-kilter images would make the service not only less useful, but also potentially distracting. It would also take quite an investment (of presumably public money) to get a network of cameras installed and to keep them properly aligned.

Traffic lights? Why not traffic walls?

Today's traffic lights are dots of colored light that appear relatively tiny from a driver's perspective, and are easily obscured by direct sunlight, rain, and obstructions. The mechanical systems required to create those "tiny" lights, however, are actually huge, and quite expensive. One local news source recently ran a story about the $450,000 price tag that came with a single new traffic light.[89] "The reason a single traffic light costs so much," the article explained, "is due to the cost of the hardware. Each traffic signal must be custom made. In addition, the cost of steel used to support the lights and the traffic signals themselves have gone up dramatically in recent years."

When the signals are virtual, however, there are no mechanical or financial constraints on their size. Instead of looking up to find the little dot of light in the sky, a driver viewing an upcoming intersection through an AR windshield could just as easily see a giant red wall stretching across the entire road – translucent enough not to obscure physical objects behind it, but visible enough to make it impossible to miss.

---

[88]New Scientist, *Transparent Wall,* YouTube, (Uploaded on January 15, 2010), available at https://www.youtube.com/watch?v=Q5O13bk7z2s (last visited on September 4, 2014).

[89]Ken Ross, *$450,000 traffic light cost eyed for Holyoke,* MassLive by the Republican Newsroom, (February 11, 2009), available at http://www.masslive.com/news/index.ssf/2009/02/450000_traffic_light_cost_eyed.html (last visited on September 4, 2014.

Floating, virtual road signs

Why stop at traffic signals? All road signs could easily be augmented just as well, and made to float right at eye-level for easy viewing. A "right-hand turn only" sign, for example, suddenly becomes a curved arrow floating in space, rather than a road-side sign or words painted on the asphalt that are too easily obscured by other cars. The same could be done for every one of the messages currently displayed by metal rectangles on poles. As long as this is done in an efficient manner that aids the driver rather than cluttering her view, safety should noticeably improve.

A system of AR road signs could also have a wealth of collateral benefits beyond driver assistance. The most obvious is reducing government spending. Virtual road signs would cost a whole lot less than tangible ones – after the network needed to project them was in place. (And creating that infrastructure would be no mean feat; it would have to be widespread, reliable, and universally adopted before physical signs could be done away with, so this is a long-term vision.) A less tangible, but perhaps more impactful result would be the beautification of our roadways – especially if physical billboards were also replaced by virtual advertisements, *a la Minority Report*. Imagine if residents, pedestrians, passengers – everyone except the AR-equipped driver – could enjoy the scenic natural beauty alongside the road, un-obstructed by a sea of signage.

Virtual speed displays

AR could be a boon to traffic cops as well. The U.S. Supreme Court has already up-held the secret installation by law enforcement of GPS beacons that track a vehicle's movement. The smarter our cars get, the more likely it will be that they'll have GPS devices of their own built in. Add AR to the mix, and it's a short distance to a world in which traffic cops come equipped with sensors that read speed data broadcast by the vehicle and display the information so that the officer sees it directly above the vehicle itself. Of course, by that point, we may not need police officers to hand out the tickets at all; our speeds would be automatically monitored by a central system that churns out tickets automatically.

Virtual speed displays could also benefit drivers. It's not always easy to immediately tell, for example, how quickly a car ahead of you is decelerating. Someone slamming on their brakes might trigger an accentuated, visual warning to other drivers behind the car, with different shades of color to indicate the degree of deceleration.

CONCLUSION

In sum, those who augment the physical world with digital imagery should always keep in mind the fact that physical objects can cause physical injury. Although it will be easy to become enamored of the various ways there will be to digitally supplement our daily experiences, designers of augmented reality experiences will have a responsibility to help their users to blend the digital and the physical in ways that minimize dangers.

Criminal Law

INFORMATION IN THIS CHAPTER:

- Unintentional encounters with law enforcement
- Criminal collaborations and tools
- Enhancing and monitoring law enforcement

INTRODUCTION

For all of the promise that any new technology brings, there will always be an element of society that seeks to exploit it for unlawful purposes. That is an inevitable characteristic of human nature. This is not to say that we should fear or suppress augmented world technologies simply because they can and will be misused. To the contrary, the best way to protect society against the abuses of AR is to anticipate and understand them, so that we are better able to minimize and react to harmful developments. The worst thing we could do is hide our heads in the sand, pretending that this will be the first technology that criminal elements will not exploit, or that talking about misuse will somehow cause it to happen.

In practice, this means talking with the AR industry about criminal misapplications, so that we can design our safeguards to make the technology more difficult to abuse. It also means educating and equipping law enforcement to understand and deal with what they are likely to encounter. At the same time, however, it also means educating and equipping the citizenry to monitor police officers and hold them accountable to the public they serve.

UNINTENTIONAL RUN-INS WITH THE LAW THROUGH AR

In most respects, law enforcement tends to lag behind the leading edge of technological innovation. Like any publicly funded agency, the average police department gets computer upgrades only so often, and many of its officers are too busy doing other things to stay abreast of the latest technological developments and fads. As a result, officers will sometimes mistake innocent activity as potentially criminal.

LOCATION-BASED GAMES

As with the other mentions of the popular location-based AR game *Ingress* throughout this book, the following discussion is directed at location-based AR games in general, not at *Ingress* specifically. It is only because *Ingress* has been the first game of its kind to gain such widespread adoption that the currently available examples of what can happen in connection with such games tend to involve that one.

In December 2012, a gamer who goes by the handle "Eheaubaut" on the social network Reddit was walking the streets of his city playing *Ingress*. The game requires players to locate and either destroy or repair virtual objects called "portals." Almost all of these portals are located on public property, for reasons that have been discussed in previous chapters. In order to manipulate a portal, however, a player needs to be physically very near to it. This can lead players to engage in behavior that is not typical of the average pedestrian, especially because, depending on one's experience level in the game, it can take some time to meaningfully affect the portal.

On this occasion, Eheaubaut was engaging a portal located over a police station. Although stopping to point his phone for a long period of time at the local police station gained him an advantage in the game, it was predictably suspicious to the officers inside. He wrote:

> *"I was out capturing some portals (I live in a medium sized city and only one other person is playing that I noticed, only one portal was taken.). And I walk by the police station and notice that the portal was still free! So I grabbed it. Then my phone locked up. I restart it, and load the game back up when a cop noticed me, shouted to me and arrested me. Apparently sitting near a police station for about 5 minutes with a GPS view of the surrounding area with little blue blips on the screen is a red flag. I was in a holding cell for nearly 3 hours explaining to them it's just a game by google, 'Strangest night ever.'[1]*

A friend alerted me to this post, writing: "Your prognostications about augmented reality legal troubles have begun to come true."

Not long after this incident, I was able to interview multiple, active *Ingress* players in my area. They retold their own stories, both personal and second-hand, of players being questioned by police. In one such incident, the player was playing while driving (which, I understand, the game discourages) and was pulled over after circling the same location at low speeds several times.

Similar incidents continue to occur. The Multi-State Information Sharing & Analysis Center – a division of the Center for Internet Security – published a notice to participating law enforcement agencies that *Ingress* "will likely increase reports of suspicious activity."[2] The publication explained the basis of the game and that the behavior and terminology associated with it (including "hacking" and "attacking") "are part of the game and not real-world malicious activity." Nevertheless, the notice also speculated that "[m]alicious actors unaffiliated with the game may attempt to

---

[1]Eheaubaut, *So I got arrested [post]*, Reddit-Ingress, (submitted 1 year ago), available at http://www.reddit.com/r/Ingress/comments/13zehg/so_i_got_arrested/ (last visited on September 5, 2014).

[2]"Google's Ingress Game Will Likely Increase Reports of Suspicious Activity," Multi-State Information Sharing & Analysis Center, Msisac.cisecurity.org/daily-tips/google-ingress-game.cfm (last visited September 13, 2014).

cover up their malicious activity and/or surveillance effort by claiming they are playing the game." It will be interesting to see if officers begin demanding to see – and are able to evaluate – players' in-game credentials to judge whether they're telling the truth.

In January 2014, a Kansas law enforcement lobbyist posted an article online purporting to describe "a number" of 911 calls in Park City, Kansas about "suspicious persons" who turned out to be playing *Ingress*. The article also cites one of my blog posts as an example of what "can go wrong" when *Ingress* players cross paths with police, and suggests that readers Google the phrase "ingress police calls" to find more. He wrote:

> *"The Park City Police Department has had a number of 911 suspicious character calls, and upon further investigation, the 'suspect(s)' were actually in the process of playing a new smart-phone 'augmented-reality' game called 'Ingress'....*
> *This game is rapidly becoming more popular. Part of this game involves actually going to a physical location, and then 'tagging/ marking/ closing/ taking over' that location. With the success of this game, it is likely that similar games will be created in the future. ...*
> *One recent confirmed experience with this game occurred at a church in Park City. A vehicle occupied by two people had been sitting in the parking lot for quite some time, but for no apparent reason. This occurred again the following day, and when church employees called 911 about 'suspicious characters', officers stopped the vehicle and found the occupants had been playing 'Ingress'....*
> *It is very likely that this game will generate even more 911 calls as it becomes more popular."[3]*

The article also noted the fact, however, that Niantic Labs had been proactive about warning players how to react to police inquiries. There are similar resources available online as well, including a page from the user-generated "Ingress Field Guide" describing the game to law enforcement officials.[4] Similar advice abounds in online player forums and Reddit threads. Handling such encounters, it seems, will continue to be a fact of life that must be dealt with by players of location-based AR games.

VIRTUAL SHOOTING GAMES

The stakes only get higher when – unlike *Ingress* – the AR game in question is one where players pretend to shoot each other.

Several years ago now, an incident happened only a few miles from my home that foreshadowed the risks of such games. A group of teens were running through

---

[3]*General Information,* Kansas Law Enforcement Information, available at http://www.kslawenforcementinfo.com/general-information-postings.html (last visited on September 5, 2014).
[4]Ingress Field Guide, "Ingress Informationor for Law Enforcement," available at <ingressfieldguide/police.php> (last visited September 13, 2014).

a neighborhood yard shooting at each other with Airsoft guns (which, if you don't know, are like paintball except more realistic and with smaller, softer pellets). A passing police officer mistook the toy guns for real ones and fired his (real) weapon at one of the teens. Fortunately, he missed. The lesson: things that you pretend to do in public might be interpreted by others as real, and that can be especially dangerous when what you're pretending to do is violent.

Nevertheless, there is good reason to think that AR companies will continue to develop games that involve virtual gunplay. First-person shooters have perennially been one of the most popular category of video games. Whatever the reasons, lots of people enjoy acting out violent scenarios within the (heretofore) safe boundaries of pretend environments. Geeks around the world are salivating in anticipation of the first truly immersive first-person shooter game in AR that takes that experience even further into the real world.[5] Therefore, as one industry observer wrote in July 2014, "there's been a huge push in the video games space towards a little something known as immersion."[6] The industry has sought to provide players with an immersive experience by introducing "a whole host of peripherals[, including] the ATOC Gaming Gun (the name stands for Advanced Tactical Oriented Controller). Designed for PC, Xbox 360, and PlayStation 3[,] it'll allow people to experience their shooters in a way they never have before: by making them get up and move around."[7] Chapter 12 further discusses these games and the effect they have on those who play them.

EFFECT ON CRIMINAL RESPONSIBILITY

One of the first things that first-year law students learn about Criminal Law is the concept of *mens rea*, which is Latin for "guilty mind." It is the measure of a person's conscious intent. Unless a person has a sufficiently culpable state of mind when committing a certain action, that action will not be punished criminally.

So it will be interesting to see whether, and under what circumstances, a criminal defendant will ever be able to demonstrate that he did not have the *mens rea* necessary to commit a crime because he thought that he was acting the virtual, rather than physical, world. There is already precedent for making such an argument. In February 2013, according to a newswire report, a 35-year-old man in the eastern Russian town of Nizhnaya Monoma got drunk, armed himself with two knives, and began breaking

---

[5]See, e.g., Chauncey Frend, *Augmented Realtiy FPS System*, YouTube, (Published on May 1, 2012), available at https://www.youtube.com/watch?v=ELt_aPLxKds (last visited on September 5, 2014); Chauncey Therelsa Canal, *Battlefield 5 on Google Glass (The Marine Revenge)*, YouTube, (Published on April 12, 2012), available at https://www.youtube.com/watch?v=-sSsRIhVYB4 (last visited on September 5, 2014).

[6]Nicholas Greene, *Want to Unlock A New Level of Immersion In Your First Person Shooters? The ATOC Gaming Gun Has You Covered*, Inventor Spot, available at http://inventorspot.com/articles/want-unlock-new-level-immersion-your-first-person-shooters-atoc- (last visited on September 5, 2014).

[7]*Id.*

into local homes. He stabbed five people, one fatally. His defense? "The suspect told investigators he had no intention of actually killing anyone. He said he thought he was committing a 'virtual reality' murder."[8]

In truth, this particular defendant's state of mind probably owed more to the alcohol he drank than to any video game he may have played, or thought he was playing. And there is, in fact, precedent for arguing that a severely drunk person cannot think coherently enough to form the state of mind necessary for some crimes.[9] The incident is likely, however, to foreshadow more sophisticated legal arguments to be made in a time when digital interactions in AR are much more commonplace. In a setting in which digital content is intentionally designed to be perceived and interacted with as if it were physical, it will not be such a stretch to argue that the defendant thought he was interacting with a digital object or person. If the action results in an otherwise criminal act, the defendant may well be able to establish his lack of *mens rea*.

INTENTIONAL CRIMINAL ACTIVITY
AUGMENTED WEAPONS

In addition to weapon-oriented video games, another contributor to augmenting the firearm experience is the trickle-down effect of military research and development. It should be no surprise that the military and its contractors are one of the leading forces behind the development of AR. An oft-repeated truism of modern society is that war, pornography, and fast food are among the leading drivers of technological innovation. And AR has a lot to offer soldiers in the field. Distinguishing enemy units from allies, visualizing the insides of buildings, and heads-up display of directions and targeting information are only a few of the more obvious applications.

Nor are these new ideas. Fighter pilots have used heads-up displays for decades, and virtually every combat-themed video game on the market demonstrates the utility of having these tools available.

In fact, the earliest example I can think of goes back to the mid-1980s animated series *Robotech* (Fig. 8.1). In one episode,[10] the character Louie Nichols develops an eyewear-based controller for a video game used for training military pilots. After

---

[8]UPI, *Man Accused in Killing Said He Thought It Was a "Virtual Reality" Game,* Breitbart, (February 7, 2014), available at http://www.breitbart.com/system/wire/upiUPI-20140207-093340-8698 (last visited on September 5, 2014).

[9]Voluntary intoxication, however, is not a defense to crimes requiring the mental state of recklessness or malice, because the defendant's decision to become that intoxicated in the first place is recognized as reckless in itself.

[10]InfoPedia, *The Hunters,* Robotech.com, available at http://www.robotech.com/infopedia/episodes/viewepisode.php?episode=53 (last visited on September 5, 2014).

FIGURE 8.1

Louie Nichols in *Robotech* episode "The Hunters."

he uses them to set a new score, an onlooker exclaims, "It's as if there's a machine gun built right into your glasses!" "Exactly," Louie explains "The glasses pick up the movements of my pupils and respond with impulses which program the memory in the cartridge. The cartridge remembers the patterns on my pupils, producing a recognizable firing zone, which is activated by organic impulses produced when my pupils intercept the reflected light from the target." He calls it Nichols's Special Vision Track Firing System (VTFS), or the "Pupil Pistol." To Nichols' chagrin, his superiors promptly copy the technology and incorporate it into their pilots' targeting computers.

It's also a truism that government-funded technologies eventually tend to filter down into the public's hands. From Tang to assault rifles to spaceflight, companies quickly figure out how to commercialize military-funded capabilities.

AR for the individual shooter will follow this same trend, sooner or later. Shooting games are already some of the most popular AR applications for mobile devices. How much longer until gun stores sell heads-up targeting accessories for real handguns? This alone, of course, is unlikely to be *per se* illegal; in fact the current political climate ensures that there will be a fierce confrontation between gun control advocates who see augmented weaponry as dangerous and Second Amendment purists who argue that the only way to stop a criminal with AR targeting capabilities is with one's own augmented gun.

It seems inevitable that AR will be used by criminals to place digital bounties on certain places or people, visible only by others using a certain AR darknet. (More on those below.) Even more unnerving would be target device that identify certain individuals based on AR information that they share about themselves, once augmented social networks gain more traction. Displaying information about ourselves as we walk down the street would make it that much easier for someone to pick targets with particular attributes out of a crowd. Even militarized versions of video game-style self-monitoring data (such as vital signs, ammunition, wind conditions and the location of nearby threats) would be enough to make criminal shooters that much more dangerous in a public setting.

Of course, none of these are reasons to ban AR from the marketplace, as if such a thing were even possible. AR, like the internet before it, will be another ubiquitous medium for data transmission. Even tying AR into private weapons is not necessarily a categorically bad or good idea. But the first time that a rogue gunman uses his digital eyewear in connection with shooting civilians, you can bet that we'll hear calls to ban the technology. So let's give some thought ahead of time to how AR can and should be used in connections with firearms.

SURREPTITIOUS DATA COLLECTION AND HACKING

The allure of wearable recording devices is the promise of being able to forever memorialize cherished sights in our field of view. What one person wishes to see, however, is often something that another wishes to hide from view. So when on-the-fly recording capabilities increase, intrusion into ostensibly private spaces will as well, unless opposing countermeasures are taken.

We have already discussed the potential for eavesdropping – which in many jurisdictions is a criminal offense as well as a civil tort – and other forms of privacy invasion in Chapter 3. Here, it is interesting to note the type of criminally surreptitious recording to which wearable technology is already being put. For example, in June 2014, *Wired* magazine reported on a study performed by researchers at the University of Massachusetts Lowell.[11] They tested the ability of various wearable cameras "to surreptitiously pick up four-digit PIN codes typed onto an iPad from almost 10 feet away – and from nearly 150 feet with a high-def camcorder." By using custom visual recognition software, they were able to determine the numbers entered merely by tracking finger movements, even when the video could not directly see the screens onto which the numbers were entered. Criminals in the field could easily use similar methods to collect ATM and device passwords from unsuspecting users. At the same time, however, the researchers also suggested an easy solution to the problem: software that randomizes the positions of the numbers on the keypad used to enter the PINs.

Of course, for as long as recording devices have existed, they have also been used for gathering more prurient images. In 2008, for example, a stalker inserted a tiny video camera into the keyhole of ESPN reporter Erin Andrews' hotel rooms in

---

[11]Andy Greenberg, *Google Glass Snoopers Can Steal Your Passcode With a Glance,* Wired, (June 24, 2014), available at http://www.wired.com/2014/06/google-glass-snoopers-can-steal-your-passcode-with-a-glance/ (last visited on September 5, 2014).

Tennessee, Wisconsin, and Ohio to capture images of her in the nude.[12] Similar incidents involving less-high-profile victims are reported with disturbing frequency in local tanning salons, dressing rooms, showers, and similar locales across the country.

Here again, increasing the prevalence of recording devices – a necessary consequences of an increasingly augmented world – will increase the number of such Peeping Toms and the ways in which they can capture the images they seek. In June 2014, a Seattle woman made national headlines by reporting a suspicious drone flying outside her window.[13] The next month, a New York man was arrested and charged with unlawful surveillance after allegedly flying his video-recording drone outside the 4th-floor examination rooms of a medical building.[14]

The complexity of this issue lies in the fact that such devices have multiple legitimate uses in addition to the perverse ones. For example, it later became apparent the owner of the Seattle drone was actually recording a panoramic image of the city skyline, and was not recording through the woman's window at all. The New York defendant likewise claimed to be recording architecture and not indoor activity.

The exponentially expanding Internet of Things that will undergird the augmented world, however, offers a tempting collection of targets for hackers. At the 2013 Black Hat security conference, "two researchers from Trustwave Security Labs discussed vulnerabilities in a number of home-automation systems, such as door locks, alarm systems, garage doors, lights, surveillance cameras and other electronic appliances that could be used to carry out covert surveillance and gain entry to buildings."[15] As mentioned in Chapter 3, the Federal Trade Commission has already taken action against one such home monitoring company for doing too little to prevent such hacking.

As this network adds more devices that perform important and sensitive functions, the consequences of that hacking escalate. "In order to avoid lurid headlines about cars crashing, insulin overdoses and houses burning," warned *The Economist*, "tech firms will surely have to embrace higher standards."[16] These are not hypothetical concerns. At the 2013 hacker convention DEF CON, security researchers Charlie Miller and Chris Valasek showed how they used a simple Mac laptop hack a Toyota

[12]Monty, *Erin Andrews Suing Peepr, Nashville Marriott for $7 Million,* Busted Coverage, (December 5, 2011), available at http://bustedcoverage.com/2011/12/05/erin-andrews-suing-peeper-nashville-marriott-for-7-million-documents/ (last visited on September 5, 2014).

[13]Gregory S. McNeal, *Alleged Drone 'Peeping Tom' Photo Reveals Perils of Drone Related Journalism,* Forbes, (July 14, 2014), available at http://www.forbes.com/sites/gregorymcneal/2014/07/14/alleged-drone-peeping-tom-photo-reveals-perils-of-drone-related-journalism/ (last visited on September 5, 2014).

[14]"NY man charged with peeping in windows with drone," WRGB July 16, 2014, available at http://www.cbs6albany.com/template/cgi-bin/archived.pl?type=basic&file=/news/features/top-story/stories/archive/2014/07/HMAM58iB.xml#.VBUF4PldV8E

[15]Fahmida Y. Rashid, *How the Internet of Things Could Kill You,* tom'sGuide, (July 18, 2014), available at http://www.tomsguide.com/us/iot-attack-physical-impact,news-19182.html (last visited on September 5, 2014).

[16]*The internet of things (to be hacked),* The Economist, (July 12, 2014), available at http://www.economist.com/news/leaders/21606829-hooking-up-gadgets-web-promises-huge-benefits-security-must-not-be (last visited on September 5, 2014).

Prius, deactivating the brakes regardless of what the driver attempts to do. They can likewise "turn off power steering, make the onboard GPS systems give wrong directions, change the numbers on the speedometer and even make the car change direction."[17] Likewise, "[t]he famed late hacker Barnaby Jack demonstrated how to hijack wireless insulin pumps to deliver potentially fatal doses from across a room, or hijack wireless pacemakers to stop hearts … or deliver electric shocks (Fig. 8.2)."[18]

The unnerving plausibility of these scenarios has spawned fictional dramatizations of such malicious IOT hacks. The television drama "Homeland" featured a hacked pacemaker, while an artificially intelligent program uses similar methods to eliminate enemies and ensconce itself in computers around the world in Daniel Suarez's AR-influenced techno-thrillers *Daemon* and *Freedom*™. As the world becomes more connected, criminal hackers will have more access points for causing more harm than they will know what to do with.

AR AS A DISCLOSURE OF "SOFT TARGETS"

Augmented reality has sometimes been referred to as a window into, or the visual "interface for[,] the Internet of Things."[19] It offers the same advantages for existing networks of other kinds as well. One of the most compelling and practical use cases for AR in both the consumer and industrial sectors will be visualizing electronic, mechanical, and organizational processes and activities that would not otherwise be apparent to the user. This could be as simple as the proverbial smart fridge that alerts its owner when food items are running low, to on-the-job visual prompts that instruct a technician on how to repair a piece of machinery or locate a particular piece of pipeline or equipment. In my neighborhood, utility companies regularly fly planes overhead to monitor the status of underground pipelines, which are marked by unsightly signs designed to be visible from the air. Similarly, homeowners are required to call 1-800-MISS-DIG before breaking ground for landscaping or construction; servicemen then come and use flags and spray paint to mark out the location of all underground pipes and wires. All of these precautions could – and someday are likely to – be rendered obsolete by an AR application that reliably displays the location of all underground structures in three dimensions.

Travelers are also likely to become more dependent on AR. In their book *Augmented Reality: An Emerging Technologies Guide to AR*, Gregory Kipper and Joseph Rampolla discuss various AR apps that track and visualize the identity and location

---

[17]Jill Scharr, *Hackers Hijack Prius with Mac Laptop,* tom'sGuide, (July 26, 2013), available at http://www.tomsguide.com/us/hackers-hijack-prius-with-laptop,review-1797.html (last visited on September 5, 2014).

[18]Fahmida Y. Rashid, *How the Internet of Things Could Kill You,* tom's Guide, (July 18, 2014), available at http://www.tomsguide.com/us/iot-attack-physical-impact,news-19182.html (last visited on September 5, 2014).

[19]Anna Leach, *When augmented reality hits the Internet of Things,* wired.co.uk., (October 10, 2014), available at http://www.wired.co.uk/news/archive/2010-10/14/augmented-reality-internet-of-things (last visited on September 5, 2014).

FIGURE 8.2

Barnaby Jack.[20]

of individual rail cars, buses, ships, planes, and more.[21] This functionality is not limited to AR apps; *FlightAware*, for instance, is a popular app that tracks nearby flights in a two-dimensional display. But conveying vehicle information to travelers by means of AR can provide real value in locating public transit routes, stations, and vehicles.

[20]© Marc Handelman / cc licensed.
[21]pp. 100–04.

As with most information, however, all of these insights could be used for nefarious purposes as well. For instance, a terrorist intent on attacking a particular vehicle (perhaps because of who is inside) or causing the maximum number of casualties would have a better chance of succeeding if he had access to a real-time, heads-up display of traffic information.

Policymakers have long fretted about the vulnerability of such "soft targets" as power grids and water purification plants (Fig. 8.3). For example, immediately after the onset of the 2003 blackout that left much of the Eastern and Midwestern United States without power for days, many of us affected by it initially assumed that it must have been the result of a terrorist attack. Attacks on such systems hit far more average citizens "where they live," so to speak, than do the more common forms of terrorism, such as bombings or mass shootings. In November 2012, the National Academy of Sciences released the results of a study finding that a successful attack on the United States' power grid could cost hundreds of billions of dollars and lead to thousands of deaths.[22] In 1993, the parasite cryptosporidium infiltrated the water distribution system in Milwaukee, Wisconsin by unknown means. In all, more than 400,000 people were

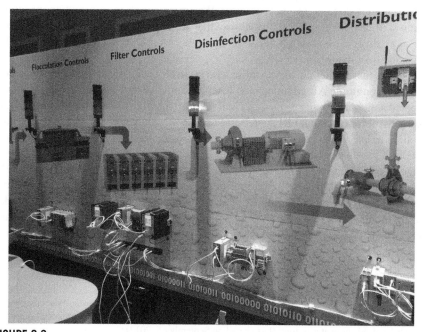

FIGURE 8.3

A mock-up at DefCon 2014 of potentially hackable computers in a water treatment system.

[22]Brian Wingfield, *Thousands Could Die If U.S. Power Grid Attacked,* BloombergBusinessWeek, (November 14, 2012), available at http://www.businessweek.com/news/2012-11-14/thousands-seen-dying-if-terrorists-attack-vulnerable-u-dot-s-dot-grid (last visited on September 5, 2014).

sickened, and at least 69 died – "the largest waterborne outbreak recorded in U.S. history."[23] Although there is no evidence to suggest that this contamination occurred intentionally, it revealed society's enormous vulnerability to adulterated water supplies.

Without a doubt, access to a three-dimensional AR display of the grid's interconnected components would make such an attack even easier to carry out and more effective in its results. Again, this sort of threat does not emerge from whole cloth; governments and utilities are (generally) already sensitive to the need to guard such information, and access to the systems that controls these networks, carefully. But with the increased transparency that AR brings comes a commensurate need to weigh carefully how much information is shared, and how well-secured the sensitive data is kept. If these high-value networks are kept as unsecured as some of the commercial IOT networks that have been cited for lax security (such as TrendNET[24]), the result could be far more catastrophic than mere embarrassment and civil fines.

REPURPOSING THE INFRASTRUCTURE OF AN AUGMENTED WORLD FOR CRIMINAL PURPOSES

One of the most exciting features of the emerging augmented world is the power it gives individuals to create and innovate. We are so awash in information, programming skill, and manufacturing capability that we already have the ability to create a far more diverse range of applications than we currently have. All that is needed is time and imagination.

Again, that applies equally to those who innovate for criminal purposes. Police officer and long-time AR commentator Joseph Rampolla sees the combination of augmented reality and flying drones as a real security threat in the near term (Fig. 8.4). In April 2014, for example, FBI agents arrested a Moroccan national who was allegedly plotting to use a consumer-grade drone to fly a homemade bomb into a Connecticut school.[25] Drone aircraft are a growth market for visual AR. The "Fat Shark" line of goggles are specifically designed to give drone pilots a bird's-eye view through the vehicle's on-board cameras, creating the illusion that they are actually on board.[26] The popular "AR Parrot" drone creates a similar effect by beaming live HD video to the mobile device used to control it, and several applications (both official and otherwise) are available to display that feed directly into various AR-capable digital eyewear. This offers a more intuitive method of controlling the craft's trajectory, but

---

[23]Marion Ceraso, *20 years after fatal outbreak, Milwaukee leads on water testing,* WisconsinWatch. org, (May 22, 2013), available at http://wisconsinwatch.org/2013/05/20-years-after-fatal-outbreak-milwaukee-leads-on-water-testing/ (last visited on September 5, 2013).

[24]See Chapter 3.

[25]Michael P. Mayko, *FBI: Drone-like toy planes in bomb plot,* ctpost, (April 7, 2014), http://m.ctpost.com/local/article/FBI-Drone-like-toy-planes-in-bomb-plot-5383658.php (last visited on September 5, 2014).

[26]FatShark RC Vision Systems home page, fatshark.com, available at http://www.fatshark.com/ (last visited on September 5, 2014).

FIGURE 8.4

Joseph Rampolla.

at the same time increases their attractiveness as a means of delivering explosives. It does not take a great deal of imagination to draw parallels between AR-enabled weaponized drones and the warhead's-eye view footage from Tomahawk cruise missiles that so captivated the American public during the war to liberate Kuwait. The military puts video cameras in its missiles and drones to better avoid interception and confirm the results of air strikes; criminals will do likewise, for the same reason.

Another component of the increasingly augmented world is the autonomous automobile. Driverless cars are already being tested on American roads, and they have been approved for deployment in the United Kingdom beginning in 2015. An internal report authored by the Strategic Issues Group within the FBI's Directorate of Intelligence and revealed to the public in July 2014 identified these as a "game-changing" weapon for criminals. For one thing, driverless cars will essentially take the place of the "getaway driver." The report notes that "bad actors will be able to conduct tasks that require use of both hands or taking one's eyes off the road which would be impossible today."[27]

Such vehicles could also be packed with explosives and weaponized as easily as airborne drones could be. Car bombings have already become a staple of terrorism and low-intensity warfare across the world. Automated vehicles – especially when their use becomes so normalized as to not raise eyebrows – offer the groups behind such attacks the option to launch target car-bomb attacks without the need to recruit suicide bombers. Some in the media have attacked the FBI's predictions as alarmist, reactionary, and anti-progress.[28] To the contrary, the history of automobiles' use in

---

[27]Mark Harris, *FBI warns driverless cars could be used as lethal weapons,* theguardian, (July 16, 2014), available at http://www.theguardian.com/technology/2014/jul/16/google-fbi-driverless-cars-leathal-weapons-autonomous (last visited on September 5, 2014).

[28]Tim Cushing, *FBI Thinks Driverless Cars Could Be Criminals' New Best Friends,* techdirt, (July 17, 2014), available at https://www.techdirt.com/articles/20140716/11432527899/fbi-thinks-driverless-cars-could-be-criminals-new-best-friends.shtml (last visited on September 5, 2014).

crime and terrorism make these predictions so self-evident as to be inevitable. The only surprise is that they were not made sooner. Rather than focusing only on the positive applications of these and similar technologies, companies and law enforcement alike should waste no time in devising means to deter and defeat their misuse.

CRIMINAL COLLABORATIONS THROUGH AR DARKNETS

Darknets all around us

In November 2002, a group of Microsoft researchers coined the term "darknet" to describe "a collection of networks and technologies used to share digital content."[29] The term has since come to be used (in both capitalized and uncapitalized form) to refer to the underground Internet – the "walled-off online databases that are off-limits to search engines and indexing software robots."[30] In popular culture and mainstream media, this realm has been likened to "private, invitation-only cyberclubs or gated communities requiring an access code to enter," as well as "the world of cybercrime, spammers, terrorists, and other underworld figures who use the Internet to avert the law."[31] Sensationalism aside, darknets are simply "closed-off social spaces – safe havens in both the virtual and the real worlds where there is little or no fear of detection."[32]

The augmented medium, of course, offers a unique opportunity to create such safe havens that combine aspects of both the digital and the physical. Daniel Suarez best captured this idea in his novels *Daemon* and *Freedom*™. There, the primary antagonist creates an encrypted virtual network simply called "the Darknet" as a means for his operatives to communicate with each other without being detected. Through digital eyewear, they share text and audio messages, recognize each other through virtual "call-out" name badges, see their assigned paths as a red line in the sky (very much like the "virtual cable" car navigation system described in Chapter 7), share programs with each other in the form of three-dimensional digital objects, and even create such objects by performing spell-like rituals inspired by the role-playing games favored by the network's creator.

With or without such artistic flare, AR darknets are sure to crop up in the near future – if they haven't already – as an extension of the same clandestine criminal organizations that exist today. Indeed, they apparently already exist in the virtual world. Since at least 2008,[33] the U.S. intelligence community has been concerned about terrorist groups collaborating in plain sight, as it were, as characters within such massively multiplayer online communities as *Second Life* and *World of Warcraft*. That was the same year that the U.S. Intelligence Advanced Research Projects Activity

---

[29]J.D. Lasica, Darknet: Hollywood's War against the Digital Generation 45 (2005) .

[30]*Id.*

[31]*Id.*

[32]*Id.*

[33]*Office of the Director of National Intelligence Data Mining Report,* (February 15, 2008), available at http://www.fas.org/irp/dni/datamining.pdf (last visited on September 5, 2014.)

(IARPA) launched its "Project Reynard" to uncover recruiting and training operations going unnoticed in these online gaming environments.[34] The use of these online communities to recruit operatives was also a key plot point in Daniel Suarez's books, as well as in the novel *MMORPG* by Dutch author Emile van Veen.[35] When these online communities begin expanding into the physical world by way of AR – as they have already begun to do – encrypted digital data tied to specific physical locations will become potential means of secret communication by underground groups.

When collaboration becomes criminal

The potential for criminal liability in these communications begins with *solicitation*. Although we usually use this term in connection with the encouragement to engage in prostitution, it also applies more generally to any communication that encourages another person to commit a felony or serious misdemeanor, with the intent that the person commit the crime. Such encouragement may take many forms, including words, writings, or combinations of the two. Mere talk about a crime is not enough; the defendant must specifically intend that the recipient commit the crime. Once the communication is made, however, the crime of solicitation is complete; it does not matter if the hearer actually acts on the encouragement.

If two or more people reach agreement between themselves to commit an unlawful act, that agreement can be punished by the law as a criminal *conspiracy*. The crime here is the mutual intent to carry out the plan, which does not necessarily need to be verbalized in order to be proven. The defendants' action can be sufficient evidence of their agreement. In some jurisdictions, the act that the conspirators agree to commit need not even be a criminal one, but simply unlawful. Moreover, once the conspiracy is formed, members can be held liable not only for the agreed-upon action, but also any foreseeable criminal actions carried out in furtherance of the conspiracy. Most jurisdictions require that at least one conspirator take some overt action in furtherance of the conspiracy before liability will be imposed, but this is not a high threshold; virtually any action will do.

Actions taken in furtherance of a crime that fall short of carrying it out can still be punished as an *attempt*. To be held liable, the defendant must have specifically intended that the crime be committed and do something that constitutes a substantial step toward completing the crime.

As current criminal behavior migrate into the augmented medium, legal liability will follow. It is easy to picture a number of scenarios in which AR messaging could be considered solicitation, conspiracy, or attempt. Instigators could digitally mark a location with symbols, virtual objects, or instructions that other members of a gaming or Darknet community would recognize as an encouragement to commit a criminal act. As in a particular scene in Daniel Suarez's books – in which several members of

---

[34]Aaron Saenz, *Al Qaeda in Azeroth? Terrorism Recruiting and Training in Virtual Worlds,* Singularity Hub, (August 24, 2011), avaialbe at http://singularityhub.com/2011/08/24/al-qaeda-in-azeroth-terrorism-recruiting-and-training-in-virtual-worlds/ (last visited on September 5, 2014).
[35]*Id.*

the Darknet receive precise instructions from an omniscient voice speaking through their eyewear to walk here, turn there, hand this package to that person at this specific time, culminating in an untraceable but impeccably coordinated mass shooting – separate instructions could be sent in sequence to various members of a Darknet community that constitute foreseeable criminal acts in furtherance of a conspiracy, even if certain members of the conspiracy are not aware of the full plan.

Again, none of these scenarios are cut from whole cloth; analogous criminality occurs every day through video messaging, SMS, telephones, and even the U.S. Mail. But each upgrade in communications technology makes it that much easier to coordinate conspiracies with increasing robustness and detail. The ability to simultaneously and remotely augment the vision and hearing of multiple individuals will be the latest step in that progression.

Augmenting personal and property crimes

Law enforcement has long foreseen the threat of criminals making use of AR in the furtherance of their crimes. In 2003, Thomas J. Cowper of the New York State Police and Michael E. Buerger of Bowling Green State University authored a paper that was published by the FBI. Entitled *Improving Our View of the World: Police and Augmented Reality Technology*,[36] it included a substantial discussion of the types of AR crimes that law enforcement personnel of the future would encounter. "It is necessary to anticipate that the bad guys will have access to the technology fairly early and will work to devise both defensive measures and counterattack strategies," the authors wrote. "Indeed," they continued, "it may be wise to anticipate that the criminal element may already be ahead of the police in these areas."[37]

Cowper and Buerger's primary concern was criminals' use of AR to gain a tactical advantage over police officers in the field. "It is only a small leap of the imagination," they wrote, "to envision the interior of a mob bar or restaurant being … outfitted to support a rudimentary AR environment.... enough to discern whether an informant is carrying a wire, or where an undercover officer has concealed a backup weapon."[38] They went on to mention such complementary technology as "cameras that spot liars," "stolen [virtual] 'Friend/Foe' signatures," and "night time thermal imaging." These are all capabilities that one could easily conceive of being added to existing or in-development digital eyewear.

Enhanced situational awareness through AR would also aid individuals in carrying out various crimes, especially those against property. There are already an endless number of apps available that cull certain types of data from social media and other public databases. In 2010, the site Please Rob Me[39] made a splash when

---

[36]Thomas J. Cowper and Michael E. Buerger, *Improving Our View of the World: Police and Augmented Reality Technology, (abstract),* NCJRS- National Criminal Justice Reference Service, (February 2003), available at https://www.ncjrs.gov/App/publications/abstract.aspx?ID=200341 (last visited on September 5, 2014).

[37]*Id.*

[38]*Id.*

[39]*Raising awareness about over-sharing,* Please Rob Me, available at http://pleaserobme.com/ (last visited on September 5, 2014).

it collected – for the purpose of raising awareness – posts by individuals indicating that they were not at home. It is not difficult to imagine an AR network dedicated to visualizing this same information over the locations in question, just to make it that much easier for the would-be burglar to find a place to rob. Around the same time, an AR industry blogger posited this scenario:

> *"[Y]our mother comes over to your house and tweets about your priceless collection of Ming dynasty vases. Your home location is geotagged and out there for all to see along with details of your most valued possession. An enterprising thief using the latest version of BurglAR would be able to see high value items worth stealing in the local area."*[40]

Cowper and Buerger highlighted similar, albeit more violent, concerns:

> *When "through-the-wall" technology becomes available, it can be used to pinpoint the location of individuals in a private home (or a police station) for rescue, kidnap, or assassination. It can identify key junctures to cripple electronics, tell when the on-duty data entry clerk has gone to the relief room on break, show the location of Evidence/Property rooms and their electronic monitors, isolate burglar alarms on private residences and send false signals to cover electronic intrusions....*
>
> *The police are not the only, nor even the most likely targets: intrusive technology in the hands of the bad guys makes the citizenry far more vulnerable and in need of protection. Leaving timer lights on in the house, even with recorded music or conversation or barking dogs, is of little consequence to a burglar who can establish electronically that the house is not occupied. The thought of portable through-the-walls technology in the hands of a child kidnapper/murderer is terrifying, as the Polly Klaas, Samantha van Dam and Elizabeth Smart cases vividly illustrate.*[41]

Speaking from experience, these authors see the technologies of the augmented world as inevitable steps in the endless cycle of escalation and countermeasure between cops and robbers. As Augmented World Expo co-founder Tish Shute is fond of saying, augmented reality is a "superpower," and it can be used for good or for evil.[42] Or, more likely, for both.

---

[40]Lester, *The Case Against Augmented Reality,* Augmented Planet, (submitted on January 27, 2010), available at http://www.augmentedplanet.com/2010/01/the-case-against-augmented-reality/ (last visited on September 5, 2014). As of this writing, more than four and a half years later, this post remains the blog's most commented upon.

[41]Thomas J. Cowper and Michael E. Buerger, *Improving Our View of the World: Police and Augmented Reality Technology, (abstract),* NCJRS- National Criminal Justice Reference Service, (February 2003), available at https://www.ncjrs.gov/App/publications/abstract.aspx?ID=200341 (last visited on September 5, 2014).

[42]Tish Shute, *Augmented Humans in an Augmented World: Quantified Desire,* slideshare, (June 14, 2013), available at http://www.slideshare.net/TishShute/augmented-humansaugmentedworld (last visited on September 5, 2014).

LAW ENFORCEMENT USAGE

AR by itself is simply a medium. Like any other medium or technology, how it is used will be up to the people using it. As Cowper and Buerger predicted, for every criminal exploitation of AR, there is likely to be a responsive counter-measure, or even an escalation, by law enforcement.[43]

ENHANCING SITUATIONAL AWARENESS

Cowper and Buerger foresaw situations in which police officers engaged in tactical law enforcement situations would rely on augmented reality data to gain the tactical upper hand over resisting suspects. "AR information can be transmitted wirelessly from a centralized computer network, accessed directly from a wearable computer carried by the individually equipped AR user, acquired from purposely embedded devices within a surrounding intelligent environment and acquired from an array of AR sensors scanning the immediate or visible location of the user. The information is then projected onto a see-through heads-up display, transmitted audibly to a headset, or felt through a haptic interface like a glove."[44] In other words, officers would essentially become the "Robocop" character that inspired so many early innovators of AR (Fig. 8.5).

Developments since their report, particularly in the area of visual AR, have brought us very close to realizing this predicted future. In 2009, the San Jose police experimented with head-mounted cameras to monitor their interactions with civilians. Officers activated the over-the-ear cameras every time they responded or made contact with a person. At the end of the officer's shift, the recording was downloaded to a central server. The pilot project was launched in response to public criticism over incidents of police violence.

More recently, several law enforcement agencies have begun to test the use of Google Glass and other digital eyewear in the field. Most prominent among these is the New York City Police Department – the country's largest police department – which began beta tests of Glass in February 2014,[45] before they became publicly accessible. Reports said that the department had obtained a few of the devices and were evaluating

---

[43]*See also* Joseph Rampolla, *Top 5 Reasons Law Enforcement Cannot Ignore Augmented Realtiy,* AR Dirt, (February 2, 2012), available at http://www.ardirt.com/general-news/top-5-reasons-law-enforcement-cannot-ignore-augmented-reality.html (last visited on September 5, 2014.)

[44]Thomas J. Cowper and Michael E. Buerger, *Improving Our View of the World: Police and Augmented Reality Technology, (abstract),* NCJRS- National Criminal Justice Reference Service, (February 2003), available at https://www.ncjrs.gov/App/publications/abstract.aspx?ID=200341 (last visited on September 5, 2014).

[45]Richard Byrne Reilly, *New York Police Department is beta-testing Google Glass,* VBnews, (February 5, 2014), available at http://venturebeat.com/2014/02/05/nypd-google-glass/ (last visited on September 5, 2014).

FIGURE 8.5

The *Robocop* films depicted the advantages of enhanced situational awareness for officers through AR.

their usefulness for officers on patrol.[46] At that time, "[t]he chief information officer of the San Francisco police department, Susan Merritt, said that her department ha[d] yet to test the wearable Google computers. But she says the applications for law enforcement are potentially huge."[47] Merritt cited facial recognition applications, instant access to records, and reduction of paperwork as potential advantages.[48] Members of the Secret Service are said to be "smitten"[49] with Glass and have been spotted in the wild testing it out. Brazilian police officers, moreover, reportedly already employed "facial-recognition camera glasses that can capture 400 facial images per second to store them in a central database of up to 13 million faces" during the 2014 World Cup.[50]

I have also spoken with Bill Switzer, head of CopTrax, a division of Stalker Radar in Georgia. CopTrax is making a name for itself as the first private company to offer a software solution to law enforcement officers based on Google Glass.

On Friday, September 13, 2013, the Byron Police Department in Georgia – a loyal Stalker Customer – captured video footage using Glass while running the Cop-Trax software application for Android (Fig. 8.6). Byron PD uses the CopTrax video system in their cars but during the field trail the goal was to capture video using CopTrax from the vantage point of the officers eyes using the new Google Glass wearable computers. In order to avoid running down Glass's battery, the CopTrax system doesn't start recording until the officer activates his car siren. Byron was able to capture footage of an arrest, a traffic stop, using radar and lidar, and firing weapons

---

[46]*Id.*

[47]*Id.*

[48]*Id.*

[49]Aliya Sternstein, *How Soon Before Obama's Bodyguards Don Google Glass?* Nextgov., (September 10, 2013), available at http://www.nextgov.com/defense/2013/09/how-soon-obamas-bodyguards-don-google-glass/70112/ (last visited on September 5, 2014).

[50]*U.S. robots, Israeli drones to help make 2014 World Cup in Brazil one of safest sporting events ever,* rt.com, (May 19, 2013), availablae at http://rt.com/news/brazil2014-us-military-robots-501/ (last visited September 5, 2014).

FIGURE 8.6

The CopTrax system on Glass.

while wearing Glass – reportedly the first time an arrest had been captured through Glass by the arresting officer (but not, as discussed below, the first time *anyone* had used Glass to film an arrest).

CopTrax is not the only outfit interested in equipping officers with Glass. A company named Mutualink demonstrated an app in August 2013 that would allow officers to communicate in real-time via streaming video from the scene, as well as to receive and view key documents, including things like building schematics, medical records of victims, live feeds of security cameras in the area and more.

The United States military – whose technological advances often trickle down to law enforcement agencies – has likewise been at work for years developing digital eyewear for soldiers. The Defense Advanced Research Projects Agency, or DARPA, has developed a prototype tactical augmented reality system called the Urban Leader Tactical Response, Awareness and Visualization, or ULTRA-Vis.[51] (Fig. 8.7) This "system overlays full-color graphical iconography onto the local scene ... [using an] integrated a light-weight, low-power holographic see-through display with a vision-enabled position and orientation tracking system."[52] The device is meant to enhance situational awareness by "visualiz[ing[the location of other forces, vehicles, hazards and aircraft in the local environment even when these are not visible to the Soldier. In

---

[51]ARPA, "URBAN LEADER TACTICAL RESPONSE, AWARENESS & VISUALIZATION (ULTRA-VIS)," available at http://www.darpa.mil/Our_Work/I2O/Programs/Urban_Leader_Tactical_Response,_Awareness,___Visualization_%28ULTRA-VIS%29.aspx (last visited September 12, 2014).
[52]*Id.*

FIGURE 8.7

DARPA's ULTRA-Vis system.

addition, the system can be used to communicate to the Soldier a variety of tactically significant (local) information including imagery, navigation routes, and alerts."[53]

A similar device, called the X6, is being developed for the Defense Department by San Francisco-based Osterhout Design Group.[54] During a June 2014 demonstration of the device, a user looked at a two-dimensional map, "and suddenly structures appeared in three dimensions related to objects of interest."[55] Here again, facial recognition capability is high on the government customer's priority list, and an Australian company called Imagus has developed a program for the X6 that provides it. [56] The Defense Department has already ordered 500 units of the device.[57] Likewise, "United Kingdom-based BAE systems built the Q-Warrior high-tech headset to live-stream more to soldiers than ever before, and provides a tremendous battlefield advantage by showing soldiers multi-dimensional, full-color displays of battle zones outside their fields of vision."[58] Similar applications for both first responders and the military are summarized in Kipper and Rampolla's book.[59]

Discussing technological developments since the publication of his book, Rampolla shared with me his eagerness to see law enforcement make use of instant three-dimensional mapping capabilities such as those offered by the Structure Sensor[60] and Google's Project Tango.[61] In particular, Rampolla envisions this functionality added to an aerial drone, allowing officers to map out in real time "the position of active shooters" during hostile encounters. A forerunner of such technology received an

---

[53]*d.*

[54]Patrick Tucker, *The Military is about to Get New Spay Glasses,* Defense One, (June 25, 2014), available at http://www.defenseone.com/technology/2014/06/military-about-get-new-spy-glasses/87292/ (last visited on September 5, 2014).

[55]*Id.*

[56]*Id.*

[57]*Id.*

[58]Giuseppi Marci, *The military's new Google Glass streams TONS of futuristic battle date,* The Daily Caller, (March 11, 2014), available at http://dailycaller.com/2014/03/11/the-militarys-new-google-glass-streams-tons-of-futuristic-battle-data/ (last visited on September 5, 2014).

[59]PP.100–03.

[60]Structure home webpage, available at http://structure.io/ (last visited on September 5, 2014).

[61]Project Tango home webpage, available at https://www.google.com/atap/projecttango/#project (last visited on September 5, 2014).

FIGURE 8.8

ARS by Churchill Navigation.

"Auggie Award" at the 2011 Augmented Reality Event[62] in Santa Clara, California. Churchill Navigation of Boulder, Colorado won the award for ARS (Fig. 8.8), a helicopter-mounted system that gives in-flight officers a heads-up overlay of street names and other navigational data over their view of the ground during a chase, giving the effect of an immersive version of Google Maps.

HARVESTING DIGITAL INFORMATION FOR CRIME INVESTIGATION AND PREVENTION

Rampolla also foresees augmented world technologies being used to harvest data in the course of investigating and preventing crimes. As the foregoing discussion highlighted, the law enforcement and military agencies who have already begun work on AR eyewear have consistently identified facial recognition technology as a top priority.

Cowper and Buerger described its utility:

A more robust example of AR technology is real-time facial recognition. A user wearing an AR system containing a dataset of business and personal contacts (or a police officer with access to a known-criminal database) that included facial recognition features would always know the names and associated information of people in his or her presence that are matched within that database. Upon approaching any person the AR system could automatically capture and compare their facial or biometric features and if found, superimpose a heads-up textual annotation of the person's name and available statistics in the user's field of view, or provide an auditory announcement into an earphone.

---

[62]The former name of what is now the Augmented World Expo.

Rampolla expects law enforcement agencies equipped with such devices to regularly harvest such data into databases for later comparison to suspects, much like agencies have begun to do with license plates in recent years.

Cowper and Buerger predicted a number of applications for AR in crime scene investigation, including "[t]he use of AR video, audio and sensing devices used to visualize blood patterns, blood stains and other sensor-detectable forensic data available at crime scenes." Similarly, they said, "[f]orensic pathology could benefit from various advanced medical imaging techniques to visualize traumatic penetrating wounds before physical autopsy." Long time AR developer Robert Rice likewise authored an entire chapter on "Augmented Reality Tools for Enhanced Forensic Simulation and Crime Scene Analysis" in the 2012 book *Working Through Synthetic Worlds*.[63] "Law enforcement and investigations officers," he wrote, "will have the ability to mark and highlight evidence with virtual markers and metadata, as well as run real-time tests and analysis through the use of dynamic tools and immediate access to key databases and other information sources."[64]

Such capabilities have since materialized. In February 2012, it was revealed that "[r]esearchers at Delft University of Technology in the Netherlands have created AR goggles that let investigators create 3D videos of crime scenes, tag evidence and then virtually re-visit the scene."[65] "With this tech, you'd be free to move and look around while you manipulate the electronic display with a pair of gloves. The left hand brings up a set of menus and tools, while the right hand acts as a pointer. By pointing to a blood splatter or bullet holes (for example), you'd be able to tag them as points of interest in a 3D-model of the crime scene."[66] "If the person wearing the glasses requires assistance, they can contact someone back in the lab who can watch their video stream, speak to the wearer through a headset and place markers in the scene using a mouse and keyboard. This would also allow a police officer to take the first look around a crime scene."[67]

Visualization in AR would be useful for more than just cataloguing physical evidence at a crime scene. Tweetaround, an AR app introduced in 2010, visualized tweets according to the geolocation from which they were posted. Rampolla observes that

---

[63]Google Books description of *Working Through Synthetic Worlds* by Morrison, Kisiel, and Smith, available at http://books.google.com/books?id=EebmDgC2bb0C&dq=augmented+reality+crime+sce ne&source=gbs_navlinks_s (last visited on September 5, 2014).

[64]*Id.*

[65]Mashable Video, *Augmented Reality Goggles Virtually Recreate Crime Scenes [VIDEO]*, Mashable, (February 1, 2012), available at http://mashable.com/2012/02/01/augmented-reality-goggles-crime/ at 201 (last visited on September 5, 2012).

[66]Kevin Lee, *Coming Soon: Augmented Reality Goggles for Crime Scene Investigations*, TechHive, (Feb. 1, 2012), available at http://www.techhive.com/article/249143/coming_soon_augmented_reality_goggles_for_crime_scene_investigations.html (last visited on Sept. 5, 2014).

[67]Jacob Aron, *AR googles make crime scene investigation a desk job*, NewScientist, (Jan. 31, 2012, available at http://www.newscientist.com/article/mg21328495.700-ar-goggles-make-crime-scene-investigation-a-desk-job.html#.U9mkhvldV8E (last visited on Sept. 5, 2014).

expanding and refining that functionality could be incredibly useful for investigators trying to reconstruct what observers saw at a particular time and place.

Police have even proposed crowd-sourcing such investigation data. In January 2014, a San Jose, California city councilman proposed a system that "would allow property owners voluntarily to register their security cameras for a new San Jose Police Department database. Officers then would be able to access the footage quickly after a nearby crime has occurred."[68] To the cash-strapped police department, such a database would save the expense of collecting security footage on an *ad hoc*, door-to-door basis in response to each crime reported. Predictably, civil rights groups raised the alarm, particularly because this was the same city in which police had also begun wearing video cameras on their persons to prevent abuses. But San Jose was not the first to create such a public-private surveillance collaboration. Cities such as Philadelphia and Chicago and small towns such as Los Gatos, California have launched similar initiatives, with significant results. The Philadelphia Police Department reports that, over the course of two years, its SafeCam program resulted in over 200 arrests.[69] With advanced AR eyewear, officers could access and view such remotely-stored footage while standing in the actual location that was filmed (as was depicted in the 2013 remake of *Robocop*).

FORCE MULTIPLICATION WITH AUTONOMOUS DRONES

Yet another development presaged by the original *Robocop* is the use of unmanned ground vehicles (i.e., robots) to amplify the force projection capabilities of human officers. By the time the movie was remade, this was already reality. For example, the "Packbots" manufactured by iRobot and used by American soldiers in Iraq and Afghanistan were employed by Brazilian police during the 2014 World Cup.[70] Various groups have experimented with adding AR visualization capabilities to robots like these to "enable better mission performance and better skill transfer from platform to platform,"[71] and such devices represent an integral component of a future augmented world.

---

[68]Mike Rosenberg, *San Jose police could tap into volunteer residents' private security cameras under new proposal*, San Jose Mercury News, available at http://www.mercurynews.com/crime-courts/ci_24979753/san-jose-police-would-tap-into-residents-private (last visited on Sept. 5, 2014).

[69]Alan Reiter, *City Police Create Personal Surveillance Database*, UBM's Future Cities, (Dec. 27, 2013), available at http://www.ubmfuturecities.com/author.asp?section_id=378&doc_id=526350 (last visited on Sept. 5, 2014).

[70]Corinna Underwood, *Packbot: Serving the Military and World Cup Football*, TechEmergence, (Feb. 19, 2014), available at http://techemergence.com/packbot-serving-the-military-and-world-cup-football/ (last visited on Sept. 5, 2014).

[71]R. Darin Ellis Ph.D., *Warfighter-Focused UGV System Design: Augmented Reality-Enhanced Human-Robot Interaction for UGV Operations*, Wayne State University—College of Engineering, available at http://engineering.wayne.edu/ise/research/interaction.php (last visited on Sept. 5, 2014).

FIGURE 8.9

The arrest that Chris Barrett captured #throughglass.

South African company Desert Wolf has taken the concept one step further with "the Skunk," the heavy-duty, semi-autonomous octocopter drone it debuted in June 2014.[72] Designed for riot control, the drone "can unleash pepper spray, plastic bullets, paintballs, strobe lights and 'blinding' lasers" – at a potential combined rate of 80 projectiles per second – as well as various audio messages.[73] "The Skunk is also equipped with FLIR thermal infrared and HD color cameras to capture the identity of those in a crowd to be controlled."[74] According to the manufacturer, dozens of units have already been ordered by police departments and other customers.[75]

TURNING THE CAMERAS BACKWARDS: WEARABLES AS A MEANS TO MONITOR LAW ENFORCEMENT

On July 4, 2013, New Jersey Google Glass Explorer Chris Barrett wore his device through what proved to be fairly raucous Independence Day celebrations. In the midst of it, he ended up capturing on video what was reported to be the first arrest filmed through Glass (Fig. 8.9).[76] "I think if I had a bigger camera there, the kid would probably have punched me," Barrett said. "But I was able to capture the action with Glass and I didn't have to hold up a cell phone and press record."[77] Perhaps

---

[72]Sean Gallagher, *Flying RoboCop is a "riot control" octocopter with guns and lasers,* arstechnica, (June 19, 2014), available at http://arstechnica.com/tech-policy/2014/06/flying-robocop-is-a-riot-control-octocopter-with-guns-and-lasers/ (last visited on Sept. 5, 2014).

[73]*Id.*

[74]*Id.*

[75]*Id.*

[76]John Koetsier, *"I filmed the first fight and arrest through Google Glass"* (VB news, (July 5, 2013), available at http://venturebeat.com/2013/07/05/i-filmed-the-first-fight-and-arrest-through-google-glass/ (last visited on Sept. 15, 2014).

[77]*Id.*

the more important question is what the arresting officer would have done if he had noticed Barrett.

Although I am not aware of any reason to suspect any irregularities with this arrest, videos taken with mobile and wearable devices have exposed all manner of officer excesses and mistakes. In July 2013, the San Francisco Fire Department rushed to the aid of those who survived an Asiana Airlines plane crash at the city's airport. Those fire fighters were wearing helmet cameras. "The footage recorded by Battalion Chief Mark Johnson's helmet camera shows a Fire Department truck running over 16-year-old Ye Meng Yuan while she was lying on the tarmac covered with fire-retardant foam."[78] The incident was then reported by journalists, leading to an internal investigation. Soon thereafter, Chief Joanne Hayes-White announced a "clarification" that a pre-existing ban on video cameras applied to devices worn by fire fighters. The Chief cited medical privacy concerns, but the timing smacked of damage control.

As the world becomes increasingly augmented, video footage of every sort – including of police officers acting in the line of duty – will proliferate. If history is any guide, law enforcement and prosecutors will continue to respond to such surveillance by arresting and prosecuting those who record them. It currently seems that every week brings another headline about yet another citizen arrested and charged with wiretapping or eavesdropping (or sued civilly for invasion of privacy) for recording police officers acting in the line of duty. Indeed, in 2011, a 41-year-old mechanic in Illinois faced *life in prison* merely for recording officers issuing a citation.

In recent years, social media has provided a new and more effective way to get those videos out to the public. Just type in the search term "police brutality" into YouTube and see how many results pop up. This trend will only accelerate as the footage is recorded by more types of wearable devices, including in three dimensions, and broadcast through augmented means. Citizens and officers across the country need to know once and for all, therefore, whether recording cops is lawful.

As an attorney, I have advocated in court that such recording is protected by the First Amendment. That said, before you run out and click the "record" button, keep in mind that not all courts (and certainly not all police officers) agree. But almost every court to consider the issue has reached the same conclusion. Here's why.

THE RIGHT TO HOLD PUBLIC OFFICIALS ACCOUNTABLE IS ENSHRINED IN THE FIRST AMENDMENT AND OUR SYSTEM OF ORDERED LIBERTY

Our democratic system of ordered liberty cannot tolerate a rule of law that permits public officials to keep "private" – and, hence, free from public scrutiny – the manner in which they choose to enforce the law against private citizens. That fundamental principle is part and parcel of the right of open debate on issues of public importance enshrined in the First Amendment to the U.S. Constitution. In 1980,

---

[78]AP, "After airliner crash, SF chief bans helmet cams," Aug. 18, 2013, available at http://bigstory. ap.org/article/after-airliner-crash-sf-chief-bans-helmet-cams

Supreme Court Justice William J. Brennan wrote: "the First Amendment embodies more than a commitment to free expression and communicative interchange for their own sakes; it has a structural role to play in securing and fostering our republican system of self-government."[79] The Court has similarly held that "[t]here is an undoubted right to gather news from any source by means within the law"[80] and "news gathering is not without its First Amendment protections,. .. for without some protection for seeking out the news, freedom of press could be eviscerated."[81] This First Amendment right to gather "news" applies equally to all citizens, not just the professional press.

When public officials restrict access to information about their official activities, they are "selectively control[ling] information rightfully belonging to the people. Selective information is misinformation. The Framers of the First Amendment 'did not trust any government to separate the true from the false for us.' They protected the people against secret government."[82] "Secret government" – law enforcement outside the scope of public scrutiny – is precisely what allowing cops to suppress video of themselves would permit.

THE FIRST AMENDMENT SEVERELY LIMITS PUBLIC OFFICIALS' ABILITY TO ASSERT PERSONAL PRIVACY IN THEIR WORK-RELATED SPEECH

Speech by public officials carries few, if any, of the personal rights and privileges associated with private speech. In 2006, the U.S. Supreme Court reiterated "that when public employees make statements pursuant to their official duties, the employees are not speaking as citizens for First Amendment purposes."[83] "Restricting speech that owes its existence to a public employee's professional responsibilities does not infringe any liberties the employee might have enjoyed as a private citizen." [84] Likewise, the landmark case of *New York Times Co v Sullivan*,[85] established that a public official could not recover for "a defamatory falsehood relating to his official conduct unless he proves that the statement was made with 'actual malice,' a nearly insurmountable burden of proof. This holding flowed from our society's "profound national commitment to the principle that debate on public issues should be uninhibited, robust, and wide-open."

Accordingly, several courts have held that recording of police officers and other public officials in the course of carrying out their duties is directly protected by the

---

[79]*Richmond Newspapers v Va*, 448 US 555, 586-88 (1980) (Brennan, J concurring)
[80]*Houchins v KQED, Inc*, 438 US 1, 11 (1978) (citations omitted)
[81]*Branzburg v Hayes*, 408 US 665, 681, 707 (1972)
[82]*Detroit Free Press v Ashcroft*, 303 F3d 681; 683 (CA6, 2002) (quoting *Kleindienst v Mandel*, 408 US 753, 773 (1972)).
[83]*Garcetti v Carbalos*, 547 US 410, 421 (2006).
[84]*Id*.
[85]376 US 254, 279-280 (1964)

First Amendment.[86] These federal constitutional principles severely curtail, as a matter of law, the conceivable range of privacy interests that on-duty officers could assert.

POLICE OFFICERS ARE PARTICULARLY SUBJECT TO PUBLIC SCRUTINY

Police officers are the epitome of a public servant, whose official words and deeds are subjects of legitimate public scrutiny. As recently as June 2010, the United States Supreme Court held that "a law enforcement officer. .. should have known that his actions were likely to come under legal scrutiny, and that this might entail an analysis of his on-the-job communications."[87]

Courts around the country universally echo this reasoning. As the Massachusetts Supreme Court explained:

> *Law enforcement officials ... necessarily exercise State power in the performance of their duties. All police officers are empowered to further the preservation of law and order in the community, including the investigation of wrongdoing and the arrest of suspected criminals. Even patrol-level police officers are vested with substantial responsibility for the safety and welfare of the citizenry in areas impinging most directly and intimately on daily living: the home, the place of work and of recreation, the sidewalks and streets. Further, although a patrol officer such as the plaintiff is "low on the totem pole" and does not set policy for the department, abuse of the office can result in significant deprivation of constitutional rights and personal freedoms, not to mention bodily injury and financial loss. All police officers have the ability and authority to exercise force. We conclude, in line with the vast majority of other jurisdictions, that the abuse of a patrolman's office can have great potentiality for social harm; hence, public discussion and public criticism directed towards the performance of that office cannot constitutionally be inhibited by threat of prosecution under State libel laws.[88]*

Likewise, the Montana Supreme Court wrote that "the position of great public trust which law enforcement officers occupy [as compared to other public officials]. Specifically, the nature of the office [job] mandates that the office holder [officer] be properly subject to public scrutiny in the performance of his duties, and the public has the right to be informed of the actions and conduct of such office holders

---

[86]See, eg, *Smith v City of Cumming*, 212 F3d 1332, 1333 (CA11, 2000) ("The First Amendment protects the right to gather information about what public officials do on public property, and specifically, a right to record matters of public interest"); *Alvarado v KOB-TV, LLC*, 493 F3d 1210, 1219-20 (CA10, 2007) (dismissing privacy lawsuit by undercover police against videographer on First Amendment grounds); *Gilles v Davis*, 427 F3d 197, 212 (CA3, 2005) ("videotaping or photographing the police in the performance of their duties on public property may be a [First Amendment] protected activity"); *Fordyce v. City of Seattle*, 55 F3d 436, 439 (CA9, 1995) (recognizing a "First Amendment right to film matters of public interest"); *Blackston v Alabama*, 30 F3d 117, 120 (CA11, 1994) (First Amendment protects right to film public meetings).

[87]*City of Ontario v Quon*, 130 S Ct 2619, 2631 (2010).

[88]*Rotkiewicz v Sadowsky*, 730 NE2d 282, 288 (Mass, 2000) (emphasis added);

[officers]."[89] Consequently, law enforcement personnel of every rank and function are public figures for First Amendment purposes, and – as illustrated below – no expectation of privacy in their official law enforcement actions.

Virtually all courts to address the issue have held that police officers cannot have a reasonable expectation of privacy in the performance of their public law enforcement duties

Courts applying the U.S. Constitution and the laws of Washington, New Jersey, Missouri, and Pennsylvania (informed and limited by the above-mentioned First Amendment principles) have held that police officers performing their law enforcement duties cannot objectively expect their actions to be private and hence free from unauthorized recording.

One of the earliest cases on point was *State v Flora*,[90] decided in 1992 by the Washington Court of Appeals. There, a private citizen recorded his own arrest "because he feared the deputies would assault him and use racial slurs as they had done in the past." He was convicted of criminal eavesdropping. In reversing the conviction, the Washington court noted a lack of authority allowing "public officers [to assert] a privacy interest in statements uttered in the course of performing their official and public duties," and held that "the police officers in this case could not reasonably have considered their words private." In *Flora* and its progeny, "Washington courts have refused to transform the privacy act into a sword available for use against individuals by public officers acting in their official capacity."[91]

Across the country, "[c]ourts have held that police officers do not have a reasonable expectation of privacy when they are interacting with suspects."[92] Such expectations are objectively unreasonable, according to the U.S. Court of Appeals for the Eight Circuit, even where officers subjectively believe their words to be private:

> *Clearly the officers' subjective expectations [were] that their communication would not be intercepted. . . . The objective reasonableness of the subjective expectations of the officers, however, is another matter. The undisputed facts show that the tape-recorded incident took place in a public jail and between police officers*

---

[89]*Bozeman Daily Chronicle v City of Bozeman Police Dep't*, 859 P2d 435, 440 (Mont, 1993)

[90]68 Wn App 802; 845 P2d 1355 (Wash Ct App, 1992)

[91]*Johnson v Hawe*, 388 F3d 676, 682 (CA9, 2004) (internal quotation omitted) (upholding a §1983 action against a police chief who arrested a citizen for videotaping the chief "in the performance of his public duties").

[92]*Hornberger v. ABC*, 799 A2d 566, 594 (N.J. Super. 2002) (dismissing eavesdropping charges against television station that used hidden cameras to record police searching a car); *see also Hart v City of Jersey City*, 308 NJ Super 487, 493; 706 A2d 256 (NJ App Div, 1998) ("police officers, because they occupy positions of public trust and exercise special powers, have a diminished expectation of privacy"); Commonwealth v Henlen, 522 Pa 514; 564 A2d 905 (Penn, 1989) (finding no reasonable expectation of privacy for police officer who was recorded interrogating a prison guard in closed room); *Rawlins v Hutchinson Pub Co,* 543 P.2d 988, 993 (Kan, 1975) ("a public official, a fortiori, has no right of privacy as to the manner in which he conducts himself in office. Such facts are 'public facts' and not 'private facts.' Hence, a truthful account of charges of misconduct in office cannot form the basis of an action for invasion of privacy.")

and a prisoner. These are the only material facts necessary to prove, as a matter of law, that it was not objectively reasonable for the officers to expect that their conversations would not be intercepted.[93]

Because society entrusts police officers with unique license to deprive others of liberty, the manner in which they use those powers vis-à-vis private citizens is inherently a subject for public scrutiny, and not the officer's own private concern.

More recent legal developments have continued this trend. In 2011, the U.S. Court of Appeals for the First Circuit ruled that "a citizen's right to film government officials ... in the discharge of their duties in a public space is a basic, vital, and well-established liberty safeguarded by the First Amendment."[94] In January 2012, the U.S. Justice Department filed a brief in the U.S. District Court for the District of Maryland expressly supporting a citizen's right to film police in public. According to the DOJ:

This litigation presents constitutional questions of great moment in this digital age: whether private citizens have a First Amendment right to record police officers in the public discharge of their duties, and whether officers violate citizens' Fourth and Fourteenth Amendment rights when they seize and destroy such recordings without a warrant or due process. The United States urges this Court to answer both of those questions in the affirmative. The right to record police officers while performing duties in a public place, as well as the right to be protected from the warrantless seizure and destruction of those recordings, are not only required by the Constitution. They are consistent with our fundamental notions of liberty, promote the accountability of our governmental officers, and instill public confidence in the police officers who serve us daily.

Later the same year, the U.S. Court of Appeals for the Seventh Circuit enjoined enforcement of Illinois' eavesdropping law. In a 2-1 decision, the court ruled that the law, which prohibits people from making audio recordings of police officers in public, "likely violates" the First Amendment.

MASSACHUSETTS SHOWS WHAT HAPPENS IF FIRST AMENDMENT RIGHTS ARE NOT PROTECTED

In the widely criticized 2001 decision *Commonwealth v Hyde*,[95] a motorist was convicted of eavesdropping for recording his traffic stop by police. A divided Massachusetts Supreme Court upheld the conviction. The court sidestepped *Flora*'s rejection of privacy protection for police acting their official capacities by noting that Massachusetts' eavesdropping statute – unlike those in most other states – outlawed all unauthorized recording, whether or not the recorded persons had a reasonable expectation of privacy.

Two of the six justices dissented, lamenting that, had the Rodney King beating occurred in Massachusetts, George "Holliday would have been exposed to criminal

---

[93]*Angel v Williams*, 12 F3d 786, 790 (CA8, 1993) (applying Missouri law).
[94]*Glik v. Cunniffe*, 655 F. 3d 78 (1st Cir. 2011)
[95]434 Mass 594; 750 NE2d 963 (Mass, 2001)

indictment rather than lauded for exposing an injustice." The majority did not disagree, but was nevertheless unmoved. It relied on the plain text of the statute "in favor of speculation as to how an imaginary scenario might have played out, had the Rodney King episode occurred in Massachusetts." Massachusetts Chief Justice Marshall saw this development as a grave threat to our Republic:

> *Citizens have a particularly important role to play when the official conduct at issue is that of the police. Their role cannot be performed if citizens must fear criminal reprisals when they seek to hold government officials accountable by recording – secretly recording on occasion – an interaction between a citizen and a police officer.*

This view has been vindicated by virtually every other court to consider a similar dispute.

REPRISALS BY POLICE AGAINST THE CITIZENS WHO RECORD THEM ARE INEVITABLE WITHOUT CLEAR JUDICIAL GUIDANCE

The instinct to suppress video recordings of their misdeeds is not unique to the law enforcement officers of any particular jurisdiction. And in light of the ever-increasing ubiquity of audiovisual recording technology in modern society, officers and other public officials will have more opportunities to initiate such reprisals. In 2010, 25-year-old motorcyclist Anthony Graber used a helmet-mounted camera to record his traffic stop by a plain-clothes officer in Maryland. After posting the clip to the internet site YouTube, police raided Graber's home, confiscated his computer and camera, and charged him with wiretapping – a felony carrying a possible sentence of 16 years' imprisonment (Fig. 8.10).

The incident sparked a torrent of news coverage and editorials decrying the charges. The same publications also note the disturbing increase in such arrests in re-

FIGURE 8.10

The wearable video recorded by Anthony Graber.

cent years.[96] Notably, those charged with interpreting the law in these States continue to reject such charges. On July 7, 2010, the Maryland Attorney General responded to the Graber incident by endorsing the conclusion that "a police stop of an individual necessarily is not a 'private conversation.'[97] Following *Flora* and similar cases – and distinguishing Massachusetts' *Hyde* decision – the Attorney General opined that a reasonable expectation of privacy is "an unlikely conclusion as to the majority of encounters between police and citizens, particularly when they occur in a public place and involve the exercise of police powers."

In a September 27, 2010 opinion, Judge Emory A. Plitt agreed and dismissed the eavesdropping charge against Graber, holding that, "[i]n this rapid information technology era in which we live, it is hard to imagine that either an offender or an officer would have any reasonable expectation of privacy with regard to what is said between them in a traffic stop on a public highway." The thoroughly researched opinion concludes with the following reflection:

> *Those of us who are public officials and are entrusted with the power of the state are ultimately accountable to the public. When we exercise that power in public fora, we should not expect our actions to be shielded from public observation. "Sed quis custodiet ipsos cutodes" i.e., "Who will guard the guards themselves?"*

Many courts, however, have yet to pass on the issue. Therefore, police and prosecutors in those jurisdictions remain free to interpret the law as they see fit. "Even if these cases do not hold up in court, the police can do a lot of damage just by threatening to arrest and prosecute people. . . . Most people are not so game for a fight with the police. They just stop filming. These are the cases no one finds out about, in which there is no arrest or prosecution, but the public's freedoms have nevertheless been eroded."[98] By contrast, thanks to the clear guidance of the *Flora* decision, police officers in Washington State know unequivocally that the conversations they have with citizens in their official capacities are not private.[99]

---

[96](USA Today, July 17, 2010) ("This is an abuse of prosecutorial authority and a misinterpretation of state law. But it's typical of the attitude of too many prosecutors and police toward people who record their encounters with law enforcement"); (ABC News, July 20, 2010) ("Arrests such as Graber's are becoming more common along with the proliferation of portable video cameras and cell-phone recorders"); (Boston Globe, Feb. 3. 2010) ("in Massachusetts and other states, the arrests of street videographers, whether they use cellphones or other video technology, offers a dramatic illustration of the collision between new technology and policing practices").

[97]Letter from Robert McDonald of the State of Maryland Office of the Attorney General to Honorable Samuel Rosenberg, (July 7, 2010), available at http://www.thenewspaper.com/rlc/docs/2010/md-youtube.pdf (last visited on Sept. 5, 2014).

[98](Time, Aug. 4, 2010).

[99]See, e.g., *Johnson, supra* ("Because it was clearly established under Washington law at the time of the arrest that recording a police officer in the performance of his public duties was not a violation of the Privacy Act and it was unreasonable for Chief Nelson to believe otherwise, we hold that the Chief is not entitled to qualified immunity"); *Barela v City of Woodland*, 358 Fed Appx 857, 859 (CA9, 2009) (same, following *Johnson* and *Flora*).

CITIZEN VIDEO RECORDINGS ARE EFFECTIVE IN CURBING UNLAWFUL CONDUCT BY POLICE

Audiovisual recording empowers citizens to document abuses of power by law enforcement officers that would otherwise never be held accountable. Data collected by the United States government suggests that most police officers will not report even serious misconduct by a fellow officer. The entire nation, of course, is familiar with the video of Rodney King's March 3, 1991 beating by Los Angeles police, which George Holliday, a private citizen, recorded with his camcorder. Without Holliday's recording, however, it is probable that the officers involved would not have been convicted in federal court, and the Christopher Commission, which revealed widespread corruption in the Los Angeles Police Department, would (by the Commission's own admission) never have been formed. Cell phone videos taken by onlookers were the key evidence against the San Francisco officer convicted of manslaughter in the January 1, 2009 fatal shooting of Oscar Grant.

Video evidence has been no less useful in holding law enforcement officers accountable in my home state of Michigan. In November 2009, a Lansing police officer was disciplined after video evidence emerged showing him tasering a handcuffed and subdued suspect. In April 2005, "videotape evidence played a key role in convincing prosecutors to charge a Michigan State Police trooper with second-degree murder in the. .. shooting of a homeless man"[100] in Detroit. Similar examples abound from across the country and the globe.

This is a public service that benefits both society and police departments. Advocacy groups have recognized the power of a camera-armed citizenry. In 2006, the ACLU responded to repeated accusations of police misconduct in St. Louis by distributing free video cameras to local residents, for the purpose of documenting any such incidents. Police departments themselves have acknowledged the social utility of such precautions. St. Louis' police chief responded to the ACLU's plan by saying, "It's legal and there's nothing wrong with it." As noted above, in 2009, San Jose police adopted a similar approach in response to incidents of police violence.

Without question, society as a whole around the country is moving toward more video recording of police officers acting in the line of duty, not less – and our democracy is healthier for it. Shielding public servants acting in official capacities from embarrassing public scrutiny simply is not worth the price of eroding our civil liberties.

---

[100]Ben Schmitt, *Acquitted In Killing, Trapper Files a Lawsuit,* Convertino and Associates webpage, (March 15, 2006), available at http://convertino.net/id21.html (last visited on September 5, 2014).

Civil Rights

INFORMATION IN THIS CHAPTER:

- Civil rights for the disabled
- How AR can help the disabled
- AR as a civil right

INTRODUCTION

With all the wonder and anticipation that surrounds augmented reality, it is easy to forget that there are already millions of people whose experience of reality through their five senses has already been involuntarily altered. More than 50 million Americans – about 18% of our population – have some form of disability. Whether their condition impairs one or more of their five senses, their freedom of movement, or their cognitive abilities, these individuals do not enjoy the same capacity to experience reality that others have.

When discussing this fact in the context of AR, it is tempting to make the observation – as I have mistakenly done in the past – that disabled persons already experience an "augmented reality." That is, until one remembers that to "augment" means to "make greater or larger." Physical and mental disabilities do anything but. They "substantially limit[] one or more of the major life activities of such individual,"[1] thereby diminishing that individual's opportunity to experience physical reality in ways that others take for granted.

Yet AR does have an important role to play for these individuals. Custom-designed augmented world devices could go a long way toward bridging the experiential gap imposed by disabilities. Although the end result may be only an approximation of typical human experience, the inherent value of the augmentation to that individual certainly could be significantly more meaningful than an equivalent improvement in a normally abled person's experience.

The United States and many other nations have various laws on the books designed to encourage providers of goods and service to make extra effort to accommodate the disabled, in order to minimize the degree to which disabilities keep people from enjoying everyday life experiences. When certain methods of accommodation become sufficiently economical and logistically feasible, they tend to become

---

[1] 28 C.F.R. §36.106.

requirements instead of suggestions. As AR technologies improve, it seems inevitable that some of them will first be encouraged, and ultimately become prescribed, methods of accommodating disabled persons.

THE CURRENT REQUIREMENTS FOR ACCOMMODATING THE DISABLED IN DIGITAL MEDIA
THE GOVERNING LEGAL FRAMEWORK

The Americans with Disabilities Act of 1990 (ADA) is the flagship of legal protection for the disabled in the United States. It was adopted to ensure, among other things, that no one is "discriminated against on the basis of disability in the full and equal enjoyment of the goods, services, facilities, privileges, advantages, or accommodations of any place of public accommodation."[2] The law has required public and private entities across the country to make a number of significant accommodations in the way they do business, and modifications to their physical structures, to assist disabled individuals. Various other Federal[3] and state laws supplement these protections.

By and large, these laws have received broad, bipartisan support, and have even been strengthened over the years. But striking the right balance between accommodating the disabled and respecting the liberty and economic interests of businesses is not always simple, especially in light of how quickly technological and economic realities change.

When regulations requiring accommodation are perceived as imposing too heavy a burden on businesses, a backlash can erupt. For example, in 2010, the Department of Justice published updated regulations under the ADA. These regulations adopted the 2010 Standards for Accessible Design, which, for the first time, contain specific accessibility requirements for many types of recreational facilities, including swimming pools, wading pools, and spas. In January 2012, the Department issued guidance titled "ADA 2010 Revised Requirements: Accessible Pools – Accessible Means of Entry and Exit" to assist entities covered by Title III of the ADA, such as hotels and motels, health clubs, recreation centers, public country clubs, and other businesses that have swimming pools, wading pools, and spas, in understanding how the new requirements apply to them. Many owners of such businesses, however, did not care at all for what they learned, sparking a firestorm of criticism. The DOJ relaxed its enforcement of the new regulations a bit, by delaying the deadline for implementation and emphasizing that "there is no need [under the ADA] to provide access to existing pools if doing so is not 'readily achievable,'[4] especially in a weak economy.

---

[2] 42 U.S.C. 12182.

[3] U.S. Department of Justice – Civil Rights Division – Disability Rights Section, *A Guide to Disability Rights Laws* (July 2009), available at http://www.ada.gov/cguide.htm (last viewed on September 5, 2014).

[4] *Questions and Answers: Accessibility Requirements for Existing Swimming Pools at Hotels and Other Public Accommodations,* ada.gov, available at http://www.ada.gov/qa_existingpools_titleIII.htm (last visited on September 5, 2014).

Pressure to provide more accommodation is building on the international level as well. The UN Convention on the Rights of Persons with Disabilities – the first human rights treaty of the twenty-first century – was opened for signature in 2007. The United States is one of the 149 member states to sign the treaty, although Congress has not ratified it as of this writing.

The same debates will continue in the augmented world. As noted above, the points of conflict in today's world are over such issues as building ramps into swimming pools and making sure sidewalks have adequate curb cuts – because these are "readily achievable" means of providing equal access to "places of public accommodation." Tomorrow, as virtual "places" become more important venues for commerce and entertainment, the fight will likely be over equal access to those experiences. It will be interesting to observe whether the law continues to view such immersive content as purely software and speech,[5] or according to the metaphors of physicality and place that we use to describe them. If the latter, then we may see laws treat massively multi-participant virtual experiences as "places of public accommodation," at least for purposes of civil rights laws. The question will then be which forms of ensuring equal access to those "places" are "readily achievable" for its creators to provide.

DIGITAL ACCOMMODATION IS STILL IN ITS EARLY STAGES

Equal access standards are only beginning to make an impact in digital technology. Section 255 and Section 251(a)(2) of the Communications Act of 1934, as amended by the Telecommunications Act of 1996, require manufacturers of telecommunications equipment and providers of telecommunications services to ensure that such equipment and services are accessible to and usable by persons with disabilities, if readily achievable. The UN Convention likewise "recognizes access to information and communications technologies, including the Web, as a basic human right,"[6] but that standard will not apply in the United States unless Congress ratifies and implements the treaty.

The Federal government actually holds itself up to a higher standard than others in this area. Section 508 of the Rehabilitation Act of 1973[7] was first added in 1986, and has been updated several times since. This legislation requires all Federal departments and agencies to "ensure … that the electronic and information technology [they develop, procure, maintain or use] allows [disabled persons] to have access to and use of information and data that is comparable to the access to and use of the information and data"[8] by individuals without disabilities. This provision applies "regardless of the type of medium of the technology,"[9] but comes with a variety of

---

[5]See Chapter 6 for a deeper elucidation of this concept.
[6]Tim Berners-Lee, *Accessibility,* W3.org, available at http://www.w3.org/standards/webdesign/accessibility (last visited on September 5, 2013).
[7]29 U.S.C. §749d.
[8]29 U.S.C. §749d(a)(1)(A).
[9]*Id.*

FIGURE 9.1

Chief Operations Officer Torsten Oberst demonstrates FEDVC's software, which reads web page content aloud at a 2011 program highlighting Section 508.[10]

caveats, including an exception for when "an undue burden would be imposed on the department or agency."[11]

Nevertheless, these standards put the Federal government ahead of most private providers in terms of access to digital materials. As applied to online resources, such as websites, Section 508 and its enabling regulations are modeled after the access guidelines developed by the Web Accessibility Initiative of the World Wide Web Consortium, or W3C (Fig. 9.1).[12] The W3C advertises that its "guidelines [are] widely regarded as the international standard for Web accessibility."[13] Indeed, some of the W3C's basic tips for making websites more accessible – such as alternative text for images, allowing for input by keyboard instead of a mouse, and transcripts for podcasts[14] – are becoming increasingly common. That said, such standards still remain largely voluntary in most circumstances.

[10]USDA/CC BY2.0 license.
[11]29 U.S.C. §749d(a)(1)(A).
[12]*Summary of Section 508 Standards,* Section 508.gov webpage, available at http://www.section508.gov/summary-section508-standards#web (last visited on September 5, 2014).
[13]*Web Accessibility Initiative (WAI),* W3.org webpage, available at http://www.w3.org/WAI/ (last visited on September 5, 2014).
[14]Tim Berners-Lee, *Accessibility,* W3.org, available at http://www.w3.org/standards/webdesign/accessibility (last visited on September 5, 2014).

Applying such laws to the digital economy, however, is tricky. For one thing, so much digital content is inherently audiovisual in nature that it may be either practically impossible, or at least very expensive, to create satisfactory accompaniments for the blind or deaf – especially in light of the sheer volume of digital data available. What is more, there is not the same tradition of access to such materials as there are for more basic functions such as climbing stairs and crossing streets. On the other hand, our society becomes more dependent on digital and online data with each passing day, meaning that those without meaningful access to that world are getting increasingly left behind.

Therefore, advocates on both sides of the issue tend to be particularly vocal when disputes arise. For example, in March 2012, a federal judge in California allowed the Greater LA Council on Deafness to proceed with a lawsuit against CNN for failing to provide close captioning for videos on its website. Similar accommodations for the deaf have become customary in many television broadcasts, which has created an expectation for similar options with online video.

To date, close captioning has been required online only for video that was originally broadcast on television. In 2012, the Federal Communications Commission required closed captioning only in full-length TV shows that were rebroadcast online. By 2016, this requirement will be extended to "so-called 'straight lift' clips using the same audio and video …. A year later, the rule will apply to montages involving multiple straight-lift clips. And by mid-2017, closed captioning will be required on live and near-live TV over the web, including news and sports."[15] Some providers already go beyond these minimum expectations, however – such as the text transcripts that YouTube auto-generates for many of its videos – and there is every reason to believe that the requirement will eventually be imposed on more, if not all, video content provided online, and perhaps other content as well.

Indeed, in June 2012, a judge in Massachusetts became the first to rule in favor of those seeking to require Netflix to close caption its online video.[16] The foundation of this ruling was the judge's finding that Netflix and other websites had become "place[s] of public accommodation" – the first time any court had reached that conclusion. The implications of this holding are not modest. Leading internet law commentator Eric Goldman, of the Santa Clara University School of Law, saw this as a dangerous and errant deviation from previously settled law that threatened to do real damage to internet commerce:

> *This is a bad ruling. Really terrible. It's … potentially ripped open a huge hole in Internet law. … If websites must comply with the ADA, all hell will break loose. Could YouTube be obligated to close-caption videos on the site? (This case seems to leave that door open.) Could every website using Flash have to redesign their sites for browsers that read the screen? I'm not creative enough to think of all the*

---

[15]David Lieberman, *FCC Creates Timetable For Closed Captioning In TV Clips That Run Online*, Deadline Hollywood (July 11, 2014), available at http://www.deadline.com/2014/07/fcc-online-tv-clips-closed-captioning/ (last visited on September 5, 2014).

[16]National Association of the Deaf v. Netflix, Inc., 3:11-cv-30168-MAP (D. Mass. June 19, 2012)

*implications, but I can assure you that ADA plaintiffs' lawyers will have a long
checklist of items worth suing over. Big companies may be able to afford the compliance and litigation costs, but the entry costs for new market participants could
easily reach prohibitive levels.*[17]

Nevertheless, that case settled a few months later, with Netflix agreeing to caption
100% of its videos by 2014, and to reduce the time the service takes to add captions
to new streaming content down to 7 days by 2016.[18] The National Association for the
Deaf, which brought the lawsuit, heralded this agreement as "a model for the streaming
entertainment industry," although it's still not clear two years later whether the Netflix
model will indeed become the norm anytime soon. As of this writing, courts remain
"split about the extent to which private websites are subject to the accessibility requirements of Title III of the Americans with Disabilities Act (ADA), and the U.S. Department of Justice (DOJ) has not yet published any clear regulations about the issue."[19]

Meanwhile, Federal regulators continue to push for greater accommodation not
only by websites, but in mobile applications as well. In June 2014, the Department
of Justice reached its first settlement agreement that included a provision requiring
the settling party to make its mobile app ADA-compliant. "The [DOJ's] investigation
found that the [Florida State University] Police Department's online application form
asked questions about a past or present disability and other medical conditions in violation of the ADA."[20] One of the steps FSU agreed to take to rectify the problem was
"ensuring that the FSU Police Department website, including its employment opportunities website and its mobile applications, conform to the Web Content Accessibility Guidelines 2.0 Level AA Success Criteria and other Conformance Requirements
(WCAG 2.0 AA)."[21]

These developments demonstrate the growing political and legal pressure to make
digital media more accessible to disabled persons. Especially in light of the increas-

---

[17]Eric Goldman, *Will the American with Disabilities Act tear a hole in Internet law?* Arstechnica, (June
27, 2012), available at http://arstechnica.com/tech-policy/2012/06/will-the-americans-with-disabilities-
act-tear-a-hole-in-internet-law/ (last visited on September 5, 2014). I'm sure Professor Goldman would
also want it known, however, that he qualified his comments as follows: "Although I believe the statute
and case law make it clear that ADA does not apply to websites, I also believe that responsible websites
should voluntarily undertake extra efforts to accommodate users with disabilities. In many cases, doing
so will actually increase profits by expanding the userbase; and even where it isn't, it's a good business
decision both as a matter of corporate ethics and for providing extra utility to all users."

[18]*National Association of the Deaf, et al., v. Netflix, Inc.,* U.S. District Court, District of MA, Consent
Decree of October 9, 2012, available at http://dredf.org/captioning/netflix-consent-decree-10-10-12.
pdf (last visited on September 5, 2014).

[19]Michael C. Wilhelm, *Are websites operated by public accommodations subject to the American with
Disabilities Act (ADA)?* ACC-Association of Corporate Counsel website, (January 9, 2014), available
at http://www.lexology.com/library/detail.aspx?g=40a950f7-8c9b-4d88-9595-5a7a6399a267 (last visited on September 5, 2014).

[20]Department of Justice Office of Public Affairs, *Justice Department Reaches Settlement with Florida
State University,* The United States Department of Justice website, (June 5, 2014), available at http://
www.justice.gov/opa/pr/2014/June/14-crt-606.html (last visited on September 5, 2014).

[21]*Id.*

ing median age in the United States and other developed nations,[22] there is every reason to expect this trend to continue. This means that those developing the augmented world should proactively include access concerns in their design strategies from the very beginning. It also suggests there will be lucrative markets available for digital solutions that enhance access to digital content.

HOW AR CAN MEANINGFULLY IMPROVE THE LIVES OF DISABLED PERSONS

Fortunately, the augmented medium provides several natural methods of enhancing disabled persons' access to digital information. Again, Google is largely responsible for sparking most of the public conversation on this topic because its Glass device was the first digital eyewear to get widespread attention. (Not to mention the "smart" contact lenses that Google announced in July 2014, which are said to be capable of "monitor[ing] the wearer's blood sugar levels.")[23] Some have said of Glass that "not since the invention of text-to-voice and other speech-recognition software has a tech invention had such potential to help the disabled."[24] The issues and opportunities Glass raises, however, apply to the entire category of wearable computing.

THE DEAF

Enormous sums of money and political capital have been spent to achieve the modest improvements in close captioning availability that resulted from the *Netflix* and *CNN* cases and related FCC regulations. Yet AR-infused eyewear could accomplish far more in terms of giving the deaf access to the everyday world.

Google Glass has already offered a glimpse of what this future might look like. Because the device (by default) conveys sound through bone conduction – i.e., through the skull directly into the inner ear – rather than headphones, it actually allows even many deaf persons to perceive the sounds. Digital marketing professional David Trahan, who is deaf in his right ear, experienced this first-hand. The audio produced by his Glass device allowed him to hear through his right ear for the first time, and now it has become an integral part of his life.[25]

---

[22]See, e.g., Congressional Research Service, The Changing Demographic Profile of the United States, March 31, 2011, available at http://fas.org/sgp/crs/misc/RL32701.pdf.

[23]Mark Scott, *Novartis Joins With Google to Develop Lens that Monitors Blood Sugar,* New York Times (July 15, 2014), available at http://www.nytimes.com/2014/07/16/business/international/novartis-joins-with-google-to-develop-contact-lens-to-monitor-blood-sugar.html?_r=0 (last visited on September 5, 2014).

[24]Marco della Cava, *Beyond a gadget: Google Glass is a boon to disabled,* USA Today (October 23, 2013), available at http://www.usatoday.com/story/tech/2013/10/22/google-glass-aids-disabled/3006827/ (last visited on September 5, 2014).

[25]Andy Meek, *Voices In Your Head: How Google Glass Lets a Half-Deaf Person Hear,* Fast Company, available at http://www.fastcompany.com/3015749/voices-in-your-head-how-google-glass-lets-a-half-deaf-person-hear (last visited on September 5, 2014).

Combining digital eyewear with speech recognition software has the potential to radically enhance life for deaf individuals by essentially close captioning *anything* and *everything* in life. People wearing such digital eyewear could potentially see the words of someone speaking to them superimposed on their field of vision in more-or-less-real time. Obviously, technological barriers to such devices still remain. Software would need to improve, and it would need to sync with directional microphones that could isolate the speaker's voice from the background noise. But the impressive quality of voice recognition products like Dragon Naturally Speaking and Siri bring hope such a product is not far off.

Voices are not the only sounds that deaf people could benefit from "hearing." Wearable devices could be programmed to recognize and alert to the telltale sales of oncoming traffic, traffic control signals, music, alarms – all the sounds that others take for granted every day – and display appropriate text notices in the user's field of view.

These solutions would allow a deaf person to understand the sounds around them, but could AR help the deaf communicate? For more than a decade, researchers have been working toward that exact goal. As early as the 2003 IEEE International Symposium on Wearable Computers, a team demonstrated the ASL OneWay, a tool designed to help the deaf community to communicate with the hearing by translating American Sign Language.[26] The device consists of a set of sensors in a hat worn by the signer, and two wristwatch-sized devices, one on each hand. The system recognizes the hand gestures that make up a sign and deduces the English phrases most closely associated with the signed phrase. The deaf person sees these phrases in his eyewear and selects the appropriate one, which the device then speaks through a speaker in the hat. As one would imagine, these prototypes were a bit cumbersome, but the concept was potentially revolutionary.

More recently, researchers at the multi-university project MobileASL have been working to develop visual recognition software capable of detecting hand gestures and transmitting them in real time over standard mobile phone networks (Fig. 9.2).[27] Other projects hope to someday be able to translate the signs in to written or spoken speech in near-real time. These projects have advanced far in the past decade, and it is feasible to imagine them installed in digital eyewear within the coming decade. Likewise, designers have at least begun to conceive of gloves that can track the wearer's gestures in three dimensions, also providing instant translation from sign to speech. Such developments could increase deaf persons' ability to integrate into society by orders of magnitude.

Once such on-the-fly captioning becomes even marginally feasible, we are likely to see political pressure grow to make the technology available to the deaf community. The first implementations will almost certainly be voluntary, by providers who seek

[26]7th IEEE International Symposium on Wearable Computers, Oct. 2003, home page, available at http://www.iswc.net/iswc03/press.html (last visited on September 5, 2014).

[27]Stuart Fox, "Targeted Video Compression Brings Cell Phones to Sign Language Users," Popular Science December 8, 2009, available at http://www.popsci.com/technology/article/2009-12/targetted-compression-brings-sign-language-cell-phones.

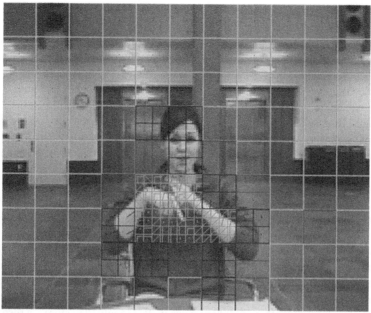

FIGURE 9.2

The MobileASL project.

to distinguish themselves from their competitors. By that time, much of the programming that we currently receive on televisions may be broadcast on eyewear instead, meaning that the same close captioning rules that currently apply to TV will be in force there as well. What is more, the deaf will not be the only market for the technology. Just like noisy bars will activate the close captioning feature of their televisions to allow patrons to follow the programming, normally abled people could encounter situations in which they too can benefit from technology originally intended for the disabled.

Once the technology gains a track record, insurance companies may begin to subsidize it for persons who lose their hearing as a result of injury or disease. Government officials and politicians who today ensure that a sign language interpreter is present with them onstage may instead make live-captioning eyewear available to those in the crowd who need it. Eventually, provisions like the Rehabilitation Act may require Federal employees to provide such "access" to their live speeches. By various means, live close captioning in the physical world will eventually become commonplace.

THE BLIND

Games like *Inception the App*,[28] which "uses augmented sound to induce dreams," already promise to digitally augment our sense of hearing. AR devices could accentuate

---

[28]Inception: The App home page, available at http://inceptiontheapp.com/ (last visited on September 5, 2014).

the hearing of blind individuals in a way analogous to the visual information it could provide for the deaf. Users could receive audible alerts when they come into proximity with a person, vehicle, traffic control device, sign, or any of a hundred other significant objects. In 2012, Japanese telecommunications giant Nippon Telegraph and Telephone Corp. developed a prototype pair of glasses designed to do just that. Running the company's "SightFinder" technology, the device "sends streaming images from a camera to one of NTT's data centers to recognize and identify street signs or potential obstacles. In real time, NTT's computers analyze the images and provide warnings – street construction causing a detour or a cone in front of a pothole – via an Internet-connected device like a smartphone to help the visually impaired to move freely."[29]

Dr. Peter Meijer, a senior scientist at Philips Research Laboratories in the Netherlands, has been working toward this goal for years. His software, called the "vOICe," is "a universal translator for mapping images to sounds."[30] Already available as a free Android app, the software uses a mobile phone's camera to take an audio snapshot of the user's surroundings, associating height with pitch and brightness with loudness. Presumably once the user grows accustomed to this system, it will become second nature and allow the blind to roam more confidently than is possible with a mere walking stick for guidance. As of this writing, the app has earned an average of 3.5 out of 5 stars from more than 77,000 reviews in the Google Play store – a respectable indication of real utility.

One could imagine similar functionality being added to Word Lens or almost any other visual recognition app, allowing the app to audibly explain to the user what it sees. The blind community has certainly imagined this future. One sight-impaired Explorer shared his thoughts after testing Glass:

> I imagine a future where Glass can read a menu to me in a restaurant. A simple glance at the menu and glass recognises the text and begins to read aloud. Or perhaps, opening a book and have it read aloud, reading a book – that is something I have not been able to do in a long time. Object recognition, the ability to identify objects in a specific scene, or recognise my friends and acquaintances, and speak their names in my ear. Essentially, Glass would allow me to more readily operate in social environments, fill in the gaps created by my lack of vision.[31]

The impact of such advances would be so profound for blind individuals that they are likely to become common and even required by the same mechanisms discussed above with respect to accommodations for the deaf.

[29]Sarah Berlow, *Google Glasses Find Unlikely Japanese Rival,* The Wall Street Journal (April 12, 2012), available at http://blogs.wsj.com/japanrealtime/2012/04/19/google-glasses-find-unlikely-japanese-rival/ (last visited on September 5, 2014).

[30]"The vOICe for Android," http://www.seeingwithsound.com/android.htm (last visited September 12, 2014).

[31]Simon, *Google Glass – A blind perspective,* andadapt, (June 27, 2014), available at http://www.andadapt.com/google-glass-a-blind-users-perspective/ (last visited on September 5, 2014).

As one step in that direction, the "vOICe for Android has already been demonstrated to run on Google Glass, letting the blind 'see' for themselves and get visual feedback in a second. A talking face detector and color identifier is included."[32] A significant caveat to this idea is the limited battery life of Glass in its current form. Users are cautioned to use an external battery, and even then "[i]t is recommended to run the vOICe for Android on Google Glass only for up to a few minutes at a time, to avoid overheating risks."[33] These present-day limitations, however, have not tempered the excitement Glass has stirred within the blind community, with some already calling it "a blind man's window into the world."[34]

Dr. Meijer has proposed an even more radical version of this idea by integrating the vOICe app directly into a dedicated eyewear device promises "synthetic sight" by essentially hacking the brain to accept audio signals as visual images. According to Meijer's website, "neuroscience research has already shown that the visual cortex of even adult blind people can become responsive to sound, and sound-induced illusory flashes can be evoked in most sighted people. The vOICe technology may now build on this with live video from an unobtrusive head-mounted camera encoded in sound."

Digital eyewear also offers a promising new platform for apps like VizWiz, which might be described as crowd-sourced AR. Currently a smartphone app, VizWiz allows blind people to upload pictures of their surroundings and ask questions about them, then get feedback from seeing persons around the globe. "Where smartphone-based VizWiz users have to contend with the inherent hassle of 'using a handheld device while blind, Glass offers the chance to provide continuous, hands-free visual assistance,'[35] according to the service's founder.

Of course, audio signals are not the only way to enhance life for the blind. Those who read Braille could still benefit from enhanced haptic technology. In theory, the feel of virtually any surface could be augmented with additional sensory feedback, including in the Braille language. Therefore, a blind person wearing a haptic glove could "feel" Braille text on any surface, without that writing physically being there.

THE PHYSICALLY HANDICAPPED

Digital information alone can't do anything to increase the mobility of those with physical impairments. Better databases and way finding applications, however, could make it a lot easier to find the accommodations designed to make their lives easier.

---

[32]"The vOICe for Android," http://www.seeingwithsound.com/android.htm (last visited September 12, 2014).

[33]Id.

[34]Vaibhav Athare, *Google Glass for Visually Impaired and Blind,* I Wanna See, (Posted on April 12, 2014), available at http://www.iwannaseee.com/google-glass/google-glass-for-visually-impaired/ (last visited on September 5, 2014).

[35]Kevin Kepple, *Beyond a gadget: Google Glass is a boon to disabled,* USA Today, (October 23, 2013), available at http://www.usatoday.com/story/tech/2013/10/22/google-glass-aids-disabled/3006827/ (last visited on September 5, 2014).

For example, Mapability,[36] an existing data layer on the Layar browser, helps the disabled locate the nearest wheelchair-accessible venue.

The introduction of Glass has also done much to illustrate how digital eyewear can improve the lives of the physically disabled. Just the simple ability to take pictures and video has been a sea change in the lives of disabled users. One Glass Explorer wrote, "[m]y injury was a spinal cord injury that occurred in 1988 and yesterday I was able to take a picture unassisted for the first time in 24 years!"[37] Similar stories abound.

The disabled have even had a hand in helping to overcome the limitations of first-generation devices like Glass. Because Glass is still (as of this writing) a beta product, its Explorers have an active voice in shaping future enhancements and revisions. Disabled users have made such suggestions as making the volume control less buried in the command menu,[38] decreasing the sensitivity of the touchpad,[39] and allowing alternate methods of controlling the video camera (because those without use of their hands cannot tap the touchpad, as is presently required).[40] Input like this allows the device (and those that come after it) to be designed with accessibility in mind.

One specific community that has benefited from Glass has been those with Parkinson's disease, which causes uncontrollable tremors. "With custom apps, experts have tuned Glass to provide subtle alerts reminding volunteers to take their medication and notify them of upcoming medical appointments. Sufferers are also prompted to speak or swallow to prevent drooling. Glass' motion sensors are put to good use too, preventing patients from 'freezing' by displaying visual cues to help them unblock their brain and regain a flow of a movement."[41] One can easily imagine those afflicted by any number of diseases with analogous physical symptoms to benefit from the same functionality.

For example, patients with ALS (Lou Gehrig's disease) and muscular dystrophy – both of which lead to loss of motor control throughout the body – have experienced increased quality of life through digital eyewear. One volunteer who works with ALS patients said, "Some patients have no use of their hands, and others are losing their

---

[36]Mapability Association, *Mapability Creates First Augmented Reality Layer for Accessibility,* Disabled World, (September 16, 2012), available at http://www.disabled-world.com/assistivedevices/apps/mapability.php (last visited on September 5, 2014).

[37]Kelly Michels, "Accessibility for physically disabled recording video," Glass Explorers Community, July 24, 2014, available at https://www.glass-community.com/t5/Wishlist-for-Glass/Accessibility-for-physically-disabled-recording-video/idi-p/147155 (Google+ authentication required).

[38]Kevin Kepple, *Beyond a gadget: Google Glass is a boon to disabled,* USA Today, (October 23, 2013), available at http://www.usatoday.com/story/tech/2013/10/22/google-glass-aids-disabled/3006827/ (last visited on September 5, 2014).

[39]*Id.*

[40]Kelly Michels, "Accessibility for physically disabled recording video," Glass Explorers Community, July 24, 2014, available at https://www.glass-community.com/t5/Wishlist-for-Glass/Accessibility-for-physically-disabled-recording-video/idi-p/147155 (Google+ authentication required).

[41]Matt Brian, *First UK Google Glass trial gives Parkinson's sufferers more independence,* engadget, available at http://www.engadget.com/2014/04/09/google-glass-parkinsons-uk-trial/ (last visited on September 5, 2014).

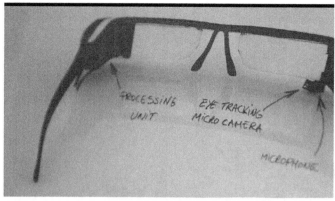

FIGURE 9.3

EyeSpeak by LusoVU.

vocal abilities. But they talk to Glass and it understands them."[42] In July 2014, the Portuguese company LusoVU successfully completed a Kickstarter campaign for its own "augmented reality glasses" called EyeSpeak (Fig. 9.3).[43] This device – which was inspired by the CEO's father being diagnosed with ALS – is designed to capture in a wearable device the same eye-tracking technology currently used by desktop computers to turn patient's eye movements into written letters and words.

Because the impairments suffered by these communities are more often the result of injury, disease, or advanced age, they are more likely to receive AR devices through their health insurance provider or medical professional.

THOSE WITH COGNITIVE IMPAIRMENTS, LEARNING DISABILITIES, AND EMOTIONAL TRAUMA

One study in Ohio created simulated virtual environments to aid the rehabilitation of those with traumatic brain injuries and other cognitive impairments.[44] Similarly, Dr. Helen Papagiannis – a designer, researcher, and artist specializing in AR – has written an AR pop-up book designed to let those suffering from phobias directly encounter their fears in augmented space[45] called "Who's Afraid of Bugs?" the book

[42]Kevin Kepple, *Beyond a gadget: Google Glass is a boon to disabled,* USA Today, (October 23, 2013), available at http://www.usatoday.com/story/tech/2013/10/22/google-glass-aids-disabled/3006827/ (last visited on September 5, 2014).

[43]LusoVU-Usa, *Eye Speak: Beyond Communication,* Kickstarter request, available at https://www.kickstarter.com/projects/886924859/eyespeak-beyond-communication (last visited on September 5, 2014).

[44]Maurissa D'Angelo, S. Narayanan, *A Virtual Reality Environment to Assist Disabled Individuals,* paper submitted for Virtual Rehabilitation 2007 Conference, available at http://www.wright.edu/lwd/documents/virtual_rehabilitation_dangelo.pdf (last visited on September 5, 2014).

[45]Helen Papagiannis, *New Work: First AR Pop-up Book for iPad 2 and iPhone 4 using image recognition,* Augmented Stories, (June 27, 2011), available at http://augmentedstories.wordpress.com/2011/06/27/new-work-first-ar-pop-up-book-for-ipad-2-and-iphone-4-using-image-recognition/ (last visited on September 5, 2014).

FIGURE 9.4

Sension app for autistic users.

features various insects that appear to come alive through a companion AR app. It "was inspired by AR psychotherapy studies for the treatment of phobias such as arachnophobia. AR provides a safe, controlled environment to conduct exposure therapy within a patient's physical surroundings," Papagiannis writes, "creating a more believable scenario with heightened 'presence' and greater immediacy than Virtual Reality (VR)."[46]

Wearable devices even hold promise for those with severe neuro-psychological impairments. The startup company Sension, for example, develops software that recognizes people's emotional state by analyzing their facial expression (Fig. 9.4). The company's Glass software maps 78 points on the face and labels the faces with on-screen keywords like "happy" and "angry."

"Emotional recognition (software) is still in its early days, at about the state of a 3-year-old, but I still felt passionate about trying to do something meaningful," says Sension founder Caitalin Voss. "From my personal experience, I know that the issues (for my cousin) are recognizing an expression, and then smiling back. Glass is good for the first, and can help with the second."[47] Here, too, health insurance companies and medical professionals will be the most likely source AR-based treatments.

The possibilities for AR in the educational field are seemingly endless. Brad Waid and Drew Minock have been at the forefront of this topic for some time. They were each elementary school educators in Bloomfield Hills, Michigan, when they began touring the country teaching other educators how to use AR in the classroom. Now employed by Daqri to do the same work on a broader scale, they have seen countless educators break down barriers to learning and open up exciting new pedagogical

[46]*Id.*

[47]Kevin Kepple, *Beyond a gadget: Google Glass is a boon to disabled,* USA Today, (October 23, 2013), available at http://www.usatoday.com/story/tech/2013/10/22/google-glass-aids-disabled/3006827/ (last visited on September 5, 2014).

possibilities with AR applications. For example, AR allows kinesthetic learners their best opportunity yet to interact with digital objects in a way that fits their learning style.

Although these techniques offer new worlds of possibilities for all kids, the potential is particularly tantalizing for kids with learning disabilities and other barriers to comprehension. Educators are currently limited in what they can offer by such pesky constraints as budgets, resources, and the laws of physics. AR overcomes those barriers by virtually replicating and allowing students to meaningfully interact with anything they can imagine. Kids who need to learn through particular senses can have their instruction tailored to those needs.

Driven by such legal mandates as the Individuals with Disabilities Education Act (IDEA), which was reauthorized in 2004, the public education system is constantly searching for alternative methods to teach kids who do not respond to traditional pedagogical techniques. For example, the IDEA requires that a meeting of parents, educators and other professionals be convened for each student with special needs, resulting in an Individualized Education Plan (IEP) designed to accommodate the child's specific disabilities.

IDEA 2004 already requires IEP teams to consider the use of "assistive technology" so as "to maximize accessibility for children with disabilities."[48] An "assistive technology device" is defined as "any item, piece of equipment, or product system, whether acquired commercially off the shelf, modified, or customized, that is used to increase, maintain, or improve functional capabilities of a child with a disability."[49] IDEA defines an "assistive technology service" as:

> "any service that directly assists a child with a disability in the selection, acquisition, or use of an assistive technology device. Such term includes

(A) the evaluation...
(B) purchasing, leasing, or otherwise providing for the acquisition of assistive technology devices...
(C) selecting, designing, fitting, customizing, adapting, applying, maintaining, repairing, or replacing...
(D) coordinating and using other therapies, interventions, or services with assistive technology devices...
(E) training or technical assistance for such child, or ...the family of such child...
(F) training or technical assistance for professionals..."[50]

The Act also requires schools to provide training in the assistive technology for the teachers, child, and family.[51]

These statutory provisions already provide the legal foundation for requiring AR-based tools as part of a disabled child's IEP. Once educators have a sufficient track record with AR pedagogical tools to prove their effectiveness – which, thanks to

---

[48] 20 U.S.C. 1400(c)(5)(H).
[49] 20 U.S.C. 1401(1).
[50] 20 U.S.C. 1401(2).
[51] 20 U.S.C. 1400(2)(E) & (F).

passionate educators like Waid, Minock, and many others, will not be long – we could very soon see conversations about augmented reality happening in IEP meetings across the country.

The incredible promise of augmented world devices and experiences to improve the lives of the disabled suggests that legal incentives and sanctions will soon encourage or require its use in various contexts. The concepts discussed in this chapter highlight some of the rationales by which that may be accomplished.

Litigation Procedure

INFORMATION IN THIS CHAPTER:

- Evidence and V-Discovery
- In the courtroom
- Exercising personal jurisdiction

INTRODUCTION

On the whole, the legal profession is a conservative institution. It does not move quickly to adopt new technologies or change the way it does things. To the contrary, it serves to bring some semblance of balance and consistency to a rapidly changing society by applying the lessons of the past to solve today's disputes. Change does come even within the legal system, however, and like everything else in contemporary life, change seems to be coming at a faster rate than it did before.

So it will be with augmented reality. As of this writing, only a handful of disputes involving AR have made it through the legal system. It will be some time before use of the technology becomes anywhere near commonplace within the system itself. Nevertheless, some legal innovators have already begun to see the value AR can add in the way they do their jobs and represent their clients' interests. As the ability to tell stories in AR improves, it should become a more frequently used tool for legal persuasion. And before any of that change sets in, lawyers will likely be scrambling to understand and adapt to the AR data that their clients create in the course of their more-rapidly adapting businesses.

GATHERING EVIDENCE FOR USE IN LEGAL PROCEEDINGS

One of the main attractions of digital eyewear is its ability to capture users' experiences from their own first-hand perspective, in a hands-free manner that prevents the device from interfering with what it's recording. The advertisements and popular apps in this space emphasize the use of such capabilities for recording fun, recreational activity, like playing with kids, shopping, and even skydiving. As with anything else in AR, though, these devices simply provide a platform. It's up to the user to determine the content.

One group of people that cares quite a bit about accurately reproducing scenes from everyday life as accurately as possible is the legal profession. Law enforcement officers, detectives, inspectors, and lawyers all seek to gather and preserve evidence of what other people are doing in order to be able to accurately retell that story in the neutral context of a courtroom. Just as wearable technology holds the promise of being able to capture moments more accurately and uniquely than other methods, so too does it stand to enhance the ability to introduce those experiences into evidence.

MOBILE VIDEO AS AN INTENTIONAL MEANS OF GATHERING EVIDENCE

United States courts already have a predisposition in favor of video evidence. In the landmark case *Scott v. Harris*,[1] decided in 2007, the United States Supreme Court announced what almost amounts to a *per se* rule of deference. The plaintiff in that case alleged that the defendant police officer had used excessive force by ramming the plaintiff's car during a high-speed chase, causing a crash that badly injured the plaintiff. The lower courts had allowed the lawsuit to proceed, determining that a reasonable jury could rule for either party based on its interpretation of the evidence.

The Supreme Court in *Scott* reversed, holding as a matter of law that the evidence could only support a judgment in favor of the officer. Its primary basis for reaching this conclusion was the "existence in the record of a [dashcam] videotape … [that] quite clearly contradicts the version of the story told by [plaintiff.]"[2] Specifically, the video demonstrated that plaintiff's driving had "resemble[d] a Hollywood-style car chase of the most frightening sort, placing police officers and innocent bystanders alike at great risk of serious injury,"[3] and therefore justifying the degree of force used by the defendant officer. The guiding principle for future cases set forth by *Scott* is one that commands deference to unrebutted video evidence:

> *When opposing parties tell two different stories, one of which is* blatantly contradicted by the record, *so that no reasonable jury could believe it, a court should not adopt that version of the facts for purposes of ruling on a motion for summary judgment.*
> *That was the case here with regard to the factual issue whether respondent was driving in such fashion as to endanger human life. [Plaintiff's] version of events is* so utterly discredited *by the record that no reasonable jury could have believed him. The Court of Appeals should not have relied on* such visible fiction; *it should have viewed the facts in the light depicted by the videotape.*[4]

Of course, video recordings can be altered. "There [were] no allegations or indications that [the *Scott*] videotape was doctored or altered in any way, nor any

---

[1] 127 S. Ct. 1769.
[2] *Id.* at 1775.
[3] *Id.* at 1775–1776.
[4] *Id.* at 1776.

contention that what it depicts differs from what actually happened."[5] Video editing technology has come a long way even in the years since *Scott*, such that litigants in later cases may have to do a little more work to prove the authenticity of their records. But *Scott*'s rule of deference still governs.

Meanwhile, one of the predominate features of augmented world technology is the proliferation of devices that can record audiovisual footage. It is little wonder, therefore, that people have already begun using these devices for the purpose of gathering evidence to use in court. In April 2014, New York City – which had already experimented with giving its police officers digital eyewear – next decided to give the devices to their restaurant inspectors.[6] Around the same time, the Phoenix, Arizona personal injury law firm Fennemore Craig launched a program it called "Glass Action" (groan), through which the firm lent its digital eyewear devices to its clients. "The idea is to let the clients communicate with their lawyers via Glass to show how their injuries impact their daily lives. Ultimately, Fennemore Craig hopes to turn these communications into evidence."[7] The program is a testament to the fact that the intimacy generated by first-person-perspective video can also subtly influence a jury to empathize with the person behind the recording, "see[ing] the nuances of a victim's daily challenges firsthand." [8] It is as close as video evidence can come to putting the viewer in the victim's shoes.

PRESERVING THREE-DIMENSIONAL EXPERIENCES IN AR

Writing in 2003, police futurists Thomas J. Cowper and Michael E. Buerger foresaw "[a]utomatic sensor readings that calculate distance and height and directly create digital and AR maps for court presentation."[9] By 2011, private accident reconstruction firms in the United States were already beginning to employ 3-D laser scanner for just this purpose, although only on a small scale.[10] "Mounted on a tripod, a laser scans the horizon and records up to 30 million separate data points, down to sub-millimeter resolution. Each sweep takes four minutes, and investigators will typically

---

[5]*Id.* at 1775.

[6]Matthew D. Austin, *NYC eyes Google Glass for restaurant inspections, is OSHA next?* Association of Corporate Counsel website, (April 23, 2014), available at http://www.lexology.com/library/detail. aspx?g=71a587d3-12ab-40d3-88cf-68fa2001be3f (last visited on September 5, 2014).

[7]Lily Hay Newman, *Use of Google Glass to Win your Next Personal Injury Lawsuit,* Slate (April 7, 2014), available at http://www.slate.com/blogs/future_tense/2014/04/07/law_firm_fennemore_craig_is_giving_google_glass_to_clients_so_they_can_create.html?sf24910004=1 (last visited on September 5, 2014).

[8]*Id.*

[9]Thomas J. Cowper and Michael E. Buerga, *Improving Our View of the World: Police and Augmented Reality Technology,* FBI.gov publication, available at http://www.fbi.gov/stats-services/publications/police-augmented-reality-technology-pdf (last visited on September 5, 2014).

[10]Rebecca Boyle, *3-D Scanning and Reconstruction of Crash Scenes Will Save Cops and Drivers Time and Money,* Popular Science (Posted July 15, 2011), available at http://www.popsci.com/cars/article/2011-07/3-d-crash-scene-reconstruction-lasers-will-save-cops-time-and-money?cmp=tw (last visited on September 5, 2014).

make four sweeps.... The image can then be processed into a 3-D computer model, allowing investigators to see where the vehicles are located relative to each other, tire skid marks, and other evidence."[11]

The following year, as discussed in Chapter 9, Danish researchers presented a multi-sensory system designed to allow investigators to capture a full crime scene in AR:

> *"The goggles consist of two head mounted 3D-cameras feeding video to a back-pack with laptop. With this tech, you'd be free to move and look around while you manipulate the electronic display with a pair of gloves. The left hand brings up a set of menus and tools, while the right hand acts as a pointer. By pointing to a blood splatter or bullet holes (for example), you'd be able to tag them as points of interest in a 3D-model of the crime scene. The system is also set up to completely document the crime scene with a video and audio track. This sort of virtual record would allow a new investigator to explore the crime scene and it may also be accepted as evidence in future court cases."*[12]

Such technology, however, would be just as useful for civil litigation as for criminal prosecutions, as discussed further below.

GATHERING EVIDENCE FROM DIGITAL REMNANTS

Of course, a fundamental characteristic of digital data is its permanence. Once created – and especially once it is uploaded to a server – digital information is notoriously difficult to ever truly, permanently delete. Therefore, it will not always be necessary or even preferable to use wearable devices to capture events as they happen. Rather, most AR evidence used in legal proceedings will likely be found after the fact, often because it was shared socially by the very person against whom it is to be used.

The bounty of evidence being collected in social media today bears this out. Three particular examples serve as interesting transitional species, so to speak, in the evolution from social media to the augmented world. First, as discussed in Chapter 7, California bicyclist Chris Bucchere struck and killed an elderly pedestrian while Bucchere was competing for the fastest recorded time on the competitive bicycling social network Strava. At a hearing in his prosecution for manslaughter, "data from Bucchere's Strava account ... had been used to show how fast he had been going and to prove he had ignored stop signs."[13] Likewise, Bucchere's comments made through the social network after the crash – in which he lamented the "heroic" loss of his helmet – helped establish his reckless disregard for the consequences of his actions.

---

[11]*Id.*

[12]Kevin Lee, *Coming Soon: Augmented Reality Goggles for Crime Scene Investigations*, TechHive (February 1, 2012), available at http://www.techhive.com/article/249143/coming_soon_augmented_reality_goggles_for_crime_scene_investigations.html (last visited on September 5, 2014).

[13]Kashmir Hill, *Google Glass Will Be Incredible for the Courtroom*, Forbes (March 15, 2013), available at http://www.forbes.com/sites/kashmirhill/2013/03/15/google-glass-will-be-incredible-for-the-courtroom/ (last visited on September 5, 2014).

FIGURE 10.1

Alleged excerpt from Cecilia Abadie's Google+ account appearing to show a picture taken through Glass while driving.

Another case discussed in Chapter 7 was the first-ever traffic citation for wearing Google Glass while driving, issued to software developer and avid Glass Explorer Cecilia Abadie. She was found not guilty because the officer could not prove that the device was actually turned on while she was behind the wheel. This prompted some internet sleuths to investigate her Google+ and YouTube social media accounts, where they found photos and recordings that appeared to have been taken while driving (Fig. 10.1). Apparently, they also found a message Abadie had posted saying "I just received a message … while driving." Of course, none of this "evidence" would have been likely to make a difference in the actual hearing on Abadie's citation, nor is it conclusive proof that she was the one who made the recordings, or that she did so while driving (which, it should be observed, is not necessarily unlawful or even dangerous; see the discussion in Chapter 7). But it does illustrate the fact that there are evidentiary goldmines online, and that wearable devices will create even more opportunities for lawyers to discover such gems – if they have the stamina and wherewithal to sift through all the available data.

A third, almost-real example came in August 2014, when online news outlets reported that Gainesville, Florida police had used a murder suspect's interactions with his iPhone to prove he committed the crime, including the "fact" that he had asked Siri where to hide the victim's body.[14] "In addition to the Siri query, [the suspect's] phone had no activity between 11:31pm and 12:01am on the night [the victim] disappeared. [The suspect] also used the flashlight app on his phone for a total of

---

[14]Casey Johnson, *Murder suspect's phone held screenshot of "hide my roommate" Siri query [updated]*, arstechnica (August 13, 2014), available at http://arstechnica.com/gadgets/2014/08/murder-suspect-asked-siri-where-to-hide-my-roommate/ (last visited on September 5, 2014).

48 minutes that day…"[15] Although later reports recanted much of this narrative, the fact of its plausibility demonstrates just how many digital remnants we leave behind already using today's technology. As the world becomes more augmented, even more of our everyday actions will be preserved, allowing others to come back after the fact and reconstruct – or misinterpret – our actions in litigation.

V-DISCOVERY
THE PRECEDENT OF e-DISCOVERY

As these examples demonstrate, advances in digital and computing technologies can make litigation, like anything else, more effective and efficient. Lawyers have so many more tools at their disposal for crafting and communicating persuasive arguments than they did 10, or even five years ago.

But this rapid expansion of technology has also been giving lawyers a whole lot more to do. Generally speaking, any documents, files, emails, spreadsheets, or information that is reasonably likely to reveal evidence that could be admissible in court is fair game for discovery during litigation.[16] Increasingly, the digital data stored and exchanged by the people and companies involved in lawsuits are becoming important to the issues being fought over. Especially over the past decade, that has meant that lawyers and their staff often have to gather "electronically stored information" (ESI) during the discovery phase, in addition to the paper documents and testimony – a phenomenon we call "e-discovery." Therefore, lawyers end up with even more data to sift through in order to figure out what happened than they used to a lot more.

"Perhaps no case could be a more monumental example of the reality of modern e-discovery," says a 2011 article in the *ABA Journal*, "than the [then-]ongoing Viacom copyright infringement lawsuit against YouTube filed back in 2008. In that dispute, the judge ordered that 12 terabytes of data be turned over"[17] – more than the printed equivalent of the entire Library of Congress. Even after a few years, this example still remains a prodigious monument to the burdens of e-discovery. "Experiences like these," the article continues, "have left law firms and in-house attorneys scrambling to make sense of the new risks associated with the seemingly endless data produced by emerging technologies like cloud computing and social media."

How will law firms and litigants cope, then, when augmented reality becomes mainstream, and digital technology leaps off the computer monitor to overlay the physical world? At least four potential problems seem apparent.

---

[15]*Id.*

[16]Legal Information Institute, *Federal Rules of Civil Procedure: Rule 26. Duty to Disclose, General Provision Governing Discovery,* Cornell University Law School, available at http://www.law.cornell.edu/rules/frcp/Rule26.htm (last visited on September 5, 2014).

[17]Joe Dysart, *As Bulging Client Data Heads for the Clud, Law Firms Ready for a Storm,* ABA Journal, (Posted April 1, 2011), available at http://www.abajournal.com/magazine/article/as_bulging_client_data_heads_for_the_cloud_law_firms_ready_for_a_storm/ (last visited on September 5, 2014).

ORDERS OF MAGNITUDE MORE DATA

The first problem will be one of volume. Consider this: in 2013, it was calculated that "[a] full 90 percent of all the data in the world has been generated over the last two years."[18] And that was before the wave of wearable communications and health-monitoring devices that began shortly thereafter.

Companies such as Vuzix and Google already have digital eyewear on the market, and several more are in development. If a site like YouTube can amass enough video footage to make the prospect of reviewing it all seem (quite rightly) ridiculous, how about when everyone is wearing digital eyewear that is capable of recording more or less everything we look at? Will paralegals be sifting through days and weeks worth of mundane, first-person audio and video to find the relevant portions of a litigant's experiences? As more of our reading takes place on digital devices, we are already creating troves of data about our activities in browser caches and RAM memory. But how much larger will our digital footprints be when everyday physical objects become opportunities (even necessities) for encountering and creating geo-tagged data?

TRACKING IT ALL DOWN

The second, and closely related, problem will be locating and collecting all of this data. As recently illustrated by the comedic film *Sex Tape*, it is hard enough nowadays to locate data stored in "the cloud," which actually means some remote server farm nestled somewhere in the distant hills. Presumably, that data will be stored in even more diffuse ways in an AR world, in which our digital experience is likely to be generated by a mesh of interconnected devices. Whether or not my eyewear will require a centrally broadcast "signal" or "network" in order to function, it will certainly be interacting with any number of signals sent to and from objects that I physically encounter, leaving digital traces of my physical presence behind.

We are already halfway there. Consider Color, the social media startup that gathered a lot of attention for a brief period in 2011. Its premise was to give users access to other people's photo streams merely by coming into physical proximity to those people. Foursquare, Waze, and similar sites likewise track users' locations in real time and offer them discounts to businesses near their current, physical location. Once transactions like this become the centerpiece of a lawsuit, will it require lawyers to pinpoint where particular people where when they accessed these apps?

If it becomes relevant in litigation to retrace someone's steps through an augmented reality, how would one do it? That will depend on how and where the data is stored. If, as is the case today, almost all data resides either on central servers or on the mobile device itself, there will be obvious points for collecting the data. But as the data disperses, it may become necessary to actually visit the locations where

---

[18]Ase Dragland, *Big Data, for better or worse: 90% of world's data generated over last two years*, Science Daily (May 22, 2013), available at http://www.sciencedaily.com/releases/2013/05/130522085217.htm (last visited on September 5, 2014).

the person being investigated traveled, in order to retrieve the bits of digital data they left behind in nearby connected devices. Or perhaps we will all be equipped with personal "black boxes" that keep track of our digital experiences – all too often, probably, for the purpose of uploading them to lifelogs, or whatever social media has by then become.

MAKING SENSE OF FIRST-PERSON AR DATA

A third problem will be one of triangulation. Today, ESI may take various forms, but it all has one thing in common: it's almost always viewable on a two-dimensional screen. That will not be universally true for much longer. How one perceives augmented reality will depend first on how they're looking at their physical surroundings. It may not be possible to interpret digital data stored in a server somewhere without knowing exactly where the individual(s) viewing it were located, the direction they were facing, what other data they had open, and so on.

As an example, take the situation discussed in Chapter 5: a trademark infringement lawsuit in which the plaintiff alleges that a virtual version of his trademark was geo-tagged onto the brick-and-mortar location of his competitor's store, leading confused customers to patronize his competitor instead of his own business. (This is a fairly straightforward extrapolation of all the lawsuits being filed nowadays over sponsored ads in search engine results.) That plaintiff's claim will rise or fall in part based on how that geotag actually looked to customers. That, in turn, may depend on where the potential customers were when they looked at the logo. Was it visible through the trees, or in the sun? On which AR platforms was it viewable (assuming that there will be multiple service providers)? Did different brands of eyewear render it in the same way? Was it a static display, or did it sense and orient itself toward each individual viewer?

Even more complex issues come into play with other forms of AR, such as haptic feedback. A server or device memory may record that a glove or other haptic device delivered a series of electrical impulses, but determining with any reliability exactly how that *felt* to the user may not be possible without recreating the experience.

PRESERVATION

Fourth, after courts and the Federal Rules of Civil Procedure began to acknowledge the significance of electronically stored information, it also became clear how easily and frequently individuals and companies were deleting potentially significant evidence – whether intentionally or merely out of ignorance. Out of this realization came the recognition of a duty that every person has to preserve evidence relevant to a potential legal claim – including ESI – whenever that person "reasonably anticipates" litigation over the claim. *When* someone ought to have that anticipation is necessarily fact-dependent; it could be by receiving a formal complaint or warning that a lawsuit is coming, or when a disagreement becomes sufficiently contentious that a reasonable person would see litigation as a distinct possibility. If the duty is triggered in a corporate setting, the company's lawyers or other representative will often issue an internal "litigation hold" warning, putting all employees on notice not to delete digital information that could relate to the issues in the potential lawsuit.

Just when corporate officers were beginning to wrap their brains around the idea of preserving vast amounts of emails, spreadsheets, and word processing documents, the duty of preservation expanded to such platforms as social media accounts, voicemails, and text messages. The introduction of wearable devices, AR interfaces and v-discovery will expand the burdens of preservation yet another order of magnitude. There will come a time in the near future when companies will need to catalog, or at least query their employees when needed on, the types of wearable devices they use and the data those devices accumulate. When one employee sues over stressful or discriminatory workplace conditions, for example, it may become necessary to collect the health-monitoring data of each employee in the office to establish the average level of stress and the factors that tended to increase it. If some individuals delete such information about themselves during the relevant timeframe, however, the company could find itself sanctioned for destroying evidence.

These are just a few of the potential issues; rest assured, there will be others. But it all comes with a silver lining. Just a few minutes contemplating the complexities of virtual (or "v-") discovery makes the current fuss over e-discovery seem not so bad after all.

ASSISTING LAWYERS WITH LEGAL RESEARCH

At a 2014 legal technology conference at Harvard Law School, Wayne Weibel presented his own customized "citation extraction" software for Google Glass.[19] Although public details on the project are scarce, it appears to recognize legal text that the person wearing Glass is looking at and find the case law citations in the document. From there, the software could presumably look up and display the case being cited. More advanced versions might even detect the name of a case when spoken in the courtroom, and provide the wearer with instant intelligence on the cited opinion.

Of course, finding a legal opinion only tells half the story. Lawyers regularly rely on one of two databases – Shephard's® and Keycite® – to determine whether the holding of a particular opinion remains valid law in light of subsequent interpretations and rulings by other courts. A really useful Glassware app, then, would be one that could also run a case citation through one of these databases, and superimpose the user's view of the written text with the databases' red, yellow, and green flags, allowing the user to easily spot potential weak points in a legal argument on the fly.

---

[19] Wayne Weibel, *Law in the Wild: Citation Extraction and Glassware,* Conference for Law School Computing, available at http://conference.cali.org/2014/sessions/law-wild-citation-extraction-service-and-glassware (last visited on September 5, 2014).

AUGMENTED REALITY IN THE COURTROOM
TELEPRESENCE

Public speakers have traditionally honed their presentations by performing in front of a mirror, but digital eyewear will provide lawyers with a whole new level of self-analysis. The personal injury law firm of "Fennemore Craig is … considering using Glass with expert witnesses, or putting Glass on 'jurors' in mock trials to see court presentations from that perspective."[20] The lawyers could then analyze the footage to determine how well a presentation is playing to the jury.

Other trial lawyers plan to use the technology as a teaching or client-relations tool. "Just before the clerk calls our case," speculated trial lawyer Mitch Jackson, "I command Glass to 'go live' and a real time audio and video feed displays back at the office and private Youtube, Google Hangout, and Spreecast channels so that the new associates can watch the law and motion and oral argument from our various offices across the U.S. A private link is also shared with the clients so they can watch the procedure poolside from their hotel in the Bahamas where they are vacationing."[21] Presumably, lawyers outside the office could also watch the argument in real time (on their own headset, of course), and offer the in-court attorney real-time input that affects the outcome of the hearing. Similar methods are already being used to give medical students a unique, first-person perspective of surgeries from the surgeon's own perspective, and to allow treating physicians to collaborate in real time. Applied in the courtroom, such techniques could ultimately save clients significant sums on travel expenses and allow greater collaboration at times when it could make a critical difference in the outcome of an argument.

Telepresence in the courtroom may also expand the concept of "testifying in court." Today, when a witness gives testimony outside of the courtroom, there are only two commonly-used methods for preserving it: having it typed by a stenographer or video recorded. Adding the ability to record and play back testimony in three dimensions would certainly add to its persuasive effect in the courtroom. By the same token, witnesses who now (in rare circumstances) are allowed to testify in court by means of live videoconferencing could instead someday soon "appear" on the witness stand by means of a life-size, interactive hologram, a device frequently seen in *Star Wars* films (Fig. 10.2).

Without a serious shift in legal precedent, however, telepresence testimony is not likely to be widely adopted in criminal proceedings. At least four of the United States Courts of Appeal have decided that criminal defendants must be physically present in the courtroom when being sentenced, regardless of how effective

---

[20]Lily Hay Newman, *Use of Google Glass to Win your Next Personal Injury Lawsuit,* Slate (April 7, 2014), available at http://www.slate.com/blogs/future_tense/2014/04/07/law_firm_fennemore_craig_is_giving_google_glass_to_clients_so_they_can_create.html?sf24910004=1 (last visited on September 5, 2014).
[21]*Id.*

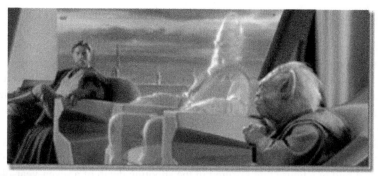

FIGURE 10.2

The *Star Wars* films have perfected the concept of telepresence.

videoconferencing technology may be. "Being physically present in the same room with another has certain intangible and difficult to articulate effects that are wholly absent when communicating by video conference. As written, the Rule [43(a) of the Federal Rules of Criminal Procedure] reflects a firm judgment in favor of physical presence and does not permit the use of video conferencing as a substitute,"[22] wrote one such court in 2011.

Similarly, the Confrontation Clause of the Sixth Amendment to the United States Constitution provides that "in all criminal prosecutions, the accused shall enjoy the right...to be confronted with the witnesses against him." This bedrock provision of constitutional law is already posing obstacles to the use of videoconferencing in criminal trials,[23] and would likely also hinder the use of telepresence technology. Recent Supreme Court case law interpreting the Confrontation Clause, however, has suggested that courts may soon begin opening the door a little wider to the possibility of "[using] remote testimony as a method to satisfy the Confrontation Clause when a witness cannot be present at trial."[24]

IMMERSING JUDGES AND JURORS IN THE EVIDENCE

I described above how lawyers might use digital eyewear to capture video footage of a scene or of an injured person's experiences from a first-person perspective. Capturing the footage, however, is only half the process. Ultimately, the footage must be conveyed to the judge or jury who will decide its significance. Here again, digital

---

[22]*United States v. Williams*, 641 F.3d 758 (6th Cir. 2011).

[23]Valerie Werse, *The Confrontation Clause in Video Conferencing,* Rutgers Computer and Technology Law Journal (October 11, 2012), available at http://www.rctlj.org/2012/10/the-confrontation-clause-in-video-conferencing/ (last visited on September 5, 2014).

[24]Jessica Smith, *Remote Testimony and Related Procedures Impacting a Criminal Defendant's Confrontation Rights,* UNC School of Government Administration of Justice Bulletin (No. 2013/12 February 2013), available at http://sogpubs.unc.edu/electronicversions/pdfs/aojb1302.pdf (last visited on September 5, 2014).

eyewear could be a great assistance. For example, if each member of the jury were given a set of digital eyewear, they could all simultaneously experience the content first-hand, rather than viewing it on a two-dimensional monitor. The immersive experience would draw the jurors into the experience, necessarily increasing its emotional resonance and hence its persuasive effect. This would likely be best accomplished with eyewear meant to deliver a wide, stereoscopic field of view like the Epson Moverio or the Meta Space Glasses, rather than smaller displays like Glass or Vuzix devices.

Such immersion could also go beyond video footage to include additional senses. In 2012, a Detroit police officer stood trial on involuntary manslaughter charges after a botched raid of a house that resulted in the shooting death of a seven-year-old girl. A critical fact in the case was that the police had set off a flashbang grenade, which "is a non-lethal device meant to disorient and give an advantage to police during a raid."[25] Arguing that "words alone can't describe the [disorienting] effects [this type of grenade] has,"[26] the prosecutor in the case argued that the jurors could only understand the circumstances of the shooting by experiencing the explosion first-hand. The judge agreed, and assembled all of the jurors in a room where a flashbang grenade was detonated.[27]

Though the experience was doubtless enlightening, such extreme measures are also exceedingly rare, as well as expensive. Equipping courtrooms to deliver multi-sensory experiences through haptic and audio-visual AR could revolutionize the practice of presenting evidence in court at least as much as the introduction of video recordings and computer-generated reconstructions have done. Jurors could feel the chill of a dark city street, hear sounds from specific directions, and generally put themselves in the shoes of those of whose actions they sit in judgment. If done correctly, such juries would gain a much more precise understanding of the evidence, presumably leading to better-informed verdicts.

The various technical difficulties in accomplishing that precise re-enactment, however, coupled, with the inherent subjectivity involved in how competing parties present their respective cases, may lead to more arguments over the permissibility of such experiences. These arguments are likely to center on Federal Rule of Evidence 403, under which a "court may exclude relevant evidence if its probative value is substantially outweighed by a danger of one or more of the following: unfair prejudice,

---

[25]Gus Burns, *Aiyana Jones trial jurors to witness flashbang grenade detonation Wednesday,* Mlive (June 11, 2013), available at http://www.mlive.com/news/detroit/index.ssf/2013/06/aiyana_jones_trial_jurors_to_w. html (last visited on September 5, 2014).

[26]*Prosecutor Wants to Simulate Explosion in Court: Detroit Police Officer Faces Manslaughter Charge in Fatal Shooting of 7 year old Black Girl,* The Brown Watch (June 16, 2012), available at http://brownwatch.squarespace.com/police-brutality-watch/2012/6/16/prosecutor-wants-to-simulate-explosion-in-court-detroit-poli.html (last visited on September 5, 2014).

[27]*Jurors in trial of officer accused in death of Aiyana Stanley-Jones see stun grenade demonstration,* Channel 7 abc WXYZ Detroit (posted June 12, 2013), available at http://www2.wxyz.com/web/wxyz/news/state/jurors-in-detroit-cop-trial-to-see-stun-grenade-demonstration (last visited on September 5, 2014).

confusing the issues, misleading the jury, undue delay, wasting time, or needlessly presenting cumulative evidence." In particular, intense, immersive demonstrations may be argued to "prejudice" the jury by arousing a strong emotional reaction. Some jurors may even have physical conditions that would make it dangerous to view the augmented content.

Moreover, appellate review of cases involving such evidence could be particularly difficult. Typically, legal appeals are fairly sterile processes, involving oral arguments in pristine halls based on the written transcripts of trial court proceedings. Video and other electronic evidence can be preserved and re-examined by appellate courts easily enough. The uniquely experiential nature of multisensory AR evidence, however, would presumably make it very difficult, or at least complicated, to recreate after the fact. When the admissibility or weight of such evidence is the subject of an appeal, appellate judges may find themselves with no other choice but to strap on the same equipment used by the jurors to experience the AR evidence, more than likely with assistance from the parties or their experts.[28]

PERSONAL JURISDICTION

Picture this: a California based software company writes an augmented reality program that allows people to engage in a digital experience tied to their respective locales. An end user in New Jersey downloads the app, and is injured while using it. (Maybe it gives her bad directions that cause a traffic accident, or maybe it gives her improper instructions for how to use a product.) She sues the California company in a New Jersey state court. Has she sued in the correct court? Is the California company subject to the New Jersey court's authority?

This is a question of "personal jurisdiction" – the power of a court to exercise authority over a specific person (or company). As a general rule, state courts may not exercise judicial power over a person or company not located in that state unless the defendant "purposefully avails itself of the privilege of conducting activities within the forum State, thus invoking the benefits and protections of its laws."[29] U.S. courts have spilled a lot of ink over hundreds of years trying to define the circumstances under which it is "fundamentally fair" for a state court to exercise jurisdiction over a person or company not located in that state.

Augmented reality media will give digital data a physicality that it has never had before, allowing creators and users of software to project their influence in specific, remote locations like never before. As this means of interaction expands, courts will have new opportunities to explore when it is fair for courts in one state to assert jurisdiction over someone in another state.

---

[28]As of this writing, the prosecution of the Detroit police officer remains pending, as the first proceeding ended in mistrial. It remains to be seen, therefore, whether a three-judge panel of the Michigan Court of Appeals will one day find it necessary to experience a flashbang grenade for themselves.

[29]*J. Mcintyre Machinery, Ltd. v. Nicastro*, 131 S. Ct. 2780 (2011).

JURISDICTION REQUIRES A MEANINGFUL CONNECTION BETWEEN THE DEFENDANT AND THE FORUM STATE

As of this writing, the most recent and definitive word on the subject of personal jurisdiction comes from the United States Supreme Court's 2014 decision in *Walden v. Fiore*.[30] The Court's unanimous opinions described the issues as follows:

> *The Due Process Clause of the Fourteenth Amendment constrains a State's authority to bind a nonresident defendant to a judgment of its courts. Although a nonresident's physical presence within the territorial jurisdiction of the court is not required, the nonresident generally must have certain minimum contacts such that the maintenance of the suit does not offend traditional notions of fair play and substantial justice.*[31]

The inquiry into whether a defendant has sufficient "minimum contacts" with a State "focuses on the relationship among the defendant, the forum, and the litigation."[32] That "relationship must arise out of contacts that the defendant himself creates with the forum State,"[33] and "looks to the defendant's contacts with the forum State itself, not the defendant's contacts with persons who reside there."[34] "[T]he plaintiff [who lives in the forum State] cannot be the only link between the defendant and the forum. Rather, it is the defendant's conduct that must form the necessary connection with the forum State that is the basis for its jurisdiction over him."[35]

A line of cases beginning with the Supreme Court's 1984 decision in *Calder v. Jones*[36] found sufficient minimum contacts, and hence jurisdiction, by focusing the *effect* that a defendant's remote conduct had in the forum State. In that case, the Florida-based defendant published a newspaper article that libeled a California celebrity; the Court upheld the exercise of jurisdiction in California because the "brunt" of the injury caused by that libel was felt in California.

The Court's 2014 decision in *Walden* reigned in the application of this "*Calder* effects test." In *Walden*, a Georgia policeman seized funds at an airport belonging to a Nevada resident. The Nevada resident sued in Nevada, and argued it was fair to subject the officer to jurisdiction there because he knew that his actions would have consequences in Nevada. Relying on *Calder*, the Court of Appeals agreed. But the Supreme Court unanimously reversed, holding that "[t]he proper question is not where the plaintiff experienced a particular injury or effect but whether the defendant's conduct connects him to the forum in a meaningful way."[37] This officer's actions, the Court explained, were not inherently aimed at Nevada. The connection to Nevada existed only because that was "where respondents chose to be at a time when

---

[30]134 S.Ct. 1115 (2014).
[31]*Walden v. Fiore*, 134 S. Ct. 1115, 1121 (2014) (citations, internal quotations, and alterations omitted).
[32]*Id.* (internal quotation omitted).
[33]*Id.* at 1222.
[34]*Id.*
[35]*Id.*
[36]465 U.S. 783 (1984)
[37]*Walden v. Fiore*, 134 S. Ct. 1115, 1125 (2014).

they desired to use the funds seized by petitioner. Respondents would have experienced this same lack of access in California, Mississippi, or wherever else they might have traveled and found themselves wanting more money than they had."[38]

Because mobile apps can be downloaded and used anywhere, this principle will be particularly instructive in applying personal jurisdiction law to digital content. Applied to AR and its particular connection to distinct places, however, *Walden* may actually increase the likelihood of jurisdiction being exercised.

THE PRECEDENT OF TODAY'S INTERNET LAW

Courts have developed various tests for determining whether a defendant's activities online meaningfully connected him to another forum so as to allow a court in that forum to exercise jurisdiction over him. In the early days of the public internet, the predominate test focused on a website's "interactivity." Under this approach – sometimes called the "*Zippo* sliding scale" analysis, after the case that coined it – courts place a website on a spectrum from "passive" to "interactive." The more interactive the site is, the more likely it is that the site owner is using it to intentionally interact with users in distant states.

As "interactivity" online has become more common, however, the *Zippo* sliding scale analysis has become less useful. Writing in 2010, for example, the Seventh Circuit Court of Appeals, ruled that "a defendant [should] not be haled into court simply because the defendant owns or operates a website that is accessible in the forum state, even if that site is 'interactive.' Beyond simply operating an interactive website that is accessible from the forum state, a defendant must in some way target the forum state's market."[39] Other courts were quick to "generally agree"[40] with this holding, but "[c]ourts differ … regarding which Internet activities constitute conduct 'purposefully directed' at the forum state."[41]

These "interactivity" or "sliding scale" tests proved to have especially little utility when applied to individual users of social media, which is the predominate online activity as of this writing. "While the websites at issue in this case may themselves be considered interactive," the Texas Court of Appeals explained, "a third party's use of the website may, in effect, be a 'passive' usage of the internet, i.e. an act of simply posting information which is accessible anywhere the internet is accessible. Such passive usages of the internet do not support jurisdiction over a non-interactive website under a sliding-scale analysis."[42] Similarly, in the case *Capitol Records, LLC v. VideoEgg, Inc.*,[43] a New York federal judge did not exercise jurisdiction over a video-sharing website just because New York residents were able to share and view videos on it. Because the site did not charge its users, the court concluded, the site's

---

[38]*Id.*

[39]*Illinois v. Hemi Group, LLC*, 622 F.3d 754, 760 (7th Cir. 2010).

[40]*Revision Military, Inc. v. Balboa Manufacturing Company*, No. 5:11-cv-149 (D. Vermont 2011)

[41]*Illinois v. Hemi Group, LLC*, 622 F.3d 754, 760 (7th Cir. 2010).

[42]*Wilkerson v. RSL FUNDING, LLC*, 388 SW 3d 668 (Tex. Ct. App. 2011).

[43]*Capitol Records, LLC v. VideoEgg, Inc.*, 611 F. Supp. 2d 349 (S.D.N.Y. 2009).

relevant "business" activity for purposes of personal jurisdiction was not video sharing, but selling advertising.

Yet the court did ultimately exercise jurisdiction in the case, because the specific advertising on the site was targeted at New York residents. "Documents produced in discovery show that [defendant's] employees touted the company's large New York user base to potential advertisers and responded directly to advertising inquiries from New York-based companies, including companies seeking to promote recording artists. Documents also support Plaintiffs' allegations that [defendant] either actively sought or actually consummated advertising sales transactions that targeted New York users."[44] The specific business conducted by the site, therefore, tied it in a meaningful way to New York, supporting the exercise of jurisdiction there.

EXERCISING JURISDICTION OVER PROVIDERS OF AUGMENTED REALITY EXPERIENCES

These precedents offer some inkling of when courts will be allowed to exercise jurisdiction over an AR service provider in another State or country. The mere fact that a particular AR app obtains information from the online cloud in order to perform its function, for example, does not distinguish it from any other use of the internet, and therefore is quite unlikely to support the exercise of jurisdiction over the data provider by a court in the user's forum. Like the defendant in *Walden*, the fact that an app user happens to be in a particular State when using a generally accessible mobile app is purely the consequence of the user's choice, not the provider's, and does not meaningfully connect the provider to that forum.

What makes AR different from other digital experiences is the way it enhances a user's physical experience of the world around them. This could be a general enhancement of a particular sense regardless of surroundings – such as, for example, an aid for deaf individuals to read sign language. In that circumstance, there would still be nothing in particular about the experience that tied the experience provider to the user's location.

Many visual AR applications, however, will be tied to a specific physical location. That could include augmented advertising through particular physical signs, providing an interactive game tied to particular physical landmarks, a travel app designed to lead tourists around a certain city, or any one of a thousand other applications. In these cases, the experience provider has targeted its services toward the residents of a particular location as in the *VideoEgg* case, and is "meaningfully connected" to that location as discussed in *Walden*, because the experience will not work properly anywhere else. In these cases, even if the data for the AR experience is provided from a remote location, there is a much more persuasive basis for arguing that the experience provider will be subject to jurisdiction in the users' forum.

Whether courts apply *Walden* to AR experiences in this manner, however, remains to be seen.

---

[44]*Id.*

AR & Society

C

11 Politics & Civil Society. 277

12 Personal Ethics. 293

13 Addiction & Pornography. 311

Politics and Civil Society

11

INFORMATION IN THIS CHAPTER:

- AR as a vehicle for social change
- AR as a mechanism for enforcing political correctness
- AR's potential to exacerbate groupthink on political and social issues

INTRODUCTION

The medium of augmented reality holds almost boundless potential for sharing information, potentially eclipsing even the advances in communication made to date by the internet. As our experience with the internet has amply demonstrated, however, people do not often do an admirable job at taking advantage of such potential. Instead, we often seek out only that which we already know will please or entertain us. Humans are, after all, finite beings with pleasures, preferences, and opinions that are often quite deeply ingrained.

Digital media can mobilize people to accomplish remarkable things, often to the benefit of society. When individuals use digital media to further ensconce themselves in their preferred, pre-selected points of view, however, they have less opportunity or desire to interact with, understand, or find common ground with others of a different persuasion. This harms the fabric of relationship and common purpose that binds societies together. By expanding the reach of digital media into our previously non-digitized daily experiences, augmented world technologies will inevitably carry the potential to further exacerbate these negative social developments.

AR AS A MEANS OF MOBILIZING PEOPLE FOR SOCIAL GOOD
REDISCOVERING AND REBUILDING CIVIC IDENTITY

Beginning in September 2010, the city of Christchurch, New Zealand was rocked by a series of devastating earthquakes. As a result, several longstanding, historical buildings have been destroyed or demolished, and reconstruction efforts are underway. "Even for people who have lived in Christchurch all their lives it is difficult to

FIGURE 11.1

The CityViewAR app from Hit Lab NZ.

walk through the earthquake damaged city and remember what buildings used to be there."[1]

It happens, however, that Christchurch is also the home of Dr. Mark Billinghurst – one of the world's most pedigreed experts in AR – and his Hit Lab NZ organization. His team reacted to the earthquakes by developing "CityViewAR," a "mobile Augmented Reality application that allows people to see how the city was before the earthquakes and building demolitions. Using an Android mobile phone people can walk around the city and see life-sized virtual models of what the buildings looked like on site before they were demolished, and see pictures and written information" (Fig. 11.1).[2] The team intends future updates of the app to enable users to not only view past buildings, but also see and comment on proposed future construction. In this way, the app has the potential to encourage greater civic participation and ownership in the community's reconstruction.

PROTESTS AND SOCIAL CHANGE

Superimposing digital data on the physical world is not just for "the one percent" social elite. As more of our innovators, artisans, and marketers experiment with augmented reality, the tumultuous politics of our times are beginning to follow suit.

2011's "Occupy" movement broke new ground in various ways that will keep sociologists and political scientists busy for decades. One example is how some of the protestors resorted to free AR apps to keep the public informed about related events and locations. Using Metaio's location-based AR browser Junaio, one AR developer launched an "Occupy channel" that provides locations, contact information, and resources for all the Occupy protests in various cities across the country. The

---

[1]Hit Lab NZ, "CityViewAR," http://www.hitlabnz.org/index.php/products/cityviewar#sthash.lGTOfwrT.dpuf.

[2]*Id.*

Occupy Wall Street group in New York took this idea one step further, using Junaio to superimpose signs, placards, and related imagery over areas from which they were restricted from physically protesting. A related site called "AR Occupy Wall Street" styled itself as a "call to all AR activists," and collects a series of protest-themed images from various AR designers.

Of course, the utility of these apps to the overall movement remains an open question. One first has to have a compatible device and software, then download the app (or subscribe to the right channel inside an app), then be in the correct location, then use the app, all before one can encounter the experience that the apps intend to convey. Someone who jumps through those hoops is likely to be someone already sympathetic to the cause – which means these may be the first real-world examples of AR's tendency to entrench existing political divisions.

Nevertheless, these examples do illustrate AR's power to crowd source a movement's message. They allow individual artists located anywhere in the world to add their own spin on the group's message – using different perspectives, images, and even languages – in a way that no mere physical demonstration could ever hope to accomplish. If even one of those protest "filters" catches on with a critical mass of individuals, it could change the entire course of the movement.

This technique of spurring social change isn't limited to protesters, either. The Dutch government recently used AR billboards as a form of experiential Public Service Announcement. The goal was to avoid a situation like one that occurred in New York City, where passersby left a "homeless hero" to die in public after he saved a woman from a mugging. The billboard superimposed a violent criminal encounter over live video footage of the area where viewers stood. The onlookers could do nothing to interact with the scene or stop the crime. But they got a stark visual reminder of how appalling doing nothing can look.

POLITICAL CAMPAIGNS

Just as Barack Obama proved in 2008 that social media could be an effective means of rallying support, so too are political parties beginning to discover AR's potential value in political campaigns. The Green Party in Germany partnered with Metaio to launch an app that lets constituents leave comments geo-tagged to specialized billboards and specific physical locations and that represent a certain issue – and to hear pre-recorded statements by party officials about those very issues.

Just in time for the 2012 presidential campaign in the US, AR startup GoldRun announced a feature called "Visualize the Vote" that lets users pose for a picture with their favorite presidential candidate – super imposed over the user's physical location – then share that photo with their friends.

NEW AUGMENTED COMMUNITIES

Several of the previous chapters have discussed different aspects of AR games. In Chapter 6, we saw how these experiences are giving players new reasons to get off their couches and intermingle, often forming genuine communities in the process. This is a tangible example of how AR can contribute to social cohesion.

As society grows more accustomed to engaging with customizable layers of reality, AR's ability to affect social change will deepen exponentially. For example, GoldRun also announced plans to launch a location-based reminder service that automatically alerts you to a particular cause when you come within a certain distance of a related location. (Virtual personal assistants and similar apps offer analogous functionality.) The first example that was mentioned is showing you the image of a dog or cat when you walk within a mile of an animal shelter.

But this same technique could easily be applied to any social or political issue. Driving over a bridge might bring you a layer of information about the "pork barrel spending" that went into funding it. Entering a road construction area might prompt data on "your tax dollars at work," or perhaps information about that company's safety record. And whether a particular geotagged location sends you negatively or positively spun information could well depend on which political group's channel you've already subscribed to (reinforcing a tendency toward political groupthink, as discussed below.)

Perhaps the most radical vision of AR's impact on society can be found in Daniel Suarez's books *Daemon* and *Freedom*™. In that two-part story, members of the AR-driven "Darknet" form a networked society that begins to subvert and supplant the existing political and economic order. Members of the community wear AR eyewear that allows them to see the information on which their Darknet society is based. All manner of virtual information like that described above is available to these people, except in a fully immersive, always-on manner. If someone writes a virtual protest sign on the side of a building, for example, that sign is equally visible to Darknet members as if it had been written with physical paint.

But Suarez's meditation on how AR would affect society goes deeper than virtual graffiti. Each of these people develop "reputation scores" that are visible to other Darknet members as numbers floating in midair above their heads. These scores are the cumulative averages of the "rating" that person has received from other Darknet members based on their credibility, honesty, proficiency, and the like. The higher that score – especially as the "base" number of ratings increases – the more trustworthy that individual is considered. It would be like living in a world where everyone judged you by your rating on eBay.

Even more interesting is Suarez's concept of the power meter. In addition to reputation scores, Darknet members achieve experience levels by accomplishing various tasks – exactly as in a video game. The higher one's experience level, the more abilities they unlock within the Darknet, and the more data to which they gain access. In order to keep any one person or faction from gaining too much power over others in this way, however, all Darknet members are able to see not only the experience levels of others around them, but also the distribution of power within a given community. If power is concentrated in too few hands, the needle tips to the right. But if it's dispersed too thinly – i.e., if there are no potential leaders within the group – the needle leans left. The optimal distribution of power is considered to be somewhere in between those extremes.

In this way, Daniel Suarez posited a solution to the inequities protested by the Occupy movement well before that group existed. But is that the way in which AR is likely to shape society?

AR AND THE EROSION OF CIVIL SOCIETY
THE DEVALUATION OF PHYSICAL PROXIMITY AND INTERPERSONAL COMMUNITY

As a powerful new communications platform, it seems inevitable that AR will increase the amount of interaction between individuals and draw them closer together. As mentioned above, we have already seen examples of this in the context of AR gaming. It is tempting to believe that these deeper interactions will be to the benefit of all, but that may be naïve. Instead, the shadowy netizens of Daniel Suarez's Darknet may be a more realistic example. By its very nature, AR is an invisible medium in that, in most cases, it is not immediately recognizable by our unaided physical senses. It requires a digital device to decode physical objects and reveal the digital message hidden in plain sight. In this way, AR rewards the discovery of *gnosis*, i.e., metaphysical knowledge that cannot be derived through ordinary physical senses. One might refer to this particular means of divining special knowledge as "aug-gnosis."

For this reason, AR *is* likely to build communities – but more often than in other types of groups, they may be isolated, bespoke communities that do not directly interact with the general populace around them. Marshall McLuhan's famous maxim that "the medium is the message" captures the fact that the means we use to convey information tends to shape how that information is understood and applied. Although it may be too severe to call AR "anti-social" or "anti-democratic," a society in which AR is a prevalent or predominate mode of communication is, at best, a gated community that can only be accessed using some sort of digital key. Indeed, a closer metaphor would be that AR enables the creation of multiple gated neighborhoods amidst and on top of each other, and that the neighborhood in which any given individual resides depends on which keys he holds.

We have already seen this to a degree in the way mobile devices have come to dominate our lives over the past decade. Most Americans today use a smartphone, tablet, or similarly interactive mobile device. A 2013 study found that the average person checks their mobile phone approximately 150 times per day, for such purposes as messaging, voice calls, and even just to get the time – to say nothing of internet use. During peak times, this amounted to once every six seconds for the highest-frequency users.[3] In 2014, another study found that the average American adult spent 34 hours

---

[3]Victoria Woollaston, *How often do you check your phone?* Mail Online (October 8, 2013), available at http://www.dailymail.co.uk/sciencetech/article-2449632/How-check-phone-The-average-person-does-110-times-DAY-6-seconds-evening.html (last visited on September 5, 204).

FIGURE 11.2

Mobile devices now permeate the lives of many individuals in contemporary society.

per month on mobile internet applications, seven more hours than they spend in front of desktop or laptop computers. Forty-seven percent of those used social media on their mobile devices on a daily basis.[4] Therefore, as a result of today's digital media, the gross number of social interactions may well be on the rise, but the increase in digital communication is coming at the expense of face-to-face conversations. (Fig. 11.2)

Accessing digital content via digital eyewear may liberate us from looking down at a hand-held device, but there is no reason to suspect that it will necessarily lead to more in-person interactions. Rather, our physical surroundings will take the place of our smartphone screens. If the other human beings in our vicinity are not part of the same digital simulation that we see through our eyewear, then we are more likely to look *through* them than *at* them. We may come to think of them as distractions from our personal realities rather than cohabitating the same physical plane.

At the very least, there will be fewer reasons to think of ourselves as being part of the same society as others just because they are in close physical proximity to us. Again, this is simply a continuation of a trend that is already well underway. When we sit in a crowded room ensconced in our mobile Facebook app, it is because we would rather interact (however obliquely) with our online friends than with the human beings to whom we are physically near. The more time we spend in digital worlds – whether through a social media platform or a massively multiplayer online

---

[4]Greg Sterling, *Nielsen: More Time on Internet Through Smartphones Than PCs,* Marketing Land (February 11, 2014), available at http://marketingland.com/nielsen-time-accessing-internet-smartphones-pcs-73683 (last visited on September 5, 2014).

roleplaying game – the more we come to consider the members of those groups (who could be actual people, virtual assistants, or AI-driven fictional characters) our "real" community, to the exclusion of the other people we encounter. A persistently augmented world frees (or "enslaves," if you prefer) us from ever having to leave that digital world in which our digital friends live, even when we look away from a particular device with its two-dimensional screen. It is only natural, then, to expect that many of us will come to accord even more personal significance to the people with whom we interact digitally, and less to those in our physical proximity.

In the abstract, there may be nothing inherently wrong with this idea. The real-world consequences, however, may include a fraying of the already-worn bonds and social contract that holds us together as a society. In communities where those bonds are already in danger of breaking, developments like these may be enough to bring them to an end.

POLITICAL GROUPTHINK, OR THE "ECHO CHAMBER" EFFECT

Another socially deleterious consequence of digital media that we already see at work by virtue of today's technology is *groupthink*: the reinforcement of our pre-existing opinions and the filtering out of anything that is inconsistent with those opinions. Psychologists for Social Responsibility define groupthink as follows:

> *Groupthink, a term coined by social psychologist Irving Janis (1972), occurs when a group makes faulty decisions because group pressures lead to a deterioration of "mental efficiency, reality testing, and moral judgment" (p. 9). Groups affected by groupthink ignore alternatives and tend to take irrational actions that dehumanize other groups. A group is especially vulnerable to groupthink when its members are similar in background, when the group is insulated from outside opinions, and when there are no clear rules for decision making.*[5]

To be sure, we do not need to wait for an augmented world to make political groupthink a reality in the United States. Commentators are already bemoaning the sharp rise in political partisanship and rancor, and the corresponding dysfunction of civil society.

The diversity of media channels and news sources makes such polarization orders of magnitude easier than it used to be. Whatever your political leaning, you can find a customized website, satellite radio station, news channel, and talk show host who will give you the news filtered through that perspective. Opposing viewpoints are increasingly things to be mocked, shouted down, or ignored, not to be respected, understood, or even considered. To see the consequences of this trend, one need look no further than the record-breaking level of gridlock in the United States Congress.[6] On

---

[5]Groupthink webpage, Psychologists for Social Responsibility website, available at http://www.psysr.org/about/pubs_resources/groupthink%20overview.htm (last visited on September 5, 2014).

[6]Zach Carter and Will Wrigley, *Do-Nothing Congress Challenges Record for Low Levels of Legislation In Fist Weeks of 2013*, Huffington Post (Posted February 26, 2013), available at http://www.huffingtonpost.com/2013/02/26/do-nothing-congress-house_n_2744597.html (last visited on September 5, 2014).

the issue of the national debt ceiling, for example, two parties with deeply entrenched political ideologies played an unprecedented game of chicken while the threat of a sovereign debt default loomed, triggering a downgrade of the country's creditworthiness and a stock slide.

Even some of the most ardent and hard-working AR advocates acknowledge this concern. As hard as artist BC Biermann is working to enable ubiquitous AR experiences, he freely acknowledges the drawbacks that would come with it. I asked him whether this ability to filter one's experience of reality could lead to more political groupthink. "The question is right on target," says BC, "and honestly, I have no good answer for it right now." Eventually, he suggests, there should be a way to combine filtering with an avenue for unfiltered information as well. But the echo chamber problem is already inherent in our current media environment, he notes, and on balance, he believes that ending what he sees as commercial dominance of public spaces will still be a net-positive.

Others are more bullish on the conviction that the augmented medium will do much more foster education and open minds rather than box them in. Daqri CEO Brian Mullins is one such person. His favorite example is the scene in *The Matrix* where Trinity needs to learn how to fly a helicopter. "She just calls up the instructions," he recounts, "and they're delivered to her on the spot." AR will likewise deliver information on the spot when needed. "AR will become a way to get knowledge in people's heads much faster than any other way that we've done education," Brian says. "It could possibly allow the sum total of human knowledge to be presented in the most effective way possible. Everybody should have access to that."

ENFORCEMENT OF POLITICAL CORRECTNESS

One disturbing outgrowth of groupthink that is already becoming increasingly more evident by the day is the growing use of social media to enforce homogeneity of thought and shaming of minority (and even majority) views. Ubiquitous AR has the potential to carry this trend forward as powerfully as it could some of the other social phenomena described in this chapter.

In March 2014, for example, Mozilla's co-founder and CEO Brendan Eich was driven to resign his position after a short but passionate online campaign seeking that result. His crime? Having made a donation in 2008 to support California's Proposition 8, a law that a then-majority of the state's voters passed to prohibit the recognition of same-sex marriage. Eich's donation had been public knowledge since 2012, but the Supreme Court's 2014 decision striking down Proposition 8 had emboldened those who sought to punish those who had supported it.

In the immediate aftermath of Eich's resignation, even many of those who denounced Proposition 8 distanced themselves from the shaming campaign against him. In the words of the popular marketing executive Ashley Brown, who is vocal in his support for same-sex marriage, what happened to Eich was "wrong. … While in hindsight Eich's contribution to the Prop 8 campaign was probably unwise," Brown wrote, "he is by all accounts a great, fair, and passionate leader. He also ~~doesn't~~ shouldn't have to check his freedom of speech at the Mozilla front door. As long as it's not a workplace matter, it's as fine for someone to oppose same-sex marriage as to support it."[7]

Yet the same story played out in the following weeks when a *Duck Dynasty* cast member (crudely) voiced a similar position on the same topic, and when HGTV cancelled *Flip This House* before it ever aired, because a little-known blog managed to stoke controversy over year-old comments of a similar nature made by the show's would-be hosts, David and Jason Benham. After the latter incident, Brown wrote that "[t]he Eich disaster, the Duck Dynasty kerfuffle, and now this fiasco make clear that no one in business or entertainment can expect privacy of personal belief. We urgently need to settle as a society where our fundamental freedoms meet our professional lives. Until then, we're living in the wild west ...."[8]

To be sure, there has been vociferous disagreement on political and social issues since the dawn of civilization. What is unique about these examples, however, is both the degree of access that the entire world has to virtually every recorded statement ever made by a particular person, and the ease with which any other individual can make their ire over those statements known to the rest of society. The internet – and particularly social media – makes all of this not only possible, but so easy as to be inevitable.

The same ability of digital media to impose a viewpoint is seen in more subtle ways as well. For decades, courts and litigants have wrestled with the question of how accessible law enforcement booking photos – i.e., mug shots – should be to the public. For many years, courts (and most police departments) generally sided with newspapers and other media outlets who argued that the photos were public documents that should be made freely available under Freedom of Information laws. This is why we are accustomed to seeing such photos prominently displayed in news reports of a celebrity's arrest.

Then the internet and big data came along and changed the equation. In recent years we have seen an explosion of mug shot websites that obtain huge troves of the photos, post them online, then demand extortionate "takedown fees" from embarrassed individuals. As a result, the legal status of mug shots has become a bit murkier.

Those campaigning to restrict access to the photos, however, have found an easier solution to litigation. They have instead put social pressure on the companies that make the mug shot websites possible. As a result, many credit card companies stopped processing payments for the sites, and search engines changed their algorithms to lower the sites' popularity in search results.[9] Overnight, the ability of these sites took a massive – and in some cases, lethal – hit.

---

[7]Ashley Brown, *Brendan Eich's Resignation Is Why We Need ENDA,* The Dash (April 7, 2014), available at http://www.ashbrown.org/2014/04/brendan-eichs-resignation-is-why-we.html#.VAPLUfldV8F (last visited on September 5, 2014).

[8]Ashley Brown, *What C-Suite Leaders Need to Understand About the Benham Brothers Fiasco,* ashbrown.org (May 10, 2014), available at http://www.ashbrown.org/2014/05/what-c-suite-leaders-need-to-understand.html?m=1 (last visited on September 5, 2014).

[9]David Segal, *Mug-Shot Websites, Retreating or Adapting,* The New York Times (November 9, 2013), available at http://www.nytimes.com/2013/11/10/your-money/mug-shot-websites-retreating-or-adapting.html?_r=0 (last visited on September 5, 2014).

FIGURE 11.3

The game *Othello*.[10]

Or consider the cases in which e-book publishers have unilaterally deleted copies of purchased books from customers' mobile devices, along with any notes or annotations the user may have made.[11] Such incidents have usually been commercially driven, because of disputes over intellectual property rights and the like. But there is no reason that internet-driven social pressure could not lead to similar decisions, echoing Rage Against the Machine's lyric about modern thought control: "They don't gotta burn the books, they just remove 'em."[12]

Ubiquitous AR will not fundamentally change this tendency to enforce a particular stance of particular political and social issues, but it will enhance the temptation and ability to do so. This phenomenon has become so much more prevalent in recent years only because, for the first time in millennia, virtually all of society interacts through the same platform – the internet. Like a late-game move in board game *Othello*, applying social pressure online is often the easiest way to flip the positions of the greatest numbers of individuals with the least amount of effort (Fig. 11.3). By extending the degree to which the internet envelops our daily activities, AR will magnify our exposure to digitally reiterated social messages.

[10]© flickr user donger / cc by-nd 2.0 license. See http://creativecommons.org/licenses/by-nd/2.0/.

[11]Brad Stone, *Amazon Erases Orwell Books From Kindle*, The New York Times, (July 17, 2009), available at http://www.nytimes.com/2009/07/18/technology/companies/18amazon.html (last visited on September 5, 2014).

[12]Rage Against the Machine Lyrics, *Bulls on Parade*, azlyrics.com, available at http://www.azlyrics.com/lyrics/rageagainstthemachine/bullsonparade.html (last visited on September 5, 2014).

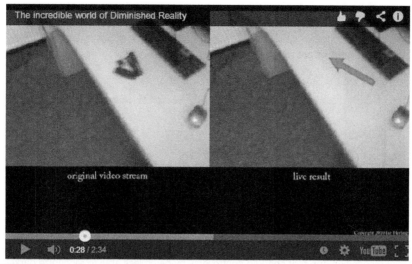

FIGURE 11.4

An example of "diminished reality."

DIMINISHED REALITY

AR apps will contribute to partisanship and polarization as much with what they prevent us from seeing as with what they display. In November 2009, Jamais Cascio published a spot-on piece in *The Atlantic* called "Filtering Reality: How an emerging technology could threaten civility."[13] Cascio saw in AR the potential to "strike a fatal blow to American civil society," as people use their immersive AR eyewear "to block any kind of unpalatable visual information, from political campaign signs to book covers." Moreover, as those devices become more able to give us information about particular individuals in our field of view (perhaps based on facial recognition technology, social media-linked RFID tags, or nanotaggants), we can start blocking those people as well. "You don't want to see anybody who has donated to the Palin 2012 campaign?" Cascio writes. "Gone, their faces covered up by black circles."

Again, we can already see the results of similar motivations today. A photo taken in the White House situation room on the day Osama Bin Laden was killed appeared on newspapers and websites across the world. *Di Tzeitung*, a Brooklyn-based Hasidic newspaper, wanted to use it as well – but its religious rules do not allow it publish photographs of women. Their solution? They simply edited out the two women present in the picture, and said nothing about it to their readers – until they got caught.

People are already talking about the ability of AR to do the same thing to our everyday lives, in real time. They call it "diminished reality" (DR) – augmenting our view of the world not to *add* more data, but to make things we don't want to see *disappear*. (Fig. 11.4)

---

[13]Jamais Cascio, *Filtering Reality,* The Atlantic (November 1, 2009), available at http://www.theatlantic.com/magazine/archive/2009/11/filtering-reality/307713/ (last visited on September 5, 2014).

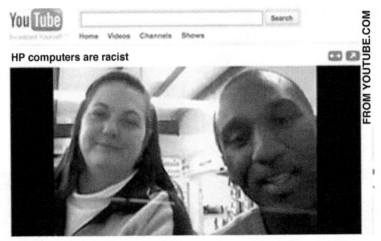

FIGURE 11.5

A facial recognition app that sparked controversy by being less able to recognize darker-skinned faces.

AR/DR apps would not have to be directly related to politics in order to have a negative effect on civil society. Suppose someone does not want to see evidence of poverty in their neighborhood. AR could make those ratty foreclosures look like splendid estates, and the homeless panhandler on the corner appear as if he's wearing a tuxedo. DR apps could simply block them from view altogether, using an algorithm to extrapolate the background view behind them and show you that instead. The less we see of the negative aspects of society, the less motivated we will be to remedy them. Out of sight, out of mind.

The same technology has implications for race relations as well. In 2009, Hewlett Packard stepped into a firestorm of criticism when consumers discovered that its facial recognition technology did not work very well on people with dark skin (Fig. 11.5). Now consider more malicious apps intentionally designed to produce the same result – apps that recognize a particular shade of melanin and replace it with another – so that the user can live in their own artificial version of a racial utopia. Such augmentations would make it that much harder to ever moderate, reform, or even challenge an individual's racist attitudes.

LABELING OTHERS – LITERALLY

Perhaps even more corrosive to civil society than ignoring people with opposing viewpoints or different ethnicities is the ability to (literally, in this case) label and objectify people. Cascio asks, "You want to know who exactly gave money to the 2014 ban on SUVs? Easy – they now have green arrows pointing at their heads." Even more probable are labels that AR users choose for themselves. Social media is likely to be one of the primary forces driving the adoption of AR. As soon as the technological capacity is there, expect to see Facebook profiles and Twitter feeds floating over their authors' heads.

Again, we already have real-world precedents. Cascio highlighted one:

After California's Prop 8 ban on gay marriage passed, opponents of the measure dug up public records of donors supporting the ban, and linked that data to an online map. Suddenly, you could find out which of your neighbors (or the businesses you frequent) were so opposed to gay marriage that they donated to the cause. Now imagine that instead of a map, those records were combined with an AR system able to identify faces.

This precise scenario is all too likely in light of what happened to Brendan Eich and others for supporting the same measure.

There is an endless array of other labels that users may want to see hovering over other peoples' heads as well – including tags identifying religious affiliations, club memberships, socioeconomic background, alumni groups, fraternal orders, or sexual proclivities. That would be as simple as importing one's Facebook or other social media profile into AR space, something that will certainly happen as soon as technologically possible. And if we choose to see such labels in a real-time AR display, it is probably because we either want to associate with, or disassociate from, "those kinds" of people.

Or worse. Recall the case of Michael Enright, the New York college student who, in August 2010, went out looking for a Muslim to kill. According to Enbright's confession,[14] when he asked his cabbie, Ahmed Sharif, if he was a Muslim and the driver said "yes," Enbright stabbed him several times. If Enbright had been wearing AR eyewear that tagged Sharif (or anyone else, rightly or wrongly) as a Muslim, he would not have even had to ask. Instead, Enbright or someone like him could seclude themselves on a hidden perch with a rifle and wait for their chosen victims to come into view – lit up with targeting information just like a video game.

With apps like these running in our AR eyewear, literally everyone we meet during the course of a day could come pre-labeled as a friend or enemy – or at least as interesting or uninteresting. What space will that leave for getting to know someone as an individual? For learning from someone with experiences that are different than ours? For taking seriously a viewpoint that doesn't already fit into our worldview?

Such a world would certainly "diminish" our realities – in more ways than one. When I was in high school, we often read the *Opposing Viewpoints* series of booklets, each one of which summarized differing views on a particular subject. I've always remembered the slogan printed on those books: "Those who do not know their opponents' arguments do not completely understand their own." It's a good reminder that a truly critical thinker is never 100% convinced that his own perception and understanding of any given issue is entirely complete or correct. Even strong opinions can be further nuanced, modified, reconsidered – or, if nothing else, strengthened – by confronting an opposing viewpoint. And even the most passionate advocate can still

---

[14]Shayna Jacobs, *"Cabbie Slasher" Michael Enright pleads guilty to Muslim hate attack,* New York Daily News (June 11, 2013), available at http://www.nydailynews.com/new-york/cabbie-slasher-michael-enright-pleads-guilty-muslim-hate-attack-article-1.1369610 (last visited on September 5, 2013).

acknowledge the basic human dignity and worth of someone who disagrees with him. Disagreement and debate can – and should – be a respectful, constructive process.

People who understand that concept are a necessary prerequisite to a healthy civil society and a functioning democracy. And at this point in American history, we could use many more such people.

HOPE REMAINS

Simply banning AR or DR applications is not the answer. That is not a realistic option in a free society, nor should we throw the baby of progress out with the bathwater of misuse even if it were possible to do so. The only question is how we as individuals will apply these tools, and how we allow them to shape our society.

It is not inevitable that widespread use of AR will visit upon us all of the social ills listed in this chapter. As BC Biermann encourages and present-day AR games show is possible, those developing the medium should be intentional about using AR to draw people into genuine community and real conversations – interactions with more depth than what today's two-dimensional screen-based social media allow. Will Wright, who created such acclaimed games as *SimCity*, *The Sims*, and *Spore*, gave a similar admonition in his keynote address to the 2013 Augmented World Expo. He said, "I'm less interested in putting zombies on the real world and more interested in how we focus in on what's actually there."[15] He went on to extoll the "tremendous value" that diminished (or "decimated," as he called it) reality has to remove the excess information that society already throws at us, in order to train our focus on the things most important to us. With tongue only halfway in cheek, Wright even suggested that the Amish were the group of people who have done the best job to date about being intentional in selecting only the technology that enhances, rather than distract from, the way in which they desire to experience the world around them.

Wright ended his speech by encouraging developers to design AR media that allows us to experience the physical world more viscerally, in a way that works with the user's intuition instead of against it. In sum, the AR he wants to experience is that which "helps me see beauty in the world, and not to see the world as just a better way to browse the internet."[16]

A few hours' drive south of the Santa Clara-based AWE conference, educators at Fuller Theological Seminary reached remarkably similar conclusions about the promise of AR.[17] Examining an educational program of theirs that interwove digital interaction with interpersonal contact, and contrasting it against wholly online learning experiences such as those offered in bespoke virtual worlds like *Second Life*,

---

[15] AugmentedRealityOrg, *Will Wright –Keynote AWE 2013,* YouTube (Published on June 9, 2013), available at https://www.youtube.com/watch?v=4d0k_7pdPGg (last visited on September 5, 2014).
[16] *Id.*
[17] *Augmented Reality: Technology and Personal Presence,* Seminary of the Future (December 21, 2011), available at http://future.fuller.edu/Discussion_Points/Discussion_Point_6__Augmented_Reality__Technology_ and_Personal_Presence/ (last visited on September 5, 2014).

opened their eyes to the power of augmented education.[18] "Augmented reality," wrote the Fuller authors, "recognizes that the most meaningful experiences and relationships in human beings' lives take place in the created world, and that no artificial, sub-created world will ever be able to approach the created world for richness, depth, and meaning. Technology's role, including information technology, is not to replace this world but unearth its latent wealth of potential."

The types of AR experiences that Wright and the educators at Fuller describe could greatly strengthen, rather than fray, the bonds of civic society, not to mention our own individual abilities to appreciate life experiences. The more we think through questions like these ahead of time, the better our chances will be of using AR in a mature, constructive manner.

---

[18]Reading the entire Fuller article in context shows that they used the term "augmented reality" a bit more broadly than how I have chosen to do in this book. The Fuller authors use it as a synonym for mixing online interactions with in-person education, not necessarily for the narrower, more technologically oriented understanding of superimposing digital information on the physical world. That said, the reasoning of the article – especially in the way that it contrasts AR to VR – is apt here.

Personal Ethics

12

INFORMATION IN THIS CHAPTER:

- Eroding our ability to make ethical decisions
- Corrupting our ethical decisions
- Forming bad habits

INTRODUCTION

"You have a responsibility …: to understand what you are doing and how you are doing it and obey [social rules] appropriately …."[1] That is what Google's executive chairman Eric Schmidt was quoted as saying in an interview about the impact Glass will have on social etiquette. As a genre-creating device, Glass has served as the poster child for the ways in which wearable computing – and eventually AR—will shape individual behavior and social norms. Schmidt's point was that, as the ones helping to induce the change, Glass users should accept responsibility for their actions and for the way those actions make others feel. They should behave with an appropriate level of self-awareness and caution, lest they actually become the "Glasshole" that others may accuse them of being.

The same advice will apply with equal, if not greater, force as true AR becomes ubiquitous. As discussed in the previous chapter, the very nature of AR is to provide access to secret knowledge, which inherently affords some measure of power. Users must be cautious and transparent about their exercise of that power, lest it become a corruptive influence on their own ethical and moral sensibilities.

WILL AUGMENTED WORLD TECHNOLOGIES ERODE OUR ABILITY TO MAKE ETHICAL DECISIONS?
SELF-MONITORING APPS ARE INCREASINGLY GIVING US ETHICAL GUIDANCE

The "quantified self" movement is all the rage as of this writing. Dozens of wearable devices currently on the market or about to launch are designed to sense information

---

[1] Keerthi Chandrashekar, *Google Glass: Schmidt Admits 'We'll Have to Develop Some New Social Etiquette,'* LATINOS POST (posted April 24, 2013), available at: http://www.latinospost.com/articles/17372/20130424/google-glass-schmidt-admits-well-develop-new-social-etiquette.htm (last visited on Sept. 9, 2014).

about their user's physical condition, such as heart rate, physical activity, and hours slept. Popular entries in this category include the Fitbit and Jawbone Up bracelets; there are new lines of beds that track the same information.[2] Mobile app stores are awash with health monitoring software. Apple's HealthKit—the newest and most high-profile example as of this writing—promises an entire ecosystem of apps that it says "just might be the beginning of a health revolution."[3]

To be sure, having more and better information about ourselves has the potential to help us improve our lives. Futurist and author John C. Havens has dedicated a good portion of his professional career to advocating this view. He is the founder of the H(app)athon Project, an organization dedicated to "identifying how our actions affect our wellbeing [so] we can track what behaviors increase our happiness.'[4] In March 2014, Havens also released the book *Hacking Happiness: Why Your Personal Data Counts and How Tracking It Can Change the World*, in which "Havens proposes that [the increased collection of 'quantified self' data] will lead to new economic policies that redefine the meaning of 'wealth,' allowing governments to create policy focused on purpose rather than productivity."[5] Through several personal interactions, I have gotten to know the sincerity with which Havens pursues these goals, and I am encouraged by the potential his work has to make a meaningful difference in people's lives.

But he has his work cut out for him. The trouble so far is that very few people currently seem to know what to do with all this self-tracking information. In the summer of 2014, *Fortune* magazine reported that as many as "[85%] of fitness tracking devices [sold] had become inactive,"[6] because people had simply stopped using them. Although these devices and apps offer encouragement and superficial feedback on how we're doing, it turns out that people's habits are not changing very much as a result.

This is not to say that the industry is giving up on the quantified self. Quite to the contrary, observed *Fortune*, the newest wave of devices is taking a harder line with their users. "Instead of incentivizing users to exercise or sleep or eat healthy, and rewarding them for it with virtual badges and digital high-fives, this new class of devices use shame, guilt, and in one case, a physical shock, to keep their owners in line."[7]

[2]Dana Wooman, *Sleep Number's x12 Smart Bed Monitors Your Sleeping Habits*, ENGADGET, available at: http://www.engadget.com/2014/01/07/sleep-number-x12-bed/ (last visited on Sept. 9, 2014).
[3]*Health: An Entirely New Way to Use Your Health and Fitness Information*, Apple's iOS 8 web page, available at: https://www.apple.com/ios/ios8/health/ (last visited on Sept. 9, 2014).
[4]http://happathon.com/about/.
[5]Amazon book summary, available at: http://www.amazon.com/Hacking-Happiness-Personal-Counts-Tracking/dp/0399165312.
[6]Erin Griffith, Introducing iPhone Masochism: Soon Everything You Own Will Judge You, FORTUNE, June 9, 2014, available at: http://fortune.com/2014/06/09/introducing-iphone-masochism-soon-everything-you-own-will-judge-you/ (last visited on Sept. 9, 2014).
[7]*Id.*

As one mild example, take the devices currently offered by Palo Alto start-up Lumo. Each is focused on encouraging proper posture. The Lumo Back is a strap worn around the lower back, while the Lumo Lift clips to a user's shirt underneath the collar bone. Each monitors the user's posture, and gives a gentle vibration whenever their wearer slouches. Analogous devices from other companies provide haptic feedback to discourage speed eating[8] or too much sitting.[9] "But the most punishing device," says *Fortune*, "is the Pavlok, its name a nod to the father of classical conditioning research". According to its creators, this bracelet "doesn't just track what you do. It transforms *who you are*."[10] Users can program it to track any number of goals, including when they wake up, their physical activity, how they use the Internet, whether they meditate, and so on. "If the user hasn't completed their goal [by 7 p.m. each day], they get a shock through the bracelet and charged money through the app."[11] It can also "shame post" automated messages to the user's Facebook page, letting their friends know that the user is a slacker, or deny the user access to their phone.[12] "If [users] complete their goal, [however,] they get rewards like lottery tickets or money."[13] "This is an expensive spin on the idea of wearing an elastic band that you ping when you have thoughts or behavior you want to change."[14] The device's creator, Maneesh Sethi, offers his own social science research to justify his approach, arguing that real consequences are necessary in order to incentivize users to actually meet their goals. Sethi practices what he preaches; he gained his initial infamy by paying a woman $8 an hour to slap him in the face whenever he wasted time on Facebook (Fig. 12.1).

When such applications run on digital eyewear, they may very well resemble an active, three-dimensional version of the content filters that can be found in most Internet browsers today. Family-friendly applications will likely take advantage of "diminished reality" techniques to remove from the user's field of view material deemed objectionable. The next chapter discusses the availability of pornography in the augmented medium, but digital eyewear could just as easily remove or regulate such fleshly temptations that we encounter in the physical world. A married man

---

[8]*HAPIfork: Eat Slowly, Lose Weight, Feel Great*, HAPI.com webpage, available at: http://www.hapi.com/product/hapifork (last visited on Sept. 9, 2014).

[9]*Darma Sitting Wisdom*, darma.co webpage, available at: http://darma.co/ (last visited on Sept. 9, 2014).

[10]*Pavlok: A Personal Coach on Your Wrist*, pavlok.com webpage, available at: http://pavlok.com/ (last visited on Sept. 9, 2014) (emphasis original).

[11]Erin Griffith, *Introducing iPhone Masochism: Soon Everything You Own Will Judge You*, FORTUNE, June 9, 2014, available at: http://fortune.com/2014/06/09/introducing-iphone-masochism-soon-everything-you-own-will-judge-you/ (last visited on Sept. 9, 2014).

[12]*Pavlok: A Personal Coach on Your Wrist*, pavlok.com webpage, available at: http://pavlok.com/ (last visited on Sept. 9, 2014).

[13]Erin Griffith, Introducing iPhone Masochism: Soon Everything You Own Will Judge You, FORTUNE, June 9, 2014, available at: http://fortune.com/2014/06/09/introducing-iphone-masochism-soon-everything-you-own-will-judge-you/ (last visited on Sept. 9, 2014).

[14]Dr. Sheri Jacobson, clinical director of Harley Therapy, London, quoted in James Trew, *Pavlok is a Habit-Forming Wearable That Will Shock You*, Engadget, available at: http://www.engadget.com/2014/07/04/pavlok-wearable/ (last visited on Sept. 9, 2014).

FIGURE 12.1

The inspiration for Pavlok.

wearing such glasses may see black rectangles interposed over his view of passing women in short skirts, for example—or, if the glasses are made by Pavlok, he may receive an electric jolt each time the glasses catch him looking.

On one level, external reinforcements, both negative and positive, have always had their place in shaping our decisions. But contemporary ethicists are troubled by the inexorable growth in outsourcing our ethical decision making to digital assistants. Professors Thomas Seager and Evan Selinger (of Arizona State University and Rochester Institute of Technology, respectively) have studied the new wave of behavior-reinforcing apps, and predict that "the range of ethical dilemmas they can weigh in on will only increase. At this rate, Siri 5.0 may be less a personal assistant than an always-available guide to moral behavior."[15] They refer to such apps as "digital Jiminy Crickets," after the omnipresent voice of reason in Disney's *Pinocchio*. With good reason, however, they do not view this possibility as a positive one.

The belief that "endurance builds character"[16] is ancient wisdom that is still repeated throughout popular culture (though often in a less-than-sincere manner[17]). At its root, this concept recognizes that exercising one's will to choose a course of action that one believes to be morally right, even though it results in less immediate

---

[15]Evan Selinger and Thomas Seager, *Digital Jiminy Crickets*, article from FUTURE TENSE ON SLATE (July 13, 2012), available at: http://www.slate.com/articles/technology/future_tense/2012/07/ethical_decision_making_apps_damage_our_ability_to_make_moral_choices_.html (last visited on Sept. 9, 2014).
[16]ROMANS 5:4-6, BIBLE GATEWAY, available at: https://www.biblegateway.com/passage/?search=Romans+5%3A4-6&version=CEV (last visited on Sept. 9, 2014).
[17]*Build character* entry, URBAN DICTIONARY, available at: http://www.urbandictionary.com/define.php?term=builds%20character (last visited on Sept. 9, 2014).

gratification than the alternatives, strengthens the individual's ability to make similarly virtuous choices in the future. In this sense, it is directly analogous to physical exercise. Repeatedly lifting heavy objects results in short-term injury to muscle fibers, but when the body repairs itself, the muscles grow larger and stronger. No pain, no gain. Consistently relying on another person (or robot) to do the heavy lifting, however, leaves us with no opportunity to develop our own physical strength, so our muscles atrophy. We get weaker and less healthy.

So it is with exercising our ethical muscles. Consistently relying on others—whether other people or digital Jiminy Crickets—to make the hard decisions for us leaves us with less ability in the next situation to decide correctly for ourselves. That is not to say that advice and counsel are necessarily debilitating. To the contrary, both ancient[18] and modern[19] philosophers have praised individuals who choose to consider the input of others when making ethical decisions. But the decision must ultimately be made by the individual in order for that person to gain any moral benefit. Deferring instead to the advice of a piece of software does nothing to challenge an individual's moral convictions, and therefore threatens to atrophy the person's ability to resist temptations to decide otherwise the next time they encounter a similar ethical dilemma.

Philosopher Robert J. Howell of Southern Methodist University took this trend to its logical conclusion in the 2012 scholarly essay "Google Morals, Virtue, and the Asymmetry of Deference."[20] As a hypothetical example, Howell posited an app he called "Google Morals"—the ultimate digital Jiminy Cricket. "When faced with a moral quandary or deep ethical question," went Howell's thought experiment, the users of this app "can type a query and the answer comes out forthwith …. Never again will I be paralyzed by [an ethical dilemma]. I'll just Google it."[21] Realized in augmented reality, such an app may very well take the form of an angelic adviser seated visibly on the user's shoulder; Evan Selinger even suggests that alerts from the app could take the form of "the sound of angelic harps playing."[22]

Summarizing Howell's essay, Selinger tells us that the most obvious concerns with this scenario are not its most troublesome features. For the sake of argument, he explains, "[l]et's imagine [the app] is infallible, always truthful and 100%

---

[18]PROVERBS 15:22, BIBLE HUB, available at: http://biblehub.com/proverbs/15-22.htm (last visited on Sept. 9, 2014).

[19]Evan Selinger, *Would Outsourcing Morality to Technology Diminish Our Humanity?* HUFFPOST TECH ON HUFFINGTON POST (posted Sept. 19, 2012), available at: http://www.huffingtonpost.com/evan-selinger/google-morals_b_1895331.html (last visited on Sept. 9, 2014).

[20]ROBERT J. HOWELL, *Google Morals, Virtue, and the Asymmetry of Deference*, NOUS 48(3), 389–415, WILEY ONLINE LIBRARY (Sept. 2014), available at: http://onlinelibrary.wiley.com/doi/10.1111/j.1468-0068.2012.00873.x/abstract;jsessionid=90CA5DF6B071148314493533F8D7D437.f01t02 (last visited on Sept. 10, 2014).

[21]*Id.*

[22]Evan Selinger, *Would Outsourcing Morality to Technology Diminish Our Humanity?* HUFFPOST TECH ON HUFFINGTON POST (posted Sept. 19, 2012), available at: http://www.huffingtonpost.com/evan-selinger/google-morals_b_1895331.html (last visited on Sept. 9, 2014).

hacker-proof. The government can't mess with it to brainwash you. Friends can't tamper with it to pull a prank. Rivals can't adjust it to gain competitive advantage. Advertisers can't tweak it to lull you into buying their products."[23] What is more, use of the app is not compulsory, so it is not a question of losing individual autonomy. "Even so, Howell contends, depending on it is a bad idea."[24]

Why? Because "deferring to [an app to make moral decisions] can reveal pre-existing character problems and stunt moral growth, both short and long term."[25] In other words, it would demonstrate just how ethically immature the user is. Even *asking* some questions would reveal more about the user than the user could ever hope to gain from the app. "For example," says Selinger, "if you need to ask Google Morals whether it is wrong to tell a lying promise to your best friend, you display callousness and disloyalty. This, in turn, reveals poor habituation and the influence of an underdeveloped character."[26]

Deference to such an app could also prevent the user from ever gaining the experience necessary to flex, let alone strengthen, his or her moral muscles. Among the hazards that Selinger (elaborating on Howell's argument) identifies[27] are that users: "might not exert the effort to learn why a course of action is good or bad"; might become intellectually lazy; might fail to see the broader principles behind distinct moral decisions; and might, by virtue of having delegated away all of the higher reasoning functions that distinguish us from other creatures, ultimately lose their humanity. Howell's highly technical essay and Selinger's summary of it examine these arguments in much greater detail, but the implications are clear. People are increasingly relying on wearable devices and mobile apps to help them make decisions. Taking advantage of useful tools is fine, but the temptation to abdicate even more of our personal decision-making responsibility to software will only increase as augmented interfaces make interacting with them all the more intuitive and frictionless. If we are not careful, such habits could easily detract from our ability to fulfill our human potential, leaving us with a morally diminished reality.

Even for individuals who opt not to use ethical-advice apps, their mere availability could radically alter what *others* expect of us. "Much the same way the rise of Blackberries and mobiles has raised expectations around instant reachability and response," writes MIT research fellow Michael Schrage, "the pervasiveness of [such software] seems sure to reset expectations about self-monitoring and interpersonal behaviors. It may be considered rude—and/or remarkably unprofessional—not to have your devices make sure you're behaving yourself."[28] "[L]arge-scale adoption[,

---

[23]*Id.*

[24]*Id.*

[25]*Id.*

[26]*Id.*

[27]*Id.*

[28]Michael Schrage, Managing Yourself With Your Smartphone, Harvard Business Review, June 6, 2011, available at: http://blogs.hbr.org/2011/06/managing-yourself-smartphone/ (last visited on Sept. 10, 2014).

then,] might do more than change personal behavior. It could transform ethical norms—the very fabric of what members of a society expect from one another."[29]

WILL AUGMENTED WORLD TECHNOLOGIES CORRUPT OUR ETHICAL DECISIONS?

Tish Shute, cofounder of the Augmented World Expo, is fond of referring to augmented reality as a "superpower"—and of pointing out that there is nothing to guarantee that those with such powers will become superheroes as opposed to supervillains.[30] After all, "power tends to corrupt,"[31] as Sir John Dalberg-Acton first said and social science has repeatedly confirmed.[32] As discussed in Chapter 11, AR is, by its very nature, a "secret" medium, accessible only to those with access to the necessary decoding device. And as another famous maxim puts it, "knowledge is power." It seems logical, then, that the more tightly the access to a particular augmented medium remains controlled, the more the power to access the secret knowledge within that medium will tend to corrupt those who have it.

It is somewhat foreboding, therefore, that three completely separate short films about augmented reality released between 2012 and 2014 depict nearly identical visions of that exact prospect.

SIGHT

The first is a 7-min short film called *Sight*, released in August 2012 (Fig. 12.2). It follows a young man in his late 20s/early 30s as he prepares for and goes out on a date. Both he and his date wear the "Sight" line of AR contact lenses, which in that future has become commonplace. The main character, it turns out, works for the Sight company, and the plot centers around his use of a "dating app" installed on his contacts. The app acts as his wingman, reading the woman's body language for signs of interest and intoxication, and giving helpful suggestions such as "act interested" and "suggest different location."

These tips become vital for helping him overcome some early *faux pas* in the date and in eventually persuading her to come home with him for a nightcap. The system apparently even "keeps score" of his successes and awards badges for in-date

---

[29]Evan Selinger and Thomas Seager, *Digital Jiminy Crickets*, article from Future Tense on Slate (July 13, 2012), available at: http://www.slate.com/articles/technology/future_tense/2012/07/ethical_decision_making_apps_damage_our_ability_to_make_moral_choices_.html (last visited on Sept. 9, 2014).
[30]Tish Shute, *Augmented Humans in an Augmented World: Quantified Desire*, SlideShare (June 14, 2013), available at: http://www.slideshare.net/TishShute/augmented-humansaugmentedworld (last visited on Sept. 10, 2014).
[31]*John Dalberg-Acton, 1st Baron Acton*, Wikipedia, available at: http://en.wikipedia.org/wiki/John_Dalberg-Acton,_1st_Baron_Acton (last visited on Sept. 9, 2014).
[32]Christopher Shea, Why Power Corrupts, Smithsonian Magazine, Oct. 2012, available at: http://www.smithsonianmag.com/science-nature/why-power-corrupts-37165345/?no-ist (last visited on Sept. 10, 2014).

FIGURE 12.2

The brilliant short film *Sight*.

accomplishments. It's those badges that ultimately give him away; when his date sees the virtual icons with her own contacts and recognizes that she's being played, she storms off toward the door. That's when the lead character's creepiness goes from subtle to overt. He commands her to stop, and she freezes. Exactly why is unclear; there is debate in my circles as to whether the system somehow takes control of her body, or whether she was a virtual character all along, a test run of the dating program. In any event, his mastery over her actions is clearly against her will. The video ends with him intoning, "Let's try this *again*."

INFINITY AR

The second video, released June 12, 2013, is remarkably similar to *Sight*—except that it is a 3-min concept video by what held itself out as an actual AR company (complete with its own OTC stock symbol) working on *actual* AR products (Fig. 12.3). This video (which echoes elements of *Sight*, Google Glass promos, and the real AR Pool[33] application) also follows a hip young man who uses a nondescript pair of AR glasses to augment his night on the town. Our hero begins his evening by using the 3D instructions given to him by his AR glasses to hustle other competitors in a billiards contest, all of whom appear unaware that he's being guided by prompts from his glasses overlaid onto the pool table. He then follows up his conquest of the pool table by approaching a svelte, young bartender and wowing her with the secret knowledge conveyed to him by his eyewear. First, the glasses read her face to (somehow) determine her astrological sign, and register her as being "intrigued" by his ability to discern it. A little conversation and a Facebook friend request later, she shows up at his house, where (as in *Sight*) he watches virtual TV programs projected

---

[33] 3D Perspectives, *"AR Pool" @ Laval Virtual 2010*, YouTube (uploaded on April 7, 2010), available at: https://www.youtube.com/watch?v=p_onAohGmrs (last visited on Sept. 9, 2014).

FIGURE 12.3

A scene from the creepy concept video posted by Infinity AR.

on his empty wall. The glasses then somehow figure out her favorite wine, and read her as being "impressed" by his selection. The video ends there, but with the clear implication that the protagonist's luck will not.[34]

EX POST FACTO

"Living in a world of grey, two M.I.T. graduates invent a gadget that will not only rival one of the world's largest tech companies but the morality of our society as a whole." That is how first-time filmmaker Antonio R. Cannady summarizes *Ex Post Facto*, the 13-min short film he published on YouTube on August 5, 2014. The film's subtitle is even more direct: "If rape was legal, would you do it?"

Most of the film is dialogue between the two aforementioned recent college grads who have invented a new digital eyewear device with great commercial potential. Exactly what it does isn't made clear at first, but what is clear is the stock role that each character plays in the story. One is the Voice of Greed and Amorality; he actually says "morals hinder progress; do yourself a favor and dump 'em." The other is the Good Guy With the Conflicted Conscience about what effect the device might have on others.

From both the dialogue and the characters' nonverbal interactions, we soon get the idea that the device does something that women will find creepy and invasive. The characters are told that "women's rights groups, religious groups, civil rights groups" and others will be up in arms over the device. The Voice of Greed brushes

[34]Interestingly, this initial version of the video was later removed by YouTube for violating its terms of service. https://www.youtube.com/watch?v=8GcYWdg81BQ. On April 23, 2014, Infinity AR reposted a new version of the same video with most of the interaction between the protagonist and the bartender removed. Infinity AR, *Infinity Augmented Reality Concept Video*, YouTube (published on April 23, 2014), available at: https://www.youtube.com/watch?v=fJI8tNG1rbQ (last visited on Sept. 9, 2014).

FIGURE 12.4

A scene from *Ex Post Facto*.

these comments off. Then another character makes an offhand remark that the device "basically rapes" people—a characterization already foreshadowed in the film's promotional material. This comes off as a figure of speech, and at this point in watching the film, I was sure that the fictional device does exactly what I have often predicted: capture the three-dimensional images of unsuspecting strangers so they can be made into digital avatars for prurient uses by others.

Sure enough, that's exactly where the plot goes. When Good Guy can no longer take being spurned by the Girl Next Door, he spies her through the window using his invention (Fig. 12.4). The eyewear recognizes the woman and processes her three-dimensional image. In seconds, Good Guy sees, through his eyewear, a digital version of the scanned woman walk into his apartment door with a sexy outfit and a come-hither look (Fig. 12.5). You can guess where their interactions go from there.

The final moments of the film then take an unexpected and unnecessary twist that leapfrogs well beyond the degree to which any reasonable viewer would be willing to suspend disbelief. By some magical plot device that is never explained, the real-life woman whose image was scanned by the glasses actually feels, physically and in real time, what Good Guy is doing to her digital avatar. So, whether he realizes it or not (and the whole moral dilemma leading up to this moment suggests that he does), he ends up *actually raping* this woman, albeit from a distance.

Inexplicable and disturbing though this plot device is, Mr. Cannady intended it to drive home his conviction that AR will seduce many of its users into unethical behavior. As he told me:

> Yes, it was a very intentional and harsh commentary on the morality of this technology. … [T]he bad apples that populate our society who will most likely turn this fun device

FIGURE 12.5

The wish-fulfilling avatar created by the AR eyewear in *Ex Post Facto*.

into something of a nightmarish proportions. Everyone from hackers, pedophiles and morally bankrupt individuals will find ways to misuse [digital eyewear] for their own personal and misguided use. I wanted my film Ex Post Facto *to paint a harsh and cold reality to get people to think before embarrassing this technology.*

Whatever other logical or artistic disagreements I may have with Mr. Cannady about this film, these concerns certainly ring true.

A DISTURBING UNANIMITY

Knowledge is power. And in each of these three videos, the male protagonist uses it to gain an advantage—specifically, sexual dominance—over an unsuspecting female character, through either subtle influence or overt force. In each case, if the woman had known that the man was using the app, it would have completely undermined the effect. We see that in the female *Sight* character's angry reaction to discovering the app, and it's safe to assume that the Infinity AR video's bartender would not have been particularly "intrigued" or "impressed" to know that her suitor was simply using his glasses to scour her social media accounts. The woman in *Ex Post Facto* expressly rejects the male character's advances, and never anticipates her impending augmented assault.

Of course, sex sells, and there's a bit of wish fulfillment going on here too. Men have been imagining ways to increase their odds with women throughout human history. Nor are these videos the first to wonder how digital eyewear might be used in dating. The fact that the Infinity AR video got more than 1.5 million YouTube views suggests that viewers liked what they saw. *Ex Post Facto*, on the other hand, leaves no room for private titillation, and instead forces viewers to confront the stark moral consequences of this power imbalance.

But underneath each of these videos is the suggestion that AR offers clever users the ability to gain secret information about—and, thus, power over—those around them. That same dynamic plays out with con men, stalkers, rapists, Peeping Toms, burglars, and similarly ill-intentioned types. And it's this association that can make AR feel creepy.

So it's one thing when a fictional film such as *Sight* or *Ex Post Facto* posits such a future, but it's another thing entirely when an actual company does it, and when others in the industry trumpet the video—which they did with Infinity AR's video—as "the future of AR." No wonder today's pioneers of digital eyewear sometimes encounter such resistance from the general public. If those in the AR industry are highlighting the underhanded ways in which the technology could be used, you can bet that the general public will as well.

There are mitigating factors, of course. For one thing, it's hard to believe that any product as revolutionary as the one depicted in the Infinity AR video—which is light-years ahead of today's capabilities—would be as unrecognizable as it would have to be to fool anybody. As with today's digital eyewear, others would see the digital data flashing on the lenses, alerting them that the device is active. And even if the device's camera wasn't visible, most people would either have seen the product advertised or be so accustomed to the technology that they'd instantly suspect what was going on. But the industry as a whole still has work to do in convincing the public that these devices don't facilitate deception—at least, not any more than any other consumer electronics on the market—and in promoting safeguards and social norms to combat such misuse.

If, on the other hand, such a profound imbalance of power really is inherent to the augmented medium, then the industry has an altogether different problem. In that case, the best hope for introducing AR in a societally healthy way is to do so cautiously, with plenty of safeguards built in to both devices and AR networks to ensure that users cannot gain an undue amount of leverage over unsuspecting individuals—for the benefit of those users who could otherwise be ethically corrupted by the devices' power as much as for those who would be hurt by their actions.

WILL AUGMENTED WORLD TECHNOLOGIES LEAD US TO FORM BAD HABITS?
THE INSEPARABILITY OF FANTASY AND REALITY

Beloved American author Kurt Vonnegut wrote, "We are what we pretend to be, so we must be careful about what we pretend to be."[35] The values and aspirations on which we focus our attention reveal what is truly inside us. We may be drawn to think and behave in a certain way in augmented (or any other) media that we would have never done anywhere else. But if we nurture that second life to the point that it becomes what we truly desire, the role becomes our true self, both inside and out.

---

[35]Kurt Vonnegut, Mother Night, HarperCollins (1966).

Few issues are more hotly contested in contemporary social science as the question of whether violent video games contribute to violent behavior in children. If we are honest, much of the resistance to the conclusion that there is a link comes from the fear of having to give up our own ability to play such games. "Approximately 90% of children in the U.S. play video games, and more than 90% of those games involve mature content that often includes violence."[36] For many of us—children and adult alike—such games are a fun escape from the boundaries of real life.

There is evidence on both sides of the debate. For example, "[researchers at the] Center for the Study of Violence at Iowa State University found hints that violent video games may set kids up to react in more hostile and violent ways,"[37] according to a study they published in the journal *JAMA Pediatrics*. "What this study does is show that it's media violence exposure that is teaching children and adolescents to see the world in a more aggressive kind of way,"[38] said study leader Craig Anderson. In other words, the more someone thinks about resolving conflicts with violence, the more likely they are to choose a violent solution over a nonviolent one. As the saying goes, "when all you have is a hammer, everything looks like a nail."

The rapid rate at which this literature evolves, however, "is why some researchers, including Christopher Ferguson, chair of the psychology department at Stetson University, insist there isn't strong evidence that exposure to violent video games leads to more aggressive behavior."[39] He notes that actual rates of crime have not risen along with exposure to violent media. The truth in this debate, therefore, likely lies somewhere in between the two extremes. Although people cannot escape their personal moral responsibility by blaming their actions on video games, and most people are easily capable of distinguishing in-game escapism from real-life norms, repeated exposure to violent fantasies must have some effect on a person's manner of thinking, feeling, and acting, at some level.

AR, MUSCLE MEMORY, AND DESENSITIZATION

All of this research, however, has been confined to present-day, two-dimensional media. Although video games are interactive, they are still a 2D simulation on a flat screen. There is every reason to expect that augmented experiences will have a far more powerful effect on our habits and thought patterns, precisely because AR is designed to perceive exactly as experience actual, physical reality.

Unlike—or, at least, to a much greater extent than—traditional video games, AR can convey muscle memory. This term refers to "a form of procedural memory that involves consolidating a specific motor task into memory through repetition. When a

---

[36]Alice Park, Little By *Little, Violent Video Games Make Us More Aggressive*, TIME MAGAZINE, March 24, 2014, available at: http://time.com/34075/how-violent-video-games-change-kids-attitudes-about-aggression/ (last visited on Sept. 10, 2014).

[37]*Id.*

[38]*Id.*

[39]*Id.*

movement is repeated over time, a long-term muscle memory is created for that task, eventually allowing it to be performed without conscious effort."[40] As suggested by the common phrase "it's like riding a bike," many believe that muscle memory cannot be unlearned, but rather, at most, only covered over with new habits.[41]

Industry and the military alike have already lauded AR as a training mechanism for this exact reason. Explaining the utility of an "Augmented Reality Training System" for soldiers, Major General Thomas M. Murray of the United States Marine Corps was quoted as saying, "It's like a quarterback taking snaps; the more snaps he takes, the more ready he'll be for the game. We deal with many possible situations so the units can react like muscle memory. We want that reaction to become as routine as possible to handle situations that you can't anticipate."[42] The term shows up often in AR literature, including in reference to using haptic feedback for learning to play an instrument or read Braille,[43] practicing surgical techniques,[44] learning the texture of tumors,[45] and relearning how to walk for the elderly and neurologically injured.[46] We also see it in applications such as the "Soldamatic Augmented Training" helmet that teaches industrial workers how to weld by reproducing the look and texture of the actual welding process without using hot, dangerous metals.[47] In each of these examples, and countless others like them, the goal is to acquaint a person with the movements and sensations involved in a particular task through repetition, until it becomes second nature to them. When those tasks are (in reality) dangerous or intimidating ones, such as welding or warfighting, the goal is also to desensitize the user to that fear in the augmented simulation before they encounter it in the flesh.

---

[40]*Muscle Memory*, WIKIPEDIA, available at: http://en.wikipedia.org/wiki/Muscle_memory (last visited on Sept. 10, 2014).

[41]Eruditio Loginquitas, *Muscle Memory and Learning*, IDOS (Instructional Design Open Studio) (Feb. 16, 2009), available at: http://id.ome.ksu.edu/blog/2009/feb/16/muscle-memory-and-unlearning/ (last visited on Sept. 10, 2014).

[42]BRIAN O'SHEA, *Augmented Reality*, MILITARY TRAINING TECHNOLOGY, MT2, 17(5) (Aug. 2012), available at: http://www.kmimediagroup.com/military-training-technology/articles/424-military-training-technology/mt2-2012-volume-17-issue-5-august/5787-augmented-reality-sp-449 (last visited on Sept. 10, 2014).

[43]*Haptic Feedback and Augmented Reality Can Accelerate Skill Learning*, NEXT BIG FUTURE (June 6, 2014), available at: http://nextbigfuture.com/2014/06/haptic-feedback-and-augmented-reality.html (June 6, 2014).

[44]T. EDMUNDS & D.K. PAI, Perpetually Augmented Simulator Design (abstract), IEEE XPLORE DIGITAL LIBRARY (IEEE TRANSACTIONS ON HAPTICS, 5(1)), available at: http://ieeexplore.ieee.org/xpl/articleDetails.jsp?reload=true&arnumber=5975145 (last visited on Sept. 10, 2014).

[45]SEOKHEE JEON, SEUNGMOON CHOI & MATTHIAS HARDERS, Rendering Virtual Tumors in Real Tissue Mock-Ups Using Haptic Augmented Reality (abstract), ACM DIGITAL LIBRARY (published in JOURNAL IEEE TRANSACTIONS ON HAPTICS, 5(1), 77–84 (2012)), available at: http://dl.acm.org/citation.cfm?id=2197138 (last visited on Sept. 10, 2014).

[46]A. MIRELMAN, et al., V-Time: A Treadmill Training Program Augmented by Virtual Reality to Decrease Fall Risk in Older Adults: Study Design of a Randomized Controlled Trial (abstract), BMC NEUROLOGY, 13, 15 (2013), available at: http://www.biomedcentral.com/1471-2377/13/15 (last visited on Sept. 9, 2014).

[47]Soldamatic Augmented Training, *Soldamatic Augmented Training Technology*, YOUTUBE, available at: https://www.youtube.com/user/SOLDAMATIC (last visited on Sept. 10, 2014).

There is no principled reason why playing games in this manner would not produce exactly the same sorts of muscle memory and desensitization. Indeed, the growing use of gamification in various industries[48] suggests that many of the "serious" training programs will have game elements in them, and educational "games" are (as with today's variety) likely to include many "educational" aspects. So there will be very little practical distinction between an augmented "game" and "training program."

What will this mean for augmented video games containing violent, misogynistic, sadistic, or other escapist role-playing? We know by both intuition and actual examples that the demand for such content is, and will continue to be, high. Two-dimensional AR shooting games have been on the market for years, and in 2013 a Louisiana high school student was arrested for posting to YouTube a video of himself using the game to imagine himself shooting his classmates.[49] Concept videos of immersive AR first-person shooters[50] and hand-to-hand combat games are plentiful online (Fig. 12.6).[51] Some even involve running and jumping on a circular, omnidirectional treadmill and wearing haptic feedback clothing that delivers the sting of pretend bullet wounds, all to further simulate the battlefield experience.[52] Meanwhile, one of the world's most popular video game series, *Grand Theft Auto*, is notorious for rewarding players who commit random acts of unprovoked violence and for engaging prostitutes to gain "health" (Fig. 12.7). This is just one example in the long-running controversy over sex[53] and torture[54] in video games.

Bringing games like *these* into the augmented medium will change the debate on whether it is ethical or socially responsible for *anyone*—let alone children—to play such games. If repeated experience through AR simulation is so widely acknowledged as a training tool in every other facet of life, it will no longer be plausible to deny that similarly repeating violent and prurient actions in the same manner will have the same effect. Just as AR uses high-resolution 3D video and haptic feedback to impart muscle memory to a surgeon, welder, or soldier, so too might *Augmented Grand Theft Auto* players gain muscle memory of what it is like to steal a car, torture

---

[48]*Gamification Industries and Examples*, Gamification Wiki webpage, available at: http://badgeville. com/wiki/Gamification_Industries_Examples (last visited on Sept. 9, 2014).

[49]Caroline Moss, A Teenager Was Arrested After Using An iPhone to Go on a Virtual Shooting Spree, BUSINESS INSIDER, Sept. 16, 2013, available at: http://www.businessinsider.com/teenager-arrested-real-strike-app-virtual-shooting-spree-2013-9 (last visited on Sept. 9, 2014).

[50]Chauncey Frend, *Augmented Reality FPS System*, YOUTUBE (published on May 1, 2012), available at: https://www.youtube.com/watch?v=ELt_aPLxKds (last visited on Sept. 10, 2014).

[51]TherelsaCanal, *Battlefield 5 on Google Glasses (the Marine Revenge)*, YOUTUBE (published on April 12, 2012), available at: https://www.youtube.com/watch?v=-sSsRIhVYB4 (last visited on Sept. 10, 2014).

[52]Joseph Nettleton, *Ultimate Battlefield 3 Simulator Build and Test Video the Gadget Show YouTube*, YOUTUBE (published on Oct. 16, 2012), available at: https://www.youtube.com/watch?v=B9ioVceVlvI (last visited on Sept. 10, 2014).

[53]*Sex and Nudity in Video Games*, WIKIPEDIA, available at: http://en.wikipedia.org/wiki/Sex_and_nudity_in_video_games (last visited on Sept. 10, 2014).

[54]A.J. Glasser, *Torture in Video Games*, KOTAKU (Sep. 10, 2009), available at: http://kotaku. com/5353873/torture-in-video-games (last visited on Sept. 10, 2014).

FIGURE 12.6

Real and imagined first-person shooter games in AR.

a rival, or bed a prostitute. It seems inevitable that such training will encourage players to replicate those behaviors in real life, if only out of ingrained habit.

In some senses, though, whether that proves true will hardly even matter at that point. As a *New York Times* blogger writes, "all of this 'reality' might be a bit too

FIGURE 12.7

A scene from *Grand Theft Auto*.

much for many of us. As much as I like playing a first-person shooter game once in a while ... I'm not sure I want to run through a war zone and see lifelike brains sprayed across my face. I might need some virtual therapy after playing a game that realistic."[55] By repeatedly simulating the actions and experiencing the consequences through their own physical senses, the effect on players' own ethical sensibilities may be the same as if they had committed the actual acts. They will, as Vonnegut warned, have become what they pretended to be, with all the emotional desensitization and altered moral outlook that comes with it.

Applying the medium to the opposite sort of content, of course, stands an equal chance of producing the opposite result. Training people through AR to make right choices will build the muscle memory that makes such behavior second nature. A hybrid approach is also possible, as shown by the Dutch billboard discussed in Chapter 4. By inserting pedestrians into an augmented scenario in which they ought to come to the aid of a first responder being attacked, but cannot, the subject is meant to feel both the impulse to behave ethically and the shame that ought to come from not acting on that impulse. This is meant to serve as negative reinforcement that sensitizes the person to the need to take action in such scenarios.

The discussion in this chapter is meant to demonstrate that we cannot wield the tool of AR to change the world we live in without also changing ourselves in the process. In the next and final chapter, we will ask whether and to what extent we can trust ourselves to create our own worlds, by highlighting some of the darkest and most seductive vices with which we will be tempted to populate our new worlds.

---

[55]Nick Bilton, Disruptions: The Holodeck Begins to Take Shape, THE NEW YORK TIMES—BITS, Jan. 26, 2014, available at: http://bits.blogs.nytimes.com/2014/01/26/disruptions-the-holodeck-begins-to-take-shape/ (last visited on Sept. 10, 2014).

Addiction and·
Pornography

13

INFORMATION IN THIS CHAPTER:

- Addiction to AR
- The reality and inevitability of adult augmented media
- The socially destructive potential of AR porn

INTRODUCTION

The previous chapter ended with a discussion of the negative habits we could form by indulging in the wrong sorts of AR experiences too often. This chapter begins by acknowledging one logical consequence of that behavior: addiction. It then examines what is already guaranteed to be the most prominent vice in the augmented medium: pornography. These are emblematic of the pitfalls that an augmented society will need to overcome in order to derive the greatest value that AR has to offer.

AR ADDICTION
SOME PEOPLE WILL GET HOOKED ON AUGMENTED WORLD TECHNOLOGIES

Augmented reality is all about customizing the world around us. Through video-enabled smartphone and tablet apps, and soon directly through eyewear, AR overlays digital data over our perception of the physical world. The virtual world gets layered directly on top of the real one.

A key buzzword within the AR industry is "immersive." Immersiveness is a measure of how seamless the integration is between virtual and physical data. The more immersive a user's experience (or "UX") is, the less the user consciously perceives the augmented content as being separate from, or inferior in quality or value to, what he or she sees with his or her naked eye. For designers of almost any AR app, the more immersive an app is, the better. In a fully immersive environment, a user perceives the virtual data as being equivalent to, and indistinguishable from, his or her physical surroundings – in other words, just another part of the landscape.

Of course, no AR company is currently in a position to achieve complete immersion. Hardware limitations make that impossible. As engrossing and useful as the display on a monitor, smartphone, or tablet screen is, it only augments one small rectangle in your field of view, and only as long as you hold the device up in front of you. Looking away from the screen doesn't take much effort. Even the best AR app is no more immersive than a really good movie would be.

But what about in the not-too-distant future, when AR-capable eyewear is commonplace, and AR content is plentiful? At that point, it will be possible for a user to become totally "immersed" in a digitally enhanced view of the world. If recent experience with consumer technologies has taught us anything as a society, however, it is that the more engrossing a form of entertainment is, the more likely it is that a certain segment of the population is going to develop an unhealthy fixation with it. Whether you call it "addiction" (a diagnostic term that gets thrown around far too often, but that makes for catchy headlines), compulsive behavior, or simply a deeply ingrained habit, the fact is that people love to immerse themselves in fantasy worlds to escape the doldrums and difficulties of real life. And fully immersive AR will be orders of magnitude more engaging and attractive than even the best of today's digital content.

We see this type of behavior everywhere today. Gamers will sit in front of their consoles playing massively multiplayer online games for hours and days on end. In 2011, someone died from a blood clot after sitting too long playing *Halo 3* on Xbox. I have personally seen people dedicate the majority of their nonworking hours to online role-playing games such as *EverQuest* and *World of Warcraft*. The 2014 documentary *Web Junkie* takes place in "a division of a Beijing military hospital, where teenage boys are being treated for Internet addiction – more specifically, addiction to 'World of Warcraft' and other games like it."[1] In 2010, a South Korean couple was arrested for allowing their newborn infant to starve to death while they did 12-hour stints at an Internet café raising a virtual baby in the online role-playing game "Prius Online." "Online game addiction can blur the line between reality and the virtual world," a South Korean professor said about the case. "It seems that taking care of their on-line game character erased any sense of guilt they may have had for neglecting their daughter."[2]

I am not without sympathy for those who get absorbed into video games. There were portions of my college years when I certainly spent more than my fair share of time playing the computer strategy game *Civilization* and other games like it, although the Internet connectivity of newer games adds a social element that draws players in even further. None of these games are bad in and of themselves. Rather, they are *so good* – so immersive – that players with poor self-discipline can easily get sucked into playing them longer than they should.

The problem is not limited to games. In a 2013 TEDx talk, Dr. Zoe Chance of the Yale School of Management admitted her addiction to a wearable device – specifically, a "smart pedometer." Driven to reach the daily goal of 10,000 steps that

---

[1]Farran Smith Nehme, Internet Addiction the Focus of 'Web Junkie' Documentary, NEW YORK POST, Aug. 7, 2014, available at: http://nypost.com/2014/08/07/internet-addiction-the-focus-of-web-junkie-documentary/ (last visited on Sept. 10, 2014).

[2]CNN, *Report: South Korea Couple Starved Child While Raising Virtual Baby*, CNN WORLD (March 5, 2010), available at: http://www.cnn.com/2010/WORLD/asiapcf/03/05/korea.baby.starved/index.html (last visited on Sept. 10, 2014).

the device set for her, Dr. Chance's entire waking experience soon became filled with trying to move as much as possible. Her marriage began to suffer, she admitted, as her new obsession led her to bond instead with other compulsive users of the device, both in person and online. "They market it as a 'personal trainer in your pocket,' Chance said. "No! It is Satan in your pocket."

Silicon Valley venture capitalist Marc Andreessen predicted that, once digital eyewear goes mainstream, many of its users will have a similar degree of attachment. "The idea of having the Internet with you all the time, being able to see, literally to be able to have the Internet in your field of vision … and to be able to talk to it, it basically just wraps you in all the information you would ever need all the time," he said. "I think people are going to find they feel, basically, naked and lonely, when they don't have this at some point."[3]

The AR medium will make digital experiences even more appealing and compelling than they already are. The explosive growth in recent years of proto-AR gaming systems, such as the Wii, Kinect, and Nintendo 3DS, demonstrates that AR is the future of digital gaming.

Toward the end of a very thoughtful panel discussion on the challenges of designing AR user experiences at the 2011 ARE Conference, Brendan Scully of Metaio said, "I certainly wouldn't trust myself to design my own UX." This reminded me of some of the cautionary tales that pop culture has already given us about the drawbacks of having complete control over our surroundings. *Star Trek: The Next Generation* did this frequently (sometimes to a fault) via the "Holodeck," a holographic room capable of replicating any environment and character imaginable. In the episode "Hollow Pursuits" (and later episodes), the socially inept character Reginald Barclay literally becomes addicted to living in the artificial worlds he creates there – complete with racier versions of his real-life female acquaintances and diminutive parodies of the men that intimidate him (Fig. 13.1).

The ability to create similar scenarios of our own may not be far off. "[S]ome scientists and researchers say we could have something like holodecks by 2024."[4] This has some futurists concerned. Ernest Cline, author of the popular sci-fi novel *Ready Player One*, also commented: "Once video games become so real, when you're wearing goggles and gloves and you're completely logged in, then [it will get worse]. Once it becomes like the holodeck, how will people avoid becoming more addicted?"[5]

Then there's the classic virtual reality film *Lawnmower Man*, in which the title character conquers an artificial world and declares, "I am God here!" The special

---

[3]Cadie Thompson, 'Naked and Lonely' Without Google Glass: Andressen, CNBC, June 12, 2013, available at: http://www.cnbc.com/id/100809673 (last visited on Sept. 10, 2014).

[4]Nick Bilton, *Disruptions: The Holodeck Begins to Take Shape*, THE NEW YORK TIMES—BITS (Jan. 26, 2014), available at: http://bits.blogs.nytimes.com/2014/01/26/disruptions-the-holodeck-begins-to-take-shape/ (last visited on Sept. 10, 2014).

[5]Nick Bilton, *One on One: Ernest Cline, Author of 'Ready Player One,'* THE NEW YORK TIMES—BITS (Aug. 22, 2012), available at: http://bits.blogs.nytimes.com/2012/08/22/one-on-one-ernest-cline-author-of-ready-player-one/ (last visited on Sept. 10, 2014).

FIGURE 13.1

Reginald Barclay in the holodeck.

effects in these shows may be dated, but their message is timeless: the more control we gain over their personal environments and surroundings, the more those surroundings will tend to reflect our own narcissism.

It seems inevitable that at least some AR users will demonstrate the same tendencies, to varying degrees. For most people, AR will probably be a lot like text messaging or Facebook is today – a technological convenience that many people may actually spend too much time with and joke about being "addicted" to, but that leads to few actual cases of *bona fide* dependence. Even if it doesn't amount to "addiction," though, the potential for unhealthy behavior through AR will always be present to some degree. Even today, for example, a jilted lover or spurned suitor could use an AR app to display their desired partner's face at the physical location of every past date – reinforcing a vicious cycle of negative emotions. As discussed further subsequently, pornographic content – already ubiquitous and responsible for an array of unhealthy behavior – can be displayed anywhere in ways that standard, two-dimensional monitors won't be able to match.

As AR hardware and capabilities mature beyond today's comparatively simplistic communication technologies into a more immersive environment, the potential for abuse will grow accordingly. To those who become accustomed to living in a *Domestic Robocop*–type world, nonaugmented reality may start to seem unbearably mundane by comparison. At that point, we could very well see a number of real-world Reginald Barclays.

WHAT CAN AND SHOULD BE DONE TO PREVENT ADDICTION?

Will government or industry step in to regulate AR content and head off some of these consequences? Perhaps. Although governments have more or less lost the ability to regulate violent content, age restrictions on prurient material remain enforceable, and would certainly be applied in this new medium. Crackdowns on illegal gambling programs may well follow. Just as we see counselors specializing in addictions to such content today, we're likely to see similar services available for those who lose themselves in their own augmented worlds.

"The trouble," says Nir Eyal, author of *Hooked: How to Build Habit-Forming Products*, "is this: The attributes that make certain products engaging also make them potentially addictive. There is no way to separate the fun of gaming, for example, with its potential for abuse. Social media is exciting principally because it utilizes the same variable rewards that make slot machines compelling. Spectator sports or television watching, enjoyed by billions of people, share common traits with the primary function of illicit drugs – they provide a portal to a different reality. If what we're watching is engaging, we experience the high of being mentally elsewhere."[6]

Eyal, therefore, proposes that the creators of immersive digital experiences should bear some ethical and moral responsibility to prevent addiction. This is due in part to the unique metrics that digital technology provides about individual users. "Makers of alcoholic beverages for example, can throw up their hands and claim they have no idea who is an alcoholic. However, any company collecting user information can no longer take cover under the same excuse. Tech companies know exactly who their users are and how much time they are spending with their services. If they can hypertarget advertising, they can identify harmful abuse."[7] Eyal argues that these companies therefore "have both an economic imperative and a social responsibility to identify addicts and intervene."[8]

He proposes that tech companies establish what he calls a "Use and Abuse Policy," which helps establish the parameters of healthy use and redlines that trigger an intervention when crossed. "Of course, what constitutes abuse and how companies intervene are topics for further exploration," writes Eyal, "but the current status quo of doing nothing despite having access to personal usage data is unethical. Establishing some kind of upper limit helps ensure that users do not abuse the service and that companies do not abuse their users."[9] Some companies, he notes, already take similar measures. The technical Q&A site StackOverflow, for example, limits how often the site can be accessed by a single user. "Programmers should be out there in the world creating things too,"[10] writes cofounder Jeff Atwood, rather than spending all of their time on his website.

REASONS FOR OPTIMISM

Just because AR will be immersive does not automatically make it addictive or dangerous. No matter how convincing its digital content is, AR is, by definition, the intersection between that data and the real, physical world. The most exciting possibilities for immersing oneself in AR are also the same features that would take

---

[6]Nir Eyal, *Is Some Tech Too Addictive?* TechCrunch (posted May 31, 2014), available at: http://techcrunch.com/2014/05/31/is-some-tech-too-addictive/ (last posted on Sept. 10, 2014).

[7]*Id.*

[8]*Id.*

[9]*Id.*

[10]*Id.*

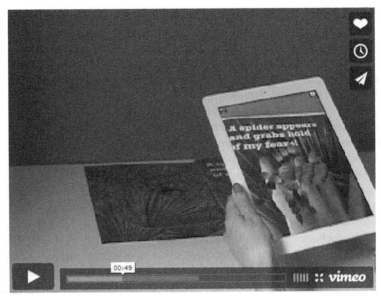

FIGURE 13.2

The AR pop-up book.

users outdoors. Therefore, augmented content may never have the same tendency to isolate users into online communities and separate them from physical interaction the way that console-based gaming systems with monitor-dependent displays do today. Proto-AR systems such as the Wii and Kinect are already heralded as getting gamers off the couch; AR could be the killer app for getting them outside and into the world around them.

Counselors, meanwhile, need not wait for AR-addled patients to start taking the technology seriously. Today's innovators are already devising ways that AR can be used to counsel patients. As mentioned in Chapter 9, Helen Papagiannis designed the world's first AR pop-up book for the iPad (Fig. 13.2).[11] It is designed to let users interact with virtual representations of their phobias – spiders, for example – in a visually convincing, but perfectly safe, way.

PORNOGRAPHIC AND PRURIENT CONTENT
PORNOGRAPHY IS ALREADY GOING MAINSTREAM THROUGH TODAY'S DIGITAL MEDIA

Regardless of your moral outlook, porn is a serious and growing presence in contemporary society. Paul Fishbein, founder of *Adult Video News*, correctly notes that

---

[11]Bruce Sterling, *Augmented Reality: Helen Papagiannis AR Pop-Up Book*, Wired (June 27, 2011), available at: http://www.wired.com/2011/06/augmented-reality-helen-papagiannis-ar-pop-up-book/.

"Porn doesn't have a demographic – it goes across all demographics."[12] An analysis of 400 million web searches demonstrated that 1 in every 8 searches of all searches was for erotic content.[13] "By 2015, mobile adult content and services are expected to reach \$2.8 billion per year, mobile adult subscriptions will reach nearly \$1 billion, and mobile adult video consumption on tablets will triple [over 2013 levels]."[14]

"It's not news, of course," the *New Yorker* wrote in 2003, "that men are into porn – or that the Internet has made it possible to delve into the dirty without slipping into the back room at a video store or hunkering down in a Times Square peep booth." But "thanks to the advent of cable modems and DSL connections," it continued, "the mass consumption of cyberporn has slyly moved from the pathetic stereotypes (fugitive perverts, frustrated husbands) into the potent mainstream (young professionals, perhaps your boyfriend) …. Porn is not merely acceptable; it's hip."[15] By 2013, "more and more adult companies [were] expanding into new fields of business. And business has been good. Hustler leads the charge in this area, having spent years building up a successful clothing line, opening casinos and even publishing the occasional mainstream magazine."[16] That is the society into which AR is being introduced.

PORN WILL BE PLENTIFUL IN AUGMENTED MEDIA

The Internet meme called "Rule 34" is a maxim that states, "If it exists, there is porn of it. No exceptions." This bit of popular wisdom reminds us that we will encounter prurient content in AR, and that such content is not unique to the medium. Nevertheless, AR's unique capabilities will bring an unparalleled degree of anonymity and accessibility to explicit content that will magnify the erotic temptation, compulsion, and dysfunction with which our society is already riddled.

Visual content

The fact that the public is already accustomed to downloading digital porn may be why, as soon as the first video teaser[17] for the first mainstream digital eyewear – Glass – was released on YouTube, a recurrent theme in the viewers' comments was how it could be used for pornographic applications. For example:

---

[12]Luke Gilkerson, *Get the Latest Pornography Statistics*, COVENANTEYES (Feb. 19, 2013), available at: http://www.covenanteyes.com/2013/02/19/pornography-statistics/ (last visited on Sept. 10, 2014).
[13]*Id.*
[14]*Pornography Statistics: Annual Report 2014*, COVENANTEYES, available at: http://www.covenanteyes.com/pornstats/ (last visited on Sept. 10, 2014).
[15]David Amsden, Not Tonight, Honey. I'm Logging On, NEW YORK MAGAZINE, available at: http://nymag.com/nymetro/news/trends/n_9349/ (last visited on Sept. 10, 2014).
[16]Chris Morris, Will Porn Become a Mainstream Business? CNBC, Jan. 15, 2013, available at: http://www.cnbc.com/id/100364346# (last visited on Sept. 10, 2014).
[17]Google, *Project Glass: One day …*, Apr. 4, 2012, available at: http://www.youtube.com/watch?v=9c6W4CCU9M4.

"you can watch porn on the go!"

"Awesome, with this remarkable device it's possible for me to watch porn while i watch porn on my computer. Life's good 😊"

"download porno on a crowded bus!"

The sentiment is easy to comprehend. Anonymity has always fueled porn consumption. First, there were magazines in slick black bags. Then pay cable stations. Then the Internet. Now, digital eyewear will enable users to take the content with them outside the house, viewing it in public while still remaining anonymous. One of the *New Yorker*'s interview subjects wrote of the thrill of danger he got by viewing porn in his university's computer lab, while others worked in adjacent cubicles. AR-equipped thrill-seekers will be able to take this one step further, and watch explicit content while actually standing in front of and talking to those same colleagues face-to-face. At school, work, home, on the bus – no setting will ever again reinforce a social stigma against watching it, because only the wearer will see what is on their AR lenses.

In the few years since Glass was first announced, independent developers have indeed been busy finding ways to apply the device to pornographic purposes. In June 2013, a small company called MiKandi released the first explicit app for the device, fittingly titled "Tits & Glass."[18] The app "allows users to view and share pornographic content from a point-of-view angle … [and] to comment and vote on their favorite content."[19] Unamused, Google promptly revised its Glassware policy to prohibit "content that contains nudity, graphic sex acts or sexually explicit material."[20] The app returned to the unofficial market of "side-loaded" Glassware, but now cautions users to share only images that are "safe for work."[21] The revised terms of service did not, however, "preclude [MiKandi] from enabling users to go buckwild in sharing their own POV creations."[22] So MiKandi launched a traditional website to store users' first-person perspective videos – the first of which was contributed by infamous porn star James Deen – and teamed up with a larger company in the industry to sell videos containing the results.[23]

Soon thereafter, a three-person team of developers caused a stir with their entry to a London-based hackathon, which they called "Sex With Glass."[24] The idea was to allow two partners, each wearing Glass, to see on their own devices the other person's point of view, in real time, during sex. With the public's imagination aroused, the developers refined the software into an app now called "Glance." As of this writing,

---

[18]*Tits & Glass*, available at http://titsandglass.com/.

[19]Cadie Thompson, X-Rated Google Glass App Gets Banned, CNBC—DISRUPTOR 50, June 4, 2013, available at: http://www.cnbc.com/id/100787343 (last visited on Sept. 10, 2014).

[20]*Id.*

[21]*How It Works*, available at: http://titsandglass.com/how-it-works.

[22]Marikia Millikan, *I Watched James Deen Make the First-Ever Google Glass Porn*, MOTHERBOARD (July 23, 2013), available at: http://motherboard.vice.com/blog/i-watched-james-deen-make-the-first-ever-google-glass-porn-1 (last visited on Sept. 10, 2014).

[23]*Id.*

[24]Glance App Action webpage, available at: http://www.glanceapp.info/ (last visited on Sept. 10, 2014).

Glance is available for the iPhone, although the version for Glass is still under development. When released, the goal is that each user will "say 'ok glass, it's time' and Glance on Google Glass will stream what you see to each other."[25] Taking a cue from Snapchat and other ephemeral social media, the app keeps the resulting video for 5 h, after which it is deleted if one of the users does not actively save it.[26]

The renewed interest in virtual reality sparked by the Oculus Rift has gotten developers working on adult content for that medium as well. "Adult-film streaming service SugarDVD announced [in March 2014] that it is working on an app for the [Rift] … that will stream adult movies and content to the device."[27] At the same time, the company was already "working with motion-capture studios in Los Angeles to generate original, VR-optimized content that will take full advantage of the Rift's technology."[28] A small California start-up called Sinful Robot announced that it was doing the same.[29] These would be fully immersive, interactive experiences that play out as a *Choose Your Own Adventure* story with benefits.

Visual recognition software and user-generated content

There is another reason that viewers are likely to take their AR porn into the public square. The ability to overlay explicit content on the real world – or, more to the point, on real *people* – will offer synergies that have been heretofore relegated only to private imaginings.

"I'm just going to say this right now," blogger Jordan Yerman wrote on the same day the first Glass teaser was released. "The dev teams for every online porn outfit on the web are watching the Google Project Glass video … and thinking, 'we can create an app that matches sex footage from our libraries to the body positions of passersby spotted by augmented-reality glasses.' I promise you, that's what they're thinking."[30]

The demand for such technology was proven in 2009, when a video advertisement[31] for the mobile app *Nude It*[32] – which purported to allow users to see through

---

[25]*Id.*

[26]Sylvia Tomayko-Peters, *Mediating Sexual Experience: A Discussion of the Glance App for Google Glass*, HASTAC (posted March 10, 2014), available at: http://www.hastac.org/blogs/sylviatp/2014/03/10/mediating-sexual-experience-discussion-glance-app-google-glass (last visited on Sept. 10, 2014).

[27]Jeffrey Grubb, *Strap on Your Oculus Rift and Get Ready: Interactive Porn Is Coming*, VB/Gamesbeat (May 21, 2014), available at: http://venturebeat.com/2014/05/21/strap-on-your-oculus-rift-and-get-ready-interactive-porn-is-coming/ (last visited on Sept. 10, 2014).

[28]*Id.*

[29]Damon Brown, *Sinful Robot: How Immersive Virtual Reality Will Transform Adult Entertainment*, Future of Sex (Feb. 28, 2013), available at: http://futureofsex.net/virtual-sex/interview-with-vr-sex-experimenter-sinful-robot (last visited on Sept. 10, 2014).

[30]The original post, which was at http://www.examiner.com/tech-biz/google-project-glass-future-augmented-reality-porn-2910206.html, is no longer available. I first quoted it here: Brian Wassom, *Augmented Reality Eyewear & the Problem of Porn*, May 2, 2012, available at: http://www.wassom.com/augmented-reality-eyewear-the-problem-of-porn.html.

[31]Whoisthebaldguy, *iPhone 6 AR App Demo: "Nude It,"* Oct. 11, 2009, available at: https://www.youtube.com/watch?v=G_AzDO_uwz8 (last visited Sept. 12, 2014, at which time the video had 3,449,910 views).

[32]Nude It Android Phone Application webpage, available at: http://www.presselite.com/iphone/nudeit/ (last visited on Sept. 10, 2014).

FIGURE 13.3

Nude It.

clothing – went viral (Fig. 13.3). Despite the obvious fact that it was a spoof – something the originators quickly acknowledged – that didn't stop thousands of eager users from demanding the ability to download it. Perhaps the most enabling development, however, has been the beta-level introduction of mobile devices able to scan three-dimensional environments in real time. Devices such as Occiptal's Structure Sensor[33] and Project Tango[34] demonstrate technology that, once perfected, will enable the masses to create their own digital avatars of anything and anyone around them. You can have three guesses as to how selfie-obsessed teens will use this technology, as long as each guess is "for sexting."

Haptic interaction

Vision will not be the only sense to be digitally augmented for prurient purposes. Digital sex toys have already been on the market for years. These include those devices traditionally intended for women – such as the music-driven OhMiBod[35] – as well as a growing market for digitized receptacles made for male use. These are sold under the brand names Fleshlight and RealTouch, and were originally designed to sync haptic pulses with the action portrayed in prerecorded videos.[36] The latter brand, however, has since introduced a service called RealTouch Interactive, which

---

[33]*The First 3D Sensor for Mobile Devices Is Here*, Structure webpage, available at: http://structure.io/ (last visited on Sept. 10, 2014).
[34]Project Tango webpage, Google, available at: https://www.google.com/atap/projecttango/#project (last visited on Sept. 10, 2014).
[35]Sylvia Tomayko-Peters, *Human Computer Interaction: Digitally Enhanced Sex and Body Exploration*, HASTAC (posted Feb. 16, 2014), available at: http://www.hastac.org/blogs/sylviatp/2014/02/16/human-computer-interaction-digitally-enhanced-sex-body-exploration (last visited on Sept. 10, 2014).
[36]*Id.*

puts male device owners in touch with live "models" for "private 1-on-1 fantasy encounters."[37] According to the company, "your RealTouch senses both the velocity and depth of motion that models perform on their joystick. This is the most realistic live sexual experience the world has ever known and we are proud to call it True Internet Sex!™"[38]

This is only one facet of the rapidly expanding genre some have labeled "teledildonics."[39] "While similar in design to the RealTouch Interactive," for example, a company called LovePalz differentiated itself by marketing its services to couples.[40] "LovePalz is intended for use by couples in long distance relationships. Rather than a single purchasable device, there is one designed for female anatomy and one for male. Partners connect via video chat software and the devices communicate information back and forth via bluetooth and the internet. What one partner does with their device, the other feels."[41] The company soon spread its marketing to a broader demographic, however; as of this writing, its website also advertises the "LovePalz Club," which promises members thereof, "Stay in your room and start meeting new people all over the world."[42] An Amsterdam-based start-up attempted to fund through Indiegogo a similar service called Kiiroo, which it billed as "the first social platform with an intimate touch." As of March 2014, however, the project fell short of its funding goal.[43]

Even the blow-up doll industry is getting into the digital age. The first commercial sexbot, called "Roxxxy," was introduced in 2010, and the company behind it now offers a wide range of units in the series. "Roxxxy is decidedly a robot ... [and] mannequin-like," offering little more nonphysical interactivity than a Teddy Ruxpin bear. "Right now, [however,] we're at an inflection point on the meaning of sexbot,"[44] says Kyle Machulis, a California-based computer scientist who focuses on sensual technologies.[45] "Henrik Christensen, founder of the European Robotics Research Network, thinks that sex with robots is only five years away."[46] In a report released

---

[37]Real Touch Interactive Beta webpage, available at: http://www.realtouchinteractive.com/how_it_works.php (last visited on Sept. 10, 2014).

[38]*Id.*

[39]Burke Denning, *Technologasm?! The Rise of Teledildonics and Adult Haptic Devices*, KINSEY CONFIDENTIAL (May 15, 2012), available at: http://kinseyconfidential.org/technologasm-rise-teledildonics-adult-haptic-devices/.

[40]Sylvia Tomayko-Peters, *Networked Bodies: Connectivity in Digitally Enhanced Sex Toys*, HASTAC (Feb. 24, 2014), available at: http://www.hastac.org/node/109248 (last visited on Sept. 10, 2014).

[41]LovePalz, available at: http://www.lovepalz.com.

[42]*Twist, the Cutting-Edge Cyber Pleasure Toy*, webpage of LovePalz, available at: https://www.love-palz.com/twist/ (last visited on Sept. 10, 2014).

[43]*Kiiroo, the First Social Platform With an Intimate Touch*, webpage on Indie Gogo, available at: https://www.indiegogo.com/projects/kiiroo-the-first-social-platform-with-an-intimate-touch (last visited on Sept. 10, 2014).

[44]Leah Reich, *Sexbot Slaves*, AEON (June 6, 2014), available at: http://aeon.co/magazine/technology/how-will-sexbots-change-human-relationships/ (Sept. 10, 2014).

[45]Nonpolynomial Labs webpage, available at: http://www.nonpolynomial.com/about/ (last visited on Sept. 10, 2014).

[46]*Robot Sex Revolution*, THE RATCHET, available at: http://theratchet.ca/robot-sex-revolution (last visited on Sept. 10, 2014).

in August 2014 by Pew Research, GigaOM Research's Stowe Boyd predicted that, by 2025, "robotic sex partners will be a commonplace."[47] By 2050, predicts artificial intelligence researcher David Levy, "Love with robots will be as normal as love with other humans while the number of sexual acts and lovemaking positions commonly practiced between humans will be extended, as robots teach us more than is in all of the world's published sex manuals combined."[48] Already, in May 2014, Florida resident Chris Sevier filed a lawsuit seeking the right to marry his pornography-laden MacBook, characterizing himself as not materially different from same-sex couples and other "sexual minorities" seeking the right to marry.[49]

The beauty of AR is that it liberates content from two-dimensional monitors and sets it free into the physical world. But we may also come to see that as AR's curse.

SOCIETY WILL SUFFER AS A RESULT

No blog post I have ever written got as much reaction – both positive and negative – as when I criticized the effects that augmented pornography could have on society. Many people agreed; yet many also responded with vigorous disdain and defensiveness. The subject strikes a chord, perhaps because so many people already consume adult content on a regular basis and cannot, or do not want to, examine it objectively. The experiences of millions, however, do not lie. One does not have to be a prude to recognize the corrosive effects adult content can have on individuals and society. To the contrary, one must try hard not to see it.

Compulsive behavior

Much of the debate over pornography's impact on the person viewing it gets hung up on terminology. As mentioned in the previous section, it is easy and commonplace to throw around the word "addiction." That is what a panel of experts did in 2004 when they testified on the subject before the Senate Commerce Committee's Science, Technology and Space Subcommittee. "Pornography really does, unlike other addictions, biologically cause direct release of the most perfect addictive substance …. It does what heroin can't do, in effect," said one witness.[50] Similarly, in 2010, "[t]he National Council on Sexual Addiction and Compulsivity estimates that 6 to 8 percent of Americans – or 18 million to 24 million people – are sex addicts. And 70 percent of sex addicts report

---

[47]Sebastian Anthony, *By 2025, 'Sexbots Will Be Commonplace' Which Is Fine, as We'll All Be Unemployed and Bored Thanks to Robots Stealing Our Jobs*, EXTREMETECH (Aug. 14, 2014), available at: http://www.extremetech.com/extreme/188047-by-2025-sexbots-will-be-commonplace-which-is-just-fine-as-well-all-be-unemployed-and-bored-thanks-to-robots-stealing-our-jobs (last visited on Sept. 10, 2014).

[48]DAVID LEVY, LOVE AND SEX WITH ROBOTS: THE EVOLUTION OF HUMAN–ROBOT RELATIONSHIPS, Harper Perennial (Nov. 4, 2008).

[49]David Millward, Florida Man Demands Right to Wed Computer, THE TELEGRAPH, May 7, 2014, available at: http://www.telegraph.co.uk/news/worldnews/northamerica/usa/10814098/marriage-gay-marriage-mac-wedding-computer-Florida-Utah.html (last visited on Sept. 10, 2014).

[50]Ryan Singel, *Internet Porn: Worse Than Crack?* WIRED (Nov. 19, 2004), available at: http://archive.wired.com/science/discoveries/news/2004/11/65772 (last visited on Sept. 10, 2014).

having a problem with online sexual behavior."[51] Yet other experts in the field scoff at the term "pornography addiction," and "the panelists themselves acknowledged [that] there is no consensus among mental health professionals about the dangers of porn or the use of the term …." "'Compulsive' is [a] more appropriate [term]" to describe those for whom pornography leads to unhealthy behaviors, said one sex therapist.[52]

This debate, however, misses the point. Whatever one calls it, adult content is easy to abuse. Just like a drug, not every encounter will necessarily lead to unhealthy or compulsive behavior, but line between use and abuse is difficult to perceive and easy to cross. Those who do fall into compulsive habits struggle mightily to overcome them, and those who cannot break free suffer a variety of negative consequences.

One of the most pernicious things about pornography is its staying power. Those addicted to drugs "can get the drug out of their system, but pornographic images stay in the brain forever." They are thoughts that cannot be unthought; the best that one can do is to try and drive the images out of one's conscious brain by training one's self in new thought patterns. That is where having constant, heads-up access to prurient content on digital eyewear will prove so destructive. It virtually ensures that one whose mind is already dwelling on adult topics will have those explicit thoughts on their mind constantly, thereby reinforcing the negative thought patterns that lead to compulsive behavior. That calls to mind the warning of seventeenth century poet Thomas Traherne, who said, "As nothing is more easy than to think, so nothing is more difficult than to think well."[53] Walking around in the wrong AR layers will make it even more difficult to think well.

There is also evidence that repeated exposure to explicit content literally messes with one's head. A recent study in Germany published in *JAMA Psychiatry*, for example, found that "[m]en who report watching a lot of pornography tend to have less volume and activity in regions of the brain linked to rewards and motivation."[54] Likewise, "[s]cientists at Cambridge University recently studied the brain scans of porn addicts and found that they looked exactly like those of drug addicts."[55]

It has also become widely understood – as was the subject of the 2013 film *Don Jon* – that habitual porn users find "less enjoyment during sex"[56] with actual people.

---

[51]Regan McMahon, Porn Addiction Destroys Lives, SAN FRANCISCO CHRONICLE, Feb. 22, 2010, available at: http://www.sfgate.com/health/article/Porn-addiction-destroys-relationships-lives-3272230.php (last visited on Sept. 10, 2014).

[52]*Is Pornography Addictive?* WEBMD—MEN'S HEALTH, available at: http://www.webmd.com/men/features/is-pornography-addictive (last visited on Sept. 10, 2014).

[53]Thomas Traherne, WIKIPEDIA, available at: http://en.wikipedia.org/wiki/Thomas_Traherne (last visited on Sept. 10, 2014).

[54]Andrew H. Seaman, Porn May Be Messing With Your Head, REUTERS ON YAHOO NEWS, May 28, 2014, available at: http://news.yahoo.com/porn-may-messing-head-202420648.html (last visited on Sept. 10, 2014).

[55]Scott Christian, 10 Reasons Why You Should Quit Watching Porn, GQ, Nov. 20, 2013, available at: http://www.gq.com/blogs/the-feed/2013/11/10-reasons-why-you-should-quit-watching-porn.html (last visited on Sept. 10, 2014).

[56]Nisha Lilia Din, How Porn Is Rewiring Our Brains, THE TELEGRAPH, Nov. 15, 2013, available at: http://www.telegraph.co.uk/men/thinking-man/10441027/How-porn-is-rewiring-our-brains.html (last visited on Sept. 10, 2014).

Psychiatrist Norman Doidge, author of the book *The Brain That Changes Itself*, observed that these men "had rewired the arousal pathways in their brains,"[57] and explained how that occurs:

> *"Pornography," writes Doidge, "satisfies every one of the prerequisites for neuro-plastic change," – that is, the brain's ability to form new neural circuitry. The most important condition is the release of dopamine, the neurotransmitter that gives us a feeling of exciting pleasure, which porn triggers. The more often you watch porn and get the dopamine hit it delivers, the more the activity and the sensation become entwined in your brain.*
>
> *Doidge puts it like this: "since neurons that fire together wire together, these men got massive amounts of practice wiring these images into the pleasure centres of the brain." And, "because plasticity is competitive, the brain maps for new, exciting images increased at the expense of what had previously attracted them."[58]*

In other words, the brain learns what it likes, and devotes more resources over time to recreating that experience instead of less-satisfying alternatives – in this case, interaction with actual people. A related consequence of the same process is the development of tolerance. Over time, it takes more and more stimulus to achieve the same amount of dopamine.[59] "It's known as the Coolidge Effect, or novelty-seeking behavior. Porn, after all, trains the viewer to expect constant newness." Whatever you call that state of being, it certainly bears a striking resemblance to what we commonly call "addiction."[60]

The impact on healthy adult relationships

For compulsive pornography users, this leads to "what Doidge politely calls 'potency problems.' Anecdotal surveys have suggested that as many as 34% of frequent porn watchers suffered performance issues with their partners, while 60% felt their performance improved after committing to stay away from adult content. Since – in the physical world – it takes two to tango, this cannot help but undermine the health of marriages and relationships.

Indeed, the deleterious impact of Internet porn on healthy adult relationships has been well documented. As early as 2003, the *New Yorker* ran a piece on mainstream, well-educated, professional men who found themselves increasingly hooked on explicit Internet imagery. This and other articles found the men correspondingly unable to relate to,[61] or maintain a healthy relationship with, the actual women in their lives.

---

[57]*Id.*

[58]*Id.*

[59]*Id.*

[60]It further calls to mind the lyrics of the 1987 Guns N' Roses hit, "Mr. Brownstone," about the band's experiences with heroin addiction: "I used to do a little, but a little wouldn't do, so the little got more and more. I just keep trying to get a little better, said a little better than before."

[61]Michael J. Formica, Female Objectification and Emotional Availability: Understanding the Social Dynamics of Pornography Addiction, PSYCHOLOGY TODAY, Aug. 22, 2008, available at: http://www.psychologytoday.com/collections/201111/the-porn-factor/pornography-emotional-availability-and-female-objectification (last visited on Sept. 10, 2014).

At the same time, those women found it increasingly difficult to find a man whose mind isn't dominated by such content. One woman interviewed in the *New Yorker* article admitted, "I think it will be really rare, and hopefully it will happen, that I can meet a guy who will be happy with only me."

Other women find themselves compromising their own standards to meet men's unrealistic ones. "Even among more casual users, porn is wreaking havoc in the bedroom." Men are increasingly reported to expect "pornified sex" from their partners. Cindy Gallop, an advertising executive, TED speaker, and founder of the website *Make Love Not Porn*, says "guys watch porn and when they go to bed with a real woman, all they think about is recreating that scenario. ... [Women, meanwhile,] start believing that that is what they have to be like in bed as well."[62] "The result is mutual unhappiness, frustration and disappointment. And, according to Doidge, [young men face] a potentially permanently addled sexuality thanks to the presence of porn during this highly plastic period of brain development."[63]

Unsurprisingly, this situation takes its toll on marriages. "According to the Web site Divorcewizards.com, huge numbers of divorce lawyers report that pornography is a big issue in divorce these days, which it never was before the advent of the Internet." What happens when erotica become available not only on computer screens and mobile devices but also 24/7 in augmented space?

Perhaps the worst-case scenario of what could happen across society is the situation already beginning to play out in Japan. According to a 2013 report, "45% of Japanese women aged 16–24 are 'not interested in or despise sexual contact.' More than a quarter of men feel the same way."[64] Although such a broad demographic trend cannot reasonably be traced back to a single cause, digital technology and the social acceptance of Internet-fueled fetishes play a strong role. "Lacking long-term shared goals, many are turning to what [some call] 'Pot Noodle love' – easy or instant gratification, in the form of casual sex, short-term trysts and the usual technological suspects: online porn, virtual-reality 'girlfriends', anime cartoons."[65] One Japanese therapist related the story of a client – a virgin in his 30s – unable to become aroused "unless he watches female robots on a game similar to Power Rangers."[66] In 2009, a Japanese man even went to the length of holding a wedding ceremony at the Tokyo Institute of Technology to solemnize his marriage to Nene Anegasaki, an anime character in the Nintendo DS video game *LovePlus*.[67] It was reported that the ceremony paid homage to the *otaku* (loosely translated as "nerd" or "geek" fans of *manga* and anime[68]) subculture "that nurtures this type of creativity."

---

[62]*Id.*

[63]*Id.*

[64]Abigail Haworth, Why Have Young People in Japan Stopped Having Sex? THE OBSERVER, Oct. 19, 2013, available at: http://www.theguardian.com/world/2013/oct/20/young-people-japan-stopped-having-sex (last visited on Sept. 10, 2014).

[65]*Id.*

[66]*Id.*

[67]Lisa Katayma, *Video: Man in Japan Weds Anime Game Character*, BOINGBOING (Nov. 29, 2009), available at: http://boingboing.net/2009/11/24/footage-from-the-fir.html (last visited on Sept. 10, 2014).

[68]*Otaku*, WIKIPEDIA, available at: http://en.wikipedia.org/wiki/Otaku (last visited on Sept. 10, 2014).

According to Japanese-American author Roland Kelts, however, it is inevitable that both young men and women in Japan will find their social relationships driven by technology. "Japan has developed incredibly sophisticated virtual worlds and on-line communication systems. Its smart phone apps are the world's most imaginative." One has to wonder how much further augmented reality, with its inherent emphasis on "immersion" into digital content, will tip that balance away from in-person interaction.

The national government sees this "celibacy syndrome" as a mortal threat to the nation's future. "Japan already has one of the world's lowest birth rates. Its population of 126 million, which has been shrinking for the past decade, is projected to plunge a further one-third by 2060."[69] If people in that society continue to find sexual satisfaction from sources other than each other, Japanese culture could quickly pleasure itself out of existence. This is not the only society in this predicament, however. "A 2010 census showed that 31.4 million Americans live alone … [which] allows people to pursue individual freedom, exert personal control and go through self-realization, but these people have fewer children."[70] That has left the United States with a birth rate just below the replacement level of 2.1, while the rate in most of the rest of the developed world is far below that. (Germany, Italy, and Spain, for example, are each at 1.4.[71]) From a demographic perspective, the last thing that any of these societies need is something else to dissuade their residents from reproducing.

Reinforcement of misogyny and sexual aggression

"Pornography itself is about the objectification of women. In this context women are treated as things, receptacles and socially dissociated objects to be used and tossed aside." The principal attraction to erotica is that the viewer (usually, but not always, a man) gets to choose a partner with the exact physical and behavioral specifications he is in the mood for at the time. And if he wants something different the next time, he can find that too. There is no mutuality, no requirement or even possibility of serving the needs of another person. It is all about the viewer and his whims. Similar to the discussion of "muscle memory" in Chapter 12, this sort of habituation cannot help but ingrain in viewers a debased understanding of sexuality as a means of conquest and self-gratification, and nothing more.

Consuming this content through the augmented medium can only deepen that habituation. We have already established that experiencing content in the augmented medium – where it seems more real to us because we experience it through our physical senses in an intuitive way – is an excellent way to train our minds and bodies to react in certain ways in a given situation. It follows, therefore, that pornographic content in the augmented medium will be even more effective in training people to objectify others than its two-dimensional counterpart.

---

[69]*Id.*

[70]Lee Kuan Yew, Warning Bell for Developed Countries: Declining Birth Rates, Forbes, Oct. 16, 2012, available at: http://www.forbes.com/sites/currentevents/2012/10/16/warning-bell-for-developed-countries-declining-birth-rates/ (last visited on Sept. 10, 2014).

[71]*Id.*

This is even more troubling with respect to content that is more graphic than simple erotica, such as rape and other sexual violence. Leaving aside the effect of consuming too much adult content *in general*, the *specific* characteristics of much of this content raise additional concerns. Already, according to one study, over 88% of explicit content online depicts some form of physical aggression, while almost half include verbal aggression.[72] Viewers already intent on viewing such content will be eager to experience it as only AR allows. The short film *Ex Post Facto* (discussed in Chapter 12) presaged this development (however imperfectly) with its tagline: "If rape was legal, would you do it?" The same question is inherent in the very concept of digital replacements for human sex partners, whether that takes the form of digital content with haptic augmentation or robotic prostitutes. "[E]ven if sexbots are not currently conscious, they do have the external markings of personhood, and we are programming them to be person-like. Indeed, we are programming them to be like a specific type of person: the type of woman who can be owned by a heterosexual man." To own and use such a device would be to habituate oneself in the experience of having a sex slave, which cannot possibly make a positive contribution to that person's general socialization.

Indeed, we already have essentially the same thing today in the form of Real-Touch Interactive and other live digital interactions. RealTouch's "models" are little more than telecommuting prostitutes, performing sex acts with a digital device for the pleasure of paying clients. The technical distinction between how they and a more traditional prostitute ply their respective trades, however, is likely to render these "models' services legal in more jurisdictions than just Nevada.

Children's access to porn

One of the most troublesome numbers in the statistics that has been gathered on pornography is "11." That is the average age at which a boy first encounters explicit material online. The *Daily Mail* recently featured an interview with a mother who told how her 11-year-old son's "entire character" changed after he began watching porn on his laptop in his own bedroom.[73] She wrote:

> *If Charlie had been on Class A drugs he couldn't have been more transformed. He became withdrawn, moody and sullen. He wasn't sleeping at night. He lost his normal gargantuan appetite. He looked hollow-eyed and listless. He had none of the boyish energy and high spirits that we were all used to.*
> *He began writing things like 'I hate myself', or 'Charlie is s***' on scraps of paper, newspapers, books, even his bedroom furniture and walls. He drew obscene cartoons with speech bubbles filled with the filthiest words in the dictionary.*

---

[72]*Internet Safety 101: Pornography Statistics*, Enough Is Enough webpage, available at: http://www.internetsafety101.org/Pornographystatistics.htm (last visited on Sept. 10, 2014).
[73]Liz Martin, *How Internet Porn Turned My Beautiful Boy Into a Hollow, Self-Hating Shell*, MAIL ONLINE (April 19, 2012), available at: http://www.dailymail.co.uk/news/article-2132342/How-internet-porn-turned-beautiful-boy-hollow-self-hating-shell.html#ixzz1scCMm8x3 (last visited on Sept. 10, 2014).

I once rolled back his sleeve to find 'I am disgusting' scrawled on the inside of his arm. I managed to stop myself from crying until I'd left the room. But the moment the door closed behind me I broke down completely.[74]

After intensive intervention, Charlie recovered. But millions of other 11-year-olds encounter similar pitfalls. In their article "Why Shouldn't Johnny Watch Porn if He Likes?," educators and authors Gary Wilson and Marnia Robinson explained that "sexual-cue exposure matters more during adolescence than at any other time in life."[75] That's because the age of 11 or 12 is "when billions of new neural connections (synapses) create endless possibilities. … By his twenties, he may not exactly be *stuck* with the sexual proclivities he falls into during adolescence, but they can be like deep ruts in his brain – not easy to ignore or reconfigure." This echoes the findings of psychiatrist Norman Doidge quoted earlier. In other words, constant, easy access to porn-on-demand conditions young men to stimuli that real-life interactions can never match, setting them up for frustration and failed relationships later in life.

And yet the Internet is already exposing kids even younger than this to adult content. One survey found that "kids start watching porn from as early as the age of 6."[76] Another found that "children aged 12 to 17 are one of the largest consumer groups of online porn … [which] can hook kids on hardcore and often violent imagery."[77] If this is what happens over desktop and mobile computers, then children will be all the more likely to find such content on digital eyewear. With no one else able to look over their shoulders to check what they are watching, kids will be even less able than adults to resist the temptation to indulge in such content anywhere and everywhere.

AR creation tools will also give already sexually frustrated teens even more ability to create and publish lewd content of their own. Social media and texting already provide ample opportunity for sexting and shaming with explicit content. In a world where all teens wore devices that allowed them to see digital content on top of the physical, bullied teens could be forced to walk in a world where they see embarrassing photos of themselves posted on literally every wall. As mentioned in Chapter 12, moreover, the instant 3D scanning technology that is already beginning to hit the market will soon be – if it has not already been – used to create digital avatars that can then be made to perform all manner of lewd acts, either with or without the permission of the person scanned.

Exploitation of children

Some of those whose physical forms will be digitally scanned – or digitally augmented with explicit content – will be minors. Some devices may (hopefully!) be

---

[74]*Id.*

[75]Oct. 5, 2011, available at: http://goodmenproject.com/families/boys/why-shouldnt-johnny-watch-porn-if-he-wants-to/.

[76]*Kids Access Porn Sites at 6, Begin Flirting at 8*, USA TODAY, available at: http://www.usatoday.com/story/cybertruth/2013/05/14/childrens-online-safety-porn/2158015/ (last visited on Sept. 10, 2014).

[77]*Teen Addiction to Pornography a Growing Problem*, 7WDAM, available at: http://www.wdam.com/story/23243124/teen-porn-addiction (last visited on Sept. 10, 2014).

programmed not to process the images of those who are obviously children, but verifying the ages of teens would be beyond its ability. And the truth is that a depressingly large number of men would use such devices for exactly that purpose. *AR Dirt* commentator Joseph Rampolla – whose day job as a police captain and consultant has included many years of cybercrime investigation – has repeatedly warned that "wherever society finds pornography, child pornography is not too far behind."[78] Experience on the Internet to date has repeatedly proven him right.

This dark rule of human nature will play out in all augmented contexts, not only with regard to digital images. The same commentators discussing human-like sexbots, for example, have already anticipated "a hypothetical company that starts producing child sex-robots to satisfy deviant sexual desires."[79] Indeed, some have even *advocated* for this development. Ron Arkin, Georgia Tech's Mobile Robot Lab director, has "said that while he doesn't approve of child sex bots for recreational use, he'd like to see them … used for pedophiles the way methadone is used to treat drug addicts."[80] Arkin's motivation – "to possibly provide better protection to society from recidivism in sex offenders"[81] – is noble enough: but the possible unintended consequences of investing in such technology (even Arkin worries about a black market for the devices), and the very idea of positively reinforcing pedophiles' impulses, are so revolting as to warrant serious hesitation in considering this approach.

Even more troubling is the distinct possibility that, if (really, when) such devices become available, they may very well be perfectly legal. In the 2002 decision *Ashcroft v. Free Speech Coalition*, the U.S. Supreme Court ruled that digital images that look like child porn, but do not portray actual children, are protected speech and cannot be punished under the laws against child porn.[82] It goes without saying that it has gotten increasingly easy to create photo-realistic digital images, and that it will get even easier in the very near future. In 2011, for example, clothing retailer H&M acknowledged that the models in its catalogs were merely digitally enhanced mannequins with the heads of real models photoshopped onto them (Fig. 13.4).[83] Yet it took a very discerning eye to notice that the images were artificial. Combining user-generated digital imagery with AR eyewear will allow anyone to immerse themselves in the objects of their desire, even if those objects happen to be in the form of children.

The best that can be said in response is that the legal lines around such content are at least fuzzy. In 2012, for example, a Georgia lawmaker proposed a statute to

---

[78]Eric Huber, *Augmented Reality: An Interview With Joseph Rampolla*, A Fistful of Dongles (Apr. 20, 2011), available at: http://www.ericjhuber.com/2011/04/augmented-reality-interview-with-joseph.html.
[79]Kashmir Hill, Are Child Sex-Robots Inevitable? Forbes, July 14, 2014, available at: http://www.forbes.com/sites/kashmirhill/2014/07/14/are-child-sex-robots-inevitable/ (last visited on Sept. 10, 2014).
[80]*Id.*
[81]*Id.*
[82]*Ashcroft v. Free Speech Coalition*, 535 US 234 (2002).
[83]Austin Considine, Invasion of the Head Snatchers, The New York Times, Dec. 16, 2011, available at: http://www.nytimes.com/2011/12/18/fashion/hm-puts-real-heads-on-digital-bodies.html (last visited on Sept. 10, 2014).

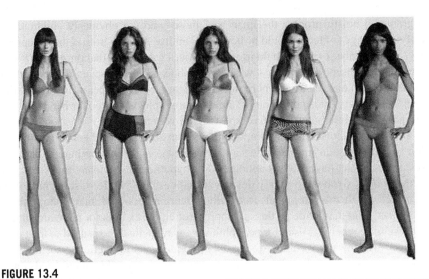

FIGURE 13.4

H&M's digital models.

outlaw superimposing a minor's head onto an explicit image,[84] and in July 2014, the United States Court of Appeals for the Eighth Circuit upheld a man's child pornography conviction for doing exactly that.[85] Using augmented world technologies to make or display explicit images blending real and digital images, then, might well be punishable. Moreover, *Free Speech Coalition* was a 6–3 decision, so it is not entirely insulated from being narrowed or reversed by a future Supreme Court, especially if an explosion of explicit AR content makes a measurable impact in the lives of many individuals. It may also prove easier to prosecute augmented child pornography in other countries. In 2013, a 48-year-old Canadian man ordered a child-sized sex doll; the shipment was intercepted and he was charged with child pornography. If the prosecution succeeds, it could stand as a potent warning to the simulation of child porn in augmented media as well, at least in Canada.

CONCLUSION

Augmented reality will be an interesting and powerful medium, with the ability to do both good and harm to individual psyches and society as a whole. It will offer users the ability to psychologically immerse themselves in artificial content to a degree

---

[84]Tim Cushing, *Georgia Lawmaker Looking to Make Photoshopping Heads on Naked Bodies Illegal*, TECHDIRT (Jan. 24, 2012), available at: https://www.techdirt.com/articles/20120122/02084717501/georgia-lawmaker-looking-to-make-photoshopping-heads-naked-bodies-illegal.shtml (last visited on Sept. 10, 2014).

[85]*United States v. Anderson*, No. 13-2337, Affirming district court order denying Anderson's motion to dismiss indictment (8th Cir., 2013), available at: http://media.ca8.uscourts.gov/opndir/14/07/132337P.pdf (last visited on Sept. 10, 2014).

unmatched by other technologies. That ability, in and of itself, is ethically neutral, but how we exercise it will ultimately be a reflection of ourselves. When our desires are personally destructive or socially unacceptable, however, augmented media will have the power to intensify those urges and the likelihood that we will act on them – to the detriment of ourselves or others. Therefore, not only must we exercise discernment and good judgment in how we choose to augment our physical surroundings, but also the consequences of making poor choices with respect to digital media will often be even more severe than they would be in other circumstances.

In the end, it comes down to the timeless wisdom of the *Spiderman* franchise: "with great power comes great responsibility." Perhaps, with a little foresight and self-awareness, we will use augmented reality to truly make our world greater.

Index

A

"Absolut Truths" app, 73
Addiction to augmented reality, 311
  compulsive behavior, 322
  exploitation of children, 328
  impact on healthy adult relationships, 324
  reinforcement of misogyny and sexual
      aggression, 326
  steps to prevent, 314
  used for pornographic and prurient content, 316
    children's access, 327
Advertising and marketing, augmented reality in, 71
  augmented content on product packaging, 73
  *Augmented (hyper) Reality: Domestic
      Robocop*, 79
  billboards and wall-sized advertisements, 77
  biometrics, 78
  business defamation and product
      disparagement, 89
  digital billboard replacement technology, 83
  disclosures, 90
  false advertising and unfair competition, 81
  future perspective, 77
  in-store kiosks, 74
  interactive print, 72
  interactive video billboards, 75
  interactivity with physical places and things, 96
  Keiichi Matsuda's vision, 79, 80
  keyword, 116
  location-based advertising, 79
  "magic mirror"-type augmented displays, 78
  "pay-per-gaze" advertising, 78
  printed targets, 71
  projection mapping, 76
  property rights and freedom of speech, 157
    models of controlling location-based
        messages, 158
  public installations, 74–76
  shocking AR ads, 178
Air Commerce Act (1926), 154
AIREAL, 27
Air rights, 154
Americans with Disabilities Act (ADA), 248
Anderson v. American Restaurant Group, 186
Anti-cybersquatting Consumer Protection
    Act (1999), 166
Apple's HealthKit, 293
Arnold v. Treadwell, 147
Ashraf, Farooq, 195

Assault, 176
  in augmented medium, 177
  defined, 176
  immersion, element of, 176
  intent to, 176
  reasonable fear of contact, 176
Assistive technology service, defined, 257
Augmented digital information, 173
Augmented graffiti, 163
Augmented methods of teaching, 38
Augmented reality
  definition, 18, 19
  different meanings of, 20
  distinction between virtual reality and, 18, 19
  in enhancing privacy, 68
  extra-sensory, 29
  false advertising and unfair competition in, 81
  innovations, 36
  legitimacy, 36
  levels of adoption, 36
  making appropriate disclosures in, 92
  Mann's, 21
  maturity, 39
  monetary transactions in, 97, 98
    consumer protection and contract law, 98
  muscle memory and desensitization, 305
  related vocabulary, 22
  synonyms, 20
  synthetic synthesis, 30
  training system, 306
  use in advertising and marketing, 71
Augmented reality devices/products,
      physical injury and
  blunt trauma, 195
  cancer, 198
  eye strain, 194
  motion sickness, 196
  retinal projection, 199
  skin irritation, 198
Augmented reality games, 290
  case of underage users, 187
  "The Game", 186
  Grand Theft Auto, 307, 308
  location-based, 187
  physical injury and, 182
    from augmented distractions, 188
    due to inaccuracy, 192
    liability on game designers, 185
    physical or digital versions of an object, 191

Augmented reality games *(cont.)*
 risks inherent in location-based, 183
 sci-fi themed AR game *Ingress*, 167–169,
  182, 185
  law enforcement, 209–211
 "SkinVaders," 183
 Splinter Cell video game, 182
 virtual shooting games, 211
 weapon-oriented video games, 213
 Witness, The, 183, 184
  risk of injury, 184, 185
Augmented weapons, 213
Augmented world technologies, 4, 31
 facial recognition technology, 35
 hand and gesture tracking, 34
 mechanical vision and sensors, 32
 mesh networking, 31
 Panternet, 31
 taggants for pinpoint-accurate perception, 32
Augmenting architectural works, copyrights of, 134
Azuma, Ronald, 19

B

Battery, 176
Biermann, B. C., 83, 284, 290
Biometrics, 78
Bluetooth Low Energy (BLE) technology, 62
 application using, 62
 next-generation, 63
 potential of, 62
 sensors, 32
Bosley, Catherine, 147
Bowery Wall project, 163
Bucchere, Chris, 186

C

Calder effects test, 272
Capability of augmented reality (AR) law, 12
Cheok, Adrian, 28
Communications Act (1934), 245
Communications Decency Act (1996), 160
Consumer protection and contract law, 98
1-800-Contacts v. Ditto Technologies, 106
Convenience of augmented reality (AR) law, 7
Copyright, 125. *See also* Patents; Trademarks
 basics, 125
 Copyright Act (USA), 125
 in defense of fair use, 137
 eligibility for, 127
 enforcement in AR medium, 138
  through licensing, 141
 fixation in a tangible medium, 126

idea/expression dichotomy and, 127
 infringement liability, 137, 175
 moral rights, 136
 obtaining, 126
 principle of originality, 127
  digital imitations of reality, case of, 130
 protection
  adding to existing work, 132
  in analogous cases, 129
  in "augmented substitution" scenario, 133
  of augmenting architectural works, 134
  duplicating copyrighted works, 131
  reproduction and derivative works, 131
 public display and performance rights, 136
 sine qua non of, 127
Courtroom, AR in
 telepresence, 268
 using haptic and audio-visual AR for evidence,
  269
Creative expression, in augmented reality
  (AR) law, 10
Cyber Navi, 204

D

Daemon and *Freedom*[TM], 132, 205, 218,
  222, 280
DAQRI Smart Helmet, 25, 30
Darknets, 138
 AR, 222
Darknet society, 280, 281
Data enhancement and privacy concerns, 55
Decimated reality, 22
Defectively designed product, injury from, 193
Designing of three-dimensional objects, 10
Digital advertising and privacy concerns, 55. *See
  also* Advertising and marketing, augmented
  reality in
Digital billboard replacement technology, 83
Digital communications networks, 172
Digital divide, 39
Digital enhancement of senses
 hearing, 27
 sight (vision), 23
 taste and smell, 28
 touch, 26
Digital eyewear, 22, 25, 26, 38
Digital lollipop, 29
Diminished reality (DR), 22, 287
Disabled persons and AR technologies
 blind, 251
 cognitive impairments, 255
 deaf, 249

emotional trauma, 255
equal access standards, 245
governing legal framework, 244
Individualized Education Plan (IEP), 257
learning disabilities, 255
patients with ALS (Lou Gehrig's disease) and
    muscular dystrophy, 254
patients with Parkinson's disease, 254
physically handicapped, 253
Disclosures in advertisement, 90. *See also*
    Advertising and marketing, augmented
    reality in
disclaimers in or with the claim, 93
distractions, 95
empirical research and analytical data, 96
FTC's enforcement, 90
Doritos Late Night campaign, 85, 86, 88
Driving, injury from wearing digital eyewear
    and, 200
    AR mobile phone apps and driving, 201
    augmented windshields and driver aids, 204
    driving amidst ubiquitous augmented
        reality, 207
        floating, virtual road signs, 208
        transparent walls, 207
        virtual speed displays, 208
        virtual traffic lights, 207
    driving with digital eyewear, 202
Dublon, Gershon, 28
Dylan, Natalie, 146, 147

E

Eavesdropping and privacy concerns, 60
"Echo chamber" effect, 283
E-discovery, 264
Electronically stored information (ESI), 264
Emotional recognition (software), 256
Enhanced reality, 20
Enright, Michael, 289
Environmental protection laws, 173
E-skin, 26
Ethics and augmented world technologies
    development of bad habits, 304
    ethical decisions, 299
    self-monitoring apps, 293
Evidence in legal proceedings, gathering, 259
    from digital remnants, 262
    mobile video, 260
    preserving three-dimensional experiences
        in AR, 261
Extra-sensory AR, 29
Eye-tracking data, 61

F

Facial recognition technology, 35, 78
    privacy concerns, 50
    regulation of, 50
Fair use, of trademark, 137
False advertising and unfair competition, 81
    business defamation and product
        disparagement, 89
    deceptive advertising methods, 85
    Doritos Late Night campaign, 85, 86, 88
    false suggestions of endorsement or
        sponsorship, 84
False light, 47
Federal Aviation Act (1958), 154
Federal Lanham Act, 80, 81
    false advertising, 81
    false endorsement, 84, 148
    false sponsorship, 84
Federal Trade Commission Act, 85, 86
    advertisement disclosures, 90, 91
    disclaimers in or with the claim, 93
    unfair practices, defined, 87
Feelings, importance of, 10
Flint, Kim, 186
Floating, virtual road signs, 208
Freedom of speech, 156
    hyperlinks, 160

G

Gartner Hype Cycles, 37
Geofencing, 22
Geolocation, 22
    privacy, 66
    sensor infrastructure, 64
Goldman, Eric, 247
Google Glass, 22, 58, 194, 195, 249, 253
Google Morals, 297
GoPro, 58
Groupthink, defined, 283

H

Hand and gesture tracking, 34
H (app)athon Project, 294
Haptic technology, 26, 320
    haptic feedback and buzzing, 27
Havens, John C., 294
Hearing, digital enhancement of, 27
    Intelligent Headset, 28
    "Voice", 27
Helmet cameras, 234
Horizontal study, 3
Horse law, 5

Horse lawyer, 5
Howell, Robert J., 297

I

Immersion, concept of, 22
Individuals with Disabilities Education Act
        (IDEA), 257
Infringement
    facial recognition as infringing rights, 145
    liability, 137
    virtual assistants as, 149
Intellectual property laws, 148
Intelligent Headset, 28
Intent, defined, 176
Intentional criminal activity, 213
    augmented weapons, 213
    criminal collaborations through AR darknets, 222
    developing infrastructure of augmented world
        for, 220
    personal and property crimes, 224
    surreptitious data collection and hacking, 215
    vulnerability of "soft targets", 218
Intentional infliction of emotional distress
        (IIED), 179
    augmented expression for harassment, 179, 180
Intentional torts, 175
    assault, 176
    intentional infliction of emotional distress
        (IIED), 179
    negligence, 180
    student bullying, 179
"Interactivity" or "sliding scale" tests, 273
Internet Corporation for Assigned Names and
        Numbers (ICANN), 166
Internet law, 5
Internet of Things (IOT), 31
    aggregating interactions with, 63
    beacons and taggants, 62
    enforcement action related to IOT-collected
        information, 65
    in innovative consumer products and services, 65
    privacy regulations and, 65
Internet protocol address system, 63
Intrusion into seclusion tort, 47
Iron Man movies, 8, 9

K

Kapture (audio recording device), 59
Keycite® database, 267
Keyword advertising system, 90. *See also* Advertising
        and marketing, augmented reality in
    AdWords, 116

Kickstarter-funded Structure Sensor, 145
Kikano, George, 196, 197

L

Landowner's rights, remedies for violations of, 155
Law enforcement
    digital information for crime investigation and
        prevention, 230
    effect on criminal responsibility, 212
    enhancing situational awareness, 226
    in location-based AR games, 209
    right to hold public officials accountable, 234
        citizen video recordings, 241
        Graber incident, 239, 240
        Massachusetts' eavesdropping statute, 238
        personal rights and privileges associated with
            private speech, 235
        police officers, 236, 237
        reprisals by police against the citizens, 239
    using autonomous drones, 232
    virtual shooting games, 211
    vulnerability of "soft targets" and, 218
    wearables for, 233
Law of the horse, 5
Legal research in AR, 267
Location-based services (LBS), 67
Longueira, Alexa, 188
Looxcie (over-the-ear camera), 58, 59
Lumo Back, 295

M

"Magic Mirror" app, 73
"Magic Mirror"-type augmented displays, 78
Mann, Steve, 20, 21, 58
Mediated reality, 20
Meijer, Peter B.L., 27, 252
Meshwerks v. Toyota Motors Sales USA, Inc.,
        129, 130, 132
Miller, Bonnie, 188
MindLight, 29
Minock, Drew, 256
Mobilizing people using AR
    building new augmented communities, 279
    contribution to partisanship and polarization, 283
    creation of multiple gated neighborhoods, 281
    devaluation of physical proximity and
        interpersonal community, 281
    "diminished reality" (DR), 287
    enforcement of political correctness, 284
    labeling others, 288
    for political campaigns, 279
    for protests and social change, 278, 280

rediscovering and rebuilding civic identity, 277
socially deleterious consequences, 283
Monetary transactions in AR, 97, 98
consumer protection and contract law, 98
Moore's law, 12
Moral rights, 136
Mullins, Brian, 284

N

Nano crystal taggants, 34
Nanotaggants, 172–174
National Policy & Legal Analysis Network to
        Prevent Childhood Obesity (NPLAN), 85
Near Field Communication (NFC) technology, 32, 62
Negligence, 180
in augmented reality games, 182
elements of claim alleging, 181
physical injury due to, 182
Newsom, Gavin, 58
Njewadda, Ajanaffy, 178
Norman, Don, 189, 190
Nuisance, 171

O

Oculus Rift, 18
Oman, Charles, 197
On-the-fly captioning, 250
"Operation SC Revelation" campaign, 182
Orthorectified image skin, 63
Ownership rights, 154

P

Panternet, 31
Papagiannis, Helen, 255
Patents. *See also* Copyright; Trademarks
nature of protection under, 101
in AR inventions, 102
AR patent infringement case, 104
rights of Lennon Image Technologies, LLC,
        107, 108
as weapons of competition, 106
Patriot Act (USA), 50
PayPal, 62
"Peeping Tom" cameras, 65
Peli, Eli, 194
Personal jurisdiction, 271
connection between defendant and forum state, 272
interactive sites, 273
over providers of augmented reality
        experiences, 274
Petkov, Jennifer, 179
Petkov, Scott, 179

Platonic Realism, 191
Porn consumption, 316, 317
children and, 327
Privacy laws, 43
AR-related technologies and, 50
eavesdropping and wiretapping statutes, 48
electronic, 48
limitations on government intrusion into privacy, 49
modern era of American privacy protection, 46
reasonable expectation of privacy, 47
right to be left alone, 46
subject-specific, 49
Projection mapping, 25, 76, 133, 134
Property rights
air rights, 154
in augmented medium
    freedom of speech and, 157
    nuisance, 171
    physical and virtual easements, 172
    sci-fi themed AR game *Ingress*, 167–169
    trespass, 169
digital graffiti, 163
easement rights, 172
environmental protection laws, 173
infringement of, 155
Madison Square Gardens arena, case of, 154, 155
real property rights, 153
scarcity and, 165
Transfer of Development Rights (TDR), 155
violations of a landowner's rights, remedies for, 155
Proto-AR systems, 315
Public Ad campaign, 83, 133
Publication of private facts, 47
Publicity rights, 143
basics, 144
commercial aspect of, 144
digital avatars and, 151
facial recognition as infringing, 145
likeness and, 145
sex appeal and, 145
    profiting from, 146, 148
as shields against prurient publications, 147

Q

QR codes, 160
Qualcomm's Vuforia software, 191
"Quantified self" movement, 293

R

Radio frequency identification (RFID) tags, 33
Ramirez, Edith, 65
Ranasinghe, Nimesha, 29

Real property rights, 153
  ownership, 153
Real-time AR display, 289
Reasonableness, 176
  believable and unexpected condition, 176
Recon's ski goggles, 58
Right to be left alone, 46

S

Sabelman, Eric, 196
Seager, Thomas, 296
Selinger, Evan, 296, 297
Senseg (Finnish company), 26
Senses, digitally augmented, 19
Shephard's® database, 267
Short films about augmented reality, 303
  Ex Post Facto, 301
  Infinity, 300
  Sight, 299
Sight (vision), digital enhancement of, 23
  billboards, 24
  computer webcams, 23
  DAQRI Smart Helmet, 25
  digital eyewear, 25, 26
  holographic projections, 23
  in-store kiosks, 24
  projection mapping, 25
  vehicle windshields, 24
  "virtual try-on" websites, 23
Smart glasses, 22
Snowden, Edward, 63
Sterling, Bruce, 19, 20, 25
Strict liability torts, 175
Suarez, Daniel, 280, 281
Surveillance and sousveillance, 57, 61
  as invasions of privacy, 60
  issue of spying, 57

T

Taggants, 32, 174
  nano crystal, 34
Taste and smell, digital enhancement of, 28
  digital lollipop, 29
Telecommunications Act (1996), 245
Thermal Touch technology, 34
Tomita v. Nintendo, 104
Tongueduino, 28
Torts, 175
  categories, 175
  intentional, 175
  of negligence, 175
  products liability, 193
  strict liability, 175

Touch, digital enhancement of, 26
  e-skin, 26
  Senseg, 26
Touch pixels, 26
Trackable nanotaggants, 64
Trademarks, 111. *See also* Copyright; Patents
  basics, 111
  emerging AR technologies and
    trademark law, 114
  fair use and free speech, 121
  third-party, 122
  unauthorized augmentation of, 123
Transfer of Development Rights (TDR), 155
Transparent walls, 207
TRENDnet, 65
Trespass, 169
  defined, 169
  legal risks for land owners, 170
  liability for physical harm and, 170
Turkewitz, Eric, 190
Tushnet, Rebecca, 81

U

Unfair competition, 80
Uniform dispute resolution policy (UDRP), 166
User-generated parody videos, 79

V

V-discovery, 140, 264
  first-person AR data, 266
  magnitude of data, 265
  preservation of data, 266
  tracking of data, 265
Veen, Emile van, 222
Veenhof, Sander, 69
Video game industry, 182, 182.
    See also Augmented reality games
Virtual reality (VR), 18, 20
Virtual speed displays, 208
Virtual traffic lights, 207
Vision-based AR devices, 32, 33
"vOICe" software, 252, 253

W

Waid, Brad, 256
"Watch Your Privacy" app, 69
Weapon-oriented video games, 213
"Wearable Marker for Passive Interaction"
    patent, 34
Wright, Will, 290

Z

Zerkin, Noah, 25